The Puritan Origins of American Sex

Religion,
Sexuality,
and
National Identity
in American Literature

TRACY FESSENDEN,
NICHOLAS F. RADEL,
and
MAGDALENA J. ZABOROWSKA,
Editors

ROUTLEDGE
NEW YORK / LONDON

A version of "A Sodom Within: Historicizing Puritan Homoerotics in the Diary of Michael Wigglesworth" was published as "A Sodom Within: Gender, Sex, and Sodomy in the Diary of Michael Wigglesworth," in *Other Americans, Other Americas: The Politics and Poetics of Multiculturalism*, ed. Magdalena J. Zaborowska (Aarhus, DK: Aarhus University Press, 1998). Reprinted with permission.

A version of "Enslaving Passions: White Male Sexuality and the Evasion of Race" appears as "Sexual Purity, White Men, and Slavery: Emerson and the Self-reliant Body" in *Prospects: An Annual of American Cultural Studies* 25 (2000). Reprinted with the permission of Cambridge University Press.

A version of "The Other Woman's Sphere: Nuns, Prostitutes, and the Medicalization of Middle-Class Domesticity" appears as "The Convent, the Brothel, and the Protestant Woman's Sphere" in *Signs: Journal of Women in Culture and Society* 25 (2000), published by the University of Chicago Press. ©The University of Chicago. All rights reserved.

Portions of "Christian Maidens and Heathen Monks: Oratorical Seduction at the 1893 World's Parliament of Religions" appear in *The Uses of Variety: Modern Americanism and the Quest for National Distinctiveness* (Cambridge, MA: Harvard University Press, 2000).

A portion of "Americanization of a 'Queer Fellow': Performing Jewishness and Sexuality in Abraham Cahan's *The Rise of David Levinsky*, with a Footnote on the (Monica) Lewinsky'ed Nation" appeard in slightly different form as "'Queer Fellows' and Other 'Victims of Circumstances': (Hetero)Sexualizing Americanization in Abraham Cahan's *The Rise of David Levinsky*," *American Studies in Scandanavia* (Spring 1997). Reprinted with permission.

Portions of "*Desert of the Heart*: Jane Rule's Puritan Outing" appeared in "Narrative Inversion: The Biblical Heritage of *Desert of the Heart* and *The Well of Loneliness*," *Journal of Homosexuality* 33 (1997). Reprinted with permission of Haworth Press.

Published in 2001 by
Routledge
29 West 35th Street
New York, New York 10001

Published in Great Britain by
Routledge
11 New Fetter Lane
London EC4P 4EE

Copyright © 2001 by Routledge

Routledge is an imprint of the Taylor and Francis Group

Printed in the United States of America on acid-free paper.

10 9 8 7 6 5 4 3 2 1

Library of Congress Cataloging-in-Publication Data

The Puritan origins of American sex: religion, sexuality, and national identity in American literature / edited by Tracy Fessenden, Nicholas F. Radel, and Magdalena J. Zaborowska.
     p.   cm.
    Includes bibliographical references and index.
    ISBN 0-415-92639-4 (hardbound) — ISBN 0-415-92640-8 (pbk.)
        1. American Literature—History and criticism. 2. Sex in literature.
    3. Christianity and literature—United States—History. 4. National characteristics, American, in literature. 5. Puritan movements in literature. 6 Puritans—United States. 7. Religion and literature. I. Fessenden, Tracy. II. Radel, Nicholas F., 1955– III. Zaborowska, Magdalena J.

PS169.S454P87 2001
3810.9'3538—dc21

00-035397

*In memory of
Jenny Franchot,
1953–1998*

Contents

Acknowledgments

The editors are grateful for generous help received from a number of sources. Tracy Fessenden wishes to thank the Department of Religious Studies and the College of Liberal Arts and Sciences at Arizona State University for supporting periods of fellowship leave in 1998, 1999, and 2000; she also wishes to thank Cory Schlosser for her help with manuscript preparation at the eleventh hour. Nicholas Radel would like to thank the Danish-American Foundation and Fulbright Commission for a teaching/research stipend at Roskilde University Center, Denmark, where much of the final work for this project was completed, and he thanks Furman University for support in the form of a sabbatical leave. Magdalena Zaborowska thanks the Center for Cultural Research and the English Department at Aarhus University and the Newcomb College Center for Research on Women at Tulane University for providing a sabbatical leave and institutional support; she thanks Crystal Kile for her help with computer problems. At Routledge, Nick Syrett provided crucial early support for the project, and Julien Devereux and Amy Reading saw it through to completion.

We have been cheered in our errand by the patience and sustenance of our families, friends, and partners, and by the gracious advice and scholarly guidance of Wai Chee Dimock, Emory Elliott, Sam B. Girgus, Miriyam Glazer, Prem Poddar, Rosemarie Garland Thomson, and Beth Willinger.

We owe a special debt to the late Jenny Franchot, who in many ways made this project possible. She moderated our first meeting as prospective editors of this book with generosity, enthusiasm, and brilliant insight, and she provided in her own work on American literature and religion a model of interdisciplinary American Studies scholarship at its best. We dedicate this collection to her memory.

Foreword

$\mathcal{A}$ *recent radio commercial* in the United States opens this way: "The seventeenth-century New England Puritans were people who devoted their entire lives to work and prayer. They would not have approved of the sensual beauty of the new Saab 500 coupe. The Puritans believed that to have fun was a sin. There was no place in their lives for the pleasure and luxury of a new Saab convertible. For the Puritans, the only reason for living was to sacrifice and prepare for an eternity of holy peace. Aren't you glad you're not a Puritan? See your nearest Saab dealer."

The New England Puritans have never fared well in American popular media. In the 1920s, H. L. Mencken tried to close the book on them with his attacks on the puritanical nabobs who were to blame for all that was wrong with American culture. Mencken's famous definition of Puritanism is that it is the suspicion that someone, somewhere, is having a good time. Even in the seventeenth century the Puritans came in for mockery both in England and the colonies. Nathaniel Ward's satire, *The Simple Cobbler of Agawam*, and Thomas Lechford's excoriating attack on ministers and magistrates, *Plaine Dealing from New England*, were notable anti-Puritan books, and they still hold a secure place in anthologies of colonial literature.

After a robust period for Puritan studies in the 1950s and 1960s generated by the works of Perry Miller, interest in the Puritans waned in the 1980s and 1990s. Reagan-era prosperity brought us discos, designer cocaine, and the creed that "greed is good." With bumper stickers declaring that "Being rich is the best revenge," "I live to shop," and "Whoever dies with the most stuff wins," the spirit of capitalism was certainly alive, but the return of the Puritan ethic seemed an unlikely prospect. It was a good time to be selling Saabs.

In the academy, meanwhile, poststructuralism had all but dismantled theories of historicism and rendered absurd such notions as national identity, historical continuities, and cultural influences. Because the study and teaching of Puritan New England had been established upon an argument about the importance of cultural connections between then and now, new theories of fragmentation and discontinuity easily won the day. At the same time, pressures on the literary and historical canons to admit the contributions of Native Americans, early Spanish explorers, and other formerly silenced voices quickly reduced the portions of literature anthologies, college courses, and doctoral examinations that had previously been accorded to the Puritans.

At one extreme, the argument emerged that Puritan studies (and even the entire study of American literature) were artificial constructions designed to promote the ideological agenda of cold war apologists who deemed it essential for American students to know something about the seventeenth-century religious debates that had helped to shape American culture. A graduate seminar that I taught at Princeton in the 1970s was called "Puritan Influences in American Literature." By 1980 I had added a question mark at the end of its title, and by 1982 I had retired it all together, never expecting to need any version of my introductory lecture for it again. With so much new reading and cultural deconstruction to do, how could we waste curricular space on the convoluted poetry of Edward Taylor who, even when explicated by a learned professor, had little to say to the present generation?

During the recent Clinton scandal and impeachment hearings, however, media commentators repeatedly invoked American Puritanism in their coverage of the "witch hunting" of Kenneth Starr and the pious outrage of Clinton's political opponents. *Hustler* magazine editor Larry Flint's exposure of the hypocrisy of some of the principals recalled Thomas Morton and his band of anti-Puritan rebels frolicking about the Maypole of Merrymount and taunting their self-righteous Puritan clergy and magistrates. Scholars of early New England were even being interviewed on talk shows and quoted in major magazines.

In an article in *U.S. News and World Report* entitled "Shifting Lines of Privacy: Today's Anxieties Mirror Earlier Debates in America's History," the reporter, Miriam Horn, solemnly quotes Mary Beth Norton, whom she describes reverently as a "colonial historian at Cornell University." Horn credits Norton with the observation that in early New England, an "orderly state was seen to depend on having orderly families. And any sex outside marriage created disorderly families." As if to warn any potential White

House interns who might be readers of *U.S. News and World Report*, the newly learned journalist goes on to inform us that in Puritan Massachusetts, "neighborly spying through windows and cracks in the wall was therefore a civic obligation, and sexual offenses were punished publicly with whippings, rebuke on church steps, or scarlet letters." Accompanying the sermon is a picture of a very sad Hester Prynne that carries the caption: "The Puritans believed the sin of one jeopardized the salvation of all." Perhaps it was this story that inspired the advertising agency handling the Saab account to entice restless Ford and Honda owners to reject Puritan austerity, rip off their scarlet letters, and buy a sexy Swedish auto.

Among the more interesting analyses of the Clinton psyche to emerge from the psychobabble generated about the affair was the one presented by Bill Moyers, which invoked the Puritan dichotomy between God and Satan in *Paradise Lost*. According to Moyers, himself a minister, Clinton has a dual personality because he is caught in a tug of war between Christ and the devil. In Hot Springs, Arkansas, where Clinton grew up, bars and brothels lined one side of the main street and churches the other. Moyers explains that when the President was a boy, he was taken on Saturday nights to the bars, where he observed the prostitutes and the hard-drinking men who visited the brothels. Then on Sunday morning, he would attend church just across the street, where he would see many of these same people praying and weeping for forgiveness and salvation. This script sounds very much like the narrative of Nathaniel Hawthorne's short story "Young Goodman Brown," which probes the psyche of a young man who cannot reconcile the contradictions he encounters on discovering that the seeming good people of his village in daytime were followers of Satan at night in the forest. In Moyers's story of a young goodman, Clinton developed a form of moral schizophrenia when he learned that one of God's elect might, indeed *would* sin, but that he could always be forgiven if his faith were strong and if he were predestined to be a Saint or a President.

I am inclined to think that it may be partly a fascination with such marvelously contradictory derivations of what was once called the American "Puritan" mentality that is leading the rising generation of scholars to Puritan studies. And returning they are with passion and intelligence. All too often, advocates of a expanded canon of the literature of the United States have suggested that a recognition of the nation's ethnic diversity should put discussions of the origin of any features of the culture to rest. However, many writers and artists, as well as countless numbers of those who live outside the

United States, continue to perceive within this society a strong component of moralism and religiosity that they identify as "puritan." Thus, it is not surprising that critics interested in such emotional issues as sexuality and violence would find associations between this strand of America's cultural heritage and broader psychological and social forces in the society at large, and would find those forces working also through characters in fiction and other features of artistic representation. The complex question of the connections between the culture of the modern United States and the world of seventeenth-century Puritan New England remains at the center of the ongoing search for a national identity. And within that set of issues, the subjects surrounding sexuality and gender identities are always of great interest to researchers.

The present volume brilliantly unfolds a set of conscious and unconscious attitudes toward sexuality and gender in America that appear to stem from New England Puritan culture and its influences through American history to the present. As several of the essays make clear, such a task presupposes no dichotomy between Puritan studies and the study of America's rich ethnic diversity. Taken together, the essays in this volume show that it is a false position to have to choose between examining the "Puritan origins" of United States culture, on the one hand, and attending to its many other "origins" in Africa, Asia, Latin America, and pre-colonial America, on the other.

Contributors to this volume have identified a wide range of approaches and a rich set of issues to be explored under the subject of the Puritan origins of American sex. The early essays in the volume take up some of the psychosocial, racial, and socio-economic consequences of certain attitudes toward sex and sexuality that appear to derive from the nation's Puritan beginnings. The first five essays examine the subject of sex and the Puritan heritage in the seventeenth and eighteenth centuries and offer a number of provocative, original readings of the events and texts of those periods. The same is true of the four essays that treat the subject in different ways in the nineteenth century. The remaining essays provide fresh and engaging readings of twentieth-century subjects and writings and offer cultural studies approaches to paradigms that have supported the traditional continuity arguments about Puritanism and American identities.

The editors of this volume are to be commended for their remarkable achievement. This is an important and exciting volume that makes a major contribution to the study of American culture.

Emory Elliott

Introduction

The Puritan Origins
of American Sex

ᗥ

Tracy Fessenden

Nicholas F. Radel

Magdalena J. Zaborowska

For the rhetoric survived, finally, not by chance but by merit, because it was compelling enough in content and flexible enough in form to invite adaptation. Colonial Puritan hermeneutics . . . evolved through an essentially symbolic interaction of perceiver and fact, thus allowing for different kinds of perceivers and a variety of historical contexts.
—Sacvan Bercovitch,
*The Puritan Origins
of the American Self*

Re: Playing the Scandal

In the introduction to the report that Special Prosecutor Kenneth Starr gave to the United States House of Representatives concerning the possible impeachment of President Bill Clinton, one section outlines "The Significance of the Evidence of Wrongdoing" in the case. Under this heading, Starr's report takes up the issue of personal privacy in the matter of the president's alleged sexual contacts with Monica Lewinsky. Of the three limits to the right to privacy[1] mentioned in the report, it is the third one that interests us, for this particular paragraph articulates clearly a relationship between Bill Clinton's "private" sex life and his public role that illustrates one of the many ways America's Puritan past haunts its present: "The third limit is unique to the President. 'The Presidency is more than an executive responsibility. It is the inspiring symbol of all that is highest in American purpose and ideals.' When he took the Oath of Office in 1993 and again in 1997, President Clinton swore that he would 'faithfully execute the Office of President.' As the head of the Executive Branch, the

1

President has the constitutional duty to 'take Care that the Laws be faithfully executed.' . . . In view of the enormous trust and responsibility attendant to his high Office, the President has a manifest duty to ensure that his conduct at all times complies with the law of the land."[2]

Quoting Herbert Hoover, the Starr report alludes to the symbolism of the U.S. presidency, thereby energizing an idea not unique to U.S. cultural imagining but one certainly defining of it: The individual American can (and in this instance must) stand as a sign of the nation's special ideals and purposes.[3] The extralegal logic of Starr's argument, it would seem, replicates a particular, Puritan hermeneutics described by Sacvan Bercovitch in his now classic study, *The Puritan Origins of the American Self.*

According to Bercovitch, the Calvinist men and women who traveled to New England from England and Holland in the early to middle seventeenth century created a fused sense of personal and historical identity through their concept of national election. America itself became a spiritually unique locale, John Winthrop's "city upon a hill," where Old Testament prophecies were unfolding and being fulfilled by the new chosen people who arrived on such ships as the *Mayflower* and the *Arabella.* The Puritan "mission in the wilderness" was a highly symbolic enterprise, and it is thus not surprising that what Bercovitch calls "the astonishing tenacity of the myth" produced a lasting vision of the state's leader as the embodiment of its highest and most abstract—indeed its most disembodied—ideals.[4]

But what exactly does sex, as we understand it today, have to do with such idealizations of the American self as the ones made glaringly evident in Clinton's trial? Sex is fully and seamlessly interwoven into Kenneth Starr's exegesis of the president's wrongdoing, reminding us explicitly of what is perhaps always the case: Sex and sexuality are part of the conditions necessary to modern subjectivity, and no less so when that subjectivity, in its American forms, can be read in relation to Puritan ideals about an elect nation (even at such a long historical remove). That the president as a national sign is necessarily gendered and sexualized in our day has been made all too clear by the tedious unraveling of the dubious "romance" that bound Starr, the descendant of Puritan persecutors of vice, to Clinton, the humbled, repentant father of the nation, and Monica Lewinsky, the fallen, unrepentant New Woman.

An unlikely ménage à trois reenacting a somewhat grotesque, modern-day *Scarlet Letter,* Starr, Clinton, and Lewinsky illustrate the continuing impact of Puritan structures of imagination on the national culture as well as the various shifts and developments of these legacies.[5] *The Scarlet Letter* is itself a part of this Puritan legacy and a continuation of it, for as Emory Elliott shows, the novel reveals "the effect of a national ideology . . . on the sense of self and personal identity of all Americans, especially sexual identity."[6] A century and a half after Hawthorne's novel was written, and three centuries after the period it invokes, Starr's fulsome narrative (as well as the president's performance in a drama of denial, confession, and repentance) points to the impossibility of separating national ideology, personal subjectivity, and sexual identity from the "representative American self."[7] We hope to show, in the essays that follow, that sex has a proper place within any exegesis of America's Puritan past, and indeed that any analysis of American Puritanism and its consequences for American subjectivities and identities will—to echo Eve Kosofsky Sedgwick—be seriously flawed to the extent that it ignores particularly American histories of sexual representation.[8]

(Post) Origins

The view that American history and culture can or must be viewed in relation to the rhetoric, ideology, and culture of Puritan New England articulated by *The Puritan Origins of the American Self* has become a dominant critical paradigm. Indeed, as Emory Elliott has written, what is distinctive about the modern study of American Puritanism—since the pioneering work of Kenneth Murdock and Perry Miller in the 1930s and 1940s—is the knowledge that New England Puritanism has had a significant impact on American literature and culture: "Not merely a negative element in our intellectual tradition against which enlightened humanists have had to rebel, Puritanism contained the seeds of political and social ideals, structures of thought and language, and literary themes which inspired both the content and the forms of much American writing from 1700 to the present."[9] While this dominant paradigm has inspired both consensus and dissent, it has certainly seemed to confirm a particular American longing for a past, a narrative of origins with a divinely inspired author. But what strikes us as peculiar about these now classic studies of America's Puritan past is their own suppression of sex.[10] While American gender conventions and sexual mores are often derided by both popular and scholarly writers worldwide as "puritanical," little sustained work has been devoted to assessing the ways that the religious and secular Protestant values of moderation, thrift, and spiritual transparency (among others) have materially shaped the American (and, increasingly, global) sex/gender system.

Sexing the Puritan(s)

Certainly, sex among the Puritans has been studied. The venerable scholar of colonial American culture Edmund Morgan long ago put to rest the idea that the Puritans were not interested in sex, that they repressed sexuality in favor of godly behavior. In an argument that has been cited repeatedly, Morgan demonstrates that Puritan sexuality was idealized as a domestic or familial and reproductive behavior. Within the family, and as part of God's plan for populating the New American Israel with His elect, sexuality had a positive and pleasurable place.[11]

More recently, in their highly influential study of the history of sexuality in America, John D'Emilio and Estelle B. Freedman follow Morgan in arguing that Puritans were not antisexual, but rather insisted on regulating sexual practice in ways that conformed to their own orthodox perceptions of the social and moral order and, indeed, in ways that suited their physical conditions in a new and dangerous land. D'Emilio and Freedman revise Morgan by giving concrete shape to the significant Foucauldian insight that sex has a history.[12] Implicit in their analysis is a particular view of America's Puritan past and its relation to subsequent history, a particular view of colonial New England as the origin of later insights about American sexual mores and habits.

Although Freedman and D'Emilio do not represent the views of New England's Puritans as the only or dominant voices about sex in early America, they do take the early Puritans' vaunted emphasis on familial and reproductive sex as the source against which future understandings can be measured and evaluated. Nevertheless, it is only recently that a sustained analysis of the productive capacity (in the Foucauldian sense of the phrase) of Puritan thought and culture on American erotic behavior and sexualities has begun to emerge in scholarship. There remains the attempt to understand how and why complex and multiply conceived Puritan and Protestant ideas about sex and religion are useful for understanding our present and historical cultural representations.

Foucault himself is, of course, germane to this discussion, and is perhaps also its greatest stumbling block. As is well known, Foucault argued in *The History of Sexuality* that sexuality as a distinct form of modern subjectivity, a mode of producing identity around the fact of one's sexual activities, only came into being in the late nineteenth century. According to Foucault, what distinguishes modern forms of sexual control from earlier prohibitions on the body or sexual activity is precisely the idea of producing discursive identities in and on bodies that can then be regimented through these identities. In the nineteenth century, Foucault argues, power directed against bodies shifted from the prohibitionary power of the law and the church to the productive power of medical and psychological discourses. Sexuality, in other words, was produced as a medical and psychological discourse with the result that its policing could be partially constituted by individuals themselves and partially through medical systems that appeared not to have the punishing force of the church or the law.[13]

Foucault's work has energized the study of sex and sexuality in at least two ways. On the one hand, it leads to more finely tuned historicizations. It has led gay- and lesbian- or queer-identified scholars, for example, to outline the uses to which a renewed historical understanding of sex in the colonial period in America can be put. In addition to the work by D'Emilio and Freedman already cited, essays by critics such as Jonathan Goldberg, Michael Warner, and Richard Goodbeer offer more nuanced assessments of America's Puritan past. Often taking their cue from historical studies of early modern England, these critics argue that modern sexual subjectivities such as homosexuality and heterosexuality are not adequate to explain American Puritan constructions of sex. Goldberg and Warner both follow Foucault in demonstrating the profound difference between modern identities that are posited around erotic desire or sexual behavior and those sexual acts that were prohibited by early modern legal and ecclesiastical institutions. They show, for example, that sodomy is a more appropriate category for understanding sexual deviance in colonial New England than homosexuality or any other modern construction of sexual identity. On the surface, at least, theirs are arguments from historical difference rather than continuity, but both show how historical misunderstandings about the nature of Puritan sex can be and are used to justify later hegemonic representations of sexuality in America.[14]

On the other hand, Foucault's work has induced a profound rescripting of what we mean when we study sex and sexuality. To a certain extent, we can see this in Warner's argument. Warner disputes Morgan's (and by implication D'Emilio and Freedman's) presumption that Puritan sexuality can be explained wholly within familial or reproductive models. Their arguments, Warner implies, tend to reproduce a way of imagining sex as a binary arrangement around normality and deviance, married copulation and sodomy, that reproduces modern constructions of heterosexuality and homosexuality. But, Warner shows, the Puritans could and did imagine potential erotic arrangements that cannot be equated with married love or sodomy. In their descriptions of relationships between men, for example, Puritan writings began to imagine what Warner calls a social erotic that located erotic feeling outside the family or the domestic sphere.[15] Whether or not such social erotics were explicitly sexual as we might conceive the term, Warner shows that what counts as the erotic and the sexual in the Puritan imaginary must be considered anew, that the location of erotic feeling or behavior cannot be presumed in advance of study. Like Foucault, he locates possibilities for bodily pleasure in discourses that would not normally, under the modern regime of fixing sexuality as identity, be considered sexual at all. While Warner does not explicitly link Puritan social erotics to contemporary constructions, the connections to alternative and utopian new sexual possibilities that evade the by-now normative identity formations of straight, gay, lesbian, and homosexual is implicit.

So, while Foucault's work tends to enforce the distinction between sexual acts and sexual identities, and while it rightly argues that the regulation of bodies in the modern age is primarily the result of the medicalization and internalization of the discourses of sexual activity, it demands, at the same time, a renewed investigation of those discursive structures by which bodies and bodily pleasures are regulated. In this way, it allows for the investigation of Puritan discourses that may bear some real or imagined relationship to more modern ones, even as it discourages arguments about historical causality or necessity and even as it envisions history as a series of discrete epistemes. Very recent scholarship, some collected here, demonstrates that the mechanisms for control of the body and the self that have developed as part of a Puritan imaginary in American culture play in complex ways around the epistemic shift Foucault sees occurring in the nineteenth century.

Further precedent for bringing the study of sex to bear on America's Puritan legacy can also be found in the work of recent feminist critics. If we consider that gender—which had long been considered without regard to its difference from or its interpellation within sexuality—belongs to a complex of ideas that Gayle Rubin labels "the sex/gender system," then the work of feminist cultural historians becomes an important precursor to our own project.[16] So, to take only a few examples, Ann Kibbey shows the effects of a Puritan sexual imaginary when she argues that colonial men were effectively able to make women a symbolic threat to their authority by equating them and their sexuality to the so-called savagery of the Pequot tribes during the War of 1637. Ivy Schweitzer argues that the Protestant paradigm of conversion was typically gendered male and tended to exclude both women and minorities from participating in what was a redeemed subjectivity—a habit of mind, she argues, that has lasting consequence for the sex/gender and racialized social system in America. And Amy Schrager Lang illustrates how early responses to Anne Hutchinson depended on monstrous constructions of her femininity and sexuality to reassert the male authority that she was presumed to undermine. Hutchinson, in fact, came to symbolize the threat of dissent against male orthodoxy and authority in American cultural production well into the nineteenth century.[17]

But even as these works touch on sexuality and the lasting effects of Puritan representations of it, they tend to figure sexuality as a function of gender and to assume that heterosexuality (and its attendant gender relations) is the primary and inevitable construction of sexual behavior, past and present.[18] The problem is perhaps most acutely seen in the book that provided the groundwork for much of what was to come, Annette Kolodny's *The Lay of the Land*. In a work whose very title is replete with sexual metaphor, and whose implicit claim is that gendered colonial and English metaphors for the American land provided the conditions of possibility for white European settlers' violent claims upon it (indeed, their "rape" of it), Kolodny explores representations not so much of sexuality as of gender. Her encounters with sexual imagery corroborate her sense that the land is gendered, and as her work moves forward, it turns away from the sexual threat of rape as an energizing trope toward a study of the gendered metaphors of nurturance and fertility in representations of the American soil.[19] Kolodny's work, of course, needs no apology, for it inaugurated the necessary woman-centered corrective to such foundational works in American Studies as those produced by F. O. Matthiessen, Henry Nash Smith, Leo Marx, and R. W. B. Lewis.[20] Still, it might be interesting to consider the sexual—and not simply gendered—possibilities implicit in a "female" land[21] when it is tilled and harvested by the many thousands of women who participated in the ambivalent conquest and settlement of North America and in engendering its various frontiers.[22]

Finally, it is surely the case that interest in American sexualities and the Puritan past has been partially shaped by recent considerations of the intersection of race with sexual and gender ideologies throughout American history. In 1991, the task of assessing the intricate relationships among these categories of identity was made especially urgent when sex entered into the public and highly publicized discussions of race and gender that ensued when Anita Hill's sexual harassment allegations were made public in the

Supreme Court confirmation hearings of Clarence Thomas. Although certainly provocative and groundbreaking in many instances, much of the preliminary response to the hearings focused on either gender or race, if not on the precariously constructed (and no-win) juxtaposition of gender *versus* race. Thus the profound complexities of the case were often shunted aside. Defended largely by "white" feminists who were championing the cause of sexual harassment, Hill came to stand for wronged womanhood. Assaulted by what he and his right-wing supporters claimed was a media-orchestrated "hi-tech lynching," Thomas came to stand for ambivalent African-American masculinity. In either formulation, the national history of race relations and postslavery sexual politics, including the systematic assault on black female sexuality under way since the nation's founding, was strangely and conspicuously elided.

Welcome correctives to these omissions came later, many in the essays collected by Toni Morrison and by Robert Chrisman and Robert L. Allen.[23] As Gayle Pemberton notes, Hill and Thomas, whatever their individual histories, were constructed as "symbolic sexual presences."[24] Both served as representatives of a historically sexualized "blackness" to be dissected by the all-white male body of governmental judges,[25] whose power and entitlement drew largely from the fact that by the end of the nineteenth century, in Paula Giddings's words, "race had become an ideology, and a basis of that ideology had become sexual difference."[26] This ideology of sexual difference was only too visible during the hearings, whose spectacle Patricia Williams interprets as a continuation of the Puritan witch trials. Like a woman of Salem, Williams's "Black Witch" cannot exist as her own self, for the American public can only see massed, multiple others: "[I]f I spill soup in a restaurant, they tend to see hundreds of me; if I have a baby, I tend to have a population explosion; if I move into a neighborhood, I come as a forward phalanx of an invading army; if I have an opinion, it is attributed to 'you people.' "[27] Williams's recounting of this obsessive, even pornographic focus on the always multiple, always threatening, and always overtly sexual African-American body sums up rather neatly the metaphorical possession and violation of the racialized, sexed Other that poignantly echoes earlier Puritan models.

A similar plight was enforced upon the original dwellers in the Virgin Land, whose "savage" sexual presence was constructed as a necessary backdrop for the Puritan mission in the wilderness. It is a habit of mind deeply ingrained, as Toni Morrison makes clear in her study of the ways America's canonical texts have tended to eclipse, erase, and relegate to spectral

status nonwhites, and especially African-Americans.[28] Although far out-
numbering the colonists in the environs of seventeenth-century
Massachusetts Bay, Native Americans are mere shadows and ghosts in *The
Scarlet Letter*, which links their presence outside the Christian settler community to Hester's transgressive sexuality and which aligns their
dangerous powers with the evil plotting and sexual frustration of the diabolical persecutor of suffering Puritan ministers, Roger Chillingworth.
Immigrants, migrant workers, and the working proletariat have also been
and continue to be seen along with African-Americans and Native Americans within this fundamentally Puritan paradigm of sexual acculturation
that would replace their communities' notions of conduct with dominant
culture's "civilized" ways, as evidenced in numerous, noncanonical early
twentieth-century novels by, among others, Anzia Yezierska, Tillie Olsen,
Abraham Cahan, and Rebecca Harding Davis.

Arising from such a historical and cultural context, the Puritan American
penchant for staging and recording for posterity public confessions of (racialized) sex has profoundly impacted the narratives and politics of national
identity. But in contrast to the actual acts of violence that have gone toward
the making of America—Native American genocide, witch trials, slavery,
rapes, lynchings, and the exploitation and rejection of immigrant labor, for
example—late-twentieth-century televised hearings about race and sex enable
a safe collective fantasy. They invoke a semireligious ritual of vicarious participation in illicit sexuality.[29] What Homi Bhabha calls the "normalization" of
shared misogynist guilt that Clarence Thomas's performance of "lynching"
made possible for the members of the all-white male Senate Judiciary Committee enabled the soap-operatic spectacle in which Anita Hill came to
represent the oversexed black female within the sanctioned discourse of the
law.[30] Like the national literature of America, the Thomas-Hill hearings
made clear that the sexed "racial persona" still haunts America's national and
sexual conscience. It also revealed that racialized sex often evokes other
specters—e.g., heterosexism and homophobia—as evidenced in allegations
about Hill's "proclivities."[31] However, in a repressive discursive turn that
again recalls Puritan evasions of impure talk, almost no scholarship chose to
examine these national-religious elements in what Lauren Berlant brilliantly
names the "counterpornography of citizenship."[32] Even as Christian religious
discourse circulated messily through the hearings (as it did through the more
recent impeachment scandal), few voices anatomized the purity of that city
upon a hill or its need for sex and race—and scandal—to mark its worth.

Pilgrims' Progress

The essays collected here attempt to do just that, bringing sex to bear on the best of traditional and recent scholarship in American cultural studies. At the same time, they are committed to demonstrating that the American sex/gender system cannot be separated from the particular forms of the American self that have been shaped by a distinct—albeit dynamic and multivalent—complex of Puritan and post-Puritan religious traditions. Indeed, the category of religious identity remains largely absent from recent scholarly conversations about American sexual, racial, and gender identities, their overlaps and discontinuities, and the flows of power among them. Given the kind of work we have been citing so far, however, it should be clear that religion and sex are wholly intertwined categories of analysis—even in the American tradition. As Janet Jakobsen and Ann Pellegrini point out in their reading of *Bowers v. Hardwick*, the 1986 Supreme Court case that upheld the constitutionality of Georgia's criminalizing homosexual and not heterosexual sodomy, "particular Christian claims undergird applications of the secular" even at the level of the Supreme Court, avowedly "the idealized representation of secularism, the site of the separation of church and state."[33]

Although the traditional intellectual and spiritual distinction between spirit and flesh in Christianity tends to obscure the relationship between religion and sex, work on medieval and Renaissance Europe by Carolyn Walker Bynum, Leo Steinberg, and, more recently, Richard Rambuss reveals what was always actually apparent in the discourses of Protestant and Catholic alike: One's relationship to one's God could be ecstatic and erotic. "In the Eucharist and in ecstasy," Bynum writes, "a male Christ was handled and loved; sexual feelings were . . . realized, not so much translated into medium as set free."[34] The eroticized ecstacy of religious devotion was not only apparent in the many pictorial representations of Christ's genitalia that Steinberg reproduces in his study of Christ's sexuality but, as Rambuss shows, was pervasive in the religious poetry of seventeenth-century England.[35] In England's American colonies, Walter Hughes shows, homoerotic—or at the very least homosocial—bonds were implicit in the Puritan male's intimate relationship with God,[36] an intimacy that would seem equally if differently charged in the devotional experience of Puritan women.

While it is certainly true that the connection between religion and sex will be different in different times and places, there is little reason to assume that it is not relatively constant in the history of Christianity. Although Foucault argues that the Christian pastoral exerted its influence on the forms of sexual discourse and behavior only up through the eighteenth century, the essays we have collected suggest that Christian discourses different from the pastoral (for example, the sermon, the diary, the execution narrative) begin to emerge around the body and sex in Puritan thought, and that these discourses prove readable in different (and sometimes the same) registers even after the epistemic shift that Foucault discerns in the nineteenth century. What we take as a matter of faith is the Foucauldian insight that there are no such things as bodies, sex, or sexuality outside power, outside discourses that produce them in particular ways in particular times and places. The question we want to ask is how these have been produced in America, given its unique religious history.

Proliferating Puritans

The essays collected in *The Puritan Origins of American Sex* represent not one particular way of theorizing history or culture but a multiplicity of ways. We have made a strategic decision in compiling the essays in this collection to interpret the notion of "origins" as flexibly as possible, neither shying away from older models of history that locate Puritan life or particular Puritan thinkers as direct sources for ideas and issues that are distinctively American, nor standing polemically against poststructuralist accounts of the impossibility of origins. To have insisted only upon such highly theorized readings of history and historical origins would have seemed to us to close off valuable interventions in the present "sexless" debate about Puritanism in America. So, working within traditional models of source study and biographical influence, two essays in this book show exactly how contemporary American writers have been shaped by Protestant or Puritan thought. Margaret Soenser Breen argues that Jane Rule's classic lesbian novel *Desert of the Heart* imitates the realist conventions of John Bunyan's *Pilgrim's Progress*, and Robert Morace shows how the moral McCarthyism of John Gardner's literary criticism is reflected in his attitudes about sexuality in his novels, and how both are determined by Calvinist influences in his childhood.

By the same token, to have insisted that all the essays in the collection reproduce the Puritan past as a simple source or origin of ideas in historical or contemporary life would have been to ignore the ways in which sex and sexuality have been imagined in the United States after Foucault and Derrida, after identity politics, after, perhaps, sexuality itself. So, two other essays implicitly critique the supposed transparency of Puritan texts in revealing a past that can be claimed as the origin of later ideas. Ed Ingebretsen argues that Puritan and post-Puritan preaching about sexual scandal produces the transgressions it aims to uncover. And Boris Vejdovsky theorizes the "spectral nature of sex" in the Puritan witch trials, and by implication its still spectral nature in modern considerations of the Puritan period.

We are aware that the competing versions of history and historiography that animate these essays may not be reconcilable, much as the (now ritually disavowed) commitment to American exceptionalism or "belief in a special providence, a destiny that is simultaneously America's utopia and its nightmare" implies an inherent, irresolvable conflict.37 And we are even more fully aware that our sometime homage to older histories of culture puts us in the tragically patriarchal position of Cotton Mather, whose work, as described by Boris Vejdovsky, instances a Hamlet-like narrative of the futile attempt to set a disordered world aright to please the fathers—under the distinct burden of imagining that the fathers' world was somehow a golden one. Judith Butler's inveighing against the possibility of origins is relevant to our enterprise: "Logically, this notion of an 'origin' is suspect: for how can something operate as an origin if there are no secondary consequences which retrospectively confirm the originality of that origin? The origin requires its derivations in order to affirm itself as origin, for origins only make sense to the extent that they are differentiated from that which they precede as derivation."38 American Puritanism, in other words, can only be seen as the origin of American identities, the origin of an American self, the origin of American sex because we have already conceived of these identities as the signs that confirm the significance and originality of a founding moment.

But there is, and remains, something profoundly suspicious about any history—whether social, intellectual, or political—that fails to acknowledge its claim to understanding the past as anything other than a retroactive superimposition of the signs of the present. As Hayden White suggests, "[o]ne can, of course, speak of the 'influence' of one thinker or another, of precursors and incarnators of intellectual traditions, and even of 'genealogies' of ideas, if one wishes; but one should do so with the full realization that such concepts are legitimate only within the epistemic presuppositions" of the age in which they appear.39 Whether or not all the essays in this volume accept that radical historiographical premise, we believe that the volume as a whole meets its challenge in articulating history as a largely presentist enterprise. It establishes, that is, "the value of the study of the past not as an end in itself but as a way of providing perspectives on the present that contribute to the solution of problems peculiar to our own time."40

With that challenge in mind, we have tended to favor essays that show how sexuality is represented at particular times in American culture and history and how that representation depends on Puritan or Protestant configurations of ideas. Many of the essays in this collection examine sex and sexuality in relation to gender, race, and class, as well as religion. In this way they reflect the contingent and historical nature of sexuality and often reveal the ways it functions only through other social institutions and discourses. In a provocative argument that links antimasturbation campaigns and the politics of slavery in the nineteenth century, Russ Castronovo shows how the obsessive policing of white bodies' pursuit of the "solitary vice" turns public attention away from the omnipresent social ill of black enslavement. In another essay, Gustavus Stadler reads Edgar Allan Poe's "The Facts in the Case of M. Valdemar" to reveal an American obsession with Jewish bodies—specifically with alien tongues and circumcised penises—and the ways in which this obsession constructs the "phantasmatic Jew" as a threat to Christian logocentrism. Linking another pair of body parts—the eyeball and the female genitalia— Renée Bergland reveals a "racialized genital landscape" that haunts the text of Nathaniel Hawthorne's "Old Manse," populating it with "Indian ghosts" and rendering the writer's wife invisible. When appropriate, the authors in this collection also reveal the entirely evanescent nature of sex—its (non) place within the social, political, and economic regimes by which the human body is regulated. So, as Darryl Dickson-Carr reveals in his analysis of the various autobiographies of Frederick Douglass, there simply was no sexuality, no sex, for Douglass outside the constraining religious and racial discourses of slavery—discourses he negotiated in an attempt to assert his "self" as a gendered and sexual being.

At the same time that we seek the historical discourses through which sexuality becomes meaningful, we eschew the notion that there is one Puritan history to which American identities and subjectivities can be linked. We recognize that in American cultural history there is no such thing as the Puritan or Puritanism. To evoke the now standard cliché of American history, there are only Puritans, Puritanisms, and Protestantisms. We, of course, accept a literal understanding of the word *Puritan* to refer to a group of white European settlers who arrived in New England in the 1630s and following. We are aware and recognize that this group propounded a highly nuanced teleology and ontology that can be shown to reverberate throughout U.S. history. But the reverberations created by the thinking of this group of European settlers

are not always the same and, as Emory Elliott shows, they change over time.⁴¹
We are also acutely aware that any narrative of American history that takes
Puritan ideas to be the source and origin of American selves and sexes threatens to replicate exclusionary notions of identity that construct the American
as a white, Anglo-American male.⁴²

We have, therefore, left it to our contributors to define what they take to be
the Puritan in American life, and we have worked to ensure that the collection
as a whole takes up the issues of Puritan sex and its impact on later history in
a variety of racial, ethnic, gender, and class formations. In some essays—such
as Jodi Schorb's reading of seventeenth- and eighteenth-century execution
narratives, Ed Ingebretsen's analysis of scandal and gossip as Puritan tropes
of social control, and Boris Vejdovsky's exploration of Cotton Mather's struggle with his fathers—the "Puritan" is fixed directly by texts and documents
from colonial New England. Other essays, such as Margaret Breen's reading
of Puritan tropes in lesbian narrative and Nicholas Radel's contextualization
of same-sex desire in the diary of Michael Wigglesworth, locate the American
"Puritan" through English histories and sources. Alternatively, the essays by
Robert Morace, Renée Bergland and Carrie Tirado Bramen find it in the general development of Calvinist thought through American Protestantism. Or
again, Russ Castronovo and Darryl Dickson-Carr find the Puritan in the
racialized reproductive and masculinist ideologies of sex that seem excep-
tional to the United States, or in the more generalized forms of social control
by which the individual American's behavior is tied to an ideal of national
morality and providential purpose.

Often, several of these essays assert, this ideal national morality is constituted as the antidote to the dangerous alterity of the non-Protestant. As
Gustavus Stadler shows the Jewish male to embody a sexualized threat to representative America as framed by Mather or Emerson, Carrie Tirado Bramen
shows the Protestant architects of the 1893 World's Parliament of Religions
to have vested a similar threat in Buddhist monks and Hindu sages. Magdalena Zaborowska finds the constellation of Jewishness and sexual excess
that besets the eponymous hero of *The Rise of David Levinsky* to be both reproduced and revised in media representations of Monica Lewinsky. In her
reading of nineteenth-century convent exposés and antiprostitution narratives, Tracy Fessenden finds a similar conflation of religious and sexual
excess in the trope of the Catholic whore, the Other to the so-called "true
woman" of Protestant domestic discourse. And, finally, Judith Wilt reads a
late-twentieth-century narrative of convent violation, Toni Morrison's *Par-*

adise, as both a cautionary revisiting and a "sex-consecrating" unwriting of the murderous racial and sexual injunctions of the Puritan past.

We do not believe that Puritanism constitutes a historical (or ahistorical) totality, and by allowing its definition to emerge as a series of statements, we hope to show that the very notion of the Puritan is, itself, a flexible category of analysis, one that can be understood both in its seventeenth- and eighteenth-century contexts and as the shifting construction of later periods in American history. It can be made to serve a variety of political and ideological ends. We believe that there are only Puritanisms, proliferating forms of an originary ideal of America that produce sexuality and sex in different ways throughout American history. Our purpose, then, is to unsettle the simple outlines of a progressive history of the origins of American sex while, at the same time, taking heed of the impact of America's Puritan past on its historical and present constructions of sexuality.

Notes

1. The report notes that while every American has the right to privacy in the conduct of personal affairs, in this instance there are limits to that right. The first is set when one is sued in federal court for sexual harassment. Starr points out that legal precedent has established the need to compel the revelation of highly personal and potentially embarrassing matter in such cases. The second limit was set when U.S. District Judge Susan Webber Wright demanded the disclosure of precise information about President Clinton's sex life.

2. *The Starr Report: The Findings of Independent Counsel Kenneth W. Starr on President Clinton and the Lewinsky Affair* (New York: Public Affairs, 1998), 26.

3. Hoover's words are quoted from Eugene Lyons, *Herbert Hoover: A Biography* (1964), 337.

4. *The Puritan Origins of the American Self* (New Haven and London: Yale University Press, 1975), 186. Expounding on some of the ways a similar myth of the presidency influenced Constitution-era formations of masculinity, Dana D. Nelson refers to the "executive body of the president" as "the concrete correlative for national manhood," which "delivers the president to the nation as a purified body, a man *in* but not *of* a body . . . who has risen above the personal passions and . . . attend[s] dispassionately to abstracted national interests." *National Manhood: Capitalist Citizenship and the Imagined Fraternity of White Men* (Durham, N.C.: Duke University Press, 1998), 218.

5. See David Yaffe, "Sex and the City," *The Nation*, 27 December 1999, 31.

6. Emory Elliott, "Art, Religion and the Problem of Authority in *Pierre*," in *Ideology*

and Classic American Literature, ed. Myra Jehlen and Sacvan Bercovitch (New York and Cambridge: Cambridge University Press, 1986), 341.

7. See Alan M. Dershowitz on how the scandal enacts a ritual of "sexual McCarthysim" that confirms the link between politics and sex ever since the times of "our founding fathers . . . [who] were a raunchy crew that included philanderers, pornographers, adulterers, and libertines." *Sexual McCarthyism: Clinton, Starr, and the Constitutional Crisis* (New York: Basic Books, 1998), 208. Although more circumspect on the question of historical precedent, J. Philip Wogaman nevertheless sees the sex scandal as a serious political crisis of a religious kind, a "struggle to define [the nation's] soul." *From the Eye of the Storm: A Pastor to the President Speaks Out* (Louisville, Ky.: Westminster John Knox Press, 1998), 63. See also Magdalena Zaborowska's essay in this collection for a discussion of how such a paradigm excludes and makes "alien" the ethnic female sexuality embodied by Monica Lewinsky.

8. Sedgwick writes that "an understanding of virtually any aspect of modern Western culture must be, not merely incomplete, but damaged in its central substance to the degree that it does not incorporate a critical analysis of modern homo/heterosexual definition." Eve Kosofsky Sedgwick, *Epistemology of the Closet* (Berkeley: University of California Press, 1991), 1.

9. Introduction to *Puritan Influences in American Literature,* ed. Emory Elliott, Illinois Studies in Language and Literature, 65 (Urbana: University of Illinois Press, 1979), xii–xiii. The literature on Protestant New England is, by this point, enormous, but the tradition Elliott refers to finds its classic statement in the work of Perry Miller, *The New England Mind: The Seventeenth Century* (Cambridge: Harvard University Press, 1954). See also *American Puritan Imagination: Essays in Revaluation,* ed. Sacvan Bercovitch (Cambridge and London: Cambridge University Press, 1974); Mason I. Lowance Jr., *The Language of Canaan: Metaphor and Symbol in New England from the Puritans to the Transcendentalists* (Cambridge, Mass., and London: Harvard University Press, 1980); and Patricia Roberts-Miller, *Voices in the Wilderness: Public Discourse and the Paradox of Puritan Rhetoric* (Tuscaloosa and London: University of Alabama Press, 1999). Although Roberts-Miller points to the lasting influence of Bercovitch's work and the tradition of seeing the Puritans as a source of American culture, it should be noted that in *Puritan Imagination* Sacvan Bercovitch himself outlines a decisive break with this tradition in criticism from the 1970s and '80s.

10. With the exception of Elliott's piece on *Pierre* quoted above.

11. The classic account is "The Puritans and Sex," *New England Quarterly* 25 (December 1942): 591–607; see also Morgan's book, *The Puritan Family: Religious and Domestic Relations in Seventeenth-Century New England* (New York: Harper and Row, 1966).

12. The most influential articulation of the historical contingency of sexuality and sex is Michel Foucault's *The History of Sexuality,* vol. 1, trans. Robert Hurley (New York: Random House, 1978), but Thomas Laqueur's *Making Sex* (Cambridge, Mass., and London: Harvard University Press, 1990), and Jeffrey Weeks's *Sex, Politics, and*

Society: The Regulation of Sexuality since 1800 (London: Longman, 1981) might also be mentioned.

13. Foucault, *The History of Sexuality*. See chapter 2, "The Perverse Implantation."

14. Jonathan Goldberg, "Bradford's 'Ancient Members' and 'A Case of Buggery . . . amongst Them,'" in *Sodometries: Renaissance Texts, Modern Sexualities* (Stanford, Calif.: Stanford University Press, 1992), 223–46; Richard Goodbeer, "'The Cry of Sodom': Discourse, Intercourse, and Desire in Colonial New England," *The William and Mary Quarterly*, 3d ser., 52.2 (April 1995): 259–85; Michael Warner, "New England Sodom," *American Literature* 64.1 (March 1992): 19–47; reprinted in *Queering the Renaissance*, ed. Jonathan Goldberg (Durham, N.C., and London: Duke University Press, 1994), 330–58. Also significant in this regard is Alan Bray, "To Be a Man in Early Modern Society: The Curious Case of Michael Wigglesworth," *History Workshop Journal* 41 (spring 1996): 158ff.

15. Warner, "New English Sodom," 352.

16. Gayle Rubin, "The Traffic in Women: Notes on the 'Political Economy' of Sex," in Rayna R. Reiter, ed., *Toward an Anthropology of Women* (New York: Monthly Review Press, 1975), 157–210.

17. Ann Kibbey, *The Interpretation of Material Shapes in Puritanism: A Study of Rhetoric, Prejudice, and Violence* (New York and Cambridge: Cambridge University Press, 1986); Ivy Schweitzer, *The Work of Self-Representation: Lyric Poetry in Colonial New England* (Chapel Hill and London: University of North Carolina Press, 1991); Amy Schrager Lang, *Prophetic Woman: Anne Hutchinson and the Problem of Dissent in the Literature of New England* (Berkeley and Los Angeles: University of California Press, 1987).

18. Recent writing on sex and sexuality has considerably complicated the field. See, for example, *The Last Sex: Feminism and Outlaw Bodies*, ed. Arthur and Marilouise Kroker (New York: St. Martin's Press, 1993), which ponders the negative effects of America's "will to purity," effects such as "the politics of the 1990s: sexual cleansing, ethnic cleansing, bodily cleansing, intellectual cleansing, racial cleansing. The politics of an entirely fictional search for a purity that never existed, and never will" (13). See also *Bodyspace: Destabilizing Geographies of Gender and Sexuality*, ed. Nancy Duncan (New York and London: Routledge, 1996); *Sexual Artifice: Persons, Images, Politics*, ed. Ann Kibbey, Kayann Short, and Abouali Farmanfarmaian (New York: New York University Press, 1994); *Feminism, the Public and the Private* (Oxford and New York: Oxford University Press, 1998), ed. Joan B. Landes; and Deborah Lupton "Talking about Sex: Sexology, Sexual Difference, and Confessional Talk Shows," in *Eroticism and Containment: Notes from the Flood Plain*, ed. Carol Siegel and Ann Kibbey (New York: New York University Press, 1994), 45–65. Although they do not address the Puritan legacy explicitly, these studies illustrate some of the cultural and historical tendencies explored in the present collection.

Similarly, we acknowledge the earlier work of Americanist scholars whose studies of sentiment, conduct, domestic fiction, and gender ideology more generally paved the way for later claims about the impact of Protestant society and literary culture on the historical constructions of sex/gender systems. These include: Jane Tompkins, *Sensational Designs: The Cultural Work of American Fiction, 1790–1860* (New York and Oxford: Oxford University Press, 1985); Nancy Armstrong and Leonard Tennenhouse, eds., *The Ideology of Conduct: Essays on Literature and the History of Sexuality* (New York: Methuen, 1987); Ann Douglas, *The Feminization of American Culture* (New York: Farrar, Strauss, and Giroux, 1998, reprinted); and Nina Baym, *Woman's Fiction: A Guide to Novels by and about Women in America, 1820–1870* (Ithaca: Cornell University Press, 1978). See also the more recent collaboration by Armstrong and Tennenhouse, *The Imaginary Puritan: Literature, Intellectual Labor, and the Origins of Personal Life* (Berkeley and Los Angeles: University of California Press, 1994).

19. Annette Kolodny, *The Lay of the Land: Metaphor as Experience and History in American Life and Letters* (Chapel Hill: University of North Carolina Press, 1975).

20. F. O. Matthiessen, *American Renaissance: Art and Expression in the Age of Emerson and Whitman* (New York: Oxford University Press, 1941); Henry Nash Smith, *Virgin Land: The American West as Symbol and Myth* (New York: Random House, 1950); Leo Marx, *The Machine in the Garden: Technology and the Pastoral Ideal in America* (New York: Oxford University Press, 1964); and R. W. B. Lewis, *The American Adam: Innocence, Tragedy, and Tradition in the Nineteenth Century* (Chicago: University of Chicago Press, 1955).

21. This vision largely excludes its native inhabitants as subjects, whose gendered, racialized, and sexualized presence complicates and disrupts both the dichotomies set up by the earlier, white-male-centered American studies scholarship and the dichotomies underlying early feminist interventions.

22. See also other works by Kolodny: *The Land before Her: Fantasy and Experience of the American Frontiers, 1630–1860* (Chapel Hill: University of North Carolina Press, 1984), "Among the Indians: The Uses of Captivity," *New York Times Book Review*, 31 January 1993, 26–28, and "Letting Go Our Grand Obsessions: Notes toward a New Literary History of the American Frontiers," in *Subjects and Citizens: Nation, Race, and Gender from Oroonoko to Anita Hill*, ed., Michael Moon and Cathy N. Davidson (Durham, N.C.: Duke University Press, 1995), 9–26.

23. *Race-ing Justice, En-gendering Power: Essays on Anita Hill, Clarence Thomas, and the Construction of Social Reality*, ed. Toni Morrison (New York: Pantheon Books, 1992). *Court of Appeal: The Black Community Speaks Out on the Racial and Sexual Politics of Thomas vs. Hill*, ed. Robert Chrisman and Robert L. Allen (New York: Ballantine Books, 1992).

24. Gayle Pemberton, "A Sentimental Journey: James Baldwin and the Thomas-Hill Hearings," *Race-ing Justice*, 179–80.

25. See also Calvin Hernton, "Breaking Silences," *Court of Appeal*, 86–91, which focuses on "the sexual and racial *smearing* of Anita Hill by members of an all-white-male Senate Judiciary Committee, along with a black man and his supporters, including a majority of the public." Hernton discusses the concept of "race first and

sex second . . . [as] a misogynist ideology that mandates male appropriation of women's bodies as objects of pornography and abuse" (88). In the same volume, see also pieces by June Jordan, "Can I Get a Witness" (120–24), Charles R. Lawrence III, "Cringing at Myths of Black Sexuality" (136–38), Melba Joyce Boyd, "Collard Greens, Clarence Thomas, and the High-Tech Rape of Anita Hill" (43–46), Julianne Malveaux, "No Peace in a Sisterly Space" (143–47), and Barbara Smith, "Ain't Gonna Let Nobody Turn Me Around" (185–89).

26. Paula Giddings, "The Last Taboo," *Race-ing Justice*, 446.

27. Patricia J. Williams, "A Rare Case Study of Muleheadedness and Men, or How to Try an Unruly Black Witch, with Excerpts from the Heretical Testimony of Four Women, Known to Be Hysterics, Speaking in Their Own Voices, as Translated for This Publication by Brothers Hatch, Simpson, DeConcini, and Specter," *Race-ing Justice*, 167.

28. Toni Morrison, *Playing in the Dark: Whiteness and the Literary Imagination* (New York: Vintage Books, 1992).

29. See especially the title story in James Baldwin's *Going to Meet the Man* (New York: Dial Press, 1965), 227–49, and Ida B. Wells's groundbreaking work on lynching in the South discussed in Paula Giddings *Where and When I Enter*, 2nd edition (New York: William Morrow and Co., 1996).

30. Homi Bhabha, "A Good Judge of Character: Men, Metaphors, and the Common Culture," *Race-ing Justice*, 232–50. "If the lynched body is black, its real color is its gender. Masked by a history of racial oppression that has become a convenience rather than a conviction, you can hear Thomas say to his interrogators, 'I may be accused of sexual harassment, but ain't I a man?'" (247–48). See also Kimberlé Crenshaw, "Whose Story Is It, Anyway? Feminist and Antiracist Appropriations of Anita Hill," *Race-ing Justice*, 402–40.

31. Jessie Givner, "TV Crisis and Confession: The Hill-Thomas Hearings," *Confessional Politics: Women's Sexual Self-Representation in Life Writing and Popular Media*, ed. Irene Gammel (Carbondale and Edwardsville: Southern Illinois University Press, 1999), 121. See also Nancy Frasier, who stresses the inclusion of class in the debates on sex, "Sex, Lies, and the Public Sphere: Reflections on the Confirmation of Clarence Thomas," in *Feminism, the Public and the Private*, 314–37.

32. Lauren Berlant, "The Queen of America Goes to Washington City: Harriet Jacobs, Frances Harper, Anita Hill," in *Subjects and Citizens* 455–80. See also Karla F. C. Holoway, "The Body Politic" in the same volume, 481–95, and Margaret A. Eisenhower and Nancy R. Lawrence's "Anita Hill, Clarence Thomas and the Culture of Romance," in *Sexual Artifice*, 94–121.

33. Janet Jakobsen and Ann Pellegrini, "Getting Religion," in *One Nation under God? Religion and American Culture* (New York and London: Routledge, 1999), 104.

34. Caroline Walker Bynum, *Holy Feast and Holy Fast: The Religious Significance of Food to Medieval Women* (Berkeley and Los Angeles: University of California Press, 1978), 248. Although Bynum later shies away, in an important dispute with Leo

Steinberg, from the idea that sexuality is implicit in representations of Christ, the connection between sex and religion is manifest. See also Bynum's "The Female Body and Religious Practice," in her *Fragmentation and Redemption: Essays on Gender and the Human Body in Medieval Religion* (New York: Zone Books, MIT Press, 1991).

35. Leo Steinberg, *The Sexuality of Christ in Renaissance Art and Modern Oblivion* (New York: Pantheon, 1983), and Richard Rambuss, "Pleasure and Devotion: The Body of Jesus and Seventeenth-Century Religious Lyric," in *Queering the Renaissance*, 253–79.

36. Walter Hughes, "'Meat out of the Eater': Panic and Desire in American Puritan Poetry," in *Engendering Men*, ed. Joseph A. Boone and Michael Cadden (New York and London: Routledge, 1990), 102–21.

37. Alan Trachtenberg, "American Studies as a Cultural Program," in *Ideology and Classic American Literature*, ed. Sacvan Bercovitch and Myra Jehler (Cambridge: Cambridge University Press, 1990), 177. See also Sam B. Girgus, *The New Covenant: Jewish Writers and the American Idea* (Chapel Hill: University of North Carolina Press, 1984), which points at links between mythic and antimythic traditions in Jewish America that run parallel to the American Jeremiad.

38. Judith Butler, *Gender Trouble: Feminism and the Subversion of Identity* (London and New York: Routledge, 1991), 313.

39. Hayden White, "The Historiography of Anti-Humanism," in *The Content of the Form: Narrative Discourse and Historical Representation* (Baltimore and London: Johns Hopkins University Press, 1987), 121.

40. Hayden White, "The Burden of History," *History and Theory* 5.2 (1966); reprinted in *Tropics of Discourse: Essays in Cultural Criticism* (Baltimore: Johns Hopkins University Press, 1978), 41.

41. Emory Elliott, "The Puritan Roots of American Whig Rhetoric," in Elliott, *Puritan Influences*, 107–27.

42. This problem is fully explicated in Toni Morrison's study of early American identity in *Playing in the Dark* and in Houston A. Baker, "Figurations for a New American Literary History," *Ideology and Classic American Literature*, 145–71.

Wigglesworth, Mather, Starr

Witch-Hunts and General Wickedness in Public

ᑐᓵ

Ed Ingebretsen

In all its unofficial aspects the history [of witchcraft] would long continue.... Its vestigial remnants could almost certainly be discovered not far from our time.
—John Demos, *Entertaining Satan*

If you are going to rely in this proceeding on a Time *magazine essay ... then I think the standards are not quite as lofty as I thought they would be this evening.*
—Kenneth Starr before the House Judiciary Committee, 19 November 1998

Congress, when the time came, pushed titillating material immediately and unthinkingly into the public domain. This howling after sex stoked the fires of Republican moralists.
—*The Economist*, 13 February 1999

𝒯*he theological underpinnings* of the Puritan civic order in the New World demanded of its citizenry interior vigilance, lest they fall prey to "sathan's wiley baites."[1] Indeed, from the Reformation onward, what might be called a spiritual narcissism seems inevitably a part of a good conscience. John Calvin himself had argued that "to know God is to be struck with horror and amazement, for . . . only then does one realize his own character."[2] If from a distance of 350 years the spiritual self-reflections of the English Puritans sound strident, even apocalyptic, that is only fitting, for the persecutions they fled in the early seventeenth century could only betoken, as they thought, the end times. Indeed, the freedom sought by the Puritans, like that sought by post-Reformation Christianity in general, was hardly freedom *from* laws but a submission to the final law, inexorably approaching. As John Winthrop explained, "[t]his liberty is maintained and exercised in a way of subjection to authority."[3] Liberty was not freedom from kings; in Winthrop's systematically gendered covenental politics, liberty was motivation for final salvific submission to ultimate kingship.

Individual self-awareness, however, was only one aspect of this spiritual ideal, and it needs to be remembered that Puritanism set out to embody the righteous community withdrawn (if not separated) from the world. Liberty was a virtue of apocalypse—to be made new the heavens and earth required, paradoxically, an emphatic *communal* vigilance. In 1630, Winthrop made the point clear to the English founders of the Massachusetts Bay Colony. Speaking aboard the *Arabella* while still at sea, and freely adapting both the image and the authority of the biblical Jesus, Winthrop linked the group to a "citee on a hill"— collectively scrutinized by friend and foe alike in the Old World. "The eyes of all people are upon us. . . . [W]e shall be made a story and a by-word through the world."[4] John Winthrop made explicit, then, what Calvin's intense interiority only implied. Bluntly put, *being watched* was as much a part of the religious program as interior vigilance, while godly affections were as necessary to *civic* duty as to religious virtue. In success—or perhaps even more in failure—not only were cities "on hills" to be watched; by implication individuals, too, were proper objects of scrutiny, gossip, and imprecation. Failure could be instructive: a pedagogy of the godly by the godless.

While the Puritans may not have invented sex, their aims, governance, and habit of moral typologizing were well suited for realizing the ideological possibilities of the body.[5] They became, in one critic's phrase, "inveterate symbolizers of sex."[6] Their post-Reformation civic rhetoric built upon an astringent moral discourse, the purifying goals of which were cast in apocalyptic terms; the body politic and the godly citizen were allegorically linked, in the words of the Mayflower Compact, as the "Civil Body Politic."[7] That is, in the Puritan mode of spiritual allegory typified in *The Pilgrim's Progress*, the body was fixed as a fleshy correlative of ultimate spiritual facts, its mortal condition transient but indicative, in Jonathan Edward's phrase, of "divine things."

Thus, one's behavior achieved significance as a visible sign of God's grace or lack thereof.[8] Further, because of the explicitly communal and eschatological nature of the Puritan settlements, "community responsibility for regulating morality"[9] was explicitly authorized: "Indeed, because of its religious utopian nature, early New England society deviated from the English pattern by creating an excess of order, based on an ideal of extreme social cohesiveness and the practice of close surveillance of personal morality."[10] Winthrop, acting in his judicial capacity, soberly puts the matter to Anne

Hutchinson, on trial for her contrary theological views: "Your conscience you must keep or it must be kept for you."[11]

A "legacy of community regulation of morality"[12] is still in place, of course, and sociologists and sexologists alike agree that the body is a pivotal symbol for the display of ideological need.[13] Nor are the Puritans alone to be blamed—or credited—for ascribing to the sexual economy a central symbolic function.[14] Sexual profligacy and its dire consequences—from the "French pox" to prostitution to the threat of AIDS—is a standard demonizing trope for unwanted or inconvenient social populations.[15] In particular, the sexual theme of seduction—not to speak of the act of sex itself—has a long history of allegorically representing religious need. In New England, for particular example, Winthrop frames the antinomian crisis of the 1630s as a crisis of persons "very loose and degenerate in their practices."[16] While in 1651, a magistrate condemned a Baptist freethinker from Rhode Island in a way that makes clear the association between sex and religion: The man is punished "for error, and going about to seduce the people."[17] As David Halperin observes, the "social body precedes the sexual body."[18] In the Puritan dispensation, that social body, and the narrative it prompted, was apocalyptic—expostulary and alarmist. Framed through its hermeneutics, unregulated sex, which was implicitly gendered feminine, signaled communal decline.

The regulation of sexual expression was an integral, even expressive, part of the Puritan commonwealths; sex explicitly became the carrier of social meaning. The marital and reproductive, familial and patriarchal order of the Puritan settlements was thought to replicate in small the larger order of the commonwealths. These, in turn, dramatized the covenantal bonds of marital love between God and His people. As John D'Emilio and Estelle Freedman explain, during the first years of the Puritan settlements "sexuality was not really a private matter, for family and community drew few boundaries between the sexual concerns of individuals and those of the group." Indeed, in the New England Way, as it was called, where theological order confirmed civil hierarchy, "intrusiveness characterized the attitude toward sexuality."[19] Sexual restraint was thought to set the Puritans significantly apart from the seeming sexual omniverousness of the natives and from the alarming profligacy of other immigrant groups.

Decrying sexual transgression—as well as other public excess—was a typical feature of Puritan preaching. Yet from Winthrop, Wigglesworth, and Mather, to Jonathan Edwards a century later, and even beyond, the preaching of sin sometimes had unintended consequences. Sex and accounts of crime—"Riots, Revels, Debauches," and "Horrid Oathes"[20]—moralized in the form of dramatic sermons and crudely printed broadsides, were publicized in ways that heightened interest in the proscribed activities. Thus, the higher good of the community was reached by appealing to the lower appetites.[21] Morality then, as well as the erotic marking of participants, was staged for various forms of profit, however much the actions were rhetorized as being for the communal good.

To the Puritan divines, more importantly, occasions of sin were emphatically moments of crisis, in the word's original sense of "opportunity." The public repudiation of "Swearing, Sabbath-breaking, Whoring, Drunkenness, and the like"[22] was often less about individual blame than about ritualizing communal cohesion. The visible scaffold in the center of town, to which grievous public sinners would be consigned, was offset by an equally apparent, if less material, ritual form: confession and repentance, an abjection conducted, sometimes literally, before the pulpit. Winthrop, says his editor, "dwelt as much on the penitential scaffold scenes as on the crime."[23] Indeed, as David Hall notes, "Confession . . . was *the* New England ritual, the one that ordinary people witnessed, read of, and reiterated countless times."[24] Public confession and repentance were signal public moments, so important that as elements in social drama the public repentance often overshadowed the acts that occasioned it. A mutual dependence thus existed between seemly and unseemly affairs, so much so that the discovery of the wrongful act, even its public orchestration, would be initiated, and sometimes directed, by those authorities who one would think had the most invested in keeping them hidden.

What is the relationship, one is drawn to ask, between public transgression and the maintenance of civil law—a collusion so often presumed by moralized, sometimes expressly religious, dramas of scandal and disclosure? How is authority complicit with the threat of its (to use a word) impeachment? This essay considers a recent case of sex, revelation, disclosure, and examines its function as authoritative public moral discourse. How was Kenneth Starr's—and the U.S. Congress's and the public media's and the general populace's—"howling after sex" a complicated public gesture, acknowledged as such even by those opposed to it (again, Starr, the U.S. Congress, and the media in general)?[25] How do moralizing and eroticizing maneuvers framing the body duplicate, even as they undercut, each other? How do they sign authority as well as signal its disruption? If in the Anglo-Protestant tradition, sexual sin is a de facto demonstration of communal failure, as Winthrop, Wigglesworth, and others affirm, what, we might ask, are the pedagogical uses of contemporary sin, and how is scandal its unofficial sacrament?

George M. Marsden observes that John Winthrop, the first governor of the Massachusetts Bay Colony, "assumed [as he cited Deuteronomy] that he could transfer the principles of nationhood found in ancient Israel to the Massachusetts Bay Company with no need for explanation."[26] Marsden concludes that the "practical confusion of church and state" logically followed this "overriding presumption." In the entangled spiritual and civil eschatology of post-Reformation governance, private experience was of great public concern since inner movements signified the presence (or absence) of God. One sees both the mundane and the eschatological import of this, for example, in the work of Jonathan Edwards, grandson of the great Puritan divine Solomon Stoddard and third-generation heir to New World Calvinist typological thinking. In "Personal Narrative," his diary that dates from 1739, Edwards charts with exquisite detail his interior spiritual movements toward, and sometimes away from, God. In A History of Redemption, published posthumously, Edwards argues the public consequences of these movements—that the apocalyptic hope underpinning the Reformation (and thus the Puritan commonwealths as well) would be brought to fruition in the New World.[27] It was against such apocalyptic urgencies that, in the example of the Massachusetts Bay Colony, "the General Court [by 1636] confined freemanship to persons who passed the new test for church membership."[28] Full citizenship thus entailed reception at the Lord's table, which first necessitated that one's spiritual movements be publicly confessed and validated. Thus, in a social order where temporal rule was intended to support a godly state, sin was as much the community's business as was visible grace.

Nonetheless, to listen to the preachers, traffic in the former seemed much more brisk. Transgression has many civic uses, as theorists of deviancy across a range of perspectives attest.[29] Bluntly put, any society must license transgression, somehow harnessing—and putting to use—its antinomian energies. Puritan society was unexceptional in this regard. Still, as Michael Colacurcio suggests, the Puritan's way of talking about sex was "different, distinctive, and revealing."[30] Colonial polemics against sin unfold a narrative that is explicitly gendered. While the male body figured as transgressive most often in scenes of public disturbance—drink or revelry, for example—all too often women bore the brunt of "private" transgression. Sexual sins were most often laid at their doors, and women were typically punished more severely than men for sexual irregularities.[31] A 1637 broadside, for example, opposes the "Cards" and "Dice" that "fill the Day" to the "sensual Joys and low Delights / That Women give . . . all their Nights."[32] Nonetheless, carnal excess of any sort was deemed to have theological consequences and was thus communally significant. "Lustful motion" implied "erroneous notion"—a link made earlier as the medieval equation of witchcraft and heresy.

Perry Miller comments that the tradition of the New England jeremiad indicates that public sinning was, to some degree at least, awarded a higher status than public sanctity. Effective preaching necessitated, as it were, the exemplum of perversity (in its older sense of "turning astray"). Yet in preaching the scandalous for its spiritual value, negativity threatened to swamp the preaching's original purpose of moral persuasion. By means of such discourse, the community would be schooled by scandal—with the consequence that it was schooled *in* it as well. As Miller remarks, moral uplift gave way to "a staggering compendium of iniquity."[33]

The ambiguous status of the transgressive act—"felix" as well as "culpa"— is, however, not new to the Puritans. The showy iniquity and the equally showy chastening are both aspects of a pervasive Christian allegory of regeneration. Under Reformed Christianity's this-worldly gaze, this allegory devolved into the equivalent of a new sacrament, an outward sign of inward grace. Accordingly, both the public keeping of the law and the public excoriation of its failures in the periodic election day, fast day, or other occasional sermon were important ritual moments in a citizen's civic life. Individual transgressions, for all they were decried, were a most direct way of binding a community to itself. Licensed, as it were, from the pulpit even as it was most vociferously repudiated there, transgression was something of a perverse *milagro*—a memorial and "monument." The marked sinner as well as the visible saint could give witness to God's powerful presence: thus the example made of Anne Hutchinson for her theological challenge in the mid-1630s, and later, of Bridget Bishop for her failure to abide by Boston's sumptuary laws. (Bishop was the first to be executed as a witch in Salem, 1692.) These women, visibly resisting authority, became witnesses to public order. For as much as Reformed Christians broke from the Roman Catholic hagiographic tradition, in the end they retained it in inverted form, replacing visibly marked saints with communally repudiated sinners.

In *Bonifacius* Cotton Mather writes, "If any person . . . fall into a scandalous iniquity, let the rebukes of the Society be dispensed unto him; and let them forbid him to come any more among them, until he bring suitable expressions and evidences of repentance with him."[34] Thus, "suitable expressions" of both sinner and spectator were sought, since the display of sin was intended.[35] One sees the public dimension of this ritual repeatedly in early Puritan accounts. John Winthrop writes about passing sentence of banishment upon Anne Hutchinson: "Mr. Cotton pronounced the sentence of admonition with great solemnity, and with much zeal and detestation of her errors and pride of spirit. The assembly continued till eight at night, and all did acknowledge the presence of God's spirit therein."[36] In another example, concluding his account of the 1672 possession of Elizabeth Knapp in Groton, Samuel Willard, the town pastor, observed, "She is a monument of divine severity, and the Lord grant that all that see or hear may fear and tremble."[37]

Scandal

Though Willard did not use the word exactly, Knapp is a "monster"—a judgment and a "wonder" upon the community, demonstrating divine disquiet.[38] Willard's identification of Elizabeth Knapp thus provides a gloss on Winthrop's "story and by-word"; both remind us that the civic use of spectacular evil is a staple of Christian discourse—especially in the history of preaching, Catholic as well as Reformed, where doctrinal orthodoxy sometimes mattered less than its colorful application. To scare the hell out of a recalcitrant or hardened sinner a preacher might use hell itself. For this reason, the obsessive retailing of sin and the close entwining of the sinful and the good in the accounts of the Puritan divines should not surprise us. In the first place, transgression is an unremarkable, even necessary feature of the Christian cosmology, its existence fundamental to its narrative and doctrine. Indeed, the Edenic fantasy of Genesis locates sin within the very act of desiring the good and the beautiful: "The tree was lovely to behold."[39]

Nor can one limit a spiritual interest in the public display of transgression to post-Reformation Christianity. The teaching value of "offense" was well understood by Jesus. For instance, Winthrop takes the image "city on a hill" from the long discourse in Matthew's Gospel where Jesus articulates the provocative dynamics by which the good functions both as moral example and as affront. The lamp, lit and placed upon the hill, shines for all to see. Conversely, that lamp shines *upon* all, illuminating the viewer as well. Indeed, throughout the Gospels, Jesus himself used scandal pedagogically to force reactions from his auditors. Blessed, he says, are those who are not offended in me, knowing full well that he has gone to great lengths precisely to elicit offense.

If Jesus used scandal to question authority, similarly, the scenes of public transgression managed by Winthrop, Wigglesworth, and Mather during the first years of the New England settlements were likewise prompted by questions of authority. From two centuries' distance the observer notes how the periodic scandals of "lay protest"[40]—the antinomians, the Halfway Covenant, or even the affair of Salem Village—erupted in times of civic crisis, almost as if the public controversy were the means by which communal distress could be represented to itself. Winthrop, Wigglesworth, and Mather each wield an authority that is, in different ways, either discredited or under threat; each wields the transgressive scene in order to define, and stabilize, the community's sense of itself. A "community in peril" facing "shipwreck" is how Winthrop framed the ragtag group of immigrants aboard the *Arabella*.[41] A parallel sense of moral peril and apocalyptic decline will inspire Wigglesworth's "The Day of Doom" (1662) and, thirty years after that, justify Mather's "Wonders of the Invisible World" (1693). If apocalypse is the occasion of virtue, the presence of sin is its enunciating, revealing sign, and as such, ideologically useful.

Michael Wigglesworth, a neurasthenic, unpopular minister in Malden, Massachusetts, suffered from what today might be called scruples about sexual impropriety in his private life and alarmist tendencies about its consequences in public. Concerned by the Halfway Covenant and what it suggested about the evidently declining morality of the time, he composed an ode to Judgment Day, "The Day of Doom" (1662). Its tone is energetically rebuking, as he addresses his congregation from a position clearly removed from theirs:

> With cords of love God often strove
> Your stubborn hearts to tame . . .
> "Your waxing worse, hath stopped the course
> of wonted clemency:
> Mercy refused, and grace misused,
> call for severity."[42]

Wigglesworth's verse is leering as well. Repudiating sin necessitated the display of sinners "Wallowing in all kind of sin" (v.2). Wigglesworth takes as his premise the fact that Winthrop's reasoned portrayal of the Christian life, covenanted in a form of marital love, was in fact duplicitous. His verses imply that orderly appearances were belied by disorderly secrets—whose existence, Wigglesworth believed, it was his ministerial duty to expose, uncover, and elaborate upon at length. God's "flaming eyes hid things doth spy, / and darkest things reveal" (v.13). Which he did, detailing for 224 eight-line verses the ruses of "Virgins unwise, who through disguise / among the best were numbered" (v.2).

Perry Miller comments that "The Day of Doom" is "the first American best-seller."[43] Another commentator suggests that the poem is "as comforting as it is frightening," which first strikes us as odd.[44] Is it Wigglesworth's salacious intimations of secrecy that were comforting, or is it his condemnatory rhetoric—which if frightening, is at least familiar, and thus perhaps comforting *as* familiar fear? Whatever the case, there was little doubt but that Wigglesworth had hit upon a formula for entertainment, if not moral uplift: "filthy facts" and "secret acts" detailed at length for spiritual edification. The private, "hidden things" and "darkest things" (feminized, as we have seen in the 1637 broadside) are uncovered, become available for public delectation. Wigglesworth's moralizing impulse here establishes, at the same time, a discourse of the titillating; in effect Wigglesworth establishes the conditions by which secrets— "however closely done"—simultaneously produce authority as well as its subversion. No wonder, as Miller remarks, that of the 1,800 copies printed, none are extant because they were "read to pieces."[45] Wigglesworth is important, then, in that he reflects the formulas still in use by which crypto-religious emotions—guilt, voyeurism and public entitlement of the private, framed apocalyptically as revelation—pass as an implicitly national moral discourse.

Thirty years later Cotton Mather likewise found himself addressing, in a similarly apocalyptic mode, an outward communal placidity in which interior duplicity is explicitly gendered. "The knot of witches," then accountably besetting Salem, prompts an epistemological crisis: What is known, and who knows it? Nonetheless, Mather's retrospective explanation of the Salem events is largely disingenuous: Despite his earnest solicitation of the readers' goodwill, his own anxieties about the crisis posed to authority are clear. The introductory "Author's Defense" concludes by saying that Mather's own thoughts on the subject "will be owned by most of the Ministers of God in these Colonies."[46] Still, the text reveals that Mather himself is not convinced by what he chronicles. Published in 1693, the year following the identifying, trying, and executions of at least nineteen persons for witchcraft, the document covertly intends to exonerate Mather for failing to protest the trials—an inaction all the more damning since Mather himself was skeptical of the evidentiary value of the "spectral" basis for the witchcraft convictions. Mather's self-perceived guilt of passivity thus becomes justified in his own mind by the epistemological threat to the text of the body politic. The situation was, in his words, "an Attempt more Difficult, more surprising, more snarl'd with unintelligible Circumstances than any that we have hitherto Encountered."[47]

Scholars note that the withdrawal of Massachusetts's royal charter in 1684 caused consequent anxiety about authority to be dramatized through class conflicts within the town; both concerns eventually became encoded in the palimpsestic body of the witch. Mather's discovery of the witches, then, did not so much give names and faces to the hapless individuals arrested for witchcraft as it gave social approbation to an eroticized public fantasy of witch conspiracy that had political usefulness: "An Army of Devils is horribly broke in upon the place which is the Center." Following the revocation of the royal charter, it could easily seem to the churches that the devil was attempting to "pull down all the Churches in the Country,"[48] and succeeding.

Even critics of the time noted that the spectacular, even theatrical content of the civil proceedings exceeded the theologies they were meant to demonstrate—and to inculcate. Still, from today's perspective this historical narrative is important for a number of reasons—not the least its anticipation of another civil proceeding whose theatrics seemed also to dwarf the morals it meant to prove. First, Mather's text effectively undoes its own authority. Mather writes, as he says, not so much as an "advocate," but as a "historian"[49]—though he admits he was not present at any of the trials. In addition, the text reflects not so much the material presence of the witches as Mather's (and the town's) high state of anxiety and obsession with them—prompted, it must be said, less by their presence than by their absence and ultimate unprovability.[50] Mather's text reveals, not the prior existence of witches, but rather how a civic order under crisis negotiated them into existence for its own purposes.[51] In this respect Mather echoes Wigglesworth and anticipates Starr. One can argue that Wigglesworth, Mather, and Starr high-mindedly *generate* the fantasy of transgression they intend to uncover. Each construes the publication of the lubricious fantasies of deviancy, sex, and hidden failure as public acts of moral worth. Each, that is, uses the trangressive act in order to clarify, explain, and defend the community's high ideal of itself. Each, also, uses the incident to bolster his own authority, oddly by invoking the very disorder he seeks to put down.

Cotton Mather's narrative, John Demos says, was "meant to reduce the Devil's influence by holding him up to public scrutiny." More to the point,

Demos observes, "as in many things 'Puritan,' the issue of *exposure* was central here."[52] Indeed, when was it not? From time immemorial, the retailing of
sin in public places was a multifaceted affair, the meaning of which was
rarely stable. The pillory, for example, until the mid-eighteenth century the
venue where sin *was* displayed as public example, could as easily be turned
against those authorities displaying it as the sympathy of the crowds aligned
with the public sinner.[53] Further, Mather's authority itself derived at some
remove from the very power he seeks to curtail. That is, Mather, as minister,
will be civilly authorized to invoke, and interpret, the wonders of the invisible
world in a way that laypersons like Hutchinson and the Quakers, for
instance, were not. A similar anxiety motivates Samuel Parris's original crying out against the witch in Salem Village. As the minister of Salem's First
Congregational Church, Parris's livelihood was directly threatened by the
witch, who challenged a metaphysical privilege that was, in practice if not in
theory, limited to the ministers' tight control. Transgression, in this case,
implied a most logically Protestant point—spiritual self-possession would
have ultimately done away with ministers entirely. It was for this possibility,
we recall, that Anne Hutchinson was banished.

Exposition

In our day the closest contemporary parallel to what I might call the rubrical
use of scandal is to be found in the industries of moralized voyeurism by which
secrets, often sexual, are discovered, and perhaps created, for a multiplicity of
purposes. Suzanne Garment notes in *Scandal* that while the public mechanics
of scandal have remained historically visible in American politics, in contemporary practice its contents and direction have changed.[54] She argues that the
epistemological basis of the scandal has shifted away from financial or bureaucratic irregularity in the 1970s and 1980s to a sexual economy. A commodity
culture that eroticizes bodies, putting them more or less explicitly up for sale,
thus conspires with an older, moralizing if not moral impulse by which sexual
conduct is deployed as the explicit sign of communal orthodoxy. In its contemporary political-moral mode, the transgressor is identified within an
apocalyptic discourse of secrets and revelations. In Mather's formidable literary pyrotechnics and in the compulsive readability of Wigglesworth, this
textual strategy braids together pseudo-judicial rhetoric, civic duty, and erotic
titillation, while the sexualized action is made to signify in socially dire ways.
That is, "lustful motion," or "unweaned affection" is apocalyptic in the truest

sense of the word; it is a revelation whose consequences are potentially world-ending. It is also, as Mather admits, the "Chief Entertainment which my readers do expect."[55]

Apocalyptic texts—including the morally dense discourse of the scandal—raise to a cosmic level the proverb that the end justifies the means. Moral collapse is, quite literally, unspeakable—Gothic, signified by a transgression of language. Words collapse into unspeakability or are devalued and exhausted through excess and overuse. This is at least one accustomed mode of high political address as it is currently practiced: from Pat Buchanan's polemic about culture collapse to Pat Robertson's linkage of lesbianism and witchery, from Jesse Helms to Newt Gingrich and the Defense of Marriage Act, from Jerry Falwell to Kenneth Starr, a gendered exposition of sex is framed, in a humorlessly literal way, as a moral end of what Matthew Ruben calls a "national-political masculinity."[56]

Of course, this begs the question of whether it is the action or its publication that is the apocalyptic moment. The public framing of the Clinton-Lewinsky episode offers a contemporary insight into the entanglement of sexual secret, authoritative public discourse, and high moralism being considered here. Starr built his moral tell-athon upon just such a foundation; he equated the public moral good with a need to tell, rather than a need to know. In his role as independent counsel he bears comparison with Winthrop—who, as a lawyer and lay preacher, was called upon to exercise a moral authority that indirectly but importantly derived from theological warrant.[57] From another perspective, the affair Starr chronicled—arguably, perhaps even orchestrated—typified the civic moral catastrophe as laid out by Wigglesworth. Like Mather, however, Starr alleges that he is an unwilling pornographer. Mather excuses his participation by noting that he was asked to compile a history of the events, while Starr finds himself, against his own protestations of disinterest, performing a sexual calculus so detailed that it found favor with *Hustler* publisher Larry Flynt.

Scandal as moral adjudication—and gossip as a social trigger—are arguably Christian tools of informal governance, as even the word "gossip" (god-sibling) suggests. Indeed, the apocalyptic scenario from which they derive still constitutes an emotional shorthand by which much of Western culture, however secularized, presents itself to itself—from Calvin, to Wigglesworth's discerning eye for public duplicity, to Mather's self-reflexive acceptance as a public moral cartographer. Clinton's "Don't ask/Don't tell" policies presume a similar disjunction between public and private in which the private, in effect unknown, has no moral status; yet known, the homosexual becomes both criminal and moral tableau, gathered up in an erotic production of secrets displayed as a debased public theater of deviancy (and gender).

The parallels between Mather and Starr are most clear in the alliance between gossip and the evidentiary aspect of law. Indeed, it is the issue of evidence (and what shall count as evidence, and of what) that drives the narrative of the Salem events as well as that of Starr's investigation. Starr implied his task was to collect information that "met the statutory standard of substantial and credible information."[58] Starr's language duplicates Mather's repeated insistence—given, as suggested earlier, because of his anxiety around spectral evidence—that the information he put forward ascertaining the presence of witches in Salem was "credible," visible, "sensible." Mather and Starr each employ a language of visible materiality, reading texts and divining secret signs by which to evaluate them. One seeks to make visible the "wonders of the invisible world" (i.e., witches), and the other to make visible—what, a spot on a dress? Mather records how "devil's marks" were found on the bodies of the accused. Ironically, unlike Mather, in this case the evidence aimed to catch not the cunning woman, but the agent with whom she was seen to be in carnal congress.

Wigglesworth, Mather, and Starr employ a rhetoric of eroticized transgression to address issues of political significance; nonetheless, each enunciates a theological *anxiety* about the nature of civil authority that remains unaddressed. Finally, Wigglesworth, Mather, even Starr show themselves aware of the fissured nature of their charges and claims, and the way that the claim itself is undercut almost by virtue of the authority it demands. Each is aware that his actions signal him as the moral superior, but in a position that is deeply conflicted, potentially fatally so. Moral credibility is implicitly undercut, in that since scandal traffics in the forbidden, the very *announcing* of scandal aligns the speaker in complicated ways with the transgressor, as Wigglesworth himself noted, saying he must "pass . . . by" speaking of divinity "less speaking should transgress"(v.16). Divinity, in the end, is as much transgressive speaking as those forces that oppose it.

"Filthy Facts and Secret Acts"

Giving public offense is a complex charge. So is its public evaluation. From New Testament times forward, the rhetoric of offense and scandal, read from the palimpsestic body of the accused, both elaborated the ideal and demonstrated its reach by showing how and where the ideal failed. Nonetheless, as Hawthorne demonstrates, the scarlet letter, emblem of sin, ever ambiguously points beyond itself to issues that ultimately energize it. So it is in the case of Bill Clinton, whose mistake was not having sex in public, but trying to have it in private. Sex, whatever else it may be in an Anglo-Puritan civil theology, is a community affair.

Colacurcio argues that this realization directs Hawthorne's revision of the Anne Hutchinson politics in *The Scarlet Letter*. He points out that Hawthorne "ascribes the opening of his most explicitly sexual romance" to "the one moment when much of colonial New England had sex on its official and conscious mind."[59] It was Mr. Clinton's misfortune that he tried to conduct a private romance under similar public conditions. Other famous persons, including presidents, have had misalliances and the occasional sexual advisory session, whether in the side rooms of the White House or elsewhere. Indeed, Clinton learned more from Kennedy than just charisma, as he remarked in a heated response to Donna Shalala.[60] It is naive to say, when justifying the extensive, even obsessively detailed narrative of Clinton's trangressions, that "times have changed." For clearly they have not, as indicated by Winthrop's musings in his *Journal* about the sexual liberties of the antinomians and how they signified, in a manner of speaking. Colacurcio sums up the situation pungently: "Lust, Winthrop must have felt, he would always have with him. But an outbreak of hermeneutics he had hoped to avoid."[61]

However, the hermeneutics are still what sex leaves us. Nor is it a new thing to find political disclosure organized by the moralized sex favored by the high-minded. The framing of sex as *the* moral moment of public electioneering is often dated to Gary Hart's abortive campaign for the presidency, although as Winthrop's *Journal* reminds us, Bellingham, briefly governor of Massachusetts Bay Colony, faced charges of inappropriate sex that resulted in his being removed from office in 1642.[62] Further, the hermeneutics of sex has its distant roots—the celebration (in a word) of scandal as a public sacrament. Edmund Morgan, himself a premier scholar of the Puritan mind, observes about sex scandals: "The role of sex in the politics of reputation . . . has a prurient element that is not easy to distinguish from its political one. Sex has a dynamic of its own that can not only reach into politics, but submerge whatever political purpose it may be put to. . . . The sexual element in the politics of reputation could not only overshadow but also outlive whatever political usefulness it may have had."[63]

Except, of course, when sex *is* politics—when, that is, a discourse of the ostensibly private moment is used to manage definitions of the public. Scholars of the witch trials conclude that the sad events at Salem derived from political pressure. A similar deflection of social anxiety through a gendered sexual narrative discourse is evident in the Clinton discourse. Sexual scandals take hybrid form, part Gothic apocalypse and part detective procedural; sex, narrated, is all in the fulsome details, in a constant press of exposure. And in this case, Clinton's prodigious sexual appetites were public before his presidency—proving that gossip, in its many public functions, need only be interesting, whatever its value as truth. For similar reasons, to many people sex *was* the point of Bill Clinton's presidency—to the extent that everything else was thought to signify this priapic prism. Yet even this must be qualified, or perhaps gendered. For from many perspectives, the point of demonizing Clinton's public relationship to sex was thereby to critique not so much his sexualizing but the way he failed gender in doing so. Demonizing Hutchinson's theology by linking it to gender inadequacy was similarly motivated.

Clinton's sexual problem stemmed from an increasingly fissured discourse around issues of sex, domesticity, and what might be called the politics of the private. Clinton helped create the problem, partly because he persisted in having it (sex and its public discussion) so often. From Clinton's campaign revelations to his initial attempt to raise the ban on gays in the military, through his dalliances with Paula Jones, Lewinsky, and unnamed, though hoped-for, hordes of others, "Don't ask/Don't tell" ironically became a compulsive national refrain. Yet, like all secrets, it generated the conditions of its own volubility, as traditionally "private" topics lurched increasingly into public discourse in an exhaustive cycle of asking and telling.

Thus, it was Clinton who indirectly gave the name to the narrative Starr would tell. The demeaning of a popular sitting president was made possible by a subtle but consistent politics of effeminization and gender failure that gained in force by being associated with, first, feminine issues, and then, more directly, with homosexuality. Under the wonderfully ironic heading, "They Ask, He Told," Al Kamen in the *Washington Post* wrote:

> There's little doubt some House trial managers are much put out over sex and the Clinton administration. "You look at what the president's policy has been from day one," Rep. Chris Cannon (R-Utah) told the *Salt Lake Tribune* recently. "The first thing he did was create a debate about homosexuality, by talking about homosexuals in the military." Another of his initial moves was

"to hire Jocelyn Elders as his Surgeon General. The whole point
was to have an advocate for weird alternative lifestyles" . . . "This
administration has had a policy goal, the public discussion of
weird sex," Cannon continued. "He did not fire Jocelyn Elders
until after she said some really weird things and said them many
times. She talked about self-abuse. Sex when you're alone."

Even so, Kamen continues, "despite the administration's focus on 'weird
alternative lifestyles' that includes [sic] 'homosexuality' and 'self-abuse' or
masturbation, said Cannon, 'There's no reason for us to talk about it.'"[64] Oh,
but there is. Sex is what a community does together in public, as Puritan governance in the "American ur-world"[65] suggests.

Suffice it to say that Clinton's penis, scandalously marked, and like the
witch, seemingly everywhere, was itself never precisely the scandal. Clinton's
sexual text produced interpretive excess. *Typologically*, his transgression (and
its emblematic sign, the letter "A" on the dress, or in this case, the spot a little lower down) pointed elsewhere to subjects and possibilities unspeakably
represented. In the fantasy life of political America, it is arguably the case that
although allegedly a chief political officer is sex addicted, it is the public, or at
least public discourse, that is truly addicted to fantasies of public, or at least
publicized, sex. Public fantasy precisely *about* the private may be a necessary
theological precondition of governance in a country, as G. K. Chesterton
famously quipped, "with the soul of a church."

Finally, this narrative of public transgression was, likewise, gendered, as
sexual excess in public is almost invariably marked as a crisis of the woman.
Anne Hutchinson's speaking her mind and having theological opinions gendered her male. She was accused and found guilty of disturbing the civil
peace and was banished to nearby Rhode Island. Clinton, on the other hand,
for all intents and purposes, was gendered as a woman. The sputterings
around Clinton's sexual body indicted as feminine, in the eyes of his critics, a
variety of other public offenses: his unmanliness in avoiding the draft; his
political alliance with issues long conceded to the "private" sphere—concerns
of care, intimacy, education, and others; his general indelicacy of treating in
public issues of intimacy; his acknowledgment of gays and lesbians in public
space; and finally, for heaven's sake, his homosexualizing of his own soft,
unmanly body by discussing underwear on MTV. His constant volubility,
sheer wordiness, and demonstrative flaunting of sexual hunger were all
excesses with public consequences in any culture that privileges the hierar-
chies of gender.

Scandal, in Mr. Clinton's case, made a woman out of him. Organized as it was by a patriarchal male political machinery, it compares with the political disturbances prompted by Anne Hutchinson, Wigglesworth's unwise virgins, and the knot of witches besieging Mather's Salem. Confession justified the legal apparatus, and no matter how heavy the penance, a properly confessed sinner could be more or less fully reinstated to the community. But what happens, asked Hawthorne, when Hester won't confess? Is the crisis having unauthorized sex in private or *not* having it in public?

Notes

1. Thomas Tilliam, "Upon the First Sight of New England," in Alan Heimert and Andrew Delbanco, eds., *The Puritans in America: A Narrative Anthology* (Cambridge, Mass.: Harvard University Press, 1985), 127.

2. Cited in Victor Sage, *Horror Fiction in the Protestant Tradition* (London: Macmillan, 1988), 74.

3. John Winthrop, *Journal of John Winthrop*, abridged version, ed. Richard S. Dunn and Laetitia Yeandle (Cambridge, Mass.: The Belknap Press of Harvard University Press, 1996), 263. Winthrop's gendering of authority is explicit: "The woman's own choice makes such a man her husband; yet being so chosen he is her lord."

4. John Winthrop, "A Model of Christian Charity," in Dunn and Yeandle, *Journal of John Winthrop*, 9.

5. See especially Sacvan Bercovitch, "Typology in Puritan New England," *American Quarterly* 19 (1968): 166–91.

6. Michael Colacurcio, *Doctrine and Difference: Essays in the Literature of New England* (New York: Routledge, 1997), 219; see also David Leverenz, *The Language of Puritan Feeling* (New Brunswick: Rutgers University Press, 1980).

7. John Demos, *A Little Commonwealth: Family Life in Plymouth Colony* (New York: Oxford University Press, 1970), 5.

8. For a discussion of the Puritans and sexual ideology see Edmund Morgan, "The Puritans and Sex," *New England Quarterly* 25 (1942): 591–607. See also his *Visible Saints: The History of a Puritan Idea* (New York: New York University Press), 1963.

9. John D'Emilio and Estelle B. Freedman, *Intimate Matters: A History of Sexuality in America*, 2d ed. (Chicago: University of Chicago Press, 1997), 29.

10. D'Emilio and Freedman, *Intimate Matters*, 29.

11. David D. Hall, ed., *The Antinomian Controversy, 1636–1638: A Documentary History* (Middletown, Conn.: Wesleyan University Press, 1968), 313.

12. D'Emilio and Freedman, *Intimate Matters*, 52.

13. R. I. Moore, *The Formation of a Persecuting Society: Power and Deviance in Western Europe, 950–1250* (New York: Basil Blackwell, 1987); Rudi Bleys, *The Geography of*

Perversion: Male-to-Male Sexual Behavior outside the West and the Ethnographic Imagination, 1750–1918 (New York: New York University Press, 1995); Claude Quetal, *History of Syphilis*, trans. Judith Baddock and Brian Pike (Baltimore: Johns Hopkins University Press, 1990).

14. Mary Douglas, *Natural Symbols: Exploration in Cosmology* (New York: Pantheon Books, 1970), 70. See also Thomas Laqueur, *Making Sex: Body and Gender from the Greeks to Freud* (Cambridge, Mass.: Harvard University Press, 1990).

15. See Mary Douglas, *Purity and Danger: An Analysis of the Concepts of Pollution and Taboo* (London: Routledge, 1966); Moore, *Persecuting Society*; Leslie Fielder, *Freaks: Myths and Images of the Secret Self* (New York: Simon and Schuster, 1979); Rosemarie Garland Thomson, ed., *Freakery: Cultural Spectacles of the Extraordinary Body* (New York: New York University Press, 1997).

16. Hall, *Antinomian*, 216.

17. Winthrop's essay is "A Short Story of the Rise, Reign, and Ruine of the Antinomians, Familists, and Libertines," in Hall, *Antinomian*, 199–310; David D. Hall, *Worlds of Wonder, Days of Judgment: Popular Religious Belief in Early New England* (New York: Knopf, 1989), 187.

18. David M. Halperin, "Is There a History of Sexuality?" in Henry Abelove, Michele Aine Barale, and David M. Halperin, eds., *The Gay and Lesbian Studies Reader* (New York: Routledge, 1993), 420.

19. D'Emilio and Freedman, *Intimate Matters*, 52, 29.

20. Hall, *Worlds of Wonder*, 184.

21. See Daniel A. Cohen, *Pillars of Salt, Monuments of Grace: New England Crime Literature and the Origins of American Popular Culture, 1674–1869* (New York: Oxford University Press, 1993).

22. Cotton Mather, *Wonders of the Invisible World* (Boston: John Smith, 1862), 11.

23. Dunn and Yeandle, *Journal of John Winthrop*, xix.

24. Hall, *Worlds of Wonder*, 184–85.

25. "The End," *The Economist* 350 (13 February 1999): 17.

26. George M. Marsden, "America's 'Christian' Origins: Puritan New England as a Case Study," in W. Stanford Reid, ed., *John Calvin: His Influence in the Western World* (Grand Rapids: Zondervan, 1982), 246.

27. Jonathan Edwards, *Concerning the End for Which God Created the World* (Boston: S. Kneeland, 1765); Jonathan Edwards, *The History of Redemption* (New York: T. and J. Swirde, 1793).

28. Morgan, *Visible Saints*, 105.

29. See, for example, Douglas, *Natural Symbols*; Moore, *Persecuting Society*; Peter Stallybrass and Alon White, *The Politics and Poetics of Transgression* (London: Methuen, 1986).

30. Colacurcio, *Doctrine and Difference*, 213.

31. D'Emilio and Freedman, *Intimate Matters*, 5.

32. Hall, *Worlds of Wonder*, 184.

33. Perry Miller, *Errand into the Wilderness* (Cambridge, Mass.: The Belknap Press of Harvard University Press), 7.

34. Cotton Mather, *Bonifacius, or Essays to Do Good* (Wilmington, Del.: Robert Porter, 1882), 410.

35. D'Emilio and Freedman note that very often grievous sinners would be returned to communal good grace by submitting to public penance; a refusal to accept the public penance could have drastic consequences, even excommunication from their community (23ff).

36. Winthrop, *Journal of John Winthrop*, 229.

37. John Demos, *Entertaining Satan: Witchcraft and the Culture of Early New England* (Oxford: Oxford University Press, 1982), 436.

38. See John Winthrop's *Journal* entry for his commentary about Mary Dyer's "monstrous" birth as well as Anne Hutchinson's—some months after her exile to Rhode Island (Dunn and Yeandle, *Journal of John Winthrop*, 141–42, 146–47).

39. From the beginning, even the theodicy of Augustine barely skirts the implication that the impulse toward sin locates itself in the source of good—i.e., God. To the point of this essay, one recalls that subsequent commentary on Genesis sexualizes the offense and thus the narrative.

40. Hall, *Wonders*, 11.

41. Dunn and Yeandle, *Journal of John Winthrop*, 8.

42. Michael Wigglesworth, "Day of Doom," in Perry Miller, ed., *The American Puritans: Their Prose and Poetry* (New York: Doubleday Anchor, 1956), 282–94, v. 137–38. Subsequently cited by verse number in the text.

43. Miller, *Errand into the Wilderness*, 282.

44. Introduction to Wigglesworth, in Nina Baym et al., eds., *Norton Anthology of American Literature*, 3d ed., vol. 1 (New York: W.W. Norton and Co., 1989), 122.

45. Miller, *Errand into the Wilderness*, 282.

46. Mather, *Wonders of the Invisible World*, 5.

47. Mather, *Bonifacius*, 14.

48. Mather, *Bonifacius*, 14.

49. Mather, *Bonifacius*, 110.

50. As a matter of statistics, the incidents of witchcraft in New England were abnormally high, Demos argues (234 indictments of complaints filed, and 36 executed persons). The panic in Salem of 1692 to 1693 was the highest concentration (19 persons executed), after which, effectively, the witch craze *in itself* died out. See Demos, *Entertaining Satan*, 10–13; also his "Appendix: List of Known Witchcraft Cases in Seventeenth Century New England" (402–9). See also Carol F. Karlsen, *The Devil in the*

Shape of a Woman: Witchcraft in Colonial New England (New York: Random House, 1987), esp. chapter 2 and "Appendix 5: Witches Accused in New England, 1620–1699."

51. See Laura Kipnis, *Bound and Gagged: Pornography and the Politics of Fantasy in America* (New York: Grove Press, 1996); Lauren Berlant, *The Anatomy of National Fantasy* (Chicago: University of Chicago Press, 1991).

52. Demos, *Entertaining Satan*, 99.

53. Anthony E. Simpson, "Spectacular Punishment and the Orchestration of Hate: The Pillory and Popular Morality in Eighteenth Century England," in Robert J. Kelley and Jess Aghan, eds., *Hate Crime: The Global Politics of Polarization* (Carbondale: Southern Illinois University Press, 1998), 177–220.

54. Suzanne Garment, *Scandal: The Crisis of Mistrust in American Politics* (New York: Times Books, 1991).

55. Mather, *Bonifacius*, 107.

56. Matthew Ruben, "Of Newts and Quayles: National-Political Masculinity in the Current Conjecture," Paul Smith, ed., *Boys* (New York: Westview Press, 1996), 255–92.

57. Winthrop's service as governor and then as lieutenant governor of the province was not always placid, and once he faced impeachment himself for abuse of authority. The movement failed. Mather writes about the incident: "Great attempts were sometimes made among the freemen to get him left out from his place in the government upon little pretenses, lest by the too frequent choice of one man, the government should cease to be by choice" (*Magnalia Christi*, 391).

58. "Excerpts from Starr's Questioning," *New York Times*, 20 November 1998, 2.

59. Colacurcio, *Doctrine and Difference*, 214.

60. One lesson not lost on Clinton was perhaps that security agents of different kinds make, in addition, good procurers—again the linkage of solicitation and elicitation.

61. Colacurcio, *Doctrine and Difference*, 20.

62. Dunn and Yeandle, *Journal of John Winthrop*, 192.

63. Edmund S. Morgan, "The Governor in Drag?" (review of Patricia U. Bonomi, *The Lord Cornbury Scandal: The Politics of Reputation in British America* [Chapel Hill: University of North Carolina Press, 1998]), *New York Review of Books* 45.4 (1998): 21.

64. Al Kamen, *Washington Post*, 3 February 1999, A15.

65. Colacurcio, *Doctrine and Difference*, 210.

A Sodom Within

Historicizing Puritan
Homoerotics
in the Diary of
Michael Wigglesworth

༄

Nicholas F. Radel

In the wake of recent understandings of the history of sexuality, it has become increasingly difficult to see the connections between premodern sexual acts and modern sexual subjectivities. As many scholars have shown, sodomy and modern homosexuality are discrete categories for regulating particular types of unauthorized sexualities, and their overlap cannot be simply assumed or easily demonstrated.[1] Nevertheless, it seems important to try to understand how these two categories might be related within an American cultural tradition, for the impress of the New England Puritans on later American social and cultural identities is, by now, a staple theme in American cultural studies and, as the present collection shows, scholars are increasingly studying the effect of America's Puritan imaginary on its historical and present sexual constructions. In this essay, then, I want to begin looking at how we might negotiate the divide between early modern, Puritan, sodomitic acts and modern sexuality in a more nuanced way, and I want to do so by looking at a text that, because of its frank revelation of sexual issues, has become something of a touchstone for the investigation of sex and gender in colonial New England, the diary that the Puritan divine and poet Michael Wigglesworth kept during the years 1653 to 1657. Wigglesworth's diary illustrates a contact point between Puritan attempts to regulate sodomy and modern discourses of sexuality. It is significant in the history of American thought neither because it provides evidence of a previous history of homosexuality now brought to light nor because it reveals the mythic origins of Anglo-American discourses of homosexuality, which are more easily located in nineteenth-century medical and psychological sources. Rather, it is important because it reveals one source in Puritan discourses for some of the regulatory strategies that have been used to produce and police sexuality in modern America.[2]

Wigglesworth, as is well known, was a preacher in Puritan Boston and a teacher at the institution that would grow into Harvard University. He was also the author of a poem, "The Day of Doom," which was, in effect, the first best-seller in America, and probably one of its most long-lasting best-sellers. The poem continued to be printed and sold widely well into the eighteenth century despite (or perhaps because of) its unique brand of Puritan didacticism.[3] Like other Calvinists in the period, Wigglesworth also wrote and left behind a diary, in which he recorded a number of sexual dreams and fantasies that troubled him deeply. What is perhaps surprising, given our common misperceptions about the Puritans, is that these dreams and fantasies concern his pupils at Harvard, the young men with whom he lived in close association. On one such occasion in 1653, Wigglesworth writes about *"[s]uch filthy lust flowing from my fond affection to my pupils whiles in their presence on the third day after noon that I confess myself an object of God's loathing as my sin is of my own; and pray God make it so more to me."*[4] Another time he writes of the "much distracted thoughts I find arising from too much doting affection to *some of my pupils*" (9). His so-called filthy lusts, confessed to his shame, cause him a great deal of distress. But, interestingly, he is able to articulate them openly, with a clarity of forethought not usually accorded homoerotic imaginings in repressed cultures later in the history of the United States. What, I would ask, are we to make of these confessions?

At first glance, they seem easy to interpret in contemporary terms. Wigglesworth's case seems to be a straightforward one in which a devout Puritan discovers his own homosexual longing and tries to repress it through confession and penitential prayer. That is exactly how one critic sees it. Walter Hughes reads the homoerotic desire to be found in the diary in terms of Wigglesworth's panicked reaction to his lust for his students, and he positions this reaction in relationship to Wigglesworth's troubled relations with God. For Hughes, Wigglesworth's desire for his students comes very close to the homoerotics of his relationship with God. As Hughes points out, and as is well known, seventeenth-century religious poetry created an erotics of domination that had homoerotic overtones.[5] This erotics was part of a larger ideology in which desire for God, the love of God, becomes the primary focus

of the believing soul, an ideology that was embodied most problematically in
the traditional exegesis of the Song of Solomon, in which the individual
Christian becomes the bride of Christ. For Hughes, Wigglesworth's diary and
poems reveal a confusion between his personal erotic orientation toward his
students and his love for God. Given the public/private dialectics of Puritan
thought, that confusion leads inevitably to a pressing question, one recorded
only at the very end of Wigglesworth's diary: "[D]o I retain," Wigglesworth
asks, "a Sodom within the temple of the holy-ghost?" (104). Hughes detects
in Wigglesworth the specter of a Sodom within, and he identifies this Sodom
with homosexuality.[6]

Yet while Hughes rightly focuses on Wigglesworth's revelation of a
"Sodom within" the temple of his body, an argument to which I will return
later, historical evidence suggests that he is wrong to equate sodomy with
homosexuality. To imagine that the Puritan teacher Wigglesworth is struggling with repressed homosexual desire, we have to imagine that there was
such a thing as homosexuality, that there was an identity configuration
around homoerotic behavior, in Puritan New England. And as recent studies
in the history of sexuality show, there simply was no such thing. The early
modern period in England and New England did not understand homosexual
behavior as we do, and it cannot be conflated in any easy or transhistorical
way with sodomy. While Wigglesworth's diary certainly proves that there was
homoerotic lust and suggests that there may have been homoerotic activities,
as well, we need to look more carefully at what it seems to be saying about
what we would call homosexuality. That, I believe, must be the starting
assumption for any examination of same-sex desire in Puritan New England.
Before turning, then, to a discussion of how we might read Wigglesworth's
diary in a way more appropriate to the period, then, let me clarify exactly what
I mean when I say that there was no homosexuality at that time.

The English social historian Alan Bray argues that from the close of the
Middle Ages until the mid-1600s, homoerotic behavior in England (and by
implication, New England) "was, quite simply, not socialized to any significant degree at all."[7] To the extent that it existed, it was not routinely identified
as the fearful sin of sodomy. It took place within social circumstances and
institutions that we do not usually associate with homosexuality (institutions
such as pedagogy and friendship), and the behavior was never taken in and of
itself to be a mark of a person's distinction from other, heterosexual, types of
people. If it was remarked at all, it was so because the behavior coincided with
some other violation of the social order. In this circumstance, and only in this

circumstance, could the behavior become identified as sodomy. It was not until the end of the seventeenth century that a subculture emerged in London in which same-sex activity could be fully socialized in the pubs and private "molly" houses that served as meeting places for men and that became the locus of repression from such agencies as the "Societies for the Reformation of Manners."

These points are clarified by the American historian Jonathan Ned Katz, who describes the age in which Wigglesworth's diary appeared as the "Age of Sodomitical Sin." He writes that "neither Wigglesworth nor any other known early colonial writer referred to 'sodomitical lust,' an emotion specific to sodomy. There was no sodomeroticism. In the early colonies there was 'sensual lust.' But no special sodomitical desire opposed an 'other,' 'different,' or 'opposite' lust. No 'homoerotic' feeling for a 'same sex' opposed a 'heteroerotic' feeling for a 'different sex,' no 'homosexual' emotion opposed a 'heterosexual.' 'Filthy lusts' and 'infamous passions' [to use Wigglesworth's terms] included a variety of feelings associated with fornication, adultery, and a variety of other sins, not just sodomy, and not just sexual."[8] So, before the late seventeenth century at the earliest and, by some accounts not until the late nineteenth century, there simply was no concept that a man's desire for another man marked him as somehow different from other men. Homoerotic desires in the period in England and New England were seen, for the most part, as sexual sins like any other, and in theory, at least, anyone was capable of committing them.[9]

What makes Wigglesworth's diary so interesting is that it does seem to reveal some of the specific ways in which discourses of sodomy were changing in the middle of the seventeenth century, and thus may provide some clues to the ways in which homoerotic desire was becoming socialized and regulated as sodomy. Nevertheless, we simply cannot begin to analyze this work with an assumption that homosexual—as opposed to heterosexual—desire or preference preceded its production. If we are going to talk about what it is that bothers Wigglesworth in his desire for his students, we have to talk about sodomy, and we have to recognize that in Puritan New England, sodomy could mean many different things. It was not (at least at first) limited by definition to male-male sexual contact, and anyone was theoretically capable of committing it. There was not a special class of people known as Sodomites whose identities were signified by their aberrant sexual desires. The sodomite was anyone who could not harness his/her sexual impulses to the norms and institutions of the social body.[10]

Given that this is the case, we would do better to follow Alan Bray, who suggests, in an article written specifically about the Wigglesworth diary, that Wigglesworth was less bothered by the fact that he felt lust for men than by his inability to control his lust or desire for them. Wigglesworth calls his lust a "fond affection" and the word "affection" in the period implied madness, unreasoned excess. (It is more akin to the modern nouns "affect" or "affectation" than to its modern equivalent.) According to Bray, Wigglesworth's desire was sodomitical not because it was directed at young men, but because it was excessive and, hence, unmanly. More than anything, the excesses of lust in the period were associated with a fear that manhood itself would unravel if the excess were not controlled.[11] In accordance with his thesis that homoerotic behavior was never singled out in and of itself as a disruptive social act, Bray links it to the social disruptions implicit in a breakdown of gender in the diary. Thus, he is able to understand the eroticism of the text as sodomy, but only insofar as it signals something else altogether: a disruption of normative gender.

The connection between gender and sodomy is, to some extent, confirmed by Eva Cherniavsky in her study of the diary. Cherniavsky sees the diary as Wigglesworth's attempt "to repossess his masculine subjectivity," which is threatened by his inability to control his errant impulses.[12] That inability, Cherniavsky argues, is an inherently feminizing position in Puritan ideology. The movement of the diary is toward marriage, a defining moment in the constitution of masculine subjectivity, and toward phallic identification with God. But Cherniavsky's study moves beyond the discussion of gender and sodomy to point toward a fundamental ambiguity in the confessional mode of the diary. Cherniavsky points out the trouble Wigglesworth goes to in order "to constitute himself in sin" while at the same time struggling to purify himself of it.[13] She shows that Wigglesworth never fully overcomes the breach. He never completely forces his errant desires to submit to the will of God, and thus he never fully achieves masculine subjectivity.

This insight, that Wigglesworth must produce himself in sin, see himself as a sinner, in order to purify himself of sin, is the one I want to follow. Not only does it provide a way to understand how sodomy in Puritan New England was increasingly linked to sexually specific misconduct, but it reveals a peculiar strategy for regulating sexual sin that has lasting consequences. So, although both Bray and Cherniavsky demonstrate the importance of gender to the spirit of this puzzling work of Protestant soul-searching, it is also appropriate to see Wigglesworth's diary as part of the increasingly specific discourse of sodomy that Gregory Bredbeck argues begins to delimit and control specifically sexual behavior in the period. As Bredbeck argues, this increasing specification marks the birth of modern sexual epistemology.[14] This is not, of course, to claim that we find the origins of modern homosexuality in the diary, and it is not my intention to use Wigglesworth's text or any Puritan text to undertake such a vexed and potentially homophobic inquiry. The diary is, however, an early example, indeed perhaps the earliest example, of what I want to call the self-articulating sodomite in Anglo-American culture and an early site for the link between sodomitical behavior and a discourse of secrecy about sex—two ways of imagining sodomy that, I wish to show, have implications for the construction of more modern sexualities in America. If I am right, then this largely artless work of self-definition may assume an important place in the history of sexuality in England and America, for it may have helped define regulatory discourses used in later constructions of sexuality, even if it did not exactly determine their meanings. Moreover, it provides evidence of how Protestant ideologies can be positioned within these later histories. Ultimately, Wigglesworth's diary can be read to suggest that Protestant culture in America is not responsible for the repression of homosexuality and homosexuals in the name of God, as it has sometimes liked to see itself. Rather, it is, at least in part, responsible for the production of sodomy (and later of homosexuality) as the sign and symbol of what must be repressed.

One critic has seen this process at work in another, more famous Puritan text. In a complex analysis of William Bradford's *Of Plymouth Plantation*, Jonathan Goldberg argues that sodomy in that document is "discovered as the repressed."[15] Reading the discourse through which Bradford uncovers a case of sodomy in Massachusetts, Goldberg argues that the sodomite is not repressed so much as produced as the thing to be repressed. In other words, Bradford's text produces the image of the sodomite in Puritan New England as the figure to be scapegoated so that this largely male-centered world can define the potentially eroticized bonds between men in ways other than the homoerotic. Bradford's text "preserves its fantasy of all-male relations precisely by drawing the line—lethally—between its sexual energies and those it calls sodomitical."[16] The repressed sodomite becomes the symbol of the denial of male-male eroticism in other locations. Goldberg's point follows the work of Eve Sedgwick in suggesting that society in Puritan New England was homosocial: that it was a society in which bonds between men assumed primary importance. But it was also a society invested in denying the erotic or potentially erotic nature of these bonds, and its evocation of the sodomite as the exclusive location of homoeroticism helped it do so.[17]

The sodomite, who is not to be confused with the homosexual, appears in Wigglesworth's text in just such a way, to draw a boundary between erotic and proper homosocial relations, to preserve the integrity of those relations. The most significant homosocial bond that Wigglesworth attempts to render outside the erotic is his bond with God. As we have already seen in Walter Hughes's discussion of the diary, the relationship of early modern men to their God was frequently eroticized in literary texts of the period. The most well-known examples are, of course, Donne's "Batter My Heart" and George Herbert's "Love III," although the tradition reaches back into the medieval period and cannot be limited to configurations of male-male desire. But despite the long-standing tradition, the sexual energies of Wigglesworth's relation to God are so close to the surface of his thinking that the evocation of the repressed sodomite seems necessary to prevent him from confusing his relationship to God with sodomy itself. As Hughes remarks, Wigglesworth's irruptions into lust occur most frequently during his devotions,[18] and the language of devotion itself is so sexually provocative that it would seem to be indistinguishable from lust. So, for example, early on, he addresses God: "The enmity and contrariety of my heart to seeking thee in earnest, with my want of dear affection to thee, these make me affraid. but thou did giue me thy self in the Lords supper, thou didst giue me a heart (though vile) to lay hold of the desiring all from thee" (3). And later, "*Ah Lord let me see thy face that will full up all my emptiness and the dissatisfaction I find in the creature. I wait and oh that I long for thy salvation O where are thy tender compassions and bowel mercies which I have been comforted with when low. . . .*" (10). Aside from our amused (or is it bemused?) concern with what, exactly, Wigglesworth means by "bowel mercies," we need to see in this language a conflation of erotic desire and religious devotion that was usual, normative, and unremarked throughout most of the period.

The intrusion of lust into the devotion of this text is so strong, however, that it seems to render the normative arrangement suspect and in need of correction. So, Wigglesworth discovers sodomy within himself, as the thing that God will help him repress, and his religious devotion can then seem free from any problematic erotic taint. It becomes, in fact, the source of his triumph over that taint. At one point, Wigglesworth reveals himself complexly: "*I find my spirit so exceeding carried away with love to my pupils that I cant tell how to take up my rest in God. Lord for this cause I am afraid of my wicked heart.*

Fear takes hold of me. God assisted me so to speak to my pupils this day that I could hardly utter my self without pouring forth tears though notwithstanding I desire to look up to the Lord and wait his time for a blessing upon it and in the mean time oh make thy face shine upon me and be thou my saviour. Suffer me not suffer me not O my God to dote upon the creature wherein is nothing but vanity and vexation of spirit. Show me thy glory O my God" (11). In this passage, Wigglesworth begins with an assertion that his lust for his students somehow interferes with his love for God. It keeps him from being able to take rest there, perhaps replacing the love he feels for God with a specific, human, and carnal image of it. But by the end, he separates the two and seeks God's help in suppressing that Other within him, the speaker who would vainly dote upon the creature. He ends with an image signifying not his potentially erotic and potentially troubling connection to God, but one in which God shows himself in his glory, separate from the speaker, to be looked at and worshiped. It is a settlement repeated at another point in the diary as well.

In this instance, Wigglesworth tells of one student, John Haines, who disobeys him, who goes to Ipswich after being denied permission to go, who indulges in pleasures with the other boys, and who rejects Wigglesworth's advice about the dangers of pleasure (26–27). The scene is full of possessive jealousy, and it recalls to Wigglesworth his own susceptibility to pleasures and lusts. But, characteristically, his recognition of his desire leads him to turn to God, and in so doing he imagines himself as Jacob wrestling with the angel: "I set my self again this day to wrestle with the Lord for my self and then for my pupils and the Lord did pretty much inlarge my heart in crying to him" (27). It is the same image that ends his poem, "Meat out of the Eater," and it is an image of the struggle to establish an intimate relationship with God in a way that seems not to be erotic, to bond with Him without fear of penetration or emasculation:

> Thus *Jacob* took fast hold, and wrestled with the Lord,
> When as he was distrest for fear of cruel *Esau*'s sword.
>
> Prince-like he wrestled and would not let him go,
> Until he had a Blessing got to shield him from his Foe.
> Thus every suffering Saint by wrestling shall prevail,
> And having overcome at last be styled *Israel.*[19]

I am arguing not that the image of struggle in the poem is not erotic, but that its potential erotics are rendered safe. They are distanced as struggle. The poem makes the safety of the image especially clear because it transforms the image of struggle into an image of union through the spiritual nation of Israel. In the struggle over John Haines, however, erotic desire itself remains invested in the student. The articulation of sodomitical lust for the student allows Wigglesworth to imagine the desire he feels for God as wholly Other, wholly nonerotic, a struggle between masculine forces, not the desire to possess one. The sodomite is thus necessary to the text, firmly within it, and even more important, as Hughes suggests, firmly within Wigglesworth himself. But he is not already there so much as he is produced, a useful actor in a drama between a man and God, the symbol of what the man ultimately triumphs over. The diary speaks the sodomite as he (or she) had never been spoken before in early modern culture: in a discourse of self-defining specificity.

The morally justified self that is produced when sodomy is revealed only as a sin to be repressed can be shown to shape other social institutions in Wigglesworth's diary as well. As many critics have shown, the institution of pedagogy itself was eroticized in the Renaissance, susceptible to a sexual charge that remained unreadable and invisible except in famous instances such as the dismissal and imprisonment of Nicholas Udall, headmaster of Eton.[20] Wigglesworth renders those erotics specific and visible in himself. In other words, if we accept Wigglesworth's professions as actually describing his carnal desires, he transforms an everyday, nonspecified desire (specified, that is, only as "pedagogy") into visible, homoerotic sodomy, by virtue of his own confession of it. While Wigglesworth's lust for his students may be, in his and the text's imagination, fully coterminous with his otherworldly longings, his recording of it represents a seemingly deliberate encroachment upon an institution in which erotic desire remained "unsocialized." The diary represents an attempt to socialize it, to give it shape and focus, to abstract and remove it from the everyday, unacknowledged erotics of teaching. As a result, as we saw in Wigglesworth's struggle over John Haines, the excessively emotional struggle to educate can be rendered free of erotic taint. On this level, the text might seem to illustrate a dialectic fundamental to the modern sexual regime: the urge to reveal sodomy, the sodomite, and sex itself as constricted, marginalized, and subject to control, especially when such restriction allows other personal investments and social institutions to appear to be free of eroticism and, consequently, to partake in a type of moral and spiritual justification. It is hard not to see in this configuration of control something distinctively modern, and perhaps distinctively Anglo-American, something related to the modern fabrication of male homosociality and homosocial institutions (even perhaps heterosexuality) as a form of sexual and spiritual self-control and "justification" dependent upon the exclusion of sodomitical (and specifically homoerotic) desires.

One other thing also makes Wigglesworth's text seem quintessentially modern. It is not the fact of its confession of sodomy, which retains about it something of the direct, medieval revelation of corporeal sin subject to guilt, punishment, and expiation. Instead, it is the diarist's tendency to speak his specific sexual "sins" obliquely, in code, secreted and already under the control of the subject who narrates. What makes it so tempting to read Wigglesworth's diary from a Freudian perspective are those moments that look like the repression of an already preexisting desire, moments that exist in this text because Wigglesworth seems to be acting through ideologies of shame and bodily control that are particularly modern. It is worth considering that when Wigglesworth details the generic lusts, pride, worldly vanities, and "spirituall adultery" (106) that define him as a sinner, he revels in a rhetoric that is effusive and obsessionally public, as Cherniavsky shows.[21] But when he discloses his "nocturnall pollutions," his carnal lusts, and his desire for his pupils—in short, those sodomitical desires of a sexual nature—he writes in a secret code that reveals even as it reveils his sexual desire. I have already cited several passages that appear in this code (signified in the text by italics), but my point can be made with another citation that appears early in the diary. This passages codifies a significant division in six short words. Talking about the passionate distempers that inwardly prevail with him, he appends a fragment: "vain thoughts *carnal lusts some also* (5)." The expression "vain thoughts" is not revealed in code; the words that refer to his carnal lusts, indicated in italics, are. Here Wigglesworth relegates sex itself to the secret paths and byways of a conscience that is under construction. He is not repressing this sex in himself so much as he is producing it as the thing to be controlled, the thing already under control, as signified in his secret code.

This relegation of sex to the secret recesses of the conscience is, furthermore, evidence that sodomy was becoming something more than a construction of the social employed against enemies of the state, as in Bradford's history *Of Plymouth Plantation*. It was becoming the mark of an inner self spoken by the self.[22] That this should be so may owe something to Puritan notions of reprobacy, for Calvin's exposition on the Epistle to the Romans, and a number of other commentaries that appear within the decade of the 1630s in England, all remark homoerotic sodomy as the sign of reprobacy—that is, as the mark of a clear disorder in the heart of the sinner. Calvin comments on Romans 24 that "[a]s the Lord's wrath is always just, it follows, that what has exposed [the Gentiles] to condemnation must have preceded it."23 It is interesting, perhaps, that this particularizing of the sin of homoerotic sodomy within an emerging concept of reprobation creates the possibility of a connection between an interiorized, persistent, and defining notion of sin and homoerotic sodomy. My point is simply that the doctrine tended to interiorize a more general idea of sin or sodomy, making it a function of the individual heart and conscience that was to be controlled not by external authorities but by the emerging self. The sodomite within, then, signified the triumph of individual self-control and justification, especially in conjunction with that social sodomite without, whose presence demarcated what was external to that self-control.

Still, Wigglesworth's diary does not tell us anything about how and when that potent symbol, the sodomite, came to be so overwhelmingly associated with the homoerotic.24 While it is certainly true that the diary marks a moment in the discursive production of sodomy as an interiorized sin, and thus seems to overlap signficantly with modern sexual subjectivity, neither the diary nor modern discourses render sodomitic sexual subjectivity exclusively homoerotic. What the diary does do, however, is produce the sodomite as a participant in an internal struggle for moral self-justification and social normality. It encodes the sodomite as a readable discursive symbol of what is to be purged and excluded from the self in order to locate a defining sense of the normal. It brings into visibility as aberration what had formerly been obscured as a simple act, putting the sodomite into play as the antagonistic "other" through which normative identities can be established. In this, the diary may provide a clue as to why sex and the concept of sexual aberration play into many different formulations of identity in America, especially those that have developed within Puritan or Protestant traditions. In these traditions, the regulation of the sodomite within may always be prerequisite to personal moral justification and normal social identity.

And just as the diary tells us nothing about when the sodomite became the homosexual, neither does it say anything about the discursive divide between homosexuality and heterosexuality that is constitutive of the modern regime. Although the specific form of sodomy revealed is often homoerotic excess, it is not always so. Sodomy is sometimes something else altogether, as when Wigglesworth refers to his vain thoughts or more generic carnal lusts. Nevertheless, the diary's strategies for articulating the sodomite within as an open secret, a force articulated within the individual and the social fabric as if it were not to be known, rehearses something like those contemporary discourses through which homosexuality (and other so-called perversions) is scapegoated as the secret but still recognized source of social and personal disorder. Like sodomy in Wigglesworth's diary, modern homosexuality is not truly "closeted." It does not exist in an empty space of what is not known. It is produced, rather, as that which is not to be known, with the result that other social institutions (including heterosexuality) can be read as known and normative.[25] What Wigglesworth's diary shows is not homosexuality but the ways in which modern discourses of homosexuality overlap with Puritan attempts to regulate sodomy. It shows how and why, perhaps, the description of sodomy as homosexuality (the confusion of homosexuality with sodomy) has become so strong in the American unconscious.

So, although Wigglesworth's diary is not about homosexuality per se, and hence cannot be read in any simple way to demonstrate the connections between America's Puritan past and its present constructions of sexual identity, it does provide evidence of how the regulation of sodomy in Protestant New England rehearses discourses that are still in play. To point to these overlaps risks obfuscating specific and important historical differences between Puritan New England and contemporary America. But to ignore them risks equally a failure to understand the important role of Puritan ideologies in the present construction of American sexual identities. Simply to accept the by-now-orthodox assertion that before the modern age there were no sexual identities, only sexual acts, threatens to write out of history those discourses that persist and that give defining shape to ideas in two different times and places. Puritan discourses did not "cause" homosexuality, and their image of sodomy cannot alone explain contemporary homophobia. But that imagining can be shown to have produced discourses that empower contemporary homophobia, and a nuanced charting of these multiple empowerments may lead to a more precise inscription of the interrelationships of religion and sexuality in the production of American sexual, and other, identities.

Notes

1. The debate over the social construction of sexuality is vexed and complicated. The history of the debate, of course, can be traced to Michel Foucault's extraordinarily

influential *The History of Sexuality*, vol. I, trans. Robert Hurley (New York: Vintage Books, 1978), and to the groundbreaking article by Mary McIntosh, "The Homosexual Role," *Social Problems* 16 (fall 1968), 182–92, both of which posit the idea that homosexuality as a modern condition that defines the nature of the individual through his or her sexual activities simply does not exist in all times and places. For Foucault, the dividing line is the nineteenth century, when "the homosexual became a personage, a past, a case history, and a childhood, in addition to being a type of life, a life form, and a morphology"(43). Before that, sodomy was nothing more than a category of forbidden acts. Foucault's position has not been adopted universally, and a useful survey of the problems associated with it can be found in Stephen O. Murray, "Homosexual Acts and Selves in Early Modern Europe," in *The Pursuit of Sodomy: Male Homosexuality in Renaissance and Enlightenment Europe*, ed. Kent Gerard and Gert Hekma (New York: Harrington Park Press, 1989), 457–77. For an overview of the theoretical issues in this debate, see *Forms of Desire: Sexual Orientation and the Social Constructionist Controversy*, ed. Edward Stein (1990; reprint, New York: Routledge, 1992), and Diana Fuss, "Lesbian and Gay Theory: The Question of Identity Politics," in *Essentially Speaking: Feminism, Nature, and Difference* (New York and London: Routledge, 1989), 97–112.

2. For a similar argument that the connections between earlier constructions of sodomy and modern sexuality may be found in regulatory discourses, see Karma Lochrie, "Don't Ask, Don't Tell: Murderous Plots and Medieval Secrets," in *Premodern Sexualities*, ed. Louise Fradenburg and Carla Freccero (New York: Routledge 1996), 137–52.

3. Perry Miller and Thomas H. Johnson, eds., *The Puritans: A Sourcebook of Their Writings*, vol. 2 (1938; reprint, New York: Harper and Row, 1963), 585–86.

4. *The Diary of Michael Wigglesworth, 1653–1657*, ed. Edmund S. Morgan (Gloucester, Mass.: Peter Smith, 1970), 31. Subsequent references to this edition will be noted in the text.

It is significant that this passage, and all those marked in italics, appear in Wigglesworth's diary in code. I will comment more fully on the significance of this code later in the essay, but for now it is worth noting that Wigglesworth uses this code to record his sodomitical lusts, which are often fully intertwined with his expressions of love for God.

5. In addition to Hughes's article, " 'Meat out of the Eater': Panic and Desire in American Puritan Poetry," in *Engendering Men: The Question of Male Feminist Criticism*, ed. Joseph A. Boone and Michael Cadden (New York: Routledge, 1990), 102–21, the reader should consult Richard Rambuss, "Pleasure and Devotion: The Body of Jesus and Seventeenth-Century Religious Lyric," in *Queering the Renaissance*, ed. Jonathan Goldberg (Durham, N.C.: Duke University Press, 1994), 253–79.

6. Hughes, " 'Meat out of the Eater,' " 107–15.

7. Alan Bray, *Homosexuality in Renaissance England* (1982; reprint, New York: Columbia University Press, 1995), 80.

8. Jonathan Ned Katz, "The Age of Sodomitical Sin, 1607–1740," in *Reclaiming Sodom*, ed. Jonathan Goldberg (New York: Routledge, 1994), 54.

9. For a fuller version of this argument, see Alan Bray, "Homosexuality and the Signs of Male Friendship in Elizabethan England," *History Workshop Journal* 29 (spring 1990): 1–19.

10. To understand how a Foucauldian reading like the one I have adopted specifically informs understandings of Puritan New England, see Michael Warner, "New English Sodom," *American Literature* 64.1 (March 1992): 19–47; and Jonathan Goldberg, "Bradford's 'Ancient Members' and 'A Case of Buggery . . . amongst Them'," in *Sodometries: Renaissance Texts, Modern Sexualities* (Stanford, Calif.: Stanford University Press, 1992), 223–46.

These assessments, however, might be usefully compared to the history of attitudes toward sodomy and homoerotic behavior in Puritan New England, in Richard Goodbeer, "'The Cry of Sodom': Discourse, Intercourse, and Desire in Colonial New England," *The William and Mary Quarterly*, 3d ser., 52.2 (April 1995): 259–85. Goodbeer describes the theological and legal discourses of sodomy that encode it, as Foucault says, as an act and not as an identity. But there is also evidence, he suggests, that among the general populace, the distinction between sodomy as an act and the sodomite as a particular person with a propensity for committing these acts was not absolute. Although his argument is fundamentally different from my own in its emphasis on the distinction in the definitions of sodomy around popular and legal or theological discourses, it ultimately supports my point in its suggestion that in Puritan New England the discourse of sodomy was more potentially multivalent than has been assumed.

I might also point out that while it seems to be the case in England that sodomy as a category of sin did not specifically exclude women, there is evidence that in Puritan New England it increasingly came to be applied only to men. See Robert F. Oaks, "Defining Sodomy in Seventeenth-Century Massachusetts," *Historical Perspectives on Homosexuality*, ed. Salvatore J. Licata and Robert P. Peterson (New York: The Haworth Press, 1981), 79–84.

11. "To Be a Man in Early Modern Society: The Curious Case of Michael Wigglesworth," *History Workshop Journal* 41 (spring 1996), 158ff.

On the fungibility of gender in early modern England, see Ann Rosalind Jones and Peter Stallybrass, "Fetishizing Gender: Constructing the Hermaphrodite in Renaissance Europe," in *Body Guards: The Cultural Politics of Gender Ambiguity*, ed. Julia Epstein and Kristina Straub (New York: Routledge, 1991), 80–111.

12. Eva Cherniavsky, "Night Pollution and the Floods of Confession in Michael Wigglesworth's Diary," *Arizona Quarterly* 45.2 (summer 1989): 30.

13. Cherniavsky, "Night Pollution," 32.

14. Gregory W. Bredbeck, *Sodomy and Interpretation* (Ithaca, N.Y.: Cornell University Press, 1991), 21–22.

15. Goldberg, *Sodometries*, 243.

16. Goldberg, *Sodometries*, 237.

17. Eve Kosofsky Sedgwick, *Between Men: English Literature and Male Homosocial Desire* (New York: Columbia University Press, 1985). In the introduction to this work, Sedgwick theorizes the relationship of the erotic to social relations between men, refusing the typical distinction between erotic (homosexual) and social (heterosexual) relations that structure modern discourses.

18. Hughes, "'Meat out of the Eater,'" 108.

19. Miller and Johnson, *The Puritans*, vol. 2, 623.

20. See Elizabeth Pittenger, "'To Serve the Queere': Nicholas Udall, Master of Revels," in *Queering the Renaissance*, 162–89, and Alan Stewart, "'Traitors to Boyes Buttockes': The Erotics of Humanist Education," in *Close Readers: Humanism and Sodomy in Early Modern England* (Princeton: Princeton University Press, 1997), 84–121.

21. Cherniavsky, "Night Pollution," 23.

22. In *The History of Sexuality*, Foucault describes the genesis of the modern notion of sexual subjectivity in the Christian confessional in a way pertinent to my discussion (22–25).

23. John Calvin, *Commentaries on the Epistle of Paul the Apostle to the Romans*, trans. and ed. Rev. John Owens (Grand Rapids, Mich.: Wm. B. Eerdmans Publishing Co., 1959), 79.

24. The discursive process by which sodomy has come to be largely associated with homosexuality in modern America reached a peak of sorts in the infamous Supreme Court case *Bowers v. Hardwick* in 1984. For an exposition of the issues involved, see Janet Halley, "*Bowers v. Hardwick* in the Renaissance," in Goldberg, *Queering the Renaissance*, 15–39.

25. As I've already suggested, the paranoid dialectic through which the homoerotic is specified in distinction to noneroticized normative homosocial bonds has been described in English literature and culture by Eve Sedgwick, in *Between Men*. The philosophical and psychological bases of the paranoid construction of modern homosexuality have been analyzed in Guy Hocquenghem, *Homosexual Desire*, trans. Daniella Dangoor (1972; reprint, Durham, N.C.: Duke University Press, 1993), and Judith Butler, *Gender Trouble: Feminism and the Subversion of Identity* (London and New York: Routledge, 1991).

"Remember Me"

The Wonders
of an Invisible World—
Sex, Patriarchy,
and Paranoia
in Early America

౿౿

Boris Vejdovsky

> Enter the Ghost
> Marcellus: *Thou art a scholar.*
> *Speak to it, Horatio.*
> —*Hamlet*

One of the characteristics of mythic figures, such as the Puritan writers of early America, is that they are disembodied. They seem deprived of a real body and to be immune to the "power structures . . . articulated directly on bodies— bodily functions, physiological needs, sensations, and pleasures."[1] Statistics indicating population increase suggest that these proto-Americans often celebrated for their seminal role in American history had sex, but sex seems to be reduced to a strictly reproductive function and tends to remain invisible like the hidden face of the moon which, we infer, must exist even though we can never see it. When we try to approach the question of sex in early colonial times to see how it is articulated on the bodies of men and women and how it affects the process of American identity formation by impinging on power structures within the culture, it seems to dissolve into thin air and become spectral, impossible to circumscribe. Even as it eludes stable identification and scholarly analysis, sex in Puritan culture tends in the same measure to disseminate in all directions and to contaminate all aspects of American identity formation. As a result, it is difficult to come up with either an ontology or an epistemology of sex in early America, difficult to separate what sex *is* (bodies, bodily functions, genetics, physiological needs) from what it represents within a complex semiotic arrangement (symbolic, metaphorical, psychoanalytical). In this essay, centered on Cotton Mather's interpretation of the spectral presence/absence of "witches" in *The Wonders of the Invisible World*,[2] I wish to explore the spectral character of Puritan sex by averting the opposition between ontology and epistemology and by seeking the originality of Puritan sex in the mutual articulation of what sex is *and* what it represents— that is, in the ways signs are articulated on bodies while bodies are constituted by sign articulations.

Recent scholarly efforts have tried to endow with a body those founding fathers and mothers whose sexual, religious, and sociopolitical practices originated "America." Feminist scholars, in particular, have contested the vaunted primacy of Puritan culture's spiritual dimension by making bodies and sex visible.[3] The rediscovery of what had been invisible or had fallen into a cultural blind spot has generated claims that, for example, "American Puritans were not the grim-faced killjoys of popular tradition but relished pleasures such as food, drink, and conjugal sex."[4] However necessary and to the point, such remarks are also problematic, for by pointing to sex so distinctly they run the risk of turning what was invisible into a blinding demonstration.

To say that sex in early Puritan culture is spectral is to find oneself in a somewhat compromising scholarly position. The task of scholars consists, it would seem, in ontologizing the world—that is, of defining what is and what is not, of separating "fictions" from the hard facts of historical reality and assuming in ontologizing responsibility for the dividing line they draw. Such scholarly formation provides little theoretical ground room for taking the spectral seriously. This is precisely what Cotton Mather, an eminent scholar of colonial America, does in *Wonders*: He addresses specters—"witches"—trying to render them visible and present in spite of the *"Metaphorical Storms"* (54) raised by the devil that have erased the clear borderline between reality and fiction. From our (post)modern point of view, Mather certainly is an exceedingly strange intellectual. He is what one may call a "tragic scholar," not only because his writing involves him in—and often indicts him for—what has come to be known as the "Salem tragedy" but, more important, because his writing, the story of the crime of witchcraft, is enmeshed with his attempt to restore justice. As a tragic scholar, Mather assumes the duty and the responsibility of revealing the elements of the crime for the benefit of his community; his "account" of the trials proposes to be a factual archival report but turns out to be an exemplary tale showing the haunting work of sex as a driving trope for identity formation in an originating protohistory of America.

When Mather senses that the history—that is, the very existence—of the American colonies is jeopardized by the spectral disturbance of witchcraft, he rallies his neighbors to vigilance: "Can ye not Discern the Signs of the Times?" (40). Like Hamlet, who says that after the supreme crime of regicide and parricide has been committed "the time is out of joint,"[5] Mather announces that New England's "*[t]ime* is upon the *wing*, and . . . will all be gone within a little while" (66). The task of the tragic scholar is to "set the time right" by writing its history, establishing a genealogy of events, and retracing those events to their causes and origins. The task is not only chronological and methodological, but also ethical, for history is to provide the moral basis without which—as Prince Hamlet's rotten Denmark suggests—no social or political structure can survive. For Mather, as for Hamlet, that task consists in rearticulating the voice and the body of the assassinated patriarchal authority by restoring it as the center of sexual, seminal, and semantic power.

In *Hamlet*, during the first encounter with the ghost that haunts Elsinore, Marcellus anxiously entreats his companion Horatio to address the ghost: "Thou art a scholar. Speak to it."[6] But modern scholars do not speak to ghosts unless the latter can be safely parked in the realm of imagination, mental disorder, or fiction.[7] The spectral character of sex in Puritan culture may be the reason its role has been so hard to define: Sex seems to be either purely fictive and akin to (para)psychological interpretations or is reduced to hard statistical facts. In order to gain some more productive understanding of the issue, we shall have to address that spectral character, to "speak" to it. We can use Mather's account of the Salem witch trials as a cautionary tale to help us revise our scholarly position, for the difficult instability of sex in Puritan culture can be accounted for by no commonsense simplification and no dead metaphor. To understand the haunting character of Puritan sex we need to renounce the firm ground where we separate fiction from historical reality, and "think the possibility of the spectre, that is, the spectre as a possibility, beyond the opposition between presence and non-presence, effectivity and non-effectivity, life and non-life; we need to be scholars 'mad enough to hope to *unlock* the possibility of such address.'"[8] What follows is an attempt to open or "unlock" the Pandora's box of the spectral and a proposal to read the presence/absence of witches in *Wonders* as a trope for the presence/absence of sex in Puritan culture. Such an understanding of sex often leads us to a *mise en abyme* of spectral representation: We think we have identified a specter only to find that it stands for an entity that is no less spectral.

An understanding of sex in early American culture as it is troped on the bodies of the "witches" and in Mather's account of the trials cannot be reached by pathologizing the "witches" or Cotton Mather and declaring either of them—or both—mad. We could even say that the source of Mather's tragic mistake regarding the "witches" was not his folly, but on the contrary the fact that, as a scholar, he was not *mad enough* to "unlock the possibility" of addressing the spectral *as* spectral. Instead he tried to control the spectral by giving it an ontological or epistemological status, as though to evade the responsibility and the dedication to the task demanded from Hamlet by his father's ghost now floating between absence and presence: "Remember me."9

For Mather, to remember is to "set right" the historical time that has been put "out of joint," but it is also to re-member the dismembered, dislocated, or disjointed body of the Father in whose name the New Jerusalem was founded, and who incarnated—through His Son—social, political, and ethical order. The mutilated body and voice of the assassinated patriarch is to be restored to its integrity through the body of the text whose syntactic and rhetorical articulations are to reconstitute them. In a process verging on incarnation, the writing of a "reasonable" account is to abate the "*Metaphorical Storms*" raised by the devil "upon the Church" (54), and restore to its place the phallogocentric body of Christ, the embodiment of patriarchal fidelity. Such is the formidable demand put on Mather, and such are the high stakes of his writing. Of course, (God) the Father cannot be brought back to life, but writing takes His place and the book is produced, as it were, under the dictation of the Father to tell His story and thereby secure the legitimacy of his successors and the perennial stability of the genealogical line. Mather's account of the trials consists in writing the Father's will, and Mather is seized by the anxiety of making mistakes, but also by the vertiginous freedom of the white page: What if he did not take everything down? What if he altered the will just a little bit?

What makes the situation even more confusing for a Puritan scholar such as Mather is the fact that the devil can plague New England only with the assent of God, "who indeed has the *Devil* in a *Chain*, but has horribly lengthened out the *Chain*" (86). In the New World, not only is the devil's chain much longer, but so also are the historical and genealogical chains that bind the Puritan settlers to the word of God. The "*American* Desart" (11) is a formidable space of liberty where the voice of the Father calling out to be remembered can no longer be heard so distinctly; indeed, it may even be altogether forgotten.

In his rewriting of the trials, Mather tries to restore and make material the summation of the patriarchal voice of authority that was left "home"—geographically, culturally—by the Puritans. Here, in the undomesticated "*howling Wilderness*" (74) of New England, in this formidable *unheimlich* space beyond the threshold of the Father's house, the Puritans are confronted with the feeling of guilt for leaving that *Heim*, that domesticity, and "embrac[ing] a voluntary Exile in a squallid, horrid, *American* Desart" (11). At the same time, they are haunted by an exhilarating historical possibility: that of *forgetting* the domestic space and the proper name attached to it. Thus, Mather's "account" of the trials presents us with a new original possibility, a new economy, in which the "accounting" for one's history is no longer submitted to the rules of the Father's *oikos*.

It is "*America's* Fate," Mather writes, to "include *New-Englands* in it," and "the design of our God . . . in bringing over so many *Europeans*" is "to make [of America] *a* seat for any *of those glorious things which are spoken of thee, O Thou City of God*" (76). Mather's text reveals the Puritans' pronounced taste for history and genealogy to be haunted by anxieties of sexual inadequacy and logocentric impotency, by fears that the seeds of the planters are no longer potent enough to dominate and subdue America's earth. Witchcraft, embodied in the flesh of the witches and their victims, threatens to unman the patriarchs of the colonies and send them back to self-doubt and impotence. The weakening of their sexual and political knowledge is the element that may break the genealogical line and halt the possibility of retracing it to a phallogocentric point of origin, namely the Word of God the Father embodied in Christ His Son, His rightful descent, and transmitted through the Scriptures to the "first Planters of [the] Colonies," the "chosen Generation of Men" (11). In a process that blurs the boundaries between psychology and Calvinistic hermeneutics, Mather's account of the trials is an attempt to restore the departed Father to His place of origin and presence, a place framed by the male Logos of the Father and the incarnation of the Word in the male body of the Son.

The story written by Mather is an exemplary tale of American patriarchal culture whose identity formation is predicated on the tragic mode and is haunted by the paranoiac feeling of sexual impotence and ignorance, here troped in terms of small-scale economy, local politics, and religious practice. The "*Halcyon* Days" (14) when New England is to become a New Jerusalem are close at hand, Mather foretells; however, those days can be reached only through successive (re)generations, which implies that the seminal power of the first "planters" must be retained. As a tragic scholar, Mather writes under the pressure of historical responsibility while cursing, not unlike Hamlet, the fate that caused him to be born to undertake "the Heart-Breaking Exercises" of setting time and history right. This means that the sons of the fathers founding the colonies have to *"Remember whence* [they] *are fallen, . . . repent and do the first works"* (13). (Or, as Derrida suggests, "There can be a tragic essence only if there is such originality [originarité], or more exactly only if there is such pre-original and precisely ghostly anteriority of the crime."[10]) For Mather, as for Hamlet, to set the time right is both a cosmological and an ethical undertaking. "[I]t is a thing," he writes, "prodigious, beyond the Wonders of the former Ages, and it threatens no less than a sort of a Dissolution upon the World" (15–16). The paranoia from which Puritan patriarchy suffers is expressed in apocalyptic terms, and suggests a definitive disjoining of time, a disarticulation of the body of history and morals, enacted on the very bodies of New Englanders: "because God said of old, *Let us make Man in our Image,* the Devil is saying, *Let us pull this man to pieces*" (47). Guilty of forgetting their Father's name, the Puritan sons are guilty thereby of dismembering the Father and disjoining the time of history as established by Protestant eschatology. The "dissolution" of the world appears as a dismemberment of man, whose torn-up constitution no longer expresses God's will and can no longer be in His image.

All this is shrewdly presented in *Wonders,* where Mather does not satisfy himself with the trite bureaucratic report the reader might expect from the opening lines of the book. His account of the trials is embedded in a series of rhetorical ploys that cannot be dismissed as a display of accumulated data or a series of provisional statements. They all serve a crafty mise-en-scène preparing the reader for the central agon of the trials themselves. Mather begins their evocation with a spectral prologue that serves as an entreaty to remember their exemplary character. "This," he writes, "will be a true History of what has occurred, respecting the WITCHCRAFTS wherewith we are at this day Persecuted" (107). As in all tragedies, the intervention of Mather the scholar and hero-writer takes place belatedly, at a time already freighted with guilt and remorse, a time when it is (almost) too late to act.

This belatedness is emphasized in *Wonders* by a preoriginal case that suggests that witchcraft in Salem is only an element of a larger historical telos:

> It was on the Second of *May* in the year 1687, that a most ingenious, accomplished and well-disposed Gentleman, Mr. J*oseph*

> *Beacon*, by Name, about Five a Clock in the Morning, as he lay,
> whether Sleeping or Waking he could not say, (but judged the
> latter of them) had a View of his Brother then at *London*, altho he
> was now himself at our *Boston*. . . . This his brother appear'd
> unto him[;] . . . his Countenance was very Pale, Gastly, Deadly,
> and he had a bloody wound on one side of his Fore-Head.
> *Brother!* Says the Affrighted *Joseph* . . . *Brother!* Answered the
> Apparition . . . *I have been most barbarously and injuriously*
> *Butchered, by a debauched Drunken Fellow, to whom I never did any*
> *wrong in my Life.* (107–8)

In this opening narrative, the ghost of the slaughtered man asks his brother
Joseph to see to the prosecution of his murderer when the latter comes to
America, where he is allegedly to flee. However, Mather reports, the mur-
derer has managed to get away with his foul action thanks to the culpable
complicity of "such friends as brought him off without the loss of his Life"
(109). Thus, the historical account of the trials is prefaced by spectral apparition and an unpunished crime. "[N]o more has been heard of the Business,"
Mather writes; but he states that he has "received [the story] of Mr. Joseph
Beacon himself," who gave it to him "written and signed with his own
Hand" (109). Through this self-reflexive move, Mather casts himself as one
of the characters of the tragedy he is describing, even as he becomes the
depository of the demand put on an American brother—as *"His brother's
keeper"* . . . "as 'tis hinted in *Gen.* 4.9," Mather himself remarks. He is now in
charge of remembering the crime, making its spectral character appear by
identifying the culprit, and seeing to it that the crime that infects the body of
the American people from the outside (Europe) and inside (complicity of
harmful friends) does not remain unpunished. *Wonders* opens, then, not
only with an uncanny apparition but also with the intimation that the scriptural injunction to the male descendants of the chosen people "to *keep* one
another from the Inroads of the Devil" (49) has not been respected, and that
there are criminals at large in America, hosted like viruses within the body
of its people and threatening the regenerative potency of the male body of
brothers.

Mather's interpretation of the "witches" is thus placed under the aegis of
the suspicion that there are enemies within and without the country plotting
for its destruction. As a result, *Wonders* turns out to be not only the account of
the trials of a few "witches" but, most important, that of all the Puritan males
who are found wanting for forgetting the name of their (fore)fathers: "The

Devil first *goes* up as an *Accuser* against us. He is therefore styled *The Accuser*; and it is on this account that his proper Name does belong unto him. There is a Court somewhere kept; a Court of Spirits, where the Devil enters all sorts of Complaints against us all" (49).

Mather is one of the sons accused of failing to maintain the generative force of the forefathers and thereby invalidating their claim for a place along the genealogical line extending from the original source of patriarchal seminal and semantic powers. *Wonders* shows how paranoia stemming from a sense of sexual inadequacy is a constitutive element of identity in American patriarchal culture, and how by investing with signification all the domains of the culture—religion, economy, politics—patriarchy becomes, in turn, an inescapable element of American identity formation.

In *Wonders* the "Body of the People" (11) constitutes a metonymy for the actual bodies of men and women "*infected* and *infested*" (15) by the spectral manifestation of the "witches" who "hideously distort and . . . disjoint all [the] members" (81) of their victims. The uncanny effects of witchcraft appear as sexual disorder and confusion caused by the devil who sexually possesses the witches, "knowing" them physically and mentally by having them sign their names in a "Spectral Book" containing "the *Devils Laws*" (82). The devil's possession of the witches disrupts the logocentric, economic, and sexual order of the domineering patriarchs of Puritan society: God, the minister, the husband. That the sexual and economic dimensions are not separate but articulated on one another is attested by the hermeneutic confusion that accompanies the apparitions of the "Witches [who] . . . have plotted the Representations of *Innocent Persons*, to cover and shelter themselves in their Witchcrafts" (17–18). Mather reports that "the Devil in Witchcrafts . . . work[s] upon the Bodies of Men and Women, . . . and that he . . . Extraordinarily afflict[s] them with such distempers as their Bodies were most subject unto" (117), while the "devil . . . make[s] a deceitful and unfaithful use of the *Scriptures* to make his *Temptations* forceable" (187). Ritualized sexual intercourse in "Hellish *Randezvouses*" (81) takes the form of orgies where another ritual, Protestant liturgy, is parodied in "Diabolical Sacraments . . . imitating the *Baptism* and the *Supper* of our Lord" (81).

The explicit sexual dimension of those nocturnal meetings is veiled by the very thing they trope: Sexual deviance is interpreted by Mather as religious and social deviance. What is at stake is not the Puritan's vaunted "conviction," as Karen Armstrong suggests, "that women had sex with demons and flew through the air to worship Satan in orgiastic parodies of the Mass";

indeed it would be almost reassuring if patriarchal identity stemmed from "a truly diabolic terror of sexuality and the female."[11] In that case, the haunting paranoia that is at work shaping American identity could be assigned a name and a shape, consigned to an unenlightened "past" and discounted. But it is not women who are the cause of the paranoia. Sexual disorder, written upon bodies and in spectral books, unsettles the seminal and semantic powers of the Father, which leads to a confusion in the world and to the disjoining of society and eschatology. It results in the suspicion that it is no longer possible to *know* what is right and wrong, to impose the phallogocentric dividing line between the fictions of the devil and the truth of God. For Mather, there can be no doubt: All this upending of the semiotic system is part of "An *Horrible* PLOT *against the Country by* WITCHCRAFT, *and a Foundation of* WITCH-CRAFT *then laid, which if it were not seasonably discovered, would probably Blow up, and pull down all the Churches in the Country*" (14).

One can only be struck by the disproportion between the petty offenses that lead to the indictment of a "witch" and what Mather announces as the apocalyptic consequences of such accusation. Even in an economic system predicated on the mutual support of all members of a community, only an exacerbated feeling of paranoia can explain the transformation of minor infringements of that rule into capital crimes belonging to a "Hellish Design of *Bewitching and Ruining* the Land" (15). The examples of witchcraft given by Mather characteristically hover over the borderline of ascertainable his-torical reality and imagination and oscillate between economic order and sexual disorder. He selects the case of Elizabeth How, who reportedly "griev-ously tortured [her neighbors] by sensible and evident *Witchcrafts*," and they "complained of [her] as the cause of their Trouble" (149). One of the charges lodged against How was that after her neighbor Isaac Cummings refused to lend her his mare, the animal "was within a day or two taken in a strange condition" and finally "dyed very suddenly" (152–53). The causal link between these events is unclear; as Bernard Rosenthal observes, the "story, related in connection with the case of Elizabeth How, had as its only link to her the visit of James How, Jr., perhaps with the implication that his visit somehow tied her to the mysterious death of the mare."[12] How's case typi-cally articulates a case of dissension within small-scale economy (the consequence of Cummings's refusal to lend the mare) with a breakdown of sexual order inscribed on the bodies of the neighbors in the form of the bites and scratches on their flesh that testify "sensibl[y]" to the nocturnal assaults of the woman/witch.

Not only in *Wonders*, but also in the proceedings on which Mather bases his own interpretation of the trials, imprints of teeth, laceration by nails, marks left by pinching or scratching recur systematically as signs of the witch on the victims' bodies. It has been argued—not unreasonably—that these signs could easily be made by the victims themselves and then attributed by them to the witches. But the repetitive character of these signs turns them into a sort of conventional catachresis that euphemistically but also unmistakably designates the sexual character of the intercourse with the witch whose presence/absence is attested by the signature she (in most cases) has left on the victims' bodies. The economic and sexual dimensions—both troped as "witchcraft"—are like two mirrors facing each other; it is impossible to decide on which side the image we see in them originated.

In these accounts, sexual intercourse with a witch is characterized by violence and pain, suggesting the unnatural character of the sexual act and the deviant dimension of the act of possession. But the marks on the bodies are also signs that potentially reveal, even as they veil, pleasure and sexual desire. The marks on the bodies are the inscription of disorderly and uncontrolled sexual behavior, a behavior beyond the ken of the community's husbands (the "planters," the "brothers"). These men are supposed to be in control of sexual practices not only when these take place as genital contact and involve actual bodies, but also when they are metonymically displaced onto the social, political, or religious scene and involve the "Body of the People."[13] Finally, the ambivalent character of these signs is coextensive with the ambivalent nature of the witch, who is both present and absent through those signs. The bodies of the witches and those of the victims are the only legible "text" where the presence/absence of the witch can be read; for the rest, the witchcraft remains spectral, and its prosecution depends on the "spectral evidence" brought by the victim/witness before the court.

For modern scholars, whose work often bears no little resemblance to that of a forensic expert, the greatest source of scandal around the Salem witch trials is probably that so many "witches" were indicted, imprisoned, morally and sometimes physically tortured, even executed on the basis of "spectral evidence"—that is, on the basis of what many see as only the witnesses' demented imagination.[14] But it is, of course, precisely the spectral quality of the evidence that makes it so damning. Mather includes the case of John Louder, who testified before the court that he "did see clearly the likeness of [Bridget Bishop] grievously oppressing him; in which miserable condition she held him, unable to help himself, till the next Day" (135). Here, unseemly sexual behavior is characterized by violence and a breaking into the private sphere of the victim. But it is one thing, perhaps, to indict Bridget Bishop for eliciting Louder's compromising desires; another to indict her "likeness": The spectral character of sex allows it to go through walls and trespass the limits between the private and the public sphere, making any infringement of the sexual order by an individual a matter of consequence for the whole community.

Mather, indeed, insists on the materiality and the corporeal reality of the phenomena he is describing; as a scholar, he desperately tries to ontologize the entities and "likenesses" that are said to have appeared to the victims. But as soon as he tries to ascertain its presence, witchcraft loses its materiality and escapes from the realm of the corporeal to take refuge in the spectral, whence it can be retrieved only through metaphor.[15] The spectral disturbances referred to as "torture" or "affliction" by the victims trope disorderly sexual practices, but the specter that leaves its marks on bodies and scars the collective psyche of the body of the people is not the witch but the haunting presence/absence of fatherly authority, which calls out to be remembered and manifests itself as repressed and uncontrolled sexual desire.

If the sexual dimension of witchcraft cannot neatly be equated with sex understood as actual genital contact, then neither is it "merely" and innocuously imaginary. *Wonders* relays the anxiety of Puritan men—husbands, brothers, planters—under the weight of patriarchal demand, and it expresses their fear in images where sex, economies—monetary as well as semiotic— and politics reflect one another. *Wonders* also illustrates how the desire for privileged access to knowledge—sexual and logocentric—is precisely what secures patriarchy's cultural dominance. Infusing male anxiety into all domains of Puritan life, public and private, *Wonders* takes its part in shaping an American individual and communal identity where masculine paranoia is—for both sexes—an essential dimension. While sex remains spectral in the account of the trials and can often be glimpsed only through the metonymies that veil it, its effects are concrete, and they contribute to determine political and social structures articulated upon and written with the bodies of the American people.

The high proportion of women accused or executed in the trials has often been noted, together with the absence of any sociological or demographic data that could satisfactorily explain this imbalance.[16] As Cornelia Hughes Wilson suggests, "Puritan legal regimes across New England unquestion-

ingly cast women as witches and condoned a prosecutorial double standard
for accused men and women such that twenty-eight women and only seven
men were hanged for the crime of witchcraft."[17] The association of women
and women's bodies with the pathology that infects the "Body of the People"
of New England revolves around male sexual fantasies of control and dependence. There are, for instance, numerous allusions to "preternatural teats"
that the witches are said to have on their bodies. In most cases, those unnatural breasts were likely to have been moles or warts, but what is significant
is their symbolic function, for the "preternatural teat" defaces and subverts
the avowed nurturing function of women.[18] The denaturing of the woman's
body perverts the genealogical line of descent by drawing lewd associations
between women and bestiality; the body of the accused woman is rewritten
as the body of a sow or a bitch giving suck to a multitude of illegitimate and
bastardly offspring. The search for some bodily deformity is also a pretext for
exposing the body of the woman and attempting to "know" her. These physical examinations, during which male inquirers were often present even
when they were conducted by women, form the fleshly counterpart to the
humiliating spiritual inventory to which the accused were subject; both constitute male paranoia as the urge and the desire to *know*.

"Although there is no denying that seventeenth-century Anglo-Americans
. . . believed women to be inferior to men," Mary Beth Norton writes, "the
specific implementation of that belief must be understood in the context of
the small politics of the neighborhood and within the nexus of gendered
power."[19] Along the same lines, the systematic victimization of women in
this primal scene of American culture makes sense only when it is read
against a paranoia in the sons of the "chosen Generation of Men," who, like
many sons within patriarchal culture, feel that they are never man enough to
live up to the memory of their (fore)fathers.

The process of identity formation as we discover it through a relatively
marginal historical event such as the Salem witch trials serves to remind us
that history is often written with a "grotesque disparity between cause and
effect"[20] and that it has been one of the most pervasive effects of American
patriarchy to erase that disparity. Significantly, modern scholars who do not
believe in witches and spectral evidence have found other ways of invoking
the patriarchal logocentric voice of authority. It has been suggested, for
example, that we "should not shrink from concluding that Elizabeth Knapp
[later executed as a witch] was truly ill—by our standards if not theirs" and
that the "literature of clinical psychiatry is full of cases evincing symptoms

immediately analogous to the bizarre actings of Elizabeth Knapp."[21] In this
clinical discourse, so pervasive in all the literature surrounding the trials, the
witches and their tormentors have both become lunatic others, lodged
together in the exclusionary category of mental disorder.[22]

The sexually charged condemnation of the "witches" in Salem appears to
have been consciously intended, but that intention is veiled in remembering
processes that begin as early as the trials themselves. No surprise, then, that
the haunting sexual character of witchcraft, repressed, now returns in the
more readily recognizable shape of schizophrenia, hysteria, or political vested
interests. The disquieting power of the witch trials manifests itself through
what Derrida calls the "helm effect" (*l'effet de visière*);[23] like Hamlet, to whom
the ghost says, "Mark me. . . . I am thy father's spirit,"[24] we can never be quite
sure that what we perceive behind the screening discourses of psychology,
politics, or economics is ever stably present. By giving an account of his
encounter with the spectral disturbance that afflicts Puritan New England,
Mather estranges himself forever from the reassuring home of the Father.
His writing is the move of exile, and that move also constitutes one of the
wobbly cornerstones of the edification of American identity. While *Wonders*
seeks to find its way "home" to fatherly authority, it also initiates an eccentric
movement into an "American Desart" where what has the appearance of the
law can often be cruel and destructive, and where the sweeping violence of
the spectral constantly threatens to turn against those who think they have
identified it.

Caught between hagiography and demonization, Puritan myths of sex are
not only hard-lived, but also self-perpetuating. Rendered spectral and then
obsessively recorporealized, sex within male Puritan culture was relegated to
the realm of the differently embodied, differently desiring other—female,
black, disabled, "oversexed," Indian, queer. Puritan sex in this way creates the
Puritan self in and through the very processes that "constitut[e] . . . [the]
Other as the Self's shadow."[25]

The 1692 Salem witch trials constitute a primal scene for American identity—even as Mather's *Wonders* constitutes a primal scene of American
writing. Far from being safely confined in an enclosed historical period
where they would constitute an interesting—if somewhat vicarious—object
of scholarly pursuit, the effects of this primal scene, where sex plays both the
role of revelation and veil, have been visited on the sons and the daughters
inhabiting the space engendered in those seminal moments of American
identity formation.

Notes

1. "[L]e but [d'Histoire de la sexualité] est bien de montrer comment des dispositifs de pouvoir s'articulent directement sur le corps—sur des corps, des fonctions, des processus physiologiques, des sensations, des plaisirs." Michel Foucault, *Histoire de la sexualité* (Paris: Gallimard, 1976), 1, 200 (author's translation).

2. Cotton Mather, *The Wonders of the Invisible World: Being an Account of the Tryals of Several Witches Lately Executed in New-England*, 1693 (Amherst: Amherst Press, 1862). Hereafter cited by page number in the text.

3. On the establishment of this received tradition Lawrence Buell writes: "Following the Puritan historians, nineteenth-century orators agreed . . . that the primary if not exclusive purpose of New England colonization was spiritual." Lawrence Buell, *New England Literary Culture: From Revolution through Renaissance* (Cambridge: Cambridge University Press, 1989), 198.

4. Frances Hill, *A Delusion of Satan: The Full Story of the Salem Witch Trials* (New York: Doubleday, 1995), 4.

5. William Shakespeare, *The Tragedy of Hamlet, Prince of Denmark*, ed. G. R. Hibbard (Oxford: Oxford University Press), 196 (1. 5. 195).

6. *Hamlet*, 1. 1. 42.

7. Hill writes that "all the English Puritans' sixteenth-century beliefs in witchcraft . . . were still current in New England in 1692. But such beliefs were the products of the human imagination with no basis in fact" (34). This may of course be true, but such a statement ignores all disquieting connections between the "facts" and the "imagination."

8. "[Un tel scholar] serait enfin capable, au-delà de l'opposition entre présence et non-présence, effectivité, vie et non vie, de penser la possibilité de spectre, le spectre comme possibilité. Mieux (ou pis), il saurait s'adresser aux esprits. Il saurait qu'une telle adresse n'est pas seulement déjà possible, mais qu'elle aura de tout temps conditionné, comme telle, l'adresse en général. Voilà en tout cas qulqu'un d'assez fou pour espérer *déverrouiller* la possibilité d'une telle adresse." Jacques Derrida, *Spectres de Marx: L'État de la dette, le travail du deuil et la nouvelle Internationale* (Paris: Galilée, 1993), 34 (author's translation).

9. *Hamlet*, 1. 5. 91.

10. "Il n'y a de tragédie, il n'y a d'essence du tragique qu'à la condition de cette originarité, plus précisément de cette antériorité pré-originaire et proprement spectrale du crime. Derrida, *Spectres*, 34 (author's translation).

11. Karen Armstrong, introduction to *A Delusion of Satan*, ix.

12. Bernard Rosenthal, *Salem Story: Reading the Witch Trials of 1692* (Cambridge: Cambridge University Press, 1993), 65.

13. On the control of sexuality by men, and by husbands in particular, Mary Beth Norton writes that "New England's emphasis on the establishment of orderly

marriages led to the legal privileging of a husband's sexual access to his wife. Accordingly, adultery (a crime defined by the marital status of the female partici- pant) was punished more severely than any other consensual heterosexual offense." Mary Beth Norton, *Founding Mothers and Fathers: Gendered Power and the Forming of American Society* (New York: Vintage Books, 1997), 348.

14. Richard Weisman provides a comprehensive account of this much debated judi- cial issue: "This form of evidence was founded on the belief that demons could assume the identity of a person, and, as a specter, inflict harm on the body of another person or simply perform general mischiefs. If this evidence were admitted, the accused would be left with virtually no means of challenge. If she were miles away from the crime or even in a large public gathering at the time of the assault, the accuser could claim that it was her specter rather than her person that established her guilt." *Witchcraft, Magic, and Religion in Seventeenth-Century Massachusetts* (Amherst: University of Massachusetts Press, 1984), 104.

15. To give further credibility to his account, Mather mentions extraordinary cases where the "bewitched" are said to have vomited nails, spindles, or pins. Mysteriously enough, however, this material can never be produced before the court. It is nonethe- less retained as proof because of the testimony of people who are said to have seen the nails: "First, One of our bewitched people, was cruelly assaulted by a *Spectre*, that, she said, ran at her with a *Spindle*: tho' no body else in the Room, could see either the *Spec- tre* or the *spindle*. At Last, in her miseries, giving a snatch at the *Spectre*, she pull'd the *spindle* away, and it was no sooner got into her hand, but the other people then present beheld, that it was indeed a Real, Proper, Iron *spindle*, belonging they knew to whom; which when they lock'd up very safe, it was nevertheless by *Demons* unaccountably stole away, to do further mischief" (162). Although Mather affirms that the spindle of "Real, Proper, Iron" had become *"Visible* to a Roomful of Spectators," in the end the "unquestionable" proof remains spectral or metaphorical. In a climax of persuasion, Mather affirms that "the very *Devils* are walking about our Streets, with lengthened *Chains*, making a dreadful Noise in our Ears, and *Brimstone* even without a Metaphor, is making an hellish and horrid stench in our Nostrils" (95). Mather's scholarly attempt in *Wonders* is to give an ontological status to the spectral, but that is the source of his tragic mistake. By refusing to address the spectral *as* spectral, he stries to endow it with a name and a face. When he writes that he can see witches in the streets of Salem without metaphor, he yields to the desire of taking figures of speech literally, and controlling the diquieting *(unheimlich)* presence of the spectral by returning them to the homely presence of the Father who guarantees knowledge and meaning.

16. Demos surveys the figures of the trials and notes: "Females outnumbered males by a ratio of 4:1." He adds that even these figures understate the association of women and witchcraft, as can be seen from a closer look at the men accused: "Twenty of the male witches were rendered suspect either by 'association' (with an accused woman) or else in a distinctly limited way (as part of a larger sequence of hostilities)." John Putman Demos, *Entertaining Satan: Witchcraft and the Culture of Early New England* (New York: Oxford University Press, 1982), 60–64.

17. Cornelia Hughes Dayton, *Women before the Bar: Gender, Law, and Society in Connecticut, 1639–1789* (Chapel Hill: University of North Carolina Press, 1995), 9.

18. Suspected "witches" were examined by female juries composed of "women who assumed leadership roles [and who] were . . . either midwives or the wives of high-ranking men or both. Such women were the focal points of the female communities, those who served simultaneously as opinion leaders, spokeswomen, and moral arbiters. Through their participation on women's juries or their work as semiofficial investigators of sexual or witchcraft offenses, they linked the communities of men and women, conveying the consensus of women's thinking to such masculine institutions as courts and legislatures" (Norton, *Founding Mothers*, 236).

19. Norton, *Founding Mothers*, 249.

20. Hannah Arendt, *The Origins of Totalitarianism* (1948; reprint, New York: Harcourt Brace & Co., 1979), viii.

21. Demos, *Entertaining Satan*, 117.

22. Rosenthal observes that "[t]he twentieth century has pursued the medical models [for the witch trials] more persistently, particularly psychological ones." He adds that "[e]choes of Freud permeate Salem accounts, popular and scholarly" and offers a comprehensive review of the numerous psychological or psychiatric explanations proposed by scholars. *Salem Story*, 33–36.

23. Derrida, *Spectres*, 26 (author's translation).

24. *Hamlet*, I. 5. 2, 9.

25. Gayatri Chakravorty Spivak, "Can the Subaltern Speak?" in *Colonial Discourse and Post-Colonial Theory*, ed. Patrick Williams and Laura Chrisman (New York: Harvester Wheatsheaf, 1993), 75. "Otherness" takes polymorphous and sometimes indistinguishable forms. The story of Tituba, the young girl who supposedly triggered the whole Salem episode, is revealing in that respect. Apart from being female, she is sometimes identified as black, sometimes as Indian, sometimes as resorting to voodoo magic, or a combination of the above. See Chadwick Hansen, "The Metamorphosis of Tituba; Or, Why American Intellectuals Cannot Tell an Indian from a Negro," in *New England Quarterly* 47.1 (1974): 3–13.

Uncleanliness Is Next to Godliness

Sexuality, Salvation,
and the Early American Woman's
Execution Narrative

ᢒᢙ

Jodi Schorb

This essay focuses on a decidedly narrow Puritan genre, the "execution narrative"—the texts produced and distributed before, during, and after a criminal's public execution. The execution genre emerged in the seventeenth century as part of a concerted effort by Puritan ministers to "document and illustrate the specific effects of declension," the widely held perception that the later generations of Puritans had fallen away from the original zeal and moral purpose of their founding fathers.[1] Beginning with Samuel Danforth's *The Cry of Sodom Enquired Into* (1674), approximately one dozen narratives were published prior to 1700, most by ministers Increase and Cotton Mather. By 1800, the genre had expanded to include over two hundred execution sermons, spiritual biographies, last words, dying confessions, lives, accounts, and ballads.[2] Until at least 1750, the vast majority of execution narratives concerned murderers, with the occasional appearance of a sodomite, pirate, or rapist. Consequently, the narratives have traditionally been discussed in the context of crime literature.[3]

Scholarship, however, has yet to highlight the significance of gender difference in these narratives. Women have the dubious distinction of being well represented in the genre,[4] and while the execution narrative was not explicitly focused on women's sexual transgressions, it nevertheless played an important role in structuring early American female sexuality. If we fail to see this fact, we eclipse the sexual nature of the women's narratives and mask the ways their murder prosecutions relate to sexual mores and (hetero)sexual expression. Women rarely murdered strangers, their masters, or even their husbands. They most often murdered their newborn children.[5] Women who murdered were usually young and unmarried. A majority of these women were servants, and a disproportionately high number of them were nonwhite, a point that reveals the biases of the criminal justice system, which tried and convicted servants and minorities at higher rates than others.[6] Crucial to my purposes, however, the overrepresentation of young servant women in these narratives reveals that these women did not fit easily into the dominant narrative of Puritan "family-centered, reproductive" sexuality.[7] Indentured servants were expressly forbidden to marry until their terms of servitude were over, and a pregnant servant faced public humiliation, fines, whippings, and extended terms of service. Consequently, a substantial proportion of the female population was denied any sanctioned form of sexual expression.

This essay attempts to locate some of these nonsanctioned forms of early American sexuality by exploring the gendered and erotic nature of the execution ritual. By considering the public execution only as an instrument of social control, a ritual that solidified the power of religious and civil authorities, we exclude other meanings—for example, the voyeuristic mix of identification and desire that drew thousands to attend public executions. Unlike other capital crimes, such as murdering a master, and unlike property theft, infanticide sexualizes the body of the woman on the gallows, most obviously because the crime marks the woman's body (mostly young, mostly unmarried) as a site of sexual knowledge, a mark bolstered by the public nature of the ritual itself. Standing on display, the woman's body functions as "a symbol, a living border of sexual deviance."[8] Ministers tried to use this to their rhetorical advantage, first arguing that the "unclean" state of the woman's body functioned as a clear, knowable sign of an unregenerate spirit, and then using her example to prompt the audience to examine their own unregenerate behaviors. Yet the ministers could never fully control what the audience "saw" during the ritual. Their anxiety over what exactly the condemned woman's body signifies grows more obvious in later execution narratives, as ministers competed with other forms of discourse (such as newspaper accounts) that offered different interpretations of the ritual. By the early 1730s, as public sentiment against neonatal infanticide began to soften, the woman on the gallows became less an object of horror and increasingly an object of empathy, even desire.

Nor has the impact of these Puritan narratives entirely disappeared from our cultural landscape. A contemporary woman's "execution narrative"—the stories told by and about Karla Faye Tucker before her 1998 execution—reveals not only the ways that the conventions of the Puritan execution narrative continue to structure discourses of sin and repentance, but also how the condemned convert becomes a complex target of identification and desire for both male and female spectators. In this sense, Tucker's narrative helps clarify the links between the spectacle of sex, the sexuality of the narrative, and the relation between sexual narratives and conversion ideology—an ideology still central to our national fantasies of self-improvement and personal transformation.

First Acts: The Wages of Sin

The narrative of Esther Rodgers nicely articulates the precarious place of the female servant. Comprising minister John Rogers's three-part sermon, and Esther Rodgers's own "Declaration and Confession," the Rogers/Rodgers text appears conventional. It is unusual, however, in that it offers competing interpretations of the same events. The minister's narrative genders and sexualizes Rodgers's crime, transforming a murder narrative into a cautionary tale of feminine stealth and corruption. Against this narrative, the more autobiographical "Declaration," ostensibly written by Esther Rodgers herself, places Rodgers's crime in a larger social nexus, locating her "sexual" crime in relation to contemporary discourses of punishment and shame, as well as to her economic status of servitude.

By all accounts, Rodgers made an unlikely saint. Accused of concealing, and then murdering, her bastard child, the twenty-one-year-old white servant initially denied the charges. She remained silent even after suspicious neighbors conducted a search, discovered a dead infant by a nearby pond, and confronted her with the evidence. Yet, the recalcitrant prisoner soon became a model of grace. After undergoing months of counseling with a host of ministers in preparation for her ensuing execution, Rodgers experienced a "remarkable conversion," confessed, and begged forgiveness. The ministers, confident in the sincerity of her conversion, used the spectacle of the penitent woman on the gallows to rouse their audiences from complacency.

In the tradition of the execution narrative, both her conversion and her death become communal events. The sermon delivered at Rodgers's execution, entitled *Death the Certain Wages of Sin*, adopts the jeremiad's tone of communal warning. The rhetorical power of the execution sermon derives largely from the concept of "shared guilt," through which the audience is encouraged to identify with Rodgers's sins, repentance, and desire for salvation. Reverend John Rogers graphically reminds both the condemned woman and the spectators of their inherent sinfulness, declaring that "Every Child of *Adam* is born a Leper, all over defiled, from the Crown of the Head to the Sole of the Foot; he is as it were one engrained spot, a lump of *Uncleanness.*" The minister does not distinguish between Esther Rodgers's criminal actions and his audience's own innate depravity.[9] Instead, he encourages his audiences to identify not only with Rodgers's sins, but also with her struggle for grace. In this way, the criminal's spiritual struggle had collective resonance, and "his or her drama to escape damnation through redemption reflected the larger drama of New England itself."[10]

While Rodgers seems to serve as a model for all, however, she is revealed more precisely as a warning to specific communities, reminding them that they are particularly unclean, weaker, and expected to transgress. The minister points a finger at women in particular by gendering Rodgers's sinfulness and suggesting that her femaleness partially accounts for her depravity: "And what shall I say unto thee, *Esther . . . Thy ways have been all filthy, thy whole Walk, a walk after the Flesh . . .* O Unclean, Unclean! As if possest with an unclean Devil, or with as many as *Mary Magdalen*, yea rather with a Legion; thou hast served the Devil an intire Prenticeship of one and twenty years in filthy ways of one sort or another" (114–15).

Reverend Rogers reads Esther Rodgers typologically as Mary Magdalen, and he links her to a whole "Genealogy . . . of loose and lewd woman," including Tamar, Rahab, and Bathsheba, the seducer of David (70). Meanwhile, his hyperbolic language casts the female body as a site of filth and pollution. This linkage of the female body with filth is, of course, part of a long Western tradition. Yet here, the minister's gendered rhetoric undermines his universalizing language of sin and positions the execution as a larger force of social control over women's sexual behavior. True to convention, the minister "accounts" for Rodgers's crime in Adam's fall; yet even his application of original sin is sexualized in the narrative. The minister constructs Adam's fall less as willful disobedience of God's command than as an adulterous affair, a sexual transgression producing spurious offspring: "*The Woman saw the Fruit was good for Food* . . . and *Adam* with complacency received the Temptation, and by the inticement of the foul Fiend of hell, committed Adultery with the Creature; from whence the cursed Race of Sin and Miseries do proceed. . . . [Thus] a hereditary Corruption is transmitted to all that naturally descend from old *Adam"* (95).

Although he focuses on Adam, rather than Eve, it is Eve's body, not Adam's, that carries the corruption from generation to generation. Ironically, such discourse constructs "repro-culture" as inherently doomed: Original sin—that old "hereditary Corruption"—lies at the heart of the reproductive imperative.

If the ministers gender Esther Rodgers's crime, they also gender her religious conversion. Here, however, the gendered language serves as a corrective ritual, providing a model of "proper" birth. Seizing upon the metaphoric resonance of Rodgers's eight-and-a-half-month confinement, the ministerial narratives depict a blood-soaked, spiritually "dead" Rodgers purified and reborn. According to Reverend Belcher's preface, Rodgers entered prison "a Bloody Malefactor, her Conscience laden with Sins of a Scarlet Die" but in the "space of Eight Months she came forth, Sprinkled, Cleansed, Comforted, a Candidate of Heaven."[11] Belcher presses the birth imagery further in his tribute to pastor John Rogers, who "saw the fruit of all his Labours, and Travels with her" (96). The tender care shown by the ministers provides a stark contrast to Rodgers's supposed parental negligence: stepping in to assist the woman through her "travail" and labor, Rogers proves a powerful midwife. In response, Esther Rodgers praised the minister for his "discourse [which] did so open and lay out my condition before me . . . so that I was smitten in my heart" (96). Thus in correcting one narrative of sexual transgression and murder, a different sort of sexual narrative gets produced, one that transforms an illegitimate birth into a legitimate spiritual renewal, but—oddly enough—only by recasting the minister as both seducer and midwife.

Rodgers's own "Declaration," however, tells a different tale. Published after her death and appended to the Sermon, the "Declaration and Confession of Esther Rodgers" emphasizes her experience of conversion and her assurance of salvation, rather than her crime and her sinfulness. The narrative, the bulk of which was supposedly narrated by Rodgers herself (albeit with assistance from her ministers) supplies some motivation for her infanticide beyond her being possessed by an unclean spirit. In the "Declaration," Rodgers charts her own slippery slide into sin with more specificity than the ministerial accounts.

After turning her back on God, she explains that God "justly gave me up to my own hearts Lusts," and that by the age of seventeen, she "f[ell]" into "that foul Sin of Uncleanness"(97). Seized by sudden awareness of her sinfulness, Rodgers makes a shocking revelation: She confesses in her narrative not only to the infanticide for which she is about to die, but also to a second infanticide five years earlier, which had never been discovered.

She explains that her primary motivation for concealing the pregnancy and birth in both cases was to avoid the public stigma of illegitimacy. Whereas the authorities consider these instances of concealment as evidence that both murders were premeditated, and as confirmation of Rodgers's weak and deceptive nature, Rodgers herself locates the problem with concealment in public discourses of shame and punishment. The stricter the social ramifications, the greater the incentive to conceal.[12] According to Rodgers, she concealed her first pregnancy "to prevent coming to Publick Shame," hiding the baby later in an upstairs room, stopping its breath, and giving it a "Private Burial" in the garden (97). When describing her second pregnancy, Rodgers again invokes social codes as the primary motivation for the infanticide. Five years later, in another household, she again "fell into the like horrible Pit (as before) viz. of Carnal Pollution" (97). Again, she seeks to avoid the social stigma of illegitimate pregnancy, claiming that "being with Child again, I was in as great concern to know how to hide this as the former." She delivered the child outdoors, "covered it over with Dirt and Snow, and speedily returned home again" (97).

Rodgers's account emphasizes her precarious identity as a household servant. The narrative is filled with references to her various apprenticeships and masters. Even her "speed[y] return" back to the house suggests that she was motivated by the wish not only to avoid the stigma of illegitimacy, but to maintain her household employment. Her narrative reveals a heightened attention to place: an early apprenticeship in the Christian home, sexual experiences "in a back part of the House," hiding her baby "in an upper room of the House" (97). The house where she committed infanticide at seventeen holds particularly painful memories for her, she says; she returns a year later to the same household, but suffers extreme remorse, "which together with other reasons"—which she does not clarify—cause her to enter service in another household (97).

By confessing the first infanticide, Rodgers contests the common Puritan belief that God swiftly brings sinfulness to light and makes evil deeds visible, suggesting that the relation of sexual transgression to visibility is dubious, at best. Without the confirming agency of female reproductive capacity, sexual transgression is notoriously hard to "see." In the absence of witnesses, only the material evidence of a child makes (certain) sexual practices "visible." And in this case, even that doesn't happen; Rodgers reveals that no one, "not so much as the Father of the child himself was privy to my disposal of it, or knew that I ever had such a Child" (97). By volunteering the information about her earlier infanticide, Rodgers exposes a gap in the dominant narrative of Puritan sexuality. How many other births went undetected? How many other kinds of sexual practices remain unseen?

While sensational, her story is in its own way "representative," but not in the morally edifying way that the ministers conceive it. Since servants were expressly forbidden to marry until their terms of indentureship were over, they were denied access to the family-based reproductive networks that scholars have seen as characterizing the whole of early American sexuality. Refused sanctioned forms of sexual expression, servants often had covert relations with other servants under the master's roof. Of course, female servants also routinely found themselves at risk of sexual exploitation at their master's hand. (Rodgers remains silent about the "other reasons" that forced her to leave the house.) Female servants had few options: stifle their sexuality altogether, engage in nonreproductive forms of sexual practices (which leave little evidence—and few historical records), or hazard pregnancy, public shame, fines, and extended terms of servitude for causing their masters "lost time." For a female servant, the punitive fines and extended terms of servitude literally constitute the "wages" of sin.

Elizabeth Colson's Empty Stage

Both of Esther Rodgers's babies were mulattos, fathered by black servants who worked with her in the household. Yet neither the minister's sermon nor Rodgers's account sensationalizes the interracial nature of her "crime." This is not to say race doesn't factor in her narrative; on the contrary, Rodgers's whiteness is foundational to her public "Declaration." Whereas the white female was often called on to speak publicly, the black female, although executed at disproportionately higher rates, was afforded neither the platform to publish her narrative nor the opportunity given to Rodgers of publicly addressing over four thousand attentive, admiring witnesses.[13] In the eyes of the church and state, the nonwhite identity of the executed woman limited her supposedly "representative" status.

When Elizabeth Emerson and a woman identified only as "Grace, 'Negro'" were jointly executed for infanticide in 1693, Cotton Mather's execution sermon, *Warnings From the Dead*, appended only Emerson's narrative. Grace never left a "warning." Neither did "Betty," executed for infanticide in 1712, or Alice Clifton, found guilty of infanticide in 1787. Although ministers didn't publish her faithful narrative, at least one black female apparently managed to leave a record. "A Short Account of the Life of Elizabeth Colson, a Molatto Woman, who now must Dye for the Monstrous Sin of Murdering her Child" was found on a slip of paper in Colson's jail cell, allegedly dictated by Colson to another prisoner before her 1727 execution in Plymouth, and was reprinted in a local newspaper "without the Addition of one Word."[14]

Despite a tone of piety and regret in Colson's narrative, no ministers publicly testified, as they did in Rodgers's case, on behalf of her "modesty," or commended her demeanor as "very grave and Christian from first to last" (105, 108). Modesty and black female sexuality, these omissions suggest, are incompatible. Nor does her narrative suggest that there was space in the conventional execution ritual for Colson to share her final words. Invited to utter her last words before the crowd, Esther Rodgers exclaimed, "O let me beg of you all to hear me! For the Lords Sake Remember me! Oh let every one Remember me!" (105–6). The centrality given Rodgers's last words in the execution ritual, and the fact of their being written and disseminated, accord an unusual degree of attention to an otherwise "insignificant" servant woman. Although Colson had no way of knowing whether her "Account" would ever become part of public discourse, she did insist on her right to narrate her case.

Clearly, Colson was familiar with the form and function of the criminal conversion genre. Her account employs many of the genre's conventions, including descriptions of her birthplace, early spiritual education and condition, descent into sinfulness, and, ultimately, her sincere repentance: "I was Born at Weymouth, and my Mother put me out to Ebenezer Prat, who was to learn me to read, but I fear they never took that pains they should have done to instruct me, my Mother being School-Mistress, was loth I should come to School with other Children, and so I had not that Instruction I wish I had in my Youth. I was carry'd very hardly too by my Mistress, and Suffer'd hunger and blows, and at last was tempted to Steal, for which I have reason to lament, for although I stole at first for Necessity as I tho't, yet the Devil took Advantage against me, and led me further into Sin"(2). Moreover, her narrative explicitly registers her knowledge of the ways the execution genre circulated publicly. She is aware that she occupies a place in the tradition of infanticide narratives, placing her story in relation to an earlier tale she heard: "I remember when I was young I heard of a Woman that Murdered her Child, and I said, I never would do so. I may Say to you as my Mistress did to me, you do not know what you may be left to"(2). Her childhood recollection reveals the extent to which execution stories circulated among various classes and races, serving—as ministers hoped—as warnings. Initially, Colson sought to define herself against the genre, but ironically, she herself became part of its discourse.

Since few, if any, black female servants left "official" execution narratives, Colson's desire to imitate the genre's conventions cannot be read simply as her wish to add her voice to its generalized warning against sin. While writing within the genre's conventions, she was also writing against its silences, using the public nature of the discourse to testify on behalf of her experience of neglect and ill use. Despite its traditional sin-to-repentance structure, the narrative's conventional piety is deceptive. Here, discourses of sin compete with more sociological discourses, for Colson's narrative suggests motivation for her descent into sin beyond the standard religious explanation of God's withdrawn grace. Colson revises the traditional "slippery slope of sin" theory, explicitly citing her lack of education, poverty, hunger, and poor treatment by her masters as social forces precipitating her descent into crime.[15] She doesn't explain why her schoolmistress mother did not want her at school with the other children, but young Colson's racial difference is a possible explanation.

Colson's account also complicates the link between sex and sin. Colson does not classify stealing food as a sin, calling it instead a "Necessity." She labels only those "further" actions of hers "sins." By implying that since she was denied food, she can justifiably steal, Colson's narrative begs a different question: Since she was denied marriage, can she justifiably have sex? If sex is a sin, then so is her hunger. Offering a twist on the traditional narrative, Colson suggests that her "sinfulness" was a last resort, rather than an innate condition— something she "[did] not know [she would] be left to" (rather than the more orthodox "led to"). Even as she embraces her punishment as just, she implies to her audience that she might have been "left to" other, less desperate circumstances had social conditions been otherwise.

The gaps in her narrative are particularly apparent in her ambiguous account of her sexual activities. She confesses to fornication, to at least two unwanted pregnancies, and to at least one infanticide: "[H]aving got a habit of

Sin, I still grew worse & worse & worse; and was left to fall into the Sin of Fornication, and after my time was out with Master *Reed,* I was in great distress,
what to do with my Child, but carried it about from place to place, till I left it
at Dighton, and ran away from it, and soon fell again to that shameful and
Soul-destroying Sin of Fornication the Second time; and not having the Fear
of God before my Eyes, I was justly left of God to this horrid Sin the Third
time, that led me, together with the Instigation of the Devil, and the
wretchedness of my own Heart, to that monstrous Sin for which I must now
Dye" (2). Although she names names earlier, in documenting harsh treatment by her masters, she doesn't name the father(s) of the children, or the
circumstances surrounding the pregnancies. Did Master Reed father the
child she abandoned? Were the encounters consensual or forced? Such gaps
urge the question: What family-based, reproductive sexuality could possibly
exist for the black servant? Where do we even locate "family," when Colson is
sold from one house to another, and must move "from place to place" when
her term of servitude expires? More dislocated than Rodgers's household narrative, Colson's account suggests that even the ability to leave the household,
and to leave indentured status, fails to provide all women with the means or
conditions for any sort of socially sanctioned sexuality.

Theaters of Mercy

The subtle tone of protest in Colson's narrative suggests another reason why
ministers may have hesitated to offer up the platform to the condemned. The
spectacle of execution also opens up the possibility of revolt, as ministers
compete with the powerful presence of the condemned to maintain control of
the event. This was particularly true in the 1730s, when attitudes toward capital punishment, particularly for neonatal infanticide, began to change.[16]
    The 1738 execution of Katherine Garret in New London, Connecticut, calls
attention to the increasing instability of the New England execution ritual.
Reverend Eliphalet Adams's sermon, *A Sermon Preached on the Execution of
Katherine Garret*, is not directed at Garret *per se*, but instead denounces Garret's supportive, sympathetic audience. As Colson's narrative suggests, and
as Adams's execution sermon for Katherine Garret makes clear, meaning can
go awry when the sympathy audiences feel for the condemned overshadows
their feelings of repulsion and horror at the crime committed. Garret's narrative highlights the voyeuristic possibilities of the power of sympathy within
the execution ritual.

Garret, a descendant of one of the most respected families of the deci-mated Pequot tribe, was now reduced to colonial servitude in the home of Reverend William Worthington. Upon learning she was pregnant, she con-cealed the birth from her master and mistress and gave birth alone. Her child was later discovered with alleged (but unspecified) "marks upon it of Vio-lence" and died soon afterward.[17] Her trial met with repeated delays, in part because ministers wanted more time to make Garret aware of her crime, and in part because witnesses were reluctant to come to court to testify against her, which triggered the ire of Reverend Adams.

Adams's sermon takes the form of a classic jeremiad but puts a twist on its contents. He gives a stern warning, chastises the audience for complacency, and ends with a note of hope. Yet the jeremiad doesn't precisely address the spiritual condition of either the audience or Garret. Distressed by their lack of zeal in bringing the criminal to justice, Adams chastises slow-moving jus-tices of the peace and their attempts to "screen [the guilty] from the punishment which they have Justly Deserved" (4). He criticizes reluctant wit-nesses and the "Numbers that have gather'd round" the condemned, declaring, "Tho [the accused's] Crimes were bloody and to the last Degree Infamous, Yet they have Interposed & Defended them" (9). Adams defends capital punishment against a criminal justice system, and a general public, who have apparently gone soft on crime.

The specific targets of Adams's rant are unclear, since the jury found Gar-ret guilty and sentenced her to death. Yet his sermon reveals an important preoccupation with the disruptive nature of spectacle, as he envisions the accused offering an extravagant performance for a rapt audience: "The Spec-tators are struck with concern; The Judges are melted into tears. . . . People Crowd to the Tryal with Eager hast, They attend the Process with Aking hearts; They gaze upon the poor Criminals after Condemnation. . . . When the Day of Execution comes, then, *Multitudes, Multitudes* flock together; And Oh! that it might be to learn Wisdom" (25).

Adams reveals his concern over the misplaced gaze. Ideally, members of the audience would see in the sinner a window to their own soul, and pangs of terror and regret would cause them to reflect upon their own sins. Instead, the audience is enraptured by the spectacle of the swooning woman, feeling "akes" and pangs in all the wrong places. The simultaneous aching, fainting, swooning, and melting suggests a mutual interplay of iden-tification, sympathy, and voyeuristic desire between the criminal and her audience.

The problem is not simply that the event is theatrical. On the contrary, execution has always relied on its theatricality for its effectiveness. When the condemned and their audiences play their appointed roles correctly, the authorities (whether church or state) solidify their power and control.[18] Esther Rodgers's ministers deliberately call attention to the theatricality of the event, inviting viewers to "draw the Curtain" on the "Tragick Scene, strangly changed into a *Theater* of *Mercy*" (95). The ministers hail Rodgers for "Her undaunted Courage and unshaken Confidence [which] . . . melted the hearts of all that were within seeing or hearing, into Tears of affection, with greatest wonder and admiration" (108). Rodgers's ministers approved of and encouraged the "tears of affection" shed by their audience because they read in those tears sincere identification, repentance, and a newfound conviction to reform.[19] But for Adams, the "concern" of spectators and the "tears" of the judges do not necessarily translate into spiritual soul-searching. By 1738, the communal nature of the sermon was no longer guaranteed. The exemplary power of a criminal like Garret no longer incited the kind of personal reflection needed to police behaviors, and thus to enforce social and sexual norms.

Cultural differences also complicate the supposedly communal function of the ritual. If the execution ritual is a carefully orchestrated event, operating on a set of shared codes and assumptions, what happens when those who don't share those codes or assumptions are brought to trial? Garret's case speaks to the ways different cultural practices, including Native American attitudes toward both infanticide and the authority of the colonial courts, create gaps of meaning that further undermine the effectiveness of the execution ritual.

Although narrated largely from Adams's biased perspective, details of Garret's cultural resistance emerge in the narrative. While given a Christian education and taught to read and write, Garret never converted to Christianity. The fact that she delivered her baby alone was used against her in the trial, for deliberate concealment of a pregnancy both gave evidence of premeditated murder (in the event of the infant's death) and violated colonial childbirthing rituals, performed commonly under the supervision of a midwife.[20] Even as late as 1779, however, Native American women typically delivered their babies alone, so far from premeditating murder, Garret may merely have been following different cultural birthing norms. She seemed perplexed by the attention her case generated; according to reports, she "seemed to Entertain a full Expectation that she should be Cleared" (38). When the verdict of guilty was announced, she "was thrown into the utmost Confusion and Distress . . . throwing blame on all sorts of persons" and letting loose a stream of "rash and unguarded" expressions (38–39). Puritans read her hostile reaction as evidence of an unregenerate spirit, yet Pequot history might certainly have taught Garret to be suspicious of the authority of colonial courts. Moreover, while Native Americans in New England were noted by colonists for their exceptionally attentive parenting, they treated infanticide with differing levels of cultural taboo, which may account for Garret's confused reaction to the charges and her anger at the verdict.[21] As a result of her resistance, officials delayed her execution "not only to allay this resentment, but to make her Sensible of the Heinousness of her Sin" (39). Fearing the ritual would lose its emotional resonance if the accused did not share their Christian religious codes of confession and repentance, the ministers and courts delayed her execution in order to make a "Praying Indian" of her. By doing so, Adams expressed his hope that "her *Country people*, in their several Tribes, whither round about us or farther off" would take notice of her example and "hearken diligently to the Offers & Proposals of the Gospel that are made to them!" (42).

Whether they did or not, we do not know. Garret, however, did convert after many months of ministerial "assistance." Her short "Confession," written "in her own Hand" and published along with Adams's sermon, enacts a newfound Christian orthodoxy and assimilation to colonial sexual values. She thanks her ministers, supporters, and those who taught her to read the Bible and extended her time in prison, "whereby I have had great Opportunity to prepare for my Death" (43). She thanks the courts for giving her a just sentence and the ministers for baptizing her and allowing her to take communion. She then piously accepts responsibility for the sin that she had so much trouble acknowledging earlier in the courtroom: "I confess myself to have been a great Sinner; a sinner by Nature, also guilty of many actual Transgressions, Particularly of Pride, and Lying, as well as of the Sin of destroying the Fruit of my own Body, for which latter, I am now to Die" (43). Yet Garret's confession is not wholly without disruptive potential. She gives the usual warnings to youth and servants to obey authority, but adds a new warning to parents and masters:

> Young People . . . Beware of all Sin, Especially of Fornication; for
> that has led me to Murder. Remember the Sabbath day to keep it

Holy. Be Sober and wise. Redeem your Time, and Improve it
well. . . . I would also Warn Servants, Either *Whites* or *Blacks*, to
be Obedient to your Masters & Mistresses.

I would also Intreat Parents and Masters to set a good Example before their Children and Servants, for You also must give an
Account to God how you carry it to them. (44)

Garret uses her platform to not only set an example, but to encourage her
authorities to set better examples themselves. Like Colson's 1726 narrative,
Garret makes a plea for greater social equity, here explicitly instructing masters and parents to behave more responsibly. Whether or not she expressly
influenced her "*Tribe*," as Adams hoped, is uncertain. Her appeal to both
white and black servants to be dutiful suspiciously omits Native Americans.

Final Acts

Rodgers, Colson, and Garret understood the theatrical nature of the execution ritual and embraced their appointed role in the "Theater of Mercy." By
adapting to the conventions of the genre, they accorded themselves an
authority otherwise disallowed to those in their present social conditions.
Together, their narratives help place the dominant narrative of Puritan
familial-based sexuality within a much broader social nexus, impacted heavily
by race and class. Provocatively, their situations also ask us to question
whether illegitimacy is a logical result, rather than an aberration, of the early
American cultural injunction to reproduce.

While locating desire within the execution ritual remains a cautious
endeavor, the difficulty of "seeing" evidence becomes foundational to other
ways sexuality functions in the narratives. The Puritan aversion to concealment permeates the narratives, particularly in the ways the ministers such
as Eliphalet Adams rail against those who "hide their *Sin* and *Shame*," the
"great Numbers [that] have Escaped Discovery in the Life and are reserved to
the final Judgment of God" (30). Concealment, as two legal historians note,
"denied personal readiness for salvation."[22] This fear of concealment
informs the legal statutes against infanticide; concealing either pregnancy or
the death of a newborn illegitimate baby was used by ministers and courts as
presumptive evidence of murder. Central to the discourses of reproduction,
especially nonnormative reproduction, were the fears that dominated the
larger society—fears of a descent into sin unless constant vigilance was

maintained. Purity demands watchfulness, concern, surveillance. If concealment itself proves guilt, then the Puritan fear of concealment produced the
necessity—and the desire— for unveiling. These executions, and the narratives produced around them, not only strove to channel Puritan sexuality
within repro-culture, they also produced alternative desires—desires to hear
and to "see" the narratives of nonnormative sexualities.

Nor is pleasure entirely confined to the spectators; the condemned women
embraced their exemplary status and took their parts in the voyeuristic ritual.
Colson's insistence on leaving a narrative, Garret's final "cooperation" in the
ritual she once resisted, or Rodgers's plea—"O let me beg of you all to hear
me! For the Lords Sake Remember me! Oh let every one Remember me!"—
also construct part of the desire in these narratives: a desire to affect, in some
way, what the spectators "saw." A brief look at Karla Faye Tucker's execution
narrative calls this complex interplay of desire into high relief and testifies to
the resonance of the early American narratives in our contemporary discourses of crime and religious conversion.

Epilogue: The Pickaxe Murderer's "Faithful Narrative"

Few recent executions have garnered as much media attention as Karla Faye
Tucker's execution for double murder on February 3, 1998. Tucker—commonly referred to as the "Pickaxe Murderer"—was the first woman put to
death in Texas since 1863 and only the second woman put to death in the
United States since the death penalty was reinstated in 1976. Her crime was
violent and sensational: Following a three-day drug binge in 1983, a twenty-
three-year-old Tucker and her boyfriend broke into an acquaintance's house
to steal motorcycle parts, unexpectedly found him in bed with a woman,
grabbed a pickaxe off the wall, and proceeded to bludgeon and axe them both
to death. Like Rodgers, Garret, and countless others facing imminent death,
Tucker underwent a Christian religious conversion while in prison. Although
her clemency appeal failed to win the favor either of the Texas Board of Par-
dons and Parole or of Governor George W. Bush, the case brought
international attention to the woman who was eventually renamed "The
Sweetheart of Death Row."

Tucker's story contains many of the formulaic features of the Puritan conversion narrative. She describes an early fall into temptation and sin, signaled
by sexual activity and disregard for authority—including marijuana at eight,
heroin at ten, and prostitution at thirteen—followed by a bottoming-out

period of gangs, fights, more drugs, and eventually, double murder. When, after her jailhouse conversion, a Christian television news show began a series of interviews with her, Tucker embraced the role of the exemplary criminal, agreeing to speak publicly so that "lives would be saved, that lives would be touched. . . . That [God] could change their life." She specifically hoped, she said, to "reach out to kids and to try to keep them from going where I went."[23] Against the media's desire to document all the sensational and grisly details of her "fall," Tucker tries in these interviews to stay vague, as though to recoup the universalizing gestures of the Puritan conversion narrative against the modern media "tell-all." When speaking to reporters about her young adulthood, Tucker emphasizes the more universal experiences of adolescence—"drugs . . . peer pressure . . . sex . . . very low self-esteem. I didn't know where I belonged"—and mutes the specifics of prostitution, heroin, and gangs.[24]

Public interest in her case was fueled by her gender, charm, and good looks. Once dark, angular, and tomboyish, the reformed Tucker now seemed soft and radiant. News reports unfailingly point to her "doe eyes," "broad smile," "dark rolling hair and soft brown eyes," "winsome" good looks, or "fresh-faced desirability."[25] Her Christian supporters argued that salvation had wrought a notable change on her body and soul, and boasted that she "put a face on death row"[26] (as if there weren't already thousands of faces on death row). Media attention to her appealing looks worried death penalty supporters, and Tucker's opponents accused her of being "a good-looking woman who's exploiting [her] gender," implying that Tucker was trading in on her femininity and sex appeal to get preferential treatment.[27] Even death-penalty opponents were distressed by the outpouring of public interest in her appeal, noting that if "Tucker were an ugly black male Muslim, no one would take as much notice."[28]

Adding to this erotic spectacle was the sexualized nature of both her crime and her religious conversion. As in the early infanticide narratives, a woman's murder case gets refigured as a "sex crime." Media accounts repeat what Tucker apparently told a friend after the killings: that she "got a nut" and "came with every stroke" of the pickaxe,[29] merging violence with desire and according her genitalia phallic power. Consistent with her reformed persona, Tucker does not discuss this detail when retelling her narrative, but the media accounts still fixate on it, rarely failing to mention how the "killings enthralled her to the point of sexual ecstasy," so that she "felt a surge of sexual pleasure with every swing of the axe."[30] Yet, consciously or unconsciously, Tucker does eroticize her relation with God and her public: Describing her moment of salvation, she melds the language of Christian conversion with modern romance fiction: "It just surrounded me, [Jesus] just put me in his arms and just said, 'I love you,' you know."[31] When asked why her ministry is so successful, Tucker explains that the "Lord has really given me a passion for the church, for his body,"[32] and when asked what she most wanted people to remember her for, she responds, "I loved the Lord with all my heart . . . that I loved people and gave that love out. That love that was in me, that I gave it out."[33] Fittingly, Tucker wed while in prison, marrying prison minister Dana Brown (by proxy), and calling into high relief the intense relation between the fallen convert and the minister who "plies his oars" on her soul.

Tucker's good looks and erotically generous demeanor seduced viewers of both genders, providing explicit lesbian content to her narratives. Preparing to interview her, *New Yorker* reporter Beverly Lowry confesses her desire: "In that cold, walled-off setting, surrounded by cold, walled-off people, Karla Faye threw her head back and guffawed—a hearty, full, genuine body-shaking guffaw—and I could see her direct, uncompromised, highly sexual charm. . . . I fell for Karla, as, I would subsequently learn, did many others: the cop who arrested her, the prosecutor who convicted her, the corrections officers and so many of the other dead-solid law-enforcement folk."[34]

Lowry's confession not only testifies to Tucker's seductive capacity, but also suggests that her desire is motivated by an epistemological quest to know, to be "touched" by the kinds of knowledge Tucker possesses. Staring at two photos, one taken before the murders and one four years afterward, Lowry says of the latter photo: "More than anything, she looked calm. I envied that calm."[35]

The condemned woman's body is infused with iconicity and knowledge. The public is invited to gaze at her, but our gaze has no singular, stable function. Her grace and piety make the orthodox observer's desire for identification safe, yet the knowledge of her sexually transgressive past also makes any gaze prurient as well. Her body indeed stands as a "border" —signaling both "deviance" and grace, sensuality and spirituality, experience and newfound innocence, life and death—and thus becomes a compelling site of knowledge. Tucker's looks, whiteness, and gender—along with the religious conversion that brings all these elements into high visibility (so much so that she "radiates" with newfound softness, beauty, and composure)—are all indispensable elements in making Tucker, for at least a few weeks, part of a national fantasy.

It would, of course, be anachronistic to accord the same level of sexual awareness and erotic content to the narratives of the Puritan women executed for murder. We have no records of men or women outwardly confessing a readiness to be seduced by these earlier women on the gallows. Yet Tucker's narrative clarifies the ways sexuality continues to surface in representations of female crime and in the execution narratives' complex interplay between the minister, the condemned woman, and their audiences.

Notes

1. Ronald A. Bosco, introduction to *Sermons for Days of Fast, Prayer, and Humiliation and Execution Sermons*, ed. Ronald A. Bosco (Delmar: Scholars' Facsimiles & Reprints, 1978), lxxiv.

2. The actual number of execution narratives is difficult to pinpoint, since a single publication might include multiple individual works, such as a sermon and a personal narrative. See Ronald A. Bosco, "Early American Gallows Literature: An Annotated Checklist," *Resources for American Literary Study* 8 (1978): 81–100, which cites 164 published works and 203 individual works published prior to 1800.

3. After 1750, a marked increase of execution narratives addressed individuals convicted of property crimes, including burglary, counterfeiting, and theft. (Nearly all those convicted of property crimes were men.) See Bosco, "Checklist."

For excellent accounts of the history of the execution genre see Daniel Cohen, *Pillars of Salt, Monuments of Grace: New England Crime Literature and the Origins of American Popular Culture, 1674–1860* (New York: Oxford University Press, 1993); Daniel Williams, *Pillars of Salt: An Anthology of Early American Criminal Narratives* (Madison: Madison House Publications, 1993); Karen Halttunen, *Murder Most Foul: The Killer and the American Gothic Imagination* (Cambridge, Mass.: Harvard University Press, 1998).

4. Roughly half of the pre-1700 narratives concern women, as do the majority of narratives between 1730 and 1740. Approximately two dozen individual execution narratives exist for women prior to 1800, including a dozen sermons and another dozen or so personal accounts, faithful narratives, dying warnings, last speeches, and/or confessions.

5. For a comparison of male and female crimes, see N. E. H. Hull, *Female Felons: Women and Serious Crime in Colonial Massachusetts* (Urbana: University of Illinois Press, 1987), 44.

6. For a detailed breakdown of gender, class, and race in relation to criminal prosecutions, see Hull, *Female Felons*, 54–58 and 100–107.

7. John D'Emilio and Estelle B. Freedman, *Intimate Matters: A History of Sexuality in America* (New York: Harper & Row, 1988), xi. D'Emilio and Freedman's account follows recent historians' focus on the social, economic, and geographical conditions in New England that made the territory amenable to a procreative, family-based sexuality, including lower infant mortality rates, more balanced sex and servant/owner ratios, a more racially and socially homogeneous culture, small clergy-centered communities, and, perhaps more important, the need for bodies to populate and provide labor in the new colony. See Edmund S. Morgan, "The Puritans and Sex," *New England Quarterly* 25 (1942): 591–607; Emil Oberholzer Jr., *Delinquent Saints* (New York: Columbia University Press, 1956); John Demos, *A Little Commonwealth* (New York: Oxford University Press, 1970); Philip Greven, *The Protestant Temperament* (New York: Alfred A. Knopf, 1977); Roger Thompson, *Sex in Middlesex* (Amherst: University of Massachusetts Press, 1986).

8. Hull, *Female Felons*, 125.

9. John Rogers, *Death the Certain Wages of Sin* (Boston: G. Green and J. Allen for Samuel Phillips, 1701), 95. Subsequent reference cited in the text. For a detailed reading of the Rodgers case, see Daniel Williams, "'Behold a Tragic Scene Strangely Changed into a Theater of Mercy': The Structure and Significance of Criminal Conversion Narratives in Early New England," *American Quarterly* 38 (winter 1986): 827–47.

10. Williams, *Pillars*, 5.

11. Esther Rodgers, "The Declaration and Confession of Esther Rodgers," appended to *Death the Certain Wages of Sin* and reprinted in Williams, *Pillars*, 95. Subsequent references cited in text.

12. For a closer look at the parallel relation between concealment rhetoric and infanticide rates, see Peter C. Hoffer and N. E. H. Hull, *Murdering Mothers: Infanticide in England and New England, 1558–1803* (New York: New York University Press, 1981), 53–54.

13. In comparison, about a dozen black male narratives were published. For statistics on conviction rates by race, see Hull, 116–20.

14. "A Short Account of the Life of Elizabeth Colson . . . " *New England Weekly Journal*, 19 June 1727, 2. Subsequent references cited in text. I wish to thank Dr. Thomas Doughton, researcher at the American Antiquarian Society, for directing me to this narrative.

15. Colson's account signals an emerging shift in the form and tone of the execution narrative. Between the Great Awakening and the Revolution the narratives began documenting the condemned's struggle as a distinct personality, impacted by real social forces (Williams, *Pillars*, 13). Colson's "Account" anticipates this important development by more than a decade.

16. This resulted from a variety of social factors, including improved material conditions, an expanding publishing industry that challenged ministerial control over infanticide discourse, and the rise of the romantic sentimental movement. See Williams, *Pillars*, 12; Hoffer and Hull, *Murdering Mothers*, 80–81.

17. Eliphalet Adams, "A Sermon Preached on the Occasion of the Execution of Katherine Garret, an Indian-servant . . . " published with "The Confession and Dying Warning of Katherine Garret" (New London, Conn.: T. Green, 1738), 38. Subsequent references cited in text.

18. On theatrical effects of execution, see Michel Foucault, *Discipline and Punish: The Birth of the Prison*, trans. Alan Sheridan (New York: Pantheon, 1977; reprint, New York: Vintage Books, 2d ed., 1995), 32–69.

19. Halttunen notes a signficant contrast. In the European ritual described by Foucault, the criminal is to enact submission and the audience is to respond with awe and fear, not sympathy (although this didn't always happen). The New England executions constructed "a more intimate drama of an exemplary sinner standing before compassionate spectators who joined with him in a collective struggle against sin" (Halttunen, *Murder Most Foul*, 23).

20. A 1624 English statute, commonly known as the "Act to Prevent the Destroying and Murthering of Bastard Children," was formally adopted into Connecticut law in 1699, making concealing a death of a bastard child a capital crime. The statute placed the burden of proof on the mother, who had to provide witnesses to prove the child was stillborn. The statute was not revised until 1808, reducing the penalty for concealment to a "fine of not more than one hundred dollars or by imprisonment of not more than one year." See Hoffer and Hull, *Murdering Mothers*, 20–38, 88–91.

21. On Native American child-rearing practices, see David Zeisberger's 1779 "Account of Indian Childrearing Practices" in *New World, New Roles: A Documentary History of Women in Pre-Industrial America*, ed. Sylvia R. Frey and Marian J. Morton (New York: Greenwood Press, 1986), 143.

On the issue of infanticide, see the oral legends recorded in William Simmons, *Spirit of the New England Tribes: Indian History and Folklore, 1620–1984* (Hanover, N.H.: University Press of New England, 1986). The Mohegan legend of Papoose Rock and the Narragansett legend of the "Bastard" or "Crying" Rocks, for example, suggest that in extreme instances mothers put unwanted infants to death on these rocks, where mournful cries remained to haunt the site. Simmons notes the moral ambiguity of the legends: Some say the children were illegitimate and cried out for justice; others claim that the cries came from the mothers who, abandoned by their husbands or lovers, saw no way to support their children (*Spirit*, 127). Other Narragansett oral histories suggest that "when a child was born deformed or crippled in any manner, it was the plan and practice of the Indian people, with proper ceremony, to put that child to death" for fear that it could not survive the "rigors of aboriginal life" (Simmons, *Spirit*, 152–53).

22. Hoffer and Hull, *Murdering Mothers*, 49.

23. Kathy Chiero, "Interviews from Death Row," Christian Broadcasting Network [http://www.cbn.org/living/christianwalk/interviews/karla-chiero.asp], June 1999.

24. Terry Meeuwssen, "Karla Faye Tucker: From Prison to Praise," Christian Broadcasting Network [http://www.cbn.org/living/christianwalk/interviews/karla-terry.asp], June 1999.

25. See, for example, Beverly Lowry, "The Good Bad Girl," *New Yorker,* 9 February 1998, 61; Florence King, "The Misanthrope's Corner," *National Review* 50.4, 9 March 1998, 72.

26. Chiero, "Interviews."

27. Daniel Pedersen, "Praying for Time," *Newsweek* 131.5, 2 February 1998, 67.

28. Ohio Northern University's Victor Streib, quoted by Pedersen, "Praying for Time," 66.

29. Lowry, "The Good Bad Girl," 60.

30. Rebecca Leung, "A Plea for Mercy," ABC News [http://more.abcnews.go.com/sections/us/DailyNews/tucker0202.html], June 1999; Pedersen, "Praying for Time," 66.

31. Chiero, "Interviews."

32. Chiero, "Interviews."

33. Chiero, "Interviews."

34. Lowry, "The Good Bad Girl," 61.

35. Lowry, "The Good Bad Girl," 61.

The Puritan Eyeball,
or,
Sexing the Transcendent

∾

Renée L. Bergland

*There was, in the rear of the house, the most delightful little
nook of a study that ever afforded its snug seclusion to a
scholar. It was here that Emerson wrote "Nature"; for he was
then an inhabitant of the Manse and used to watch the Assyr-
ian dawn and the Paphian sunset and moonrise from the
summit of our eastern hill. When I first saw the room, its walls
were blackened with the smoke of unnumbered years, and
made still blacker by the grim prints of Puritan ministers that
hung around. These worthies looked strangely like bad angels,
or, at least, like men who had wrestled so continually and so
sternly with the devil, that somewhat of his sooty fierceness had
been imparted to their own visages. They had all vanished
now . . .*

*The study had three windows, set with little, old-fashioned
panes of glass, each with a crack across it. The two on the western side looked, or rather peeped, between the willow branches,
down into the orchard, with glimpses of the river through the
trees. The third, facing northward, commanded a broader view
of the river, at a spot where its hitherto obscure waters gleam
forth into the light of history. It was at this window that the
clergyman, who then dwelt in the Manse, stood watching the
outbreak of a long and deadly struggle between two nations; he
saw the irregular array of his parishioners on the farther side of
the river, and the glittering line of the British, on the hither
bank. He awaited, in an agony of suspense, the rattle of mus-
ketry. It came— and there needed but a gentle wind to sweep
the battle smoke around this quiet house.*

—Nathaniel Hawthorne, "The Old Manse"

Let us start with a place: Concord, Massachusetts. A house: the Old Manse, home of a succession of Puritan divines, then of Ralph Waldo Emerson in the 1830s and of Sophia and Nathaniel Hawthorne in the 1840s. A room: the study on the second floor of the Old Manse. There, Emerson wrote *Nature,* Sophia and Nathaniel Hawthorne etched a dialogue onto a windowpane, and Nathaniel Hawthorne wrote many of the tales and sketches for *Mosses from an Old Manse.*

In 1775, Emerson's Puritan ancestors gathered in this room to watch the first battle of the American Revolution taking place two or three hundred yards from the house, just at the edge of the orchard. In 1835 and 1836, as Emerson was describing himself as a transparent eyeball, the view from the window was a fairly typical New England landscape. Emerson could see a bit of the river, a stone wall, and the old North Bridge, which led across to a large open field. But in 1837, a few months after the publication of *Nature,* Emerson would preside at the dedication of a large obelisk that monumentalized the battle of Concord Bridge. His dedicatory poem, "Concord Hymn" would mark the battlefield as the site of "the shot heard round the world." Six years later, in 1843, when Sophia Hawthorne incised her name on the study window with her wedding diamond, she must have seen Emerson's phallic obelisk through the glass. It is said that Sophia wrote on the glass to memorialize a miscarried pregnancy. Her husband responded by writing his name below hers. After that, the view of the battlefield (and the phallus) was always mediated by the writing on the glass.

This brief history of the window suggests that Emerson's wish to be a transparent eyeball, to transcend the local particularities of history and the body, was impossible. By locating Emerson's eyeball in the northwest corner of the Old Manse in Concord Massachusetts, I propose to reparticularize what Emerson tried to make universal. By focusing on the incised window in that room, I propose to make visible the bodies that he tried to make transparent.

In the first part of this essay, I frame Emerson's impossible transparency in terms of current visual theories that describe and debunk the notion of a disembodied yet terribly potent white male gaze. I then discuss Sophia Hawthorne and the writing on the glass. I contend that the scratched windowpane offers a concrete physical challenge to the notion of transparency, and that it offers, further, a visible physical trace of Sophia's body—not only her hand with its diamond wedding ring but also her womb, recently emptied of a dead child. Finally, I turn to Nathaniel Hawthorne's 1846 sketch, "The Old Manse," which never mentions Sophia. "The Old Manse" represses sexuality, focusing instead on violence and death. But I argue that the very landscape that the sketch maps out is also a racialized genital landscape. Nathaniel, like Sophia, eschews transparency of vision. Rather than a transparent eyeball, he offers us a Puritan one, where sexuality is repressed and rewritten as violence, and where America is generated.

Emerson's Eyeball

Nature begins and ends with vision. The first line of the introduction complains that "Our age is retrospective." Emerson wants to alter that backward-looking perspective, to replace retrospection with a new vision. *Nature* attempts to persuade readers to cease their retrospection, to stop looking through the eyes of the foregoing generations. "The foregoing generations beheld God and nature face to face; we, through their eyes. Why should not we also enjoy an original relation to the universe?" asks the first paragraph.[1] In the last sentence, Emerson holds out the promise that each of his readers will be like "the blind man . . . who is gradually restored to perfect sight."[2]

In the context of a narrative that progresses from retrospection to "perfect sight," the centrality of the image of the transparent eyeball is obvious. But what does it mean? What is a transparent eyeball? When Emerson describes himself as a transparent eyeball he claims transcendence over time, space, and the body. Transcending time and space, he transcends history and enjoys "an original relation to the universe." Transcending the body, he transcends both race and gender. When he is transparent, he is, of course, colorless. Further, he is the trans-parent, both mother and father.

He is also an eyeball. The transparent eyeball is first and foremost a paradigm for vision. Emerson's transparent eyeball makes a disembodied white male perspective into a universal perspective. As it does so, it literalizes a visual paradigm that has been dominant in America and Europe since the Renaissance. Many scholars have discussed and attacked this model of vision, which the historian Martin Jay calls "Cartesian perspectivalism." According to Jay, "the questionable assumption of a transcendental subjectivity characteristic of universalist humanism, which ignores our embeddedness in . . . the flesh of the world, is . . . tied to the 'high altitude' thinking characteristic of [the Cartesian perspectivalist] scopic regime."[3] In literary and cultural studies, Mary Louise Pratt describes a similar imperialist visual paradigm in which "the (lettered, male, European) eye" becomes "the invisible, innocent . . . 'I.' "[4] Likewise, Anne McClintock writes about the construction of what she terms the "point of privileged invisibility."[5] Film theorist Laura Mulvey is best known for her descriptions of "the determining male gaze," which Carol Clover describes as "the transcendental ideal—omniscient, omnipotent."[6]

When scholars describe these transcendent gazes, they also reproduce them to some extent. Even as they intend to contest the paradigm, many contemporary scholars and theorists continue to describe vision as monocular, hierarchical, and binary: The eye is male, white, and imperialist, while what it looks at is feminized, raced, and colonized. As Linda Williams suggests, such formulations "continue to elide the body of the viewer by making sweeping generalizations about the phallic mastery of a disembodied male gaze."[7] The paradigm may be troublingly persuasive, but it is also obviously wrong. Women, people of color, and colonized subjects all have eyes of their own. Everyone looks, just as everyone is looked at. Further, each person's eyes are physical rather than metaphysical organs. Eyes are never disembodied. Instead, they are located in time and space, as well as in bodies.

This is manifestly true of Emerson's transparent eyeball. It may present itself as a transcendent ideal—and a universal, all-powerful, all-seeing invisibleness—but it also betrays its creator's intense longings to escape his own particularity. Emerson longs to get out of his chamber, his family home, his particular (albeit particularly privileged) position. As he describes these longings, he also describes the particular circumstances by which he is circumscribed.

Chapter 1 of *Nature* begins thus: "To go into solitude, a man needs to retire as much from his chamber as from society. I am not solitary whilst I read and write."[8] This assertion of solitude is a little strange, since it's a written one. It seems important that Emerson must frame his description of the transparent eyeball by telling us that ideally he would not be in his chamber (in the northwest corner of the Manse), and also that he would not be writing. Instead he would be in a sort of an ideal vacuum, where everything had disappeared: "Standing on the bare ground,—my head bathed by the blithe air, and uplifted into infinite space,—all mean egotism vanishes. I become a transparent eyeball; I am nothing; I see all; the currents of the Universal Being circulate through me; I am part or particle of God. The name of the nearest

friend sounds then foreign and accidental: to be brothers, to be acquaintances,—master or servant, is then a trifle and a disturbance."9

The passage insists, impossibly, not only that Emerson is not writing, but
also that he is not writing in the study at the northwest corner of the Manse:
He is "uplifted into infinite space." He is not himself: "[E]gotism vanishes."
He is not part of society: "The name of the nearest friend sounds then foreign
and accidental." Since all names are "foreign," Emerson here escapes nationalism. In addition, he escapes the bonds of family, of property, and of power
relations: "[T]o be brothers, to be acquaintances,—master or servant, is then a
trifle and a disturbance."

But all the while he sits writing in the northwest corner of his grandmother's house, looking out on the national battlefield that he will
memorialize. The contradictions are many: He has returned to his family
home in order to escape egotism; he has located himself at a national historic
site in order to deny history; he is claiming to transcend gender, while he is
planning the construction of a giant phallus that will dominate the view.

And so, rather than leaving himself behind, Emerson makes his own particular self—the white man, the Harvard graduate, the propertied descendant
of Puritan clerics—into an American universal. He makes himself transparent and teaches his readers to see through him, so that his particularities—
his family history, his gender, his very ego—will become invisible. In the
guise of transparency, Emerson proposes his own New England Puritan
manhood as *the* original relation to the universe, and the lens through which
everyone should see.

In Foucault's model of panoptical surveillance, power exercises itself
through its invisibility. To be invisible is to reside at the point where power
resides. This construction is ominous and threatening, not least because at
times it also seems to be inescapable. As Robyn Wiegman contends, "modern citizenship functions as a disproportionate system in which the
universalism ascribed to certain bodies (white, male, propertied) is protected
and subtended by the infinite particularity assigned to others (black, female,
unpropertied)," a system that is "contingent on . . . visual relations."10 Emerson's transparent eyeball is the perfect emblem for these visual relations,
since it literalizes the invisible, universalized, white, male, propertied gaze.
And yet, we cannot ignore the fact that the transparent eyeball purports to
escape these very hierarchies.11

Rather than reading Emerson as celebrating his own master status, we
may want to read him as hopelessly imbricated in it. Eric Cheyfitz describes

the paradox this way: "[T]he 'I' become eyeball announces itself at once as the transparent mother, the mother effaced to 'nothing,' and the omnipresent, omniscient father who 'see[s] all.'"[12] But just as metaphors of civic "color-blindness" end up denying the experience of people of color, Emerson's metaphor of trans-parent-ness denies motherhood. Although the trans-parent may be both mother and father, as Cheyfitz explains, the *mother* is the one who is actually effaced.

But then, the rampant universalism of the transparent eyeball effaces almost everything. As a philosophical, psychoanalytic, or aesthetic metaphor, the transparent eyeball is one of the most ridiculous (and ridiculously sublime) images in literature. As Donald Pease puts it, "a 'transparent eyeball' traverses the common sense of all words."[13] It is almost nonsensical. And yet, it is central to American culture. The transparent eyeball is important because it establishes (or reestablishes) a model of vision that is necessary for the maintenance of American cultural power relations, which (as Wiegman points out) are always already visual relations. Pease describes the metaphor as an image for *"seeing seen through . . . the impossible act of sight seeing itself."*[14]

By about 1840 in America, theoretical understandings of vision had been radically reconfigured, having shifted from metaphysics to physics, and finally to physiology. Visual perception had come to be understood as carnal rather than ideal. As the historian Jonathan Crary suggests, "the body which had been a neutral or invisible term in vision now was the thickness from which knowledge of vision was derived. This opacity or carnal density of the viewer loomed suddenly into view."[15] Later in the nineteenth century, the technologies of cinema and photography would (mechanically) reconstruct vision as monocular, geometric, and disembodied. But actual vision was no longer understood in such terms. To the contrary, Crary argues, these late visual technologies offered only "a mirage of a transparent set of relations that modernity had already overthrown."[16]

When vision became physiological—thick with its own "carnal density"— and transparency was banished to the realm of the ideal, reconstructing vision as transparent and universal became necessary cultural work. In 1836, when Emerson sat down in his study in the northwest corner of the old Manse, he knew that vision was a matter of bodies; of particular eyes in particular places and times. But he hoped to transcend all of that, to offer his readers a reidealization of vision that would, as he put it in the closing sentence of *Nature*, "restore" America to "perfect sight."[17]

Sophia Hawthornes's Diamond

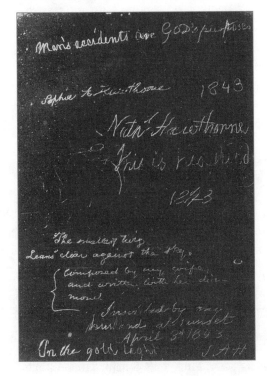

Figure 1

∽

The window of the "Old Manse" etched by Nathaniel Hawthorne and Sophia Hawthorne. Courtesy Concord Free Public Library.

Man's accidents are God's purposes
Sophia A. Hawthorne 1843

Nath Hawthorne
This is his study
1843

The smallest twig
leans clear against the sky
Composed by my wife
and written with her dia
mond
inscribed by my
husband at sunset
April 3d, 1843
In the gold light
Sun   SAH

In 1843, when Sophia and Nathaniel Hawthorne scrawled their names onto Emerson's study window, they challenged his (re)construction of transparency by making the glass visible, marking it with their own words and their own hands. I read these incisions on the study window as a dialogue about vision and perspective. It is for us to guess who initiated the dialogue. Did Nathaniel's bold proclamation "Nath Hawthorne/This is his study," (written in letters much bigger than Sophia's) precede her declaration that "Man's accidents are God's purposes"? Who wrote first?

I think she did. (She was the one with the diamond, after all.) I imagine her at the study window, looking out at the river, the obelisk, and the much-storied battlefield. She may have been thinking about death, in the context of her own recent maternal loss. The view of the battlefield could have brought back her grief and horror. But I imagine her trying to "look on the bright side," to reconstruct and discipline her gaze. "Man's accidents are God's purposes," she reminded herself.

When Nathaniel saw the writing on the glass, he must have wanted to try it too. He borrowed the diamond from Sophia, to etch his name and to assert his ownership. "Nath Hawthorne/This is his study." As he wrote, he may have been playfully chiding his wife for disfiguring *his* window. In addition, he may have been claiming the study from its previous resident, Ralph Waldo Emerson, or from its current legal owner, Emerson's cousin, Samuel Ripley. (Nathaniel, it turns out, was only renting "*his* study" after all.)

But Sophia seems to have read Nathaniel's assertion less as a challenge to Ripley's ownership than to her own authorship. She took up the diamond again and reclaimed the power to narrate her vision, describing the view through the glass from her own perspective. Her poem reads: "the smallest twig/leans clear against the sky." From her vantage, she tells us, even the smallest twig can fill the entire sky. Since the words are written on the windowpane, they demonstrate their own claim. Sophia's fine script, too, also fills up the sky.

Now Nathaniel scratches, "composed by my wife and written with her diamond." Once again, he asserts his ownership. He calls Sophia *my* wife, and calls attention to the diamond that symbolizes his proprietary relation to her. I imagine Sophia then snatching the ring. "Inscribed by my husband at sunset," she writes, giving the date, and then, seeing a little space left, she adds the line "In the gold light." Perhaps this line continues her description of Nathaniel at sunset, but it also returns us to her brief poem. In Sophia's hands, the subject returns from property to vision. At the bottom of the pane, she writes "Sun" (presumably for Sunday) and then her initials, "SAH."

On the glass, Sophia gets the last word. She has written her name. Her husband has followed with his own name, and with the assertions that it is his room, that she is his wife. But Sophia has answered his claims with lines of poetry that describe the importance of point of view, asserting that even the smallest twig can loom large from a certain angle, and that everything— including the tiny twig that fills the sky, her proprietary husband, and her own hand holding the diamond—is bathed in the same golden light. Finally, she has written her initials again, filling the last bit of glass, and claiming the entire inscription as her composition.

The writing scenario that I have reconstructed here is mostly conjectural. But what interests me is that the window demands such conjecture. Because of its singularity, the glass must be read in its particular locational context. We need to take into account the view of the battlefield and the river, the history of the study where Emerson had declared himself a transparent eyeball, and the broad cultural forces and particular marital circumstances that kept Sophia's writing singular and fixed in this place, rather than allowing it to be broadcast by means of publication.

Although Sophia Hawthorne never published a word, the archives show us a gifted woman of letters. She kept up a large correspondence, made frequent entries into the common journals that the Hawthorne family maintained, and served as Nathaniel's literary executor. But she was a private writer. Sophia was not unique in this respect; as the historian Mary Kelley explains, the denial of public voices to early nineteenth-century American women kept most of them "culturally invisible."[18] The social barriers that confined women to the private sphere were not impermeable—Sophia's sister Mary Peabody, for example, led the life of a public intellectual. In Sophia's case, however, particular marital politics combined with broad social forces: To write for publication would have been to go directly against her husband's wishes. Writing to her less retiring sister, Mary Peabody, Sophia explained that Nathaniel "cannot bear to have a woman come out of the shade, far less his wife, and never has forgiven himself for dedicating his Gentle Boy to me."[19] Since this statement uses the metaphor of "shade" to refer to privacy, it recalls us to the significance of her inscription on the glass, which ends with her words "In the gold light." As she wrote on the window, she was, for one moment in time and space, bathed in the same golden light as her husband.

But in the context of Emerson's transparent eyeball, these metaphors of invisibility and shade seem fraught and contradictory. If Emerson's transparency was a form of invisibility that guaranteed his cultural power, why didn't Sophia's invisibility guarantee hers?

Invisibility cuts both ways. In the terms of Lacanian analysis, we might explain this by arguing that in a phallocentric symbolic order, a man who is abstracted from his body *becomes* the symbolic order. The penis, abstracted, becomes the phallus, which is the central organizing principle of culture. A disembodied woman, on the other hand, becomes nothing. She personifies lack.

In other, more Foucauldian terms, we might argue that the duality of subjection makes the male subject simultaneously a sovereign "I" and an underling, subject to the constraints of the flesh. When he is abstracted from his body, he becomes pure "I," and also an invisible, omniscient eye. But in this economy of visibility and subjection, woman is defined as being always under the gaze. When she is invisible, not seen, she is, once again, reduced to nothing. In both of these models, it is impossible for a woman to be a disembodied subject. When she is invisible, she is nothing.

And so, wielding her diamond wedding ring, Sophia asserts her existence by inscribing into the glass the specificity of her maternal body. There is no symbolic universal for her, nothing to correspond to the phallus that Emerson has constructed outside the window or to the transparent vision that he has written about within the room and has broadcast to the world. In order to claim some kind of vision for herself, Sophia must, first, make herself visible. Transparency would deny her. She sticks to things: Her body. Her hand. Her diamond. The glass, whose transparency she obscures, cutting and scratching, making the invisible visible, the transparent opaque.

Nathaniel Hawthorne's Embattled Eden

Nathaniel and Sophia Hawthorne spent their wedding night in the Old Manse, and they lived there for the first four years of their married life. During that time, they repeatedly described themselves as Adam and Eve in Eden. Their imagery alluded to their nakedness, and also to their surprisingly unabashed sexual pleasure. Images of Eden, the walled garden, are often construed as images of female genitalia; Sophia and Nathaniel at play in Eden were also metaphorically at play in a private, female, sexual place.[20] But the language of Eden is tinged with inevitable loss; a flaming sword looms above the gates.

Like Adam and Eve, Nathaniel and Sophia were forced out of Paradise by their landlord. In their case, it was because they had not paid the rent. In a desperate effort to raise some cash, Nathaniel rushed a collection of stories to press soon after their departure. He titled the book *Mosses from an Old Manse*, and, from Boston, he hurriedly wrote an introductory sketch, "The Old Manse" that described the paradise from which he and Sophia had just been evicted. His sketch is impure, contingent, capitalist. It is bitter with the loss of paradise, and it reasserts the phallic vision of the flaming sword.

Like *Nature*, "The Old Manse" is structured around vision. But rather than attempting to construct new eyes for his readers, Nathaniel claims to be showing them what is actually there: "I cannot help considering [the reader] as my guest in the Old Manse, and entitled to all courtesy in the way of sight-showing," he explains.[21] This model of "sight-showing" is far different from Emerson's visionary paradigm of "seeing seen through." What Emerson had transcended, Nathaniel Hawthorne promised to show. Rather than try to inspire readers to behold nature face-to-face, Nathaniel asks readers to see through his own eyes. As host and tour guide, he re-embeds vision within the carnal densities of history.

Emerson had inveighed against his contemporaries' propensity to write history, to "build the sepulchres of the fathers," and "to grope among the dry bones of the past, or put the living generation to masquerade out of its faded wardrobe."[22] Nathaniel (who actually wore a red velvet cape as he sat at Emerson's old desk) insisted on reasserting the importance of history and on situating the house where Emerson had written in a landscape pitted with graves, beside a Revolutionary battlefield, and on the site of an Indian village. He describes the house as surrounded by stone walls, and the buried bodies of the first soldiers who had been killed in the American Revolution. Groping among the dry bones of the past, he records his own "exquisite delight" at finding Indian relics.[23]

The Manse of the sketch is also a very different place from the one Sophia and Nathaniel described in their family journals and letters. Most notably, Sophia is absent. The sketch never mentions her. The geography is very different as well. Rather than being set in Paradise, this Manse is located on a battlefield. It is haunted by Puritan ministers and Irish serving girls, while the grounds outside are haunted by the Indians who once inhabited "a thousand wigwams" on the spot, and by the British soldiers who fell at the battle of Concord Bridge (one by musket shot, the other, according to Nathaniel

Hawthorne, by having his head split open with an axe). The sketch represses sexuality, and offers its readers hellfire, class warfare, genocide, and revolutionary mayhem instead.

But this is not to say that the landscape is no longer sexualized. For one thing, its geography is still Edenic and still genital. Nathaniel describes a central house surrounded by a garden, an orchard of apple trees whose fruits taste like "those that grew in Eden,"[24] and a wall. Like the phallic sword that looms just outside the walls of Eden, "an obelisk of granite has grown up from the soil that was fertilized by British blood" just beyond the walls of the Manse.[25]

But this is a particularly American Eden, and a particularly American fashioning of the genitalized landscape. It is as violent as it is sexual: The phallus is inscribed with lines commemorating gunfire—"the shot heard round the world"—while the enclosed garden is littered with arrowheads. Each time Nathaniel picks one up, he tells us, it is as if he receives "it directly from the hand of the red hunter, who purposed to shoot it at his game, or at an enemy,"[26] The land may be an imaginary female body; more particularly, it is a female body pierced by the shots of minutemen and of Indians, its flesh studded with bullets and arrowheads.

Because of all the muskets, axes, and arrows, and also because Nathaniel has resurrected the village of a thousand wigwams within the walls of the Manse, Nathaniel's imaginary geography of the old Manse eerily recapitulates that of the Pequot massacre of 1637 (Figure 2). The Pequot map, which was published in Captain John Underhill's account of the Puritan's genocidal war, shows the Indian village enclosed by a stockade and surrounded by encircling ranks of Englishmen firing rifles and Indians shooting arrows. As Ann Kibbey famously contends, "the illustration of the Puritan men attacking the Pequot fort is also a drawing of a vagina. The circular fort with its detailed interior portrays both the Puritan men's genocidal violence and the sexual symbolism of their act."[27] Like the seventeenth-century map that it recalls, the sketch of the Old Manse conflates sexuality with violence, and even with genocide. The terrain of the Manse can be seen as a (racialized) vagina under attack.

While I am convinced by Kibbey's argument that the Underhill map figures an Indian village as a woman's genitals, I would also point out that the picture looks as much like an eyeball as a vulva. The map is about vision. It shows us a Puritan eyeball, constructed out of the carnage wrought upon bodies of women and Indians. Where a transparent eyeball purports to

Figure 2

∽

Underhill's map of the
Pequot Massacre,
1637. Courtesy of The
Library Company of
Philadelphia.

transcend, a Puritan eyeball constructs itself out of the histories of gendered
and racialized violence upon which the land has been constructed. Similarly,
"The Old Manse," which reproduces Underhill's landscape, also shows us a
Puritan eyeball.

To bring this point home, Nathaniel Hawthorne shows us the chamber in
the northwest corner of the Manse. In *Nature*, Emerson had refused to
acknowledge that he was in any chamber. Hawthorne, on the other hand, has
chosen to make public the actual chamber in which both he and Emerson
wrote. It is anything but transparent; instead, "its walls were blackened with
the smoke of unnumbered years, and made still blacker by the grim prints of
Puritan ministers that hung around. These worthies looked strangely like bad
angels, or, at least, like men who had wrestled so continually and so sternly
with the devil, that somewhat of his sooty fierceness had been imparted to
their own visages."[28] The room is "soot-blackened"; haunted by "grim," "violent" "worthies," stained by their fierce wrestling matches with a devil who

resided within the bodies of women or of people of color. These "bad angels," Nathaniel implies, were the men who shaped Emerson's vision.

When Nathaniel Hawthorne shows us the bad angels, he reasserts the power and importance of history. Since the men whom he shows us are sooty and blackened from their fierce embraces with an embodied Satan, Nathaniel also restores carnality and carnage to the American vision. Where Emerson denied his Puritan fathers, Hawthorne recapitulates them. But in the final analysis, Nathaniel Hawthorne's construction of vision is not so different from Ralph Waldo Emerson's: Both men make Sophia Hawthorne disappear.

By transcending gender and race in the images of the transcendent eyeball, Emerson effaces the female and the nonwhite. Hawthorne, by remapping his space in accordance with Puritan figures of racial, gendered violence, casts women into the shadowy realms of the Indian dead. Neither man is able to make room for a woman with eyes of her own.

As readers of the Old Manse, we are left with three images. There is the transparent eyeball, ridiculous and sublime, an image whose non-sense, and nonsensuality, betray the terrifying logic of (white, male, American) universalism. Then, there is the Puritan eyeball, mapped onto a landcape littered with bones, bullets, and arrowheads, an image that works to build America by destroying bodies that are not white, not male, and not American. Between these two eyeballs there is a thin sheet of glass on which one woman has composed a short and playful dialogue that places her body, alongside her husband's, in the golden light of a sunset shining through small twigs. It isn't much. It is mundane, and hard to see, and fragile, and it hangs between those glaring eyes. But then again, perhaps that depends on our perspective. After all, when we look through Sophia's eyes, we can see that, from her vantage, "The smallest twig/leans clear against the sky."

Notes

Thanks to Christopher Breu, Leigh Edwards, Gregory Jay, Donald Pease, Ivy Schweitzer, and Mark Williams for their help with this essay.

1. Ralph Waldo Emerson, *Nature,* in *Essays and Lectures,* ed. Joel Porte (New York: Library of America, 1982), 7.

2. Emerson, *Nature,* 49.

3. Martin Jay, "Scopic Regimes of Modernity," in Hal Foster, ed., *Vision and Visuality* (Seattle: Bay Press, 1988), 10.

4. Mary Louise Pratt, *Imperial Eyes: Travel Writing and Transculturation* (New York: Routledge, 1992), 31, 61.

5. Anne McClintock, *Imperial Leather: Race, Gender, and Sexuality in the Colonial Contest* (New York: Routledge, 1995), 37.

6. Laura Mulvey, *Visual and Other Pleasures* (Bloomington: Indiana University Press, 1989), 19; Carol J. Clover, *Men, Women, and Chain Saws: Gender in the Modern Horror Film* (Princeton: Princeton University Press, 1992), 209.

7. Linda Williams, *Hardcore: Power, Pleasure, and the "Frenzy of the Visible"* (Berkeley and Los Angeles: University of California Press, 1999), 315.

8. Emerson, *Nature*, 9.

9. Emerson, *Nature*, 10.

10. Robyn Wiegman, *American Anatomies: Theorizing Race and Gender* (Durham, N.C.: Duke University Press, 1998), 6.

11. Some may feel that Emerson's universalism succeeds in transcending the power relations inscribed onto visual relations. Richard Poirier, for example, celebrates Emerson's idealized vision, explaining that "to take possession of America in the eye, as an artist, is a way of preserving imaginatively those dreams about the continent that were systematically betrayed by the possession of it for economic and political aggrandizement" (Richard Poirier, *A World Elsewhere: The Place of Style in American Literature* [Madison: University of Wisconsin Press, 1985] 51). In this statement, Poirier offers a corrective to those of us who are tempted to attack Emerson's idealism for its impossibility. Emerson may not actually transcend the "system" that Wiegman and Poirier describe in such similar terms, but it is worth noting that he tries to do so.

12. Eric Cheyfitz, *The Trans-Parent: Sexual Politics in the Language of Emerson* (Baltimore: Johns Hopkins University Press, 1981), 53.

13. Donald E. Pease, *Visionary Compacts: American Renaissance Writings in Cultural Context* (Madison: University of Wisconsin Press, 1985), 226.

14. Pease, 225. His emphasis.

15. Jonathan Crary, "Modernizing Vision," in Hal Foster, ed., *Vision and Visuality*, 43.

16. Crary, "Modernizing Vision," 43.

17. Emerson, *Nature*, 49.

18. Mary Kelley, *Private Women, Public Stage: Literary Domesticity in Nineteenth-Century America* (New York: Oxford University Press, 1984), 182.

19. Edwin Haviland Miller, *Salem Is My Dwelling Place: A Life of Nathaniel Hawthorne* (Iowa City: University of Iowa Press, 1991), 213.

20. Nathaniel and Sophia referred to their sexual encounters as "blissful interviews," and frequently made note of them in their common journal. That shared journal is just one piece of evidence that, along with their letters, shows how strenuously both Hawthornes worked to maintain their marital paradise. The most detailed analysis of the Hawthornes' marriage is T. Walter Herbert, *Dearest Beloved: The Hawthornes and the Making of the Middle Class Family* (Berkeley and Los Angeles:

University of California Press, 1993). Herbert argues that "like other cultural formations, the domestic ideal of family life was established and sustained at a substantial
cost," and that Nathaniel and Sophia worked hard to conceal the costs and miseries of
their marriage and also to display its great rewards (xiv).

21. Nathaniel Hawthorne, "The Old Manse," in *Tales and Sketches*, ed. Roy Harvey
Pearce (New York: Library of America, 1982), 1125.

22. Emerson, *Nature*, 7.

23. Hawthorne, "The Old Manse," 1129.

24. Hawthorne, "The Old Manse," 1131.

25. Hawthorne, "The Old Manse," 1127.

26. Hawthorne, "The Old Manse," 1129.

27. Ann Kibbey, *The Interpretation of Material Shapes in Puritanism: A Study of
Rhetoric, Prejudice, and Violence* (New York: Cambridge University Press, 1986), 110.

28. Hawthorne, "The Old Manse," 1124–25.

Ejaculating Tongues

Poe, Mather,
and the Jewish Penis

∽

Gustavus Stadler

Despite its obvious ambivalence, the early New England cultural and historical imaginary placed Jews and Jewishness at the center of a dominant tradition of American self-definition. As Sacvan Bercovitch and others have shown, the ancient Israelites offered early New England an immensely valuable set of cultural terms and scripts with which to designate the significance of the Puritan errand. For the denizens of the Bay Colony, Massachussetts was a "New Jerusalem," and the Puritans' flight from England was another enactment of the Exodus. The New World was to be considered the destination of a destined, chosen people.[1] Bercovitch has traced the persistence of these notions up to the present day. In the early Republic, they manifest themselves in such forms as the frequent association of George Washington with Moses; in antebellum New England, the specific associations of Americans with the ancient Hebrew people are evident in declarations such as Emerson's that the Bay Colony founders form "a bridge to us between the . . . Hebrew epoch, & our own."[2]

Recently, Jonathan Freedman has eloquently summarized the degree to which these appropriations of Jewishness depend upon the elision of all but the most general, allegorical resonances of ancient Jewish history. In narratives such as those constructed by the Puritans, he writes, "Jewish difference becomes . . . the shadowy type whose truth is named America. In such a schema, the narrative of the biblical Hebrews and even that of the Jewish people may be privileged, but by the very conditions of that privilege, their difference—that which marks them as Jews—is extinguished."[3] In other words, in order to become consistently adaptable to the general requirements demanded by the national symbolic configuration of "America," the story of the Jews becomes departicularized, disembodied, phantasmatic, "shadowy." Their narrative has served as an ever-malleable supply of clay from which to mold figures of representative Americanness.

However, we can also identify a genealogy of manifest *struggle* with this move from Jew to American, from particular to general, from the corporeal to the abstract. Two very different gentile cultural figures, one who has for years been seen as representatively "American," and another whose integration into categories of Americanness has been persistently problematic, can be seen as exemplary figures in the mapping of a new genealogy—a record of resistances, mapped through and upon the Jewish body, to the generally despecifying, decorporealizing valences that drive the dynamics of American self-understanding.[4] Texts by both Cotton Mather and Edgar Allan Poe associate this persistence of the corporeal, its resistance to a model of signification as transcendence of the bodily, with Jewishness. In Mather's early diary, and in Poe's tale "The Facts in the Case of M. Valdemar," the "shadowy" presence of Jewishness reembodies itself. More specifically, a particularly troublesome bodily particular, the circumcised Jewish penis, reasserts and rearticulates itself as a highly animated *tongue*, issuing hyperactive outbursts—"ejaculations"—that maintain bodily presence in the act of signifying. Words, in these texts, cannot be harnessed for purely symbolic purposes; rather, they are inseparable from the tongue that issues them, and hence register resistance to the typically "American" process of abstraction and allegorization that has adapted Jewish history to its purposes.

For the young Cotton Mather, a speech impediment made the question of the corporeality of the speech act an inescapable one. Indeed, many of his diary entries around the ages of nineteen and twenty are devoted to the struggle, quite literally, to make his mouth form words in a manner adequate to God's needs. One way Mather negotiates his difficulties is by citing the example of the halting speech of Moses, who in Exodus 4:10 says, "O my Lord, I am not eloquent, neither heretofore, nor since thou hast spoken unto thy servant: but I am slow of speech, and of a slow tongue."[5] The immediate move to Moses as a site of self-validation illustrates the readiness with which the Puritans sought understanding in Hebrew history, a translatability between Puritan and Jewish experience that Mather would later do his best to *embody* by, according to Arthur Hertzberg, "wearing a skullcap and calling himself a rabbi."[6]

However, this apparent attempt to embrace Jewishness physically, rather than just symbolically, struck upon a much more obstinate barrier when it came to the translatability of practices of the penis. For Mather was in no way inclined to take up the practice of circumcision, at least as the "literalist Jews would have it."7 Mather, in a manner echoing what Daniel Boyarin has shown in early Christian negotiations of Jewish scripture and circumcision, refused to embrace a bodily practice of marking the penis. When Mather condemns Jews as "literalist," he registers suspicion that the actual, literal act that constitutes circumcision will threaten to diminish the figurative significance of the practice. Boyarin portrays a similar strain in Paul's writings, which associate Judaism with "literal interpretation" of scripture and Christianity with "allegorical interpretation." For Paul, it was necessary for Christianity to come to an understanding of circumcision as baptism, a ritual that left no mark on the body and whose signification persisted only symbolically, not literally.8

Mather effects a similar transition when he employs the term "circumcision" figuratively in his diary, as in his promise to God to "circumcise his lusts of the flesh."9 In other words, within Mather's emergent notion of American Puritanism, circumcision was to be available for figural purposes, as a word but not as a corporeal practice. Here, however, the term's metaphorical sense works specifically to address the threatening forces of corporeality: the "lusts of the flesh." It is telling of a larger dynamic evident in Mather's early diaries that this figurative use of the term is still shadowed by physicality, still addressed toward the "flesh," even somewhat suggestive of a vague urge to cut off the penis, actually to perform a more dramatic circumcision than the more traditional practice that has been rejected. Indeed, a persistent strain in Mather's citations of Jews and Jewishness resists moving completely away from the literal or physical and into the symbolic or allegorical. This phenomenon is evident, for instance, in the manner in which Mather, in his early diaries, makes reference to Moses and the precedent of his difficulty speaking: "On this particular day I pleaded; 'Lord! Thou art Hee that *made man's Mouth*; and thou wast angry with *Moses*, because hee would not make that consideration, an Argument for *Faith*, that thou wouldest *bee with his Mouth*. And now, because I would not so sin, therefore I trust in thee! Thou dost send *mee* forth, as thou didst *Moses*, in Service for thy Name among thy people; and thou who didst make *Mans Mouth* and make *my Mouth*, wilt bee with my Mouth.' "10

The base-level physicality of the passage is, of course, extreme; the question of the suitability of one's words is consistently put forth as problem of the mouth rather than the spirit, soul, or mind. But even more important, the passage conveys the particular manner in which Moses is functioning for Mather. Jay Fliegelman has noted of this passage that "Mather presents Moses's affliction as a symptom of his obstinacy rather than as a punishment for it."[11] What is perhaps most striking about this insight is that it indicates Mather's resistance to making Moses's experience perform symbolically. Mather looks to Moses not primarily as a symbol of the failure to serve God adequately, not as a site upon which God created symbolic meaning, but as a resistant physical force who repeatedly refused to comply with God's will. While Moses certainly can come to function as an affirmative abstract symbol for Mather, the way in which the ancient leader is written simultaneously maintains his presence as a physicality that stubbornly resists signification.

Indeed, virtually all of Mather's writing about his speech impediment maintains this tension between the allegorical and the physical. Fliegelman remarks on the "crucial part played [in the diary] by discipline against the stammer itself, rather than against the complacency for which it might be a punishment."[12] In other words, Mather addresses the impediment as an active, persistent physical process rather than as a *symbol* of some failure before God, some neglect of his sacred duties. Presented in this manner, the stammer begins to look analagous to the "literalist," non purely symbolic, *Jewish* approach to circumcision; the stammer, like circumcision for the Jews, is valuable in its corporeal presence, which demands continual acts of self-discipline on Mather's part.

This association gets fleshed out as more and more of Mather's diary entries about his difficulties with speech come to focus on the lips and especially the more materially penile *tongue*. His next allusion to Moses, for example, dramatizes the centrality of the tongue, among various body parts involved in producing speech: "Oh! Thou that *madest Man's Mouth*, didst Thou not make the Mouth of the Stammering *Moses* to speak? Didst thou not open the Lips of *Jeremiah*, when hee pleaded, *I cannot speak?* Did not my Lord Jesus Christ cure a man that had *an Impediment in his Speech? Oh! Lord, Oh! Lord*, I am sensible, that one Touch, one Word of thine will releeve my Infirmitie. Oh! Touch my Tongue: Say, *Ephphatha* and my mouth will bee opened!" (I, 50)

Soon after this, Mather reiterates his sentiments by pledging, "my *Tongue* is Thine. I have given it unto Thee" (I, 51). These entries both repeat and intensify the corporeal cast of Mather's approach to the problem of speaking of and for God. At issue is no longer the relatively general "mouth," but par-

ticular components of the mouth. Mather portrays the problem as one requiring direct physical contact, a process involving the opening of the lips—so
that the mouth no longer masks the problem—and, most important, the
touching of the tongue. The tongue, the source of speech, needs an actual act
of physical contact to actualize its capacity to signify.

Mather persistently surrounds the tongue with rhetoric that betrays a
desire that the tongue *not* be seen primarily as a metonym for speech, language, the Word. Rather, the literal tongue needs to be present and fit in
order to make the Word, as is clear in a diary entry from March 1682 in which
Mather makes "being *deliberate* in the Motions of my Tongue and Lip" one of
his primary "Rules of Speech" (I, 55). Mather is not only determined to train
his tongue to perform; this process of "being deliberate," of physically articulating his speech organs properly, becomes a source of grace in itself. Again,
this portrayal of the tongue closely resembles the circumcised Jewish penis
that Mather rejected. As much as it is a means to an end, speaking to and for
God, the tongue is valuable by means of its activity in physical practice. Moreover, by ideally coming under the impress of God's touch, it bears the marks
of God, rather than just producing words that symbolize Him.

But Mather's writings go still further in making an embodied penis of his
tongue. In his promise to be "deliberate in the Motions of my Tongue," as well
as in his portrayal of his tongue as something that lies ineffectual until coaxed
out of its cover by God's touch, Mather portrays this process of articulation as
strikingly similar to the physical act of erection. He needs to straighten out his
tongue, and he needs direct help from God to do it. Underlying what I am
identifying as the physicality of this writing is the sense that Mather will continue to need God's touch on his tongue. But one touch will never act
baptismally to straighten out the problem once and for all, that is to make the
issue of Speech a matter of words rather than of bodily organs. And part of
what Mather wanted his tongue to do was to issue what he called "ejaculatory
prayer." Very early in the diary he pledges "To lead a Life of heavenly *Ejaculations*," and a few years later he writes: "Every Day, and at such Minutes, as I
have not Liberty to make my more *sett Visits* unto the *God of Heaven*, I would
then ty my desires unto the *Arrowes* of *ejaculatory Prayers*, and so shoot them
over the Heads of all Interruptions." This model of prayer as projectile, as well
as the reiteration of the term "ejaculation," portray suppliance for Mather as
requiring, most important, the bodily discharge of words; content is apparently a less significant issue. To pray will be, throughout life, a recurrent
physical effort, almost a type of Olympian athleticism. This strain in Mather's

writing continually maintains the importance of *utterance*, of the individual instance of speech, within the overall divinity of the Word. Mather also connects utterance specifically with a tongue, under God's touch, projecting forth out of the lips, straightening, and finally ejaculating in a paean to God.

Taken as a whole, these dynamics differentiate the power of Mather's tongue as phallus, understood in Lacanian terms as abstract presence and authority, and its capacities as penis, a body part engaged in bodily processes that discharge material utterances. As Mather rose to greater prominence in Massachusetts, as he became more invested with symbolic power, some of this tension became less manifest. For one thing, Mather was somewhat, though not wholly, successful in smoothing over his speech impediment.[13] Additionally, one part of the Puritan mission, early on, had been to work for "the conversion of the *Jewish Nation*" (I, 200); later in Mather's career, talk about conversion took on an acknowledgedly symbolic cast. But obstinate resistance, articulated in the form of Jewishness, persisted in Mather's diary in his long-running references to his effort to convert a *specific* Jew, never named. His efforts can be seen in an entry like this from 1711: "I cried unto the Lord, that I might yett see [an opportunity to honor God], in the Conversion of that poor Jew, for whose Conversion and Salvation we have been for six or seven Years more than ten, waiting on Him."[14] Mather repeats these sentiments every few years, until they become almost a mantra. According to the editor of the diaries, they remained unsuccessful; the unnamed Jew who served as "the object of the years of prayers on the part of the Mathers . . . is said to have gone to Jamaica and died there a 'hardened wretch'" (II, 741[n1]). Yet his unrelenting, obstinate hardness also provided Cotton Mather with a valuable context in which to engage and maintain the steadfastness of his ejaculatory activities. For the religious and cultural leader whose interest was to "ty my desires unto the Arrowes of ejaculatory Prayers," this nonphantasmatic Jewish man served for decades as an alluring site for target practice.

By the antebellum era, Mather's penis/tongue had already largely retreated back behind his words. As Bercovitch has demonstrated, Mather's legacy at this point was chiefly evident in the continuing identification his New England heirs made between "America" and *mission*; in Emerson, for example, a teleology of the American self was constructed that "eliminated the tension between process and fulfillment. It gathered meaning by its proleptic identification with the destiny of the New World, of which American nature was the symbol."[15]

Edgar Allan Poe found much of this noxious. A conglomeration of aesthetic, biographical, and temperamental differences made Poe a self-willed
alien to New England literary culture. A longtime critic of allegory, Poe
cringed at the neatness of the symbolic economy underlying transcendental-
ist notions of self and nation.[16] He condemned as "didactic" writing by the
Transcendentalists as well as by the tremendously popular New England fire-
side poet Henry Wadsworth Longfellow. His roots in the South, his dislike of
English Romanticists, and his bitterness over having to devote so much time
to the commerical world of magazine editing all contributed to his rift with
the tradition often understood as largely originating in Mather's writings and
thought.

However, a series of events in 1845 shows Poe citing the obstinate corporeal presences that understandings of Mather as an originary source for the
symbolic configuration of "America" necessarily elide. A tale Poe wrote in the
late autumn of this year, "The Facts in the Case of M. Valdemar," specifically
positions him as in touch with the hidden organ behind Mather's words.
Poe's tale reanimates, I think, the particular presence of Jewishness—the
tongue, the penis, and bodily practice—that Mather had derived so much
energy from as a young man. I am not arguing that Poe sought to do this
intentionally; indeed there is no evidence I know of that Poe ever wrote or
thought about Mather. Rather, I think the story demonstrates that the "hardened" Jew had not softened with the passing of almost a century and a half,
that this specifically Jewish-cast corporeality in signification was still a presence in, and perhaps a threat to, the national culture.

The composition of this tale took place at a particularly heated moment in
Poe's conflict with the New England literary scene. After spending the early
part of 1845 making controversial accusations of plagiarism against Longfellow, Poe accepted an invitation to give a reading at the Boston Lyceum in
October. According to Kent Ljunquist, the Boston audience and reviewers
responded negatively to the New York writer, focusing largely on the weakness of his bodily and vocal style.[17] Poe, upon returning to New York,
exacerbated the conflict by announcing that he had hoaxed the audience by
reading a piece of juvenilia, the poem "Al Araaf," written when he was thirteen. Soon after, Poe produced "Valdemar," a grotesque tale about an attempt
to mesmerize a man at the point of death. Alongside the story's typically Poe-
esque preoccupation with extreme states of consciousness lay indications that
Poe was still musing over the Lyceum affair. The story's narration of Valdemar's willing subjection to P.'s desire to fill in an "omission" in mesmeristic

research—the effects of mesmerism, as P. puts it, "*in articulo mortis*"—comes to focus on the protagonist's difficulties with enunciation. While in the process of articulating death, as a literal translation of the narrator's Latin would have it, Valdemar finds it quite difficult to be articulate, uttering a host of contradictory responses to P.'s questions, issuing a long, horrific groan, and finally emitting a series of "ejaculations of 'dead! dead!'. . . from the tongue and not from the lips."[18]

Rather bizarrely, in a move that no critic I know of addresses, Poe's tale gives Valdemar a Jewish or pseudo-Jewish identity, constructing him as a literary translator whose pen name is "Issachar Marx."[19] Interestingly, in the 1840s, when Emerson and his critic Poe were at the height of their writing careers, the allegorically Jewish cast to American origin narratives was beginning to come under the pressure of a *particular* Jewish national presence. Between 1820 and 1860, the Jewish population of the United States increased from around 6,000 to 150,000.[20] So at the time Poe returned from his Boston Lyceum reading and composed a story whose protagonist had a Jewish *nom de plume*, Jewishness had taken on a newly present and embodied significance for many readers in the northeastern literary market.

Again, it is specifically Valdemar's *alias*—"Issachar Marx"—that marks him as *alien*. That his *pen* should do this effects an implicit association with the alien Jewish penis we saw Mather struggle with. Poe also creates a multilevel pun here, for Valdemar's Jewish *nom de plume* establishes him as someone whose letters—in the sense of literary writing, and in the sense of the letters of his name—make him Jewish.[21] In other words, the tale repeats the cluster of concerns reflected in Mather's problems with the "literalist" circumcised Jewish penis. Like the Jewish penis, "Marx" bears marks; his difference is inscribed, literally—through letters, and through his literary career—in his very name.

He also, as a man of letters, *makes* marks, writes, although the rationale and purpose of his writing career remain eminently unclear. When P. introduces Valdemar/Marx, he comes across as an incoherent jumble of traits, bodily features, experiences, and languages—a conglomeration of details that add up to no coherent significance beyond their individual particularities:

> In looking around me for some subject by whose means
> I might test these particulars, I was brought to think of
> my friend, M. Ernest Valdemar, the well-known compiler
> of the "Bibliotheca Forensica," and author (under the
> *nom de plume* of Issachar Marx) of the Polish versions of

> "Wallenstein" and "Gargantua." M. Valdemar, who has
> resided principally at Harlaem, N. Y., since the year 1839,
> is (or was) particularly noticeable for the extreme spareness
> of his person—his lower limbs resembling those of John
> Randolph; and, also, for the whiteness of his whiskers, in
> violent contrast to the blackness of his hair—the latter, in
> consequence, being very generally mistaken for a wig. His
> temperament was markedly nervous, and rendered him a
> good subject for mesmeric experiment. (833–34)

P.'s effort to address the particulars of his mesmeristic research yields a figure who exists almost wholly in particulars. It takes a second glance to realize just how willfully this description of Valdemar refuses to let its individual components add up to much beyond its parts. The connecting thread between the subjects of his literary work—forensics, Schiller, and Rabelais—is, so far as I can tell, quite elusive.[22] Moreover, we learn here that Valdemar knows at least four languages: Polish, German, French, and English. The passage refuses to place him nationally, locating him geographically only in the then-remote New York suburb of Harlem. We directly learn that he "had no relatives in America." The assured reference to the "lower limbs" of John Randolph, an obscure New York political figure, and the notice of the black hair and white whiskers, both conjure opaque, bodily qualities that seem to refuse to mean anything symbolically, that seem to refuse to assume the status of evidence. Even what I am taking to be the "literal" sign of Valdemar's Jewishness, his pen name "Issachar Marx," is a pseudonym, an alias, displaced from his "real" self.

But as an alias, this name is a lettered marker of alienation, and indeed the apparent pun on Marx/marks brings this home. So Poe is using a transparently Jewish name to embody otherness, to identify otherness with the very ink which, in the marks it makes, forms letters and words. To focus on the Jewishness of the name means, in a sense, to violate the story's apparent insistence on the literal; it requires an act of inference (the association of the particular name with Jewish culture), and conjures a presence that was likely to cause many readers of the time to read through a host of cultural stereotypes located, presumably, in the cultural world outside the text's letters, the Marx/marks. However, if we follow some of the inferences such a reference to Jewishness was likely to provoke, we find a pattern that continually brings us back to the persistent importance of the letter, the literal.

One of the opacities that constitutes Valdemar is the question of his "real" name. It has been read by some critics as a pun on "val de mer" (valley of the sea), and hence an allusion to other uses of the sea as a metaphor in Poe's tales. But I prefer to embrace its opacity as an invitation to read it as literally as possible—that is, as a series of marks or letters. Along these lines, the word "M. Valdemar" becomes recognizable as a near-anagram, a kind of dissolute rewriting, of the term "marveled."[23] This term bridges the *monstrative* qualities that Christian Euro-America had associated with Jews for centuries: the idea of Jews as physically spectacular *monsters*, and the association of Jews with *demonstrative* behavior and professions, especially with stage acting.[24] In either of these cultural formations, "the Jew" is linked to spectacularity, to the production of a powerfully immediate representation at which largely non-Jewish spectators can only *marvel*. And indeed, the events of the story, and the story itself, essentially work to put a monstrous body on display. Throughout, Valdemar *is* the marveled.

The name "Valdemar" also resists the symbolic in that it seems to allude to an origin in a number of national cultures, while not transparently signifying any one. Roland Barthes's reaction is typical here: "Is it German? Slavic? In any case, not Anglo-Saxon."[25] Rather than associating this array of national signs with inconsistency or reading them as Poe's extended sarcasm, we might take them to signify the complicated relationship of Jewishness to modern Western nationhood and the long-running trope of the Jews as a people without a nation. Again, though, it would seem to be contradictory of a tale focusing so heavily on "literal" interpretation to display this degree of investment in conjuring a coherent, allegorical reference to Judaism. But uncertainty continues to haunt this apparent referentiality. We can see this by looking more closely at the relationships the tale constructs among Valdemar, language, and literature.

The sense of Valdemar's shifty nationality is fortified by the allusions to his command of multiple national *languages* (or, as they are often known, "tongues"). Jews' apparent capacity for learning a variety of languages was, according to Sander Gilman, a major factor in the nineteenth-century Euro-Christian imagination of them as a people with extensive, and corruptive, *imitative* skills.[26] Valdemar's literary resumé—as well as his multifold literacy—reinforces this connotation. The story implicitly puns upon the fact that Valdemar is ripe for physical decomposition because he doesn't *compose* at all; rather, he compiles and translates. Toward the end of the tale, this pun becomes explicit, as P. describes his failed attempt to "recompose"

Valdemar (840). Not only does Valdemar's selfhood have no apparent original language in which to base itself, but it has no artistic "originality"
within the guiding principles of the post-Romantic cultural atmosphere.
Essentially, Valdemar can be seen to traffic in others' originality; he
engages in literary usury, in the circulation of texts rather than the production of them. He marks an instance of what Catherine Gallagher has called
the Jewish usurer who "is ubiquitous in nineteenth-century writing about
authorship."[27] Cultural usury associates Valdemar with a series of qualities
commonly constructed in nineteenth-century anti-Semitism that Gilman
has described as "the superficiality of the Jew, the Jew's mimicry of a world
which he could never truly enter, which produced works which were felt to
be creative but, in fact, were mere copies of the products of *truly* creative
individuals. And this degenerate creativity was marked by the stigma of disease, of madness."[28]

The coimplication of Valdemar's cultural activities and his physical condition comes into particular focus here. Gilman's observation that "degenerate
creativity" is "marked by" physical and mental disease finds a parallel in the
way Valdemar is continually characterized as both culturally useless and
sick—an association brought home most directly when P. first enters the
bedroom of the nearly dead Valdemar and finds him lying in his deathbed,
writing: "His face wore a leaden hue; the eyes were utterly lustreless; and the
emaciation was so extreme that the skin had been broken by the cheekbones.
His expectoration was excessive. The pulse was barely perceptible . . . when I
entered the room, [he] was occupied in penciling memoranda in a pocket-
book. He was propped up in the bed by pillows" (837).

The juxtaposition of these physical symptoms with this particular type of
writing inflects Valdemar's scribbling with degeneracy. We are left to wonder
what the possible point could be of his writing "memoranda" when he knows
he is on the verge of his death. Valdemar's disease thus seems associated
with pointlessness, nonproductivity, and self-directedness in writing.[29]
Indeed, the description of Valdemar's ailing physical frame resonates with
several nineteenth-century configurations of degeneration. One, the con-
sumptive, was a largely celebratory construction, familiar from female
sentimental novels and sensations surrounding the demise of boyish figures
like Paul Dombey and John Keats.[30] The others I want to focus on, however,
specifically invest the process of physical degeneration with an allegorical significance in which the one degenerating becomes *degenerate*—in the fully
moral sense with which the term is endowed today.

One of these is Gilman's culturally parasitic Jew whose "degenerate creativity" is inseparable from his physical and/or mental illness. But closely related to this is another earlier nineteenth-century pariah, the masturbator or onanist, a connection directly invited by the description of Valdemar's "leaden hue" and "lustreless eyes."[31] And the use of the term "pencilling" to describe Valdemar's odd writing process rekindles the presence of the penis in the scene. Like the Jew, the onanist's penis is stigmatized because it doesn't produce anything—or rather, it doesn't produce anything *significant* because it produces too much. It ejaculates semen indiscriminately, with no aim beyond the process of stimulation and ejaculation. Like the circumcised Jew as figured in Mather, the onanist locates value in the penis itself. His investments are still dangerously tied to the *organ* rather than to the displaced capacities of that penis's acts—capacities like procreation—or to the symbolic capacities of that penis's acts, such as maintaining a healthy, populous nation. Valdemar's "excessive expectoration" indicates that his releases of bodily fluid, like the onanist's, fail (by *over*production) to conform to the regulations guiding their quantity and purpose.

The onanist's penis doesn't produce a nation or a race; it only produces ejaculate, precisely what the term "spirit," oft-employed as a euphemism for semen, tries to dematerialize. Mather's response to the materiality of the Jewish penis was, we saw, to attempt to invest circumcision with symbolic value. But as we also saw, Mather's tongue came to take on a penislike presence as an organ—requiring physical discipline, demanding the touch or mark of God, and becoming the source of "ejaculatory" utterances. The climactic events of "The Facts in the Case of M. Valdemar" present a remarkably analagous story of a tongue's eruption into prominence.

Once P. has successfully placed Valdemar in a mesmeristic trance, he asks the patient questions designed, apparently, to ascertain his degree of consciousness. P. asks Valdemar if he is sleeping, and if he feels pain in his breast. Valdemar makes a series of brief answers, to the effect that he is "still asleep" and "dying"; with each response, his voice becomes "less audible than before" (838). P. asks Valdemar whether he is sleeping several more times, until "there came a marked change over the countenance of the sleep-waker." He blanches, "assum[ing] a cadaverous hue, resembling not so much parchment as white paper," and his mouth distorts itself grotesquely: "The upper lip, at the same time, writhed itself away from the teeth, which it had previously covered completely; while the lower jaw fell with an audible jerk, leaving the mouth widely extended, and disclosing in full view the swollen and blackened tongue" (839).

The tale's language here is strikingly reminiscent of Mather's invocation, "*O Lord, open Thou my Lips, and my Mouth shall show forth Thy Praise.*" Just as Mather's rhetoric presented his empowered tongue as emerging from the quiescence of his otherwise-closed lips, here in Poe's tale Valdemar's tongue emerges from invisibility as a grotesquely "swollen and blackened" entity. Grotesque as it is in its tumescence, the physical manifestation of Valdemar's tongue has an impact far more significant than the organ was able to achieve as the vehicle of Valdemar's faint answers to P.'s questions: "I presume that no member of the party then present had been unaccustomed to death-bed horrors; but so hideous beyond conception was the appearance of M. Valdemar at this moment, that there was a general shrinking back from the region of the bed" (839). The process by which a physical *vehicle* of sound is made into the source of impact, of signification, hearkens back to the associations of Valdemar's name and literary career with disseminating but not producing literary language, with imitating but not originating in a national language. Valdemar, we saw then, has no real tongue, in the sense that he has no national tongue. But he most certainly has a most prominent tongue, in the literal sense of the *organ*.

Indeed, the referential content of Valdemar's utterances is curiously opaque. When P. asks whether he is asleep, for example, he is asking Valdemar a question for which any answer—a grunt, even—is seemingly a reliably negative answer. That his utterances are innately contradictory and logically impossible here ("Yes; still asleep") and at the story's climax ("*I am dead!*") serves to highlight what the tale is figuring forth: a type of voicing based solely on the physical presence of sound, and not on the semiotic meaning carried by it.[32] The tale attends to the significance of the very *eruption* of vocal sound, a focus that intensifies in the tale's shocking final passage. Here P. tries desperately to awaken Valdemar from his trance: "As I rapidly made the mesmeric passes, amid ejaculations of "dead! dead!" absolutely *bursting* from the tongue and not from the lips of the sufferer, his whole frame at once—within the space of a single minute, or even less, shrunk—crumbled—absolutely *rotted* away beneath my hands. Upon the bed, before that whole company, there lay a nearly liquid mass of loathsome—of detestable putridity" (842).

By describing Valdemar's utterances here as "burst(s)"—not even "outbursts," a term more connotative of linguisitic communication—and as "ejaculations," these final two sentences corporealize Valdemar's language, powerfully identifying it with the release of bodily fluid. Valdemar the character collapses under the weight of this identification, crumbling away and leaving one giant wet spot behind. The experiment that had begun as P.'s attempt to fill in an "omission" in mesmeristic research here becomes an *emission* that leaves a smelly stain. Moreover, for us, the readers, the story is now over; there is no intervention or summing up by P. or Poe to tell us what this all means. The text is simply there, truncated, any self-actualizing allegorical resonance absent like a circumcised foreskin.

The story ends by working as hard as it can to associate significance not with the sign, the word, the phallus, but with the *embodiment* of the phallus: the penis. When P. and his associates draw back before the sight of Valdemar's tongue, and when we draw back before the text that substitutes goo for closure, we are reacting, essentially, to the sight of the penis. Presented in its literal, anatomical "fact"-hood, it is shown to do nothing more than what it can literally do—emit bodily fluid.

Daniel Boyarin has shown that this substitution of penis for phallus is one of the key threats that Jewish cultural practices, especially circumcision, pose to Christian logocentrism. Circumcision draws attention to the fact that the penis, as Boyarin puts it, "*is* divisible" and is therefore a piece of flesh, not an idealized symbol of strength, presence, and signification. He notes the "almost crude physicality" of midrashic writings on circumcision, which "register a strong protest . . . against any flight from the body to the spirit with the attendant deracination of historicity, physicality, and carnal filiation which characterizes Christianity."[33] Similarly, Poe's tale "almost crude[ly]" deploys "physicality"—both the literary illegibility of the "nearly liquid mass" and the literal truncation of the text—to prevent Valdemar's "Case" from becoming allegorically legible, from becoming anything more than a conglomeration of "Facts."

"The Facts in the Case of M. Valdemar" is a response to New England literary culture, then, to the degree that it reanimates a corporealized Jewish presence that haunted and compelled that culture's great forefather, Cotton Mather. If Poe's tale is midrashic in its physicality, it also recalls the physical intervention Mather needed to make his tongue speak of, for, and to God. Moreover, Valdemar's "ejaculations," and "Valdemar" itself *as* an ejaculation, recall Mather's idea of "ejaculatory prayer," a practice emphasizing the repeated *utterance* of supplications, the value of which lay largely in the very utterance, and the continuing quantity of utterances, rather than in the content of the prayers. Indeed, had he lived in the nineteenth century, Mather might well have found himself a target of the antionanist movement, given his freewheeling attitude toward ejaculation.

More seriously, Mather's ejaculations indicate a process in which the physical ejaculations of the tongue substitute for the physical significance of the circumcised Jewish penis. His manner of negotiating the Puritan desire to become Jewish, to be the New Jerusalem, is not *strictly* one of decorporealization. Mather's prayers, Poe's Lyceum reading, Valdemar's deathbed scene, and Poe's "Valdemar" become visible as an American genealogy of circumcised speech acts, registering a persistent resistance to any heuristic approach that completely divorces language from its source in particular bodies in particular circumstances. At an intentional level neither Mather nor Poe could be characterized as oppositional social critics—not given Mather's centrality to defining long-standing notions of self and community, and Poe's obstreperous conservatism on racial issues, as well as his general apoliticism. Yet the writings of each indicate and enact specific ethnic presences, specific heuristics, and specific parts of the body that most understandings of America would rather subordinate if not be rid of completely. In his essay "The Ritual of Consensus" and elsewhere, Bercovitch demonstrates the manner in which, for the leading New England cultural and intellectual tradition, "America" works as a transcendental signifier, becoming the category to which all discourse ultimately has reference, and subsuming the volatility of conflict into affirmation of the symbolic value of democratic "process."[34] In Poe's story, however, dissonance registers; we recall his description of Valdemar's voice: "the hideous whole is indescribable, for the simple reason that no similar sounds have ever jarred upon the ear of humanity." And indeed, "humanity," the fantasy of a timeless, coherent mass of individuals, is precisely what can't hear Valdemar. Valdemar's utterances, like Mather's prayers, are articulate chiefly in the instance, in the effort with which they are produced; as ejaculations they burst from the tip of an organ whose finer points are easily cut off.

Notes

For their insight, provocations, and suggestions, I wish to thank Tamar Adler, Kim Benston, Mackenzie Cadenhead, Anna McCarthy, and Magdalena J. Zaborowska.

1. See Sacvan Bercovitch, *The American Jeremiad* (Madison: University of Wisconsin Press, 1978), 73–80.

2. Sacvan Bercovitch, *The Puritan Origins of the American Self* (New Haven: Yale University Press, 1975), 150, 166.

3. Jonathan Freedman, "Angels, Monsters, and Jews: Intersections of Queer and Jewish Identity in Kushner's *Angels in America*" *PMLA* 113.1 (January 1998): 99.

4. On the decorporealizing tendencies of early national ideology in the United States, see Michael Warner, *The Letters of the Republic* (Cambridge, Mass.: Harvard University Press, 1990).

5. I thank Kim Benston for alerting me to this passage even before I had begun to think about Mather extensively, as well as for reminding me that George Washington, who was often compared to Moses, was also considered a poor public speaker.

6. Arthur Hertzberg, *The Jews in America: Four Centuries of an Uneasy Encounter* (New York: Simon and Schuster, 1989), 39.

7. Hertzberg, *The Jews in America*, 40.

8. Daniel Boyarin, *A Radical Jew: Paul and the Politics of Identity* (Berkeley: University of California Press, 1994), 15.

9. Hertzberg, *The Jews in America*, 40.

10. *Diary of Cotton Mather 1681–1708* (Boston: Massachusetts Historical Society, 1911), 2–3. Further citations will appear parenthetically in the main body of the essay, following the Roman numeral "I."

11. Jay Fliegelman, *Cotton Mather and Benjamin Franklin: The Price of Representative Personality* (Cambridge: Cambridge University Press, 1984), 42.

12. Fliegelman, *Cotton Mather and Benjamin Franklin*, 42.

13. See Fliegelman, *Cotton Mather and Benjamin Franklin*, 43–44.

14. *Diary of Cotton Mather, 1709–1724* (Boston: Massachusetts Historical Society, 1911), 62. Further citations will appear parenthetically in the main body of the essay, following the Roman numeral "II."

15. Bercovitch, *Puritan Origins*, 161.

16. See, for example, his review of Hawthorne's *Twice-Told Tales*, reprinted in Poe, *Essays and Reviews* (New York: Library of America, 1984), 582.

17. Kent Ljunquist, " 'Valdemar' and the 'Frogpondians': The Aftermath of Poe's Lyceum Appearance," in *Emersonian Circles: Essays in Honor of Joel Myerson*, ed. Wesley T. Mott and Robert E. Burkholder (Rochester, N.Y.: University of Rochester Press, 1997), 181–206. Ljunquist's article offers an excellent account of the affair, as well as an interesting reading of "Valdemar."

18. Edgar Allan Poe, *Poetry, Tales, and Selected Essays* (New York: Library of America, 1997), 841. Page numbers of further citations will appear parenthetically in the text.

19. There *is* an exception: Marie Bonaparte, one of Poe's earliest psychoanalytic critics, who identifies Valdemar with the trope of the Wandering Jew. However, Bonaparte makes no effort to connect this observation to any of the more literal, or literary, resonances of Valdemar/Marx's Jewishness. See Marie Bonaparte, *The Life and Works of Edgar Allan Poe: A Psychoanalytic Interpretation*, trans. John Rodker (New York: Humanities Press, 1971).

20. Hertzberg, *The Jews in America*, 105.

21. The name "Issachar Marx" comes off as an excessive, caricaturized signification

of Jewishness. But the specific connotations of each part of the name are important. Marx is commonly identified as a Jewish family name. It is derived originally from the name "Mordecai." See Benzion C. Kaganoff, *A Dictionary of Jewish Names and Their History* (New York: Schocken Books, 1977). It is conceivable, then, that the use of Marx here is a veiled reference to Mordecai Noah, probably the most well-known Jewish man in New York in antebellum culture, whom Poe referred to as a "friend" and who wrote an article supporting Poe after the Boston Lyceum incident. See Poe, *Essays and Reviews*, 1085. For information on Noah, see Hertzberg, *The Jews in America*, and Louis Harap, *The Image of the Jew in American Literature: From Early Republic to Mass Immigration* (Philadelphia: Jewish Publication Society of America, 1974). In the Old Testament, Issachar was Leah and Jacob's son; his name has been associated with the terms "ass" and "beast of burden." See Zvonko R. Rode, "The Origin of Jewish Family Names," *Names: The Journal of the American Name Society* 24.3 (1976): 167–68. The name's origins thus connect to Valdemar's literary efforts, which involve (as some would see it) the *transfer* rather than the *production* of literary words.

22. One possible connotation of the association with Schiller would be the German tragedian's philo-Semitism. See Sander Gilman, *Jewish Self-Hatred: Anti-Semitism and the Hidden Language of the Jews* (Baltimore: Johns Hopkins University Press, 1986), 133. Gilman also refers to the Polish Jewish poet Isahar Behr as a writer who was embraced by German Enlightenment figures; despite the similarity to Valdemar's alias, I do not see any evidence to suggest that Poe knew of Behr.

23. Anna McCarthy first brought this play on letters to my attention.

24. The literature on each of these topics is quite diverse. Virtually all of Gilman's work is relevant, as is Freedman's recent essay. Compelling American historical sources are Louise Mayo, *The Ambivalent Image: Nineteenth-Century America's Perception of the Jew* (Rutherford, N.J.: Fairleigh Dickinson University Press, 1988), and Harold Quinley, *Anti-Semitism in America* (New York: Free Press, 1979).

25. Barthes, "Textual Analysis of a Tale by Poe," in Robert Yound, ed., *Untying the Text: A Post-Structuralist Reader* (Boston: Routledge & Kegan Paul, 1981), 139. Barthes goes on to write, "this little enigma here implicitly formulated will be resolved at number 19 [in his lexia of analysis] (Valdemar is Polish)." But the story never actually says Valdemar *is* Polish; it only says that he translates texts into Polish.

26. Sander Gilman, *The Jew's Body* (New York: Routledge, 1991), 20–21.

27. Catherine Gallagher, "George Eliot and *Daniel Deronda*: The Prostitute and the Jewish Question," *Sex, Politics, and Science in the Nineteenth-Century Novel: Selected Papers from the English Institute, 1983–84* (Baltimore: Johns Hopkins University Press, 1986), 43.

28. Gilman, *The Jew's Body*, 129.

29. We never find out what Valdemar was writing; indeed, we never hear of these notes again, leading this moment in the story to remind us of the apparent contentlessness of the purloined letter in Poe's famous tale of that name. That contentlessness has been the basis of a fascinating series of Lacanian readings of Poe,

but it would be interesting to reconsider the degree to which various cultural formations in Poe's era, such as Jewishness, were formulated so as to register *as* emptiness
or absence.

30. Jonathan Elmer has offered a fascinating argument that "The Facts in the Case
of M. Valdemar" is in fact Poe's parody of the death scene in which so much women's
fiction and poetry of this era culminated. Although I ultimately disagree with the
schematic opposition of Poe's writing and "sentimental" literature, Elmer's reading of
the story powerfully portrays "Valdemar" as preoccupied with corporeal—as he would
have it, affective—resistance to certain notions of signification. See Elmer, *Reading at
the Social Limit: Affect, Mass Culture, and Edgar Allan Poe* (Stanford: Stanford University Press, 1995).

31. For extensive accounts of antebellum American antionanism, see G. J. Barker-
Benfield, *The Horrors of the Half-Known Life: Male Attitudes toward Women and
Sexuality in Nineteenth-Century America* (New York: Harper & Row, 1976), and
Michael Moon, *Disseminating Whitman: Revision and Corporeality in Leaves of Grass*
(Cambridge, Mass.: Harvard University Press, 1990), chap. 1. See also Russ Cas-
tronovo's essay in this volume.

32. On the "impossibility" of these utterances, see Elmer, *Reading at the Social
Limit*, and Allan White, "Death's Murmur," *Essays in Sound* (Sydney: Contemporary
Sound Art, 1999), 84–103.

33. Boyarin, *A Radical Jew*, 37.

34. See Bercovitch, *The American Jeremiad*, 132–75, and Bercovitch, *The Rites of
Assent: Transformations in the Symbolic Construction of America* (New York: Routledge,
1993), 29–67.

Now You Shall See How a Slave Was Made a Man

Gendering
Frederick Douglass's
Struggles with Christianity

∾

Darryl Dickson-Carr

Frederick Douglass's dramatic battle with Edward Covey, the brutal slave-breaker first made (in)famous in *Narrative of the Life of Frederick Douglass, an American Slave, Written by Himself* (1845), is now generally considered the pivotal moment in Douglass's development as an individual in search of his freedom. On the most obvious and essential level, the conflict taught Douglass the importance of possessing a fighting spirit to obtain his freedom. It also functions symbolically as the moment when Douglass believes his manhood has been redeemed from the physical ravages of slavery: "You have seen how a man was made a slave; you shall see how a slave was made a man."[1] This transformation is surely one of the most remarkable moments in American literature, yet reading it simply as the advent of Douglass's true "manhood" does not fully explain his personal struggles and complexities. It would be more accurate to say that this battle assures Douglass that he has become the complete heterosexual male, one who has finally purified himself of the psychological and physical corruptions of his chosen faith (Methodist Christianity), which he defines as feminine, and any evidence of homosocial bonds. This essay examines Douglass's conflicted construction of his gender, sexual, and religious identities in each of his three autobiographies: the *Narrative; My Bondage and My Freedom* (1855); and *The Life and Times of Frederick Douglass* (1881, revised 1892). In his personal narratives, Douglass interrogates the psychic and political limits of a corrupt Methodism that limited his ability to actualize his ideal of "manhood" as either a sexual or a gender identity. For Douglass, stable gender and stable sex, to use Judith Butler's terms, are found through a Puritan understanding of masculinity as penetrating, impenetrable, and heterosexual. His rhetoric emulates what Patricia Roberts-Miller identifies as a classic *masculine* approach of the Puritan sermon; he "announc[es his] stance and thrust[s his] point into the audience's mind,"[2] thereby *penetrating* it and reducing it to the feminine. By working toward his goal of penetrating both his audience and his personal enemies while muting what he might have recorded as attempts to penetrate his own body, Douglass aspires to a compulsory heterosexuality, a "gender intelligibility that assumes that for bodies to cohere and make sense there must be a stable sex expressed through a stable gender."[3] Douglass succeeds, however, only in creating an ambivalent and contingent conception of his own masculinity by positing Christianity as one manifestation of the feminine and homosocial against which he must define himself.

Despite Douglass's extensively documented championing of women's rights, his view of the feminine reveals his ambivalence. Douglass appears to have maintained the greatest respect for women as people; he had a propensity to "talk gently, particularly in [his] conversations and correspondence with women."[4] Yet he regarded any sign of femininity in himself or the institutions he upheld as anathema, even as he spoke of his relationships with men in terms that suggest homosocial desires that were not easily dismissed. An examination of Douglass's excoriation of femininity's alleged faults provides more nuanced insights into the sexual mores of a key figure who kept the details of his private life almost entirely hidden from his readers. In addition, such an analysis offers a richer sense of Douglass's personal and intellectual strengths and blind spots, particularly his unconscious desire for the security and privileges normally accorded the "impenetrable" white male in the nineteenth century.

In all of Douglass's antebellum autobiographical narratives and speeches, Christianity figures as the institution that prevents the realization of manhood (as an instrument in the hands of slaveholders) and as an equivalent to the feminine itself. In viewing Christianity as feminine, Douglass ascribes to it a decidedly negative value. As the "feminine," Christianity signals both passivity and promiscuity, a victim of sexually hyperactive males who have systematically raped the institution as if it were a slave woman. This act consequently forces antebellum Methodism to side with slavery, and so to obviate freedom and human rights for males like Douglass. Slavery, together with its new ally, Methodism, has the power to violate his body, strip him of his modesty, castrate him, and arguably rape him, thereby forcing him to the level of the feminine. By using the pattern of the conversion narrative as the structure for the recollection of his own experiences, Douglass attempts to reify, and thereby to claim, a purified—not to say a Puritan—Christian male gender identity, with all of the privileges such an identity includes. That is to say, if Douglass "converts" from the "sins" of fear, despair, and fright found at each nadir within his narratives to a semblance of personal freedom, he does so by rejecting all ties to the feminine, as both subject and gender. Simultaneously, Douglass's representation of his own relationships to other males reveals a distinct fear of acknowledging the homosocial bonds to fellow enslaved Africans, and perhaps also to his enslavers.

William McFeely reminds us that "[n]ineteenth-century men, living before Freud taught us to leap at every signal, could write with great openness about certain of their emotional relationships. With the words 'homosexuality' and 'incest' unspoken, such sexual acts, in a sense, did not exist. Douglass could therefore write openly about Henry Harris without betraying even a hint of any sexual activity that might have been a component of that friendship."[5] Similarly, if forcible sexual contact or penetration was part of Douglass's personal experiences, we are not likely to find any clear historical documentation of such acts. As Robert Richmond Ellis correctly points out, the "sexual violation of male slaves" is a "kind of abuse largely unacknowledged by historians of slavery and critics of slave narratives."[6] Although Ellis is speaking of colonial Cuba, his discussion of the absence of information regarding male-male rape is widely applicable, for in all slave societies, "[m]ale victims of slave rape left behind no biological record in the form of offspring, and, given the gender roles in their cultures, were even more constrained than female slaves from verbalizing the experience of sexual abuse" since "male sexual passivity (not simply male-male sex) was particularly stigmatized insofar as it was seen as entailing a loss of masculinity."[7] Yet emotional ties between men did not receive the same form of scrutiny, since any implication of male sexual passivity would be so deeply encoded as to be invisible. The same is true of male-male rape.[8]

To convince his or her audience that slavery's violations were truly evil, authors of slave narratives typically positioned themselves as noble heroes or heroines who, if they were initially imperfect by the Puritan standards that often guided the narratives, ultimately emerged virtuous, triumphant, and defiant. Douglass likewise posits himself as the individual redeemed by his independent triumphs over adversities other men cast his way, an embodiment of the Puritan will to perfection.9 With few exceptions, Douglass's narratives are about *men* and *manhood*; women are included as the means to describe his anxieties about other men and their actions, specifically the men who stand in the way of Douglass's manhood rights.10 The feminine is simultaneously written into his text and written out of it to get at the heart of his relationships—whether confrontational, fraternal, or affectionate—with the men he encounters.

In this way Douglass's narratives illustrate Eve Kosofsky Sedgwick's argument that nineteenth-century texts often route homosocial desire through women.11 In Douglass's case, his texts are organized around rhetoric reifying the importance of male agency. When women enter his texts, they function as conduits through which the possibility of male agency, which originates in free whites, is diverted to black men. The few women who earn Douglass's respect do so insofar as they possess some degree of independence, and therefore the ability to dictate their destinies within the limits of a male-centered society. By the same token, Douglass identifies with such women only so long as they possess agency, and he further idealizes them to the extent that they possess and practice the highest ideals of (uncorrupted) Christianity. Thus women become visible to Douglass's critical eye only to the extent that they possess the independence normally granted only to white Christian men.

More frequently, however, women who figure in Douglass's narratives are reduced to objects that illustrate slavery's horrors or, in the case of his mother and his first wife Anna, are rendered virtually nonexistent. In these texts, a woman's invisibility is in direct proportion to her submission to slavery's power. For Douglass, submission is synonymous with the feminine; by the same token, any object or institution that submits to slavery is similarly feminized. Nowhere is this more evident than in Douglass's criticism of Christianity and particularly of the Methodist Church.

Douglass's reading of Christianity stems from a desire to see his own Methodist Church, the church that nursed and directed his spiritual self, return to an inviolate, prelapsarian state, specifically to the early steadfast opposition to slavery embodied in the Methodist *Discipline*. In *My Bondage and My Freedom*, Douglass recounts a crucial passage from the *Discipline* defining slavery as "evil" and slaveholders as "ineligible to any official station" in the church.12 Immediately preceding this passage, Douglass argues

that "[t]he highest evidence the slaveholder can give the slave of his acceptance with God, is the emancipation of his slaves."[13] This particular
Methodist doctrine descends directly from one that had developed out of
Puritanism: "sinning is not acting."[14] This premise enabled early Methodism
to condemn those parishioners who passively upheld slavery, and it gave
Douglass the grounds to declare that *slavery is alike the sin and the shame of
the American people*" precisely because they allow it to exist.[15]

By the time Douglass published even his first antislavery narrative, however, the Methodist Episcopal Church in the United States had long been
accommodating proslavery forces within its ranks, a fact Douglass knew
well.[16] But for the young, optimistic, enslaved Douglass, the intractability of
proslavery sentiment within the Methodist Church was as yet unfathomed,
so he could afford to think of it as a surrogate mother in much the same way
he looked upon his mistress Sophia Auld. Both provided, in principle, the
type of maternal affection that Douglass's mother had not been able to give.
Just twenty years prior to Douglass's estimated birthdate of February 1818,[17]
eighteenth-century Methodists were preaching that "refusal to give Negroes
the freedom which belonged to them as a human right was contrary to reason, charity, and the enlightened standards" of the time,[18] in accordance with
church founder John Wesley's General Rules, which forbade "slave trading,"
among other "self-indulgences."[19] The Methodist Church's stress upon
asceticism and implicit belief in the brotherhood of man appealed to Douglass, who learned to "[love] all mankind—slaveholders not excepted" upon
his conversion.[20]

That unconditional love was but a reflection of the love he had found earlier in the person of Sophia Auld, whom Douglass regarded "as something
more akin to a mother, than a slaveholding mistress," a "kind-hearted" and
"remarkably pious" woman who at first treated Douglass almost as though he
were her own son.[21] The principled kindness of both Sophia Auld and the
early Methodist Church, however, evaporated as the system of slavery
deprived them each of their egalitarian natures. The former was corrupted by
the remonstrance of her husband, Hugh, not to educate or coddle Douglass,
lest he begin desiring freedom, while the latter quickly compromised its
principles as it saw its fortunes rise from admitting slaveholders to its ranks.
In both cases, slavery obliterated the possibilities for Douglass to find the
maternal affection, self-determination, and brotherhood he had always
sought to define himself as a human and specifically as a *man*. His response
was to reject both *in principle* in favor of *practices* that would liberate the self

and reify his masculinity. The first of these practices was the construction of a narrative that would separate him from all phenomena that could be construed as feminine.

As Jenny Franchot notes, "Douglass often situated the image of the victimized—often 'whipped'—female body at the emotional center of his critique of slavery," a tactic common in antislavery propaganda.[22] William McFeely adds that these gruesome torture scenes not only functioned as propaganda, but also that they "were one of the most sought-after forms of nineteenth century pornography."[23] The female body thus serves simultaneously as a continuous reminder of the horrors of slavery and as an erotic object, stripped naked and brutalized so that both its passivity and femininity are foregrounded. If slavery's denial of basic freedoms were not horrific enough in and of itself, so Douglass's argument appears to run, its propensity to maim, abuse, and otherwise deform the female body should provide sufficient proof. In Douglass's rendering of the slave world, slave women are usually relegated to passive relations vis-à-vis men; that is, they are either beaten and tortured, forced to become "breeders," or silenced by being practically written out of the text. Describing the first two cases, Douglass couches his rhetoric in such a way that these violations of the female body, whether implicitly or explicitly denuded, become forms of rape. The slaveholder rips layers of clothing off the body, and then, excruciatingly, removes layers of skin, an act that necessitates *opening* the body by breaking the plane of its surface, an act of penetration and violation. This same slaveholder forbids a woman's control over her own physical space, sexuality, and reproductive abilities, thereby exerting his absolute power over her body—a power that includes the unquestioned opportunity to deform it.

All of these violations would seem to provide sufficient evidence of slavery's horrors. For Douglass, however, the abuse of the black female body is not sufficient proof of slavery's insidiousness. Rather, complete proof is to be found in slavery's tendency to violate the male body and mind, forcing men into a role that crosses gender lines. When overseer Aaron Anthony brutally whips Douglass's Aunt Esther (called Hester in the *Narrative*), Douglass regards it as the "first of a long series of such outrages, of which I was doomed to be a witness and a participant" with the fear that "it would be my turn next."[24] Douglass thus fears being placed in the same submissive, helpless position that so many women occupy in his various autobiographies.[25] Douglass's description of the events leading up to Esther's violation, as well as the whipping itself, are replete with sexual connotations that he doubtlessly intended his proper, cultured audience to grasp. The markedly different descriptions in each of his autobiographies provide a curious mixture of horror and sardonic titillation in which the female body becomes equally an object of voyeuristic lust and pity. Douglass invites his audience to see Esther as a woman of virtue, elegance, and "graceful proportions, having very few equals, and fewer superiors, in personal appearance, among the colored or white women of our neighborhood." The reader may "conjecture"—he continues with devastating irony— "[w]hy master was so careful of her."[26] Douglass then adopts a rhetoric of sadomasochistic eroticism apparently designed to arouse the reader as voyeur. Esther's loveliness—and therefore her virtue—is obliterated as her "wrists were firmly tied, and the twisted rope was fastened to a strong staple in a heavy wooden joist above, near the fireplace. Here she stood, on a bench, her arms tightly drawn over her breast. Her back and shoulders were bare to the waist. Behind her stood old master [Anthony], with cowskin in hand, preparing his barbarous work with all manner of harsh, coarse and tantalizing epithets. The screams of his victim were most piercing. He was cruelly deliberate, and protracted the torture, as one who was delighted with the scene. . . . Poor Esther had never yet been severely whipped, and her shoulders were plump and tender."[27]

Douglass also prefaces this description of bodily violation with the suggestion that an actual rape or other form of molestation might well have occurred before he entered the scene: He "saw but few of the shocking preliminaries, for the cruel work had begun before I awoke."[28] Having vividly described what of the "cruel work" he did see, Douglass declares that "language has no power to convey a just sense of [the whipping's] awful criminality."[29] In this way he relegates the scene's psychological terrorism to the realm of the unspeakable, an unspeakability into which Douglass's dread of becoming the master's next victim is enfolded.

Hence Douglass's fear of being subject to "the fate of Esther."[30] To endure Esther's condition could mean homosexual rape or similar violence to the body, thereby ensuring Douglass's loss of potential masculinity. To claim a masculine identity, Douglass must prevent at least three likely affronts to his body: being stripped, if only partially; receiving a whipping or beating of any sort; and submitting to any person or institution that could administer such treatment. When Edward Covey whips Douglass several years later, all of Douglass's fears and anxieties regarding these affronts have been realized. Covey forces Douglass to submit by systematically depriving him of any sense of agency or stability. Covey thus places out of Douglass's reach all of the criteria that define white middle-class masculinity: "nobility, intelligence, strength, articulateness, loyalty, virtue, rationality, courage, self-control, courtliness, honesty, and physical attractiveness as defined in Western European terms"[31] as well as "mastery of one's environment."[32] When Covey prepares to beat Douglass after he fails at an impossible task, he makes a point of ordering Douglass "to take off [his] clothes," eliciting Douglass's last vain attempt to protect his bodily space: "To this unreasonable order I made no reply, but sternly refused to take off my clothing. 'If you will beat me,' thought I, 'you shall do so over my clothes.' After many threats, which made no impression on me, he rushed at me with something of the savage fierceness of a wolf, tore off the few and thinly worn clothes I had on, and proceeded to wear out, on my back, the heavy goads which he had cut from the gum tree. This flogging was the first of a series of floggings; and though very severe, it was less so than many which came after it, and these, for offenses far lighter."[33]

McFeely argues that Douglass's description of this encounter comes "as close as a Victorian author could come to speaking about the sadistic abuse of males by males," and that it "strongly suggests a perversion of homosexual attraction into vicious cruelty."[34] Certainly, the experience and indeed his entire relationship with Covey shades into the unspeakable, for as Douglass soon informs us, he "shall never be able to narrate the mental experience through which it was my lot to pass during my stay at Covey's. I was completely wrecked, changed and bewildered; goaded almost to madness at one time, and at another reconciling myself to my wretched condition."[35]

Noting that Covey's brutal whipping was administered at least weekly, Douglass demurs further by declaring: "I have no heart to repeat each separate transaction, in which I was a victim of [Covey's] violence and brutality. . . . I am only to give the reader a truthful impression of my slave life, without unnecessarily affecting him with harrowing details."[36] If we take Douglass at his word, the twists and turns of the path to his psychological nadir are either too tedious or horrifying to recount. But as David Van Leer argues, "this reticence does alter significantly the nature of his account as a conversion experience. After all, the traditional Puritan conversion narrative succeeded by being explicit and public about its sinful experiences; reticence in this context would be read not as decorousness but as false pride."[37] It is not unreasonable to assume that Douglass's elision covers the same unspeakable violations that Esther suffered. Whether or not this is the case, Douglass clearly has trouble devoting space in his narratives to events that could potentially eviscerate the image of the masculine figure purified by trials of fire. To include such scenes would undermine the puritanical drive informing Douglass's personal definitions and the purification process he proposes to have undergone.

Moreover, the details of these bodily violations—so easily given in the case of other slaves, especially females—would involve Douglass in confronting some of the ways in which his body was visibly broken and *penetrated,* if only to the extent that a flogging rips opens the flesh. We are, in fact, made privy to only two graphic descriptions of Douglass's tortured body. This first entails no human torturer; it is the description of his feet so scarred by frostbite "that the pen with which I am writing might be laid in the gashes."[38] The second incident is Douglass's beating at the hands of carpenters in Baltimore's ship-yards, which leads to a grotesque black eye. Disturbing as these incidents are, neither involves the surface of Douglass's body *opened* by other humans' direct actions. It stands to reason that Covey's treatment of Douglass far exceeded these incidents in both duration and sheer brutality, yet the same Douglass who is willing to publish the names of his tormentors does not allow us to view what are arguably his worst torments in any detail. If the middle-class conception of manhood for African-Americans in the nine-teenth century was most consistently expressed as "a belief in their own humanity, a sense of dignity, and a determination to control their own bod-ies," Douglass achieves manhood by controlling the *description* of his own body to make it as impenetrable as those of his white male oppressors.[39]

As R. J. Young argues, Douglass inhabited the same social milieu and embodied the same social values as other northern free blacks, who "formed their understanding of manhood in a white dominated society . . . in a period that may have been characterized by acute distress about gender due to changing gender roles . . . resulting from the economic transformation of America beginning in the 1820s."[40] Maleness or masculinity meant becom-ing part of the economic marketplace as a *self-made* man; hence Douglass's desire to be rid of his master Hugh Auld, who would not let Douglass keep his own wages. To tolerate such an arrangement, Douglass reminds us, would mean that he "[ceased] to be a *man.*"[41] Equally important, such an entry into the marketplace as a regular wage earner would allow him to ful-fill a principle inherited from American Puritanism, articulated in John Robinson's 1625 argument that "though we are to be able to bear poverty if God send it, yet should we rayther desire riches, as a man, though he can go afoot, yet will rayther chuse to ride."[42] Douglass seeks this same *choice,* one

obviously denied him at the whim of his master. So long as he is deprived of
this and other choices, Douglass can never be complete, whole, and *pure*,
and therefore cannot become like the middle-class white men blessed with
agency. His greatest resentment stems from the role his owners' personal
and religious codes play in their rescinding from the black man the privileges of middle-class manhood.

   The motive for Douglass's personal purification is indelibly linked to his
coincident desire for purifying the Methodist Episcopal Church. If Methodism was founded upon the Wesleyan reformist principles revolving around a
"scriptural holiness" consisting of "obedience and love"[43] as well as ascetic
discipline, Douglass seeks a return to the church's English roots where these
principles might be found intact, most prominent among them the "love"
that has been written out of the Methodist text. In Douglass's reading of contemporary Methodism, church members have clearly mastered the principle
of obedience—so long as it is another who is forced to obey—but agape love,
containing the possibility of homosocial bonds, is glaringly absent. Douglass's early introduction to Christianity—missing from the *Narrative* but
bitterly remembered in *My Bondage* and *Life and Times*—serves as one of the
earliest connections in Douglass's life between the cruel physicality of slavery
and Christian spirituality's ambivalent compensations, for it yielded the
insight that "[s]laves know enough of the rudiments of [their master's] theology to believe that those go to hell who die slaveholders; and they often fancy
such persons wishing themselves back again to wield the lash."[44]

   Curiously, though, in his later *Life and Times*, Douglass's retrospective
view of foreign churches, including Methodist congregations that profited
from slavery, is considerably softer than the stance he maintains against antebellum slaveholding Christianity. While visiting Edinburgh, Scotland, in
1846, Douglass witnessed the Free Church of Scotland's debate over accepting contributions from American slaveholders, a debate that ended in both
the Free Church's and the slaveholders' favor. Yet Douglass tempered his initial opposition to the Free Church, a shift attributable to the fact that while in
Scotland and much of Great Britain, he was not subjected to the same humil-
iations that inevitably awaited him in the United States. In a letter to William
Lloyd Garrison, he notes that in Britain "the chattel becomes a man! I gaze
around in vain for one who will question my equal humanity, claim me as a
slave, or offer me an insult. . . . I find no difficulty here in obtaining admis-
sion into any place of worship, instruction, or amusement, on equal terms,
with people as white as any I ever saw in the United States. I meet nothing to

remind me of my complexion."45 Douglass, therefore, also meets little reason
to condemn the church. Even if race still played a problematic role in
Britain,46 Douglass finds that his political status as a "raced" subject—that is,
circumscribed with the marker of marginality that black skin constituted—is
subsumed within his class status in mid-nineteenth-century British society.
In addition, the later narrative's retrospective stance allows Douglass to
retreat slightly from his earlier views of the connections between Christianity
and slavery.

We see this in Douglass's accounts of his friendship with the elder,
revered slave Sandy Jenkins. Jenkins provides Douglass with more reasons to
reject the type of Christianity that Douglass sees as depriving him of stable
manhood, since he introduces a religious paradigm that problematizes Douglass's earlier beliefs about the African portion of his heritage. That
alternative paradigm simultaneously extends and counters European religious and cultural ideals that Douglass had internalized via his conversion to
Methodism.

As with other events in Douglass's autobiographies, each encounter with
Jenkins is narrated with noticeable changes in tone and intent. Most telling is
the account in *Life and Times of Frederick Douglass*, which provides additional
information about Jenkins's background. Here Douglass first frames Jenkins
as a conjure-man, a "genuine African" who "had inherited some of the so-
called magical powers said to be possessed by the eastern nations."47 Jenkins
becomes Douglass's "old adviser" whose abilities to counsel his protégé stem
from his being an *African* "religious man" in possession of magical roots and
practices unknown to both Western rationalism and the corrupt Methodist
Christianity Douglass then ambivalently espoused. As Van Leer has noted,
"Douglass's relation to the root [proffered by Jenkins for its protective pow-
ers] is ambiguous" since "[g]enerally, he views it with scorn and implies that
superstition is one of the ways in which whites keep blacks enslaved. Yet
these 'mature' views are superimposed on the sixteen-year-old Frederick's
belief that the root may in fact be powerful."48 Douglass accepts the root but
denies its power, since it is "heathen" and "superstitious" to him and suggests yet another belief system with the potential to emasculate him. The root
is nonetheless intimately connected with his defiance, with his self-conscious
"manhood," since with the root's protection Douglass subsequently resisted
Covey and thereafter enjoyed freedom from his worst abuses. Again, in his
own words, the "slave" became a "man," one endowed with a new sense of
his own agency and ability to control his self-representation.49 Yet he refuses

to acknowledge openly the root's psychological power, as though by veering too close to the belief systems of those enslaved Africans with the least contact with the middle class Douglass seeks to emulate, he would find himself that much further removed from white male privilege. To draw openly on the spiritual power of the "genuine African" conjurer, moreover, would risk accentuating the differences between the African and the European, thereby undermining Douglass's project of moral suasion.

Nonetheless, Douglass finds his agency in the battle with Covey not only through the root, but also by drawing blood, thereby piercing, penetrating, and *violating* Covey in at least one way that Douglass himself was violated. In this moment Douglass becomes the dominant actor; he pointedly relishes Covey's physical weakness and his piercing of Covey's skin. As Douglass recounts the incident, "[Covey] trembled like a leaf. This gave me assurance, and I held him uneasy, causing the blood to run where I touched him with the ends of my fingers. . . . Covey at length let me go, puffing and blowing at a great rate, saying that if I had not resisted, he would not have whipped me half so much. The truth was, that he had not whipped me at all. I considered him as getting entirely the worst end of the bargain; for he had drawn no blood from me, but I had from him."[50]

Although Douglass originally attributed Covey's reluctance to whip him after the epic struggle in the barn to a chastened Covey's desire to safeguard his reputation as a top-notch slave-breaker,[51] in *Life and Times* an older, more mature, and markedly more pious Douglass ascribes Covey's change of heart to the power of "the *Sabbath*, not the root," though "had the day been other than Sunday I should have attributed Covey's altered manner solely to the power of the root."[52] Whereas the prior accounts imply that Jenkins's root and character provided Douglass with the grounding and inspiration to embrace his masculinity and avenge his earlier bodily violations, *Life and Times* shifts agency to Western religion's influence on Covey, hypocritical though he may be.

Douglass's rejection of Sandy Jenkins's role may have other motives as well. Jenkins was part of the same close group of enslaved friends who later plotted with Douglass to attempt an escape from slavery. This group included John and Henry Harris, toward whom Douglass "felt a friendship as strong as one man can feel for another; for I could have died with and for them."[53] Douglass soon downgrades Jenkins's membership, inasmuch as "[w]e were all, except Jenkins, quite free from slaveholding priestcraft,"[54] a way of accusing Sandy of being corrupted by slavery. Since Sandy is also the one member of the group whom Douglass suspects of betraying the plot,[55] Douglass has further grounds to reject him and any close homosocial bond he might have formed with his "old adviser." Ironically, once betrayed, Douglass is so distraught when separated from his friends that "[t]hirty-nine lashes on my naked and bleeding back would have been joyfully borne, in preference to this separation."[56] Here Douglass avows that he would rather be penetrated than separated, yet once separated, he draws upon his personal fortitude and endures prison until his master frees him, a testament to his masculine endurance.

Despite his shifting loyalties, Douglass's tepid allowance of the powers of the root and of the "genuine African" Jenkins produces an ironic conversion experience, one that defies and denies Christianity's power, even as his account draws upon the paradigmatic Christian narrative. It is, moreover, the cornerstone of Douglass's newfound manhood. Defiance is, after all, the polar opposite of the submission that allows the slave to be beaten. By allowing the possibility that the root may, in its African qualities, contain the key to defiance, freedom, and manhood, Douglass ambivalently appropriates a new paradigm of Christianity. Douglass rejected the notion, dear to Christian slaveholders, that whites were meant to be slaveholders and blacks were meant to be slaves. As Douglass tells us, he easily observed that not all whites were slaveholders and not all blacks were enslaved. "Race," then, is clearly an arbitrary marker used to cast the world of the slave into social chaos. And since there is no guarantee that race should mark one as a slave, there is consequently no guarantee that Christianity and Methodism, which harbored slave owners and slaves alike, are logically or legally consistent across denominations or denominational change. Thus one of Douglass's first desires after converting to Methodism is "to have the world converted" to the same uncorrupted, idealized form of the denomination that made him "[abhor] slavery more than ever."[57]

As Van Leer notes, every condemnation of slaveholding Christianity follows some profession of Douglass's faith.[58] Hence the Appendix to the *Narrative*, which contains one of Douglass's most powerful catalogs of the sins of "slaveholding religion," even as it offers an apologia for his vehemence. Douglass explicitly denies that he is "an opponent of all religion," pointing out that his castigation applies only to hypocrites like the Aulds and Covey, those most responsible for denying him the rights and privileges of middle-class identity.[59] Douglass's ambivalent embrace of Christianity parallels his ambivalent embrace of women's causes. At the various women's rights conventions and rallies Douglass attended in his antebellum years, he brilliantly compared the status of free women to that of slaves and declared that women should demand and claim their rights, including their right to education equal to that available to men.[60] Douglass demurred, however, at the idea of women having property rights equal to men and generally believed that women should assimilate to become closer to men, rather than stress their difference from men.

Similarly, as Van Leer notes of the women who figure in Douglass's narratives, his "use of female guides to chart the progress of male development may show no real interest in the engendered individuality of their experience as women."[61] On the contrary, women and Methodism play almost identical roles in Douglass's construction of himself as male; their perceived penetrability and willingness to submit to power mark them as oppressive forces. They are foils against which he defines his sexuality and masculinity, which depend upon his ability to repudiate all he holds in contempt about the feminine and homosocial. Although Douglass did not espouse black nationalism to the same degree that his contemporary Henry Highland Garnet did, his struggle anticipates twentieth-century black nationalism's fear of homosexuality among African-American males as a damning marker of weakness, femaleness, and racial submission.[62] Contained within this struggle is Douglass's tragic difficulty in separating his view of the feminine from his view of both slavery and slaveholding Christianity, a separation that might have enabled him better to reconcile his sexual and gender identities to his racial and religious identities. Without this reconciliation, we are left with haunting silences between Douglass's cries for his personal identity that echo in current discourse about the formation of black male identity.

Notes

1. *Narrative of the Life of Frederick Douglass, An American Slave, Written by Himself* (Boston: Anti-Slavery Office, 1845; reprint, New York: Signet, 1968), 77.

2. Patricia Roberts-Miller, *Voices in the Wilderness: Public Discourse and the Paradox of Puritan Rhetoric* (Tuscaloosa and London: University of Alabama Press, 1999), 108.

3. Judith Butler, *Gender Trouble: Feminism and the Subversion of Identity* (New York: Routledge, 1990), 151.

4. William S. McFeely, *Frederick Douglass* (New York and London: Norton, 1991), 95.

5. McFeely, *Frederick Douglass,* 66. McFeely's argument about incest, however, sits

somewhat uneasily with the historical record. While the *word* "incest" was certainly unspoken, the incestuous and frequently forced relationships between slaveholders, their slaves, and the slaveholders' black and white children were documented by black and white abolitionists well before Douglass wrote and published his *Narrative*. Lydia Maria Child, for example, recorded the 1842 speech of fugitive slave Lewis Clarke, who testified that he, his mother, and grandmother were all children of his former master. For this account and others detailing forced sexual liaisons between masters and slaves, see John Blassingame, ed., *Slave Testimony: Two Centuries of Letters, Speeches, Interviews, and Autobiographies* (Baton Rouge: Louisiana State University Press, 1977), 152.

6. Robert Richmond Ellis, "Reading through the Veil of Juan Francisco Manzano: From Homoerotic Violence to the Dream of a Homoracial Bond," *PMLA* 113.3 (1998): 422.

7. Ellis, "Reading," 422.

8. In researching this essay, I searched diligently for sources that conclusively offered evidence of male-male rape in slavery, with no luck. This is not to say, of course, that rape of male slaves did not occur; we should be surprised if it did not. Robert Richmond Ellis's article cites sources that detail male sexuality under slavery; none of them, however, explicitly document homosexual rape.

9. Jan C. Dawson, *The Unusable Past: America's Puritan Tradition, 1830 to 1930* (Chico, Calif.: Scholars Press, 1984), 137.

10. James Oliver Horton, "Freedom's Yoke: Gender Conventions among Antebellum Free Blacks," *Feminist Studies* 12.1 (spring 1986): 55.

11. Eve Kosofsky Sedgwick, *Between Men: English Literature and Male Homosocial Desire* (New York: Columbia University Press, 1985), 49.

12. Frederick Douglass, *My Bondage and My Freedom* (henceforth cited as *MBMF*) (New York: Miller, Orton & Mulligan, 1855), 196. See also the Appendix to Donald Mathews's excellent *Slavery and Methodism: A Chapter in American Morality, 1780–1845* (Princeton: Princeton University Press, 1965). The Appendix traces changes in the American Methodist *General Rules* regarding slavery from 1789 until the fissure of 1844 and the formation of the American Methodist Episcopal Church, South, which adopted its own rules in favor of slavery. It is at once amazing and disgusting to observe the church's legal and (il)logical dance around its original position. While the church consistently declared slavery evil, it made gradual allowances for members to enter official stations within the church while remaining slaveholders. Starting from a position of complete condemnation, the church then amended the *Rules* to allow slaveholders to join the church as long as they agreed to emancipate their slaves within a given period. The church later forbade slaveholding members only from selling their slaves; then it required them merely to treat their slaves well, and finally it granted local churches the privilege of deciding when and how slaves would be bought, sold, or emancipated. Mathews's book in its entirety is a more detailed analysis of this regression.

13. Douglass, *MBMF*, 196.

14. Dawson, *The Unusable Past*, 41.

15. Frederick Douglass, "Inhumanity of Slavery," in *MBMF*, 438. Emphasis in the original.

16. Mathews, *Slavery and Methodism*, 247. In 1844, the year before Douglass published his *Narrative*, the American Methodist Episcopal Church held its general conference, which revolved in part around the issue of whether the church would condemn, tolerate, or condone slavery. The disagreements within the church body over the issue led to its disjunction following the general conference, when the southern churches split from the northern, anticipating the later secession of the Confederacy. The American Methodist Episcopal Church, South, remained split ideologically from the northern churches. Not until 1939 did the southern and northern bodies reunify, and only then under the cloud of an arrangement that allowed African-American members to be segregated by race. See Harry V. Richardson, *Dark Salvation: The Story of Methodism as It Developed among Blacks in America*, C. Eric Lincoln Series on Black Religion (Garden City, New York: Anchor Press/Doubleday, 1976), 270–78. For Douglass's key speeches on Methodism's hypocrisies, see Frederick Douglass, *The Frederick Douglass Papers: Series One, Speeches, Debates, and Interviews*, ed. John W. Blassingame et al., 3 vols. (New Haven: Yale University Press, 1979–85).

17. McFeely, *Frederick Douglass*, 294. Douglass's master, Thomas Auld, rumored to be his father, remembered Douglass's being born at this time.

18. Mathews, *Slavery and Methodism*, 15.

19. Mathews, *Slavery and Methodism*, 5.

20. Douglass, *MBMF*, 167.

21. Douglass, *MBMF*, 142–43.

22. Jenny Franchot, "The Punishment of Esther: Frederick Douglass and the Construction of the Feminine," in Eric J. Sundquist, ed., *Frederick Douglass: New Literary and Historical Essays*, Cambridge Studies in American Literature and Culture (Cambridge: Cambridge University Press, 1990), 141.

23. McFeely, *Frederick Douglass*, 15.

24. Douglass, *Narrative*, 25–26.

25. Franchot, "Punishment," 142.

26. Douglass, *Narrative*, 25.

27. Douglass, *MBMF*, 87–88.

28. Douglass, *MBMF*, 87.

29. Douglass, *MBMF*, 88.

30. Douglass, *MBMF*, 88.

31. Richard Yarborough, "Race, Violence, and Manhood: The Masculine Ideal in Frederick Douglass's 'The Heroic Slave,'" in Sundquist, ed., *Frederick Douglass: New Literary and Historical Essays*, 168.

32. Robert Staples, *Black Masculinity: The Black Male's Role in American Society* (San Francisco: Black Scholar, 1982), 2, quoted in Yarborough, 168.

33. Douglass, *MBMF*, 214.

34. McFeely, *Frederick Douglass*, 44.

35. Douglass, *MBMF*, 221.

36. Douglass, *MBMF*, 222.

37. David Van Leer, "Reading Slavery: The Anxiety of Ethnicity in Douglass's *Narrative*" in Sundquist, ed., *Frederick Douglass: New Literary and Historical Essays*, 120.

38. Douglass, *Narrative*, 43.

39. R. J. Young, *Antebellum Black Activists: Race, Gender, and Self* (New York: Garland, 1996), 60.

40. Young, *Antebellum Black Activists*, 61.

41. Douglass, *Narrative*, 103–4. Emphasis mine.

42. John Robinson, "Diligent Labor and the Use of Gods Creatures" (1625), reprinted in Richard Reinitz, ed., *Tensions in American Puritanism* (New York: John Wiley & Sons, 1970), 73.

43. Mathews, *Slavery and Methodism*, 5.

44. Douglass, *MBMF*, 68.

45. Douglass, *Life and Times*, 248–49.

46. The relatively few blacks in nineteenth-century Great Britain tended to be consigned to the working classes and subjected to various forms of racism that were still disturbing, albeit not entirely identical to those found in the United States. See, for example, Paul Gilroy, *The Black Atlantic: Modernity and Double Consciousness* (Cambridge: Harvard University Press, 1993), and Paul Gilroy, *There Ain't No Black in the Union Jack: The Cultural Politics of Race and Nation* (Chicago: University of Chicago Press, 1991).

47. Douglass, *Life and Times*, 134.

48. Van Leer, "Reading Slavery," 125.

49. Douglass, *Narrative*, 77.

50. Douglass, *Narrative*, 81–82.

51. Douglass, *Narrative*, 83.

52. Douglass, *Life and Times*, 135.

53. Douglass, *MBMF*, 274.

54. Douglass, *MBMF*, 275.

55. Douglass, *MBMF*, 297.

56. Douglass, *MBMF*, 301.

57. Douglass, *MBMF*, 167.

58. Van Leer, "Reading Slavery," 122.

59. Douglass, *Narrative*, 120–21.

60. See, for example, Douglass's addresses at the National Women's Rights Conventions in Worcester, Massachusetts, 24 October 1850, and in New York, New York, 14 May 1858; reprinted in *Frederick Douglass Papers* II: 248–49, and III: 213–14.

61. Van Leer, "Reading Slavery," 130.

62. Amy Abugo Ongiri, "We Are Family: Miscegenation, Black Nationalism, Black Masculinity, and the Black Gay Cultural Imagination" in *Race-ing Representation: Voice, History, and Sexuality*, ed. Kostas Myrsiades and Linda Myrsiades (Lanham, Md.: Rowman & Littlefield Publishers, 1998), 243. Ongiri uses as an example Eldridge Cleaver's critique in *Soul on Ice* (1968) of James Baldwin's *Another Country* (1962), wherein Cleaver misreads Baldwin's text to create a fantasy of male homosexuality.

Enslaving Passions

White Male Sexuality and the Evasion of Race

∾

Russ Castronovo

The frequently anthologized history of Thomas Granger, condemned to death in 1642 for aberrant sexual acts, stands as an origin narrative of sexual repression in America. The elders of Plymouth Plantation took stock of Granger's "lewd practices" involving "a mare, a cow, two goats, five sheep, two calves and a turkey," and ruled that his violation of Mosaic law threatened to pollute their New World community.[1] Swift and uncompromising, the retribution handed out by seventeenth-century Puritans set the tone for historiographical narratives of sex in America. From Nathaniel Hawthorne's "The May-Pole of Merry Mount," where grim Puritans punish their morally lax neighbors, to scholarly studies of purity and prudery in the Victorian United States, a prevailing story is told that the austere ethos of early America remains with us in the repression of sexual bodies.[2]

Michel Foucault suggests another history: namely, that modernity is typified by an obsessive injunction to confess, study, and speak openly about sex in ways that are neither strictly repressive nor puritanical. Foucault's contention that "there was a steady proliferation of discourses concerned with sex" is borne out in pre–Civil War America, where reformers, educators, and clergy saturated the public sphere with anxious talk about male orgasm, masturbation, semen, and excitement.[3] Despite abundant commentary on the dangers of nonprocreative sex, the target remained the same throughout hygienic reform: white male bodies. This compulsive focus on white male sexuality does not merely seek to free citizens from the enslaving passions of unregulated sexuality; more important, it effectively liberates democratic discourse from racial contradictions by suppressing the extent to which whiteness, masculinity, and liberty are cathected to unfree black bodies. As instrumental as the Puritan legacy was in fomenting concerns about corporeal practices and bodily habits, the post-Puritan regulation of sex was equally instrumental in stifling concerns about institutional practice and bodily exploitation, specifically race slavery.

Whiteness demands a "racially erotic counterpoint," writes anthropologist Ann Laura Stoler.[4] In her study of European families living in colonial Java, Stoler asserts that civilized bourgeois bodies are libidinally indebted to the category of the "savage." For Hawthorne, white sexuality in colonial America is less straightforward, involving a simultaneous confrontation with and disavowal of race. His Puritan heroine, Hester Prynne, explains her carnal sin in the following terms: "Once in my life I met the Black Man. . . . This scarlet letter is his mark!"[5] Yes, Hester symbolically links her body's transgression to blackness, but her acknowledgment construes the historical presence of the black man in America simply as her private moral crisis. To be fair, the "Black Man" here is not a person but an allegorical personage, and Hawthorne's romance is not an analysis of race in America. Yet, the individualization and privatization of blackness as Hester's sin exemplifies the ideological bad faith of post-Puritan America: Racial injustice and oppression are refracted through the crucible of white sexuality so that citizens can avoid coming to terms with the need for pervasive cultural critique.

Physiological impurity echoes with fears of political corruption, specifically the republic's toleration, support, and practice of racial bondage. Because health reform contains messages about antislavery reform, hygienic tracts reveal how the corporeal body not only provided a site of sexual regulation but also set parameters for racial discourse. The discourse against masturbation exemplifies a slippage at the heart of U.S. culture: A national policy of slavery that pollutes the body politic is privatized as the "disease" of the self-polluted body. One contributor to *The Library of Health* thus conflated physical body and national culture:

> The public mind is, at the present time, all excitement about
> slavery—the slavery of two or three millions of our fellow men,
> by a nation professing to love and regard personal liberty beyond
> any nation on the globe. And why should it not be so? . . . Yet
> admitting it to be much more dreadful than it is, what is this sort
> of slavery compared with the slavery of man to himself, or rather,
> to his own appetites and lusts? And what is freedom, dear as in
> itself it truly is, to those who are carried captives by Satan at his

will; who bow down their necks to the yoke of passion, fashion,
appetite; and even rejoice in their own bondage?[6]

Even as this rhetoric equates masturbation and slavery, it establishes a hierarchy of oppression, deeming slavery to the self more grievous than the
enslavement of blacks. The inequality of this logic reveals the workings of
power when cultural critique is embodied: In an ironic reversal, the reformer
charges that institutional injustice occupies too limited a horizon, and he
instead emphasizes the need for regeneration at the level of the body. The
corporealization of politics deeply concerns "freedom," but this "freedom"
manifests itself as a desire to evade the contradictions within national definition and concentrate on an individual sexuality untouched by politics. This
willingness to view the private corporeal self as emblematic of the public
sphere constitutes a retrograde rhetorical strategy in which the language used
to describe states of unfreedom becomes deracialized and depoliticized.

Self-Abuse or Self-Reliance?

Although Samuel Tissot's *On Onania* reveals a European tradition preceding
American preoccupations with the "solitary vice" by at least seventy years, the
masturbation phobia that burst upon the U.S. reform movement in the 1830s
and lasted to the turn of the century was no sterile echo of continental models
of sexual knowledge. To stylize masturbators as "slave[s] of sexual lust,"
"wretched slaves of the abominable habit," and "slaves of lascivious thoughts
and practices" was to inflect the language of sexuality with nativist accents of
American institutional life.[7] The role of slavery in lending a distinctive idiom
to bourgeois reform efforts was not limited to antimasturbation discourse.
Drunkards, for example, became "slaves to drink" in what David Roediger
describes as a broad tendency to configure white working-class identity
against popular understandings of race slavery.[8] Although not as widespread
as temperance campaigns, antimasturbation discourse and the confusion it
promotes between corporeal abuse and systemic exploitation, between individual vice and institutional injustice, reveals even better the evasion of race in
post-Puritan reform. Based on misreadings of the body as body politic, warnings about the "solitary vice" pinpoint an abstract individual—that is, the
white middle-class male citizen—as the ideal target of social regeneration.

The pathology of masturbation makes recourse to an array of democratic
terms—"solitary vice," "self-indulgence," "self-destruction," "self-prostitution," "self-fornication," "self-abuse," "self-pollution"—that adumbrated the

pitfalls of celebrating autonomy in a climate where the political infects the sexual. Yet this same idiom also promised a cure: Moral and health authorities agreed that deliverance from masturbation could be achieved only through "self-respect," "self-denial," "self-government," "self-emancipation," and, of course, "self-reliance."9 Educators, doctors, preachers, and quacks lavished increasing attention on masturbation not, presumably, because more people were masturbating more frequently, but because this phobia obliquely addressed vital political issues, most notably the self's relation to liberation and enslavement.

What white Americans discovered was that in democracy questions of freedom were as solitary as vice. This democratic disease shirks off contextual ligaments, existing as a singular habit practiced in isolation from others. Such a hermetic relation hardly embodies the grist of democracy, and yet it aptly expresses the particulars of a nation in which the most pressing social conflict—race slavery—was construed as an individual dilemma. Thus a Philadelphia doctor overcame shocked sensibilities to translate the case of a French adolescent as a cautionary tale for his American audience: "It is that of a young man, who, on taking a bath, indulged in Masturbation, by placing his Penis into the hole in the bottom of the tub, made for the removal of the water. The glans soon became so much swollen that he could not withdraw the Penis. His cries brought him assistance, but it was not easy to remove him from the fetters he had forged for himself."10 The movement from "his Penis" to "the Penis" registers a process of objectification, which, ironically, stems from a perversion of self-reliance. As liberty degenerated into license, health reformers aligned autoeroticism with various forms of political abjection including bondage, tyranny, and despotism. Configured as a political body, the victim of self-indulgence was deemed responsible for his own degradation; the discourse against "the slavery of man to himself"11—yet another euphemism for masturbation—legitimated a vision of slavery in which race drops out of the social equation.

This story of the misadventurous bather, as well as popular case studies of other inveterate masturbators, helped citizens read slavery as a somatic concern. Figure 1 shows three individuals afflicted by the "slavery of man to himself," their uselessness to the nation evident in postures of antibourgeois lassitude, feebleness, and loss of self-control. Such morbid symptoms induced a masturbatory fantasy of politics that sequestered the citizen in a public of one, quarantining him from a social order debased by a very different enslavement of bodies.

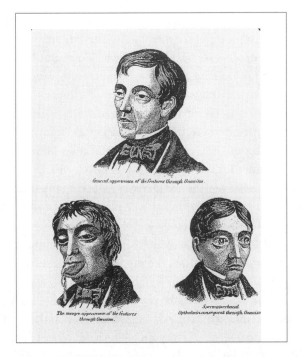

Figure 1: Portraits of Onanism

Afflicted by the onset of the "solitary vice," these three individuals suffer a range of symptoms that debilitate citizenship. His face marked by inanition and torpidity, the specimen in the upper row has forfeited the virtues of New England independence. For the candidate on the lower left, drool figures as metonym for semen. His failure to guard this precious commodity betrays his lack of self-control and loss of self-reliance. The gentleman on the lower right is a self-abuser of such habitual proportion that his optic nerve has become inflamed and blindness seems imminent. [From Seth Pancoast, *Onanism, Spermatorrhoea, Porneiokalogynomania-pathology. Boyhood's Perils and Manhood's Curse; an Earnest Appeal to the Young of America* (Philadelphia: 1858)]

As the secret sphere of white sexuality increasingly became the subject of public lectures and cheap pamphlets, political discourse retracted to an individualized space. Only frank treatment of "ruined subjects and wretched slaves of the abominable habit" could liberate the republic from a genital insurrection that threatened the virility of its citizens and the constitution of future generations.[12] As "findings" of hereditary degeneration proved, nothing less than the health of the nation was at stake. Parents searching for methods to combat physiological slavery could take their cue from the Union's response to Southern slavery: "So, parent, if you would rid your family of this pest, you must look after it; and you must not look with spectacles, glossed so, all over with love to your children, that you cannot see their faults. This will never do the work. Jefferson Davis, with his rebel crew, pleads to be let alone. But that is not the way the United States take to cure them of rebellion. Here is body and soul polluted by vice, in your very household, taught to your innocent children by one whom you are paying to take care of them; and will you shut your eyes, and cry, there is no danger? There *is* danger."[13] In crude terms, politicized body and body politic become interchangeable. The analogy between civil war and "self-pollution" argues for the need to address private vice in a public manner. At the same time, however, the comparison embodies the nation, construing political questions somatically, in essence privatizing national policy as the moral agenda of the bourgeois family.

While masturbation supposedly inflamed the optic nerve and, if unchecked, resulted in blindness, the discourse on masturbation produced blindness to institutional abuses in American culture. Medical tracts, conduct books, and bachelor guides from the 1830s to the 1860s legitimated a political vision so severely reduced in scope that representation of the "solitary vice" as slavery tended not to displace slavery altogether, but rather to occlude race as a meaningful social index. I am not suggesting that nineteenth-century discourse is a zero-sum game in which there is only so much critical energy to go around, and that it is exhausted in the treatment of the physiological individual, leaving nothing for the analysis of institutions. Instead, I contend that the voluminous talk about the "solitary vice" lays bare the conceptual limits of a prevailing cultural critique unable to address systemic abuses other than as issues of individual power and corruption, an approach that mutes the force of race as a constitutive sociopolitical category.

An 1837 article on "Physiological Vice" by William Alcott registers how white male sexuality impairs systemic awareness of social injustice. Stirred by the same mixture of Unitarian reform and Transcendentalism as his more famous cousins in Concord, Alcott agitated for a movement unconcerned with the cultural determinants of race, as though universal freedom could be attained via the cumulative emancipation of individual body after individual body:

> We say much and hear much said of the slavery of two or three
> millions of people in these United States. And much that is said
> on this subject is well said. I have surveyed, to a very consider-
> able extent, the practical enormity of this great national evil. I
> have not received my information at second hand; my own eyes
> have witnessed it. Yet I have witnessed other forms of slavery

> among us, whose effects are to me still more shocking; forms of
> slavery, too, in whose horrors twelve or fifteen, instead of two or
> three millions of my countrymen are involved. I allude of course
> to the slavery of bad physical habits; the slavery of a being made
> originally in the image of God, but now very generally subjected
> to appetite, lust, and passion. In this view, I feel justified in say-
> ing that some of the worst forms of slavery with which I am
> acquainted, exist around us in our own goodly New England, as
> well as elsewhere; yes, in the proud city of Boston itself .[14]

Democratic hygiene administers an apolitical rendition of politics, one that
masquerades as democratic practice by intimating that masturbation and
other "bad physical habits" demand reform more than slavery because a
greater portion of the populace is at risk. Racial bondage afflicts an appalling
number of people, but ultimately race becomes a restrictive category of analysis when compared to "still more shocking" forms of slavery. African
servitude exists only as a regional phenomenon, while "physiological vice"
knows no sectionalism, tainting lands that once basked in the deepest legacies of freedom. The pandemic incidence of "the slavery of man to himself"
validates a critical outlook dismissive of the particular and enraptured with
the universal—or, in this case, a nation of white men.

The Emersonian underpinnings of Alcott's posture establish a perspective
that embraces reform of the cosmos at the expense of black slaves who are
deemed unable to surpass history or culture. While curing "twelve or fifteen"
million victims poses a daunting task, these numbers fuel dreams of universal emancipation in which physiology offers the only meaningful political
index. Any other attributes that lead to the identification of a more specific
group—say "two or three" millions of slaves—would frustrate hopes of universal reform by bringing into visibility the complex forces that circumscribe
and particularize blacks in ways that implicitly figure the abstract political
subject as white. Rather than examine how racism and exploitation impinge
upon black identity, millennially minded activists adopted a perspective at
once so broad and puritanical that the target of social regeneration becomes
the single self abstracted from cultural relations.

Masturbation phobia offers an antidote to social conflict by conceiving of
citizens as ciphers unmarked by experience or contingency, tantalizingly
close to an ahistorical and prelapsarian subjectivity. "All men in the abstract
are just & good—what hinders them in the particular is, the momentary pre-
dominance of the finite," Emerson wrote in his journal.[15] Or in the terms of

popular reform: All men masturbate, revealing their lapsed goodness, but because not all men are black and enslaved, it is more difficult to intuit these particulars as having an original share of democratic virtue. Blacks—because they are not culturally normalized as white men are—cannot be recognized within the abstract language of universal reform. The vice of slavery is its irredeemable specificity; in contrast, the virtue of masturbation is its corporeal generality, which makes grappling with complexities unnecessary. Antimasturbation discourse reveals how nineteenth-century cultural critique induced a politics not of equality, but of equalization. "When all mankind are in a perfectly healthy condition, their constitutions are all alike," asserted the *Botanico-Medical Recorder*.[16] This physiological principle, echoed in more heady terms by Emerson's statement in "Self-Reliance" that "varieties are lost sight of at a little distance. . . . One tendency unites them all," acknowledges only the inequities that afflict the fantasy of the homogeneous and unmarked individual.[17]

The realization that "masturbation was equally accessible to all" inspired a brigade of moral missionaries to preach the laws of health to a citizenry—if avid consumption of antimasturbation tracts and attendance at lectures on hygiene are any indication—preoccupied with the democratic spread of onanist pleasures.[18] The data confirmed fears about links between the "solitary vice" and equality: A quick glance at the inmates of the Worcester Lunatic Asylum made clear to one medical crusader that "*no class of the young is exempt from the most melancholy and fatal results, who are, to any extent, in the habit of this secret vice.*"[19] Such "findings" support historians who contend that anxieties about all sorts of democratic tendencies—class mobility, migration to urban centers, erosive shifts in patriarchal authority—caused Americans not so much to masturbate, but to think obsessively about masturbation.

Phobic concern for white male bodies buffets a straight national politics; the discourse against masturbation legitimates examination of subjects whose racial opacity and heteronormativity remove them beyond the ken of social analysis. It is pleasurable to think about white men's bodies because white men's bodies misconnote the body of men that is the nation in all its exclusivity. Masturbation enables somatic virtue to outweigh political *virtù* because the "slavery of man to himself" invites an abstract analysis in which the universal afflictions of "man" supplant injustices stemming from specific institutions. The translation of freedom into sexual terms represents not a politicization of sectors of human activity traditionally identified as nonpolitical, but the erosion of politics to the most condensed entity imaginable—the individual. The

sterility of public culture engendered a prolix discourse on the citizen as physiological entity, ignoring possibilities of the self as a relational actor who
constantly mediates history, race, and commodification. The etiology of American masturbation is democratic, but not simply because, as various scholars
have suggested, sexual self-determination resonates with class concerns.
Instead, the antebellum epidemic of the "solitary vice" discloses the extent to
which ideals of self-culture are ambiguated by deep, unacknowledged economic, institutional, and rhetorical debts to African servitude.

If a millennial vision fueled both antislavery and health reform, then the
millennium seemed that much closer for masturbators than for slaves. The
"body in subjection," as *The Library of Health* put it in 1842, "must be self-
emancipated."[20] Emerson had staked out a position in which "all must
reform themselves" a year earlier in "Self-Reliance," and he used this stance
to denounce the Fugitive Slave Law. Calling for a solitary individual resistant
to institutions, Emerson outlined a masculinist hero: "He only who is able to
stand alone, is qualified for society."[21] Never fear that this lone figure might
degenerate into the onanist; never fear that what "Self-Reliance" championed
as the citizen's "independence of solitude"[22] might become the masturbator's
closet: Nineteenth-century social discourse privileges this privatized body
regardless of whether it is the site of virtue or vice. What matters most is that
the body standing alone furnishes an anti-institutional register promising not
only that the social critics can resist institutions, but also that the social critic
need not think about institutions at all.

Crusades against "the slavery of man to himself" emerged from a somatic
politics that embodied social conflicts as corporeal vices in order to redirect
the problem of race slavery onto the theoretically manageable site of the
atomized young man's body. The career of Sylvester Graham, temperance
advocate, dietary reformer, abolitionist, and leader of an amorphous campaign against the "solitary vice," typifies how corporeal anxieties registered
across diverse agendas of bourgeois reform, privileging the citizen's privatized body—and not the public sphere—as the location of politics. Concern
over the health of "systems of republican government" led him to take aim at
the "SEXUAL DESIRE . . . that disturbs and disorders all the functions of the
system."[23] Graham personalizes systemic knowledge, in this case embodying
the fate of the nation in white men. This bad faith was standard fare for
prominent abolitionists, many of whom lived according to the hygienic dic-
tates of what was called the "Graham System." Antislavery speakers and
supporters often lodged at Graham boardinghouses in an effort to regulate

the "living volcano of unclean propensities and passions" that they saw
erupting both below the belt and below the Mason-Dixon line.[24] "Such a
knot of Abolitionists I never before fell in with," noted an Amherst College tutor of his visit to a Graham boardinghouse. He certainly expected
to find "Grahamites" during his stay, but was pleasantly surprised to be
sharing with "Garrisonites" as well a breakfast table devoid of all stimulants from coffee to alcohol to pastry. Among the "flaming Abolitionists"
he enthusiastically glimpsed were Arthur Tappan, William Goodell, Elijah
Lovejoy, and Theodore Parker.[25] These very real overlaps—in addition to
the discursive ones that are my primary concern—signal the privatizing
pressures that transfigure national corruption into the more easily understood (and regulated) workings of the white male body. Sexuality, as an
immanent and intimate force, suggested to antislavery men the priority of
achieving personal emancipation before seeking the political freedom of
others. As one reformer wrote, "We are not fit to plead the cause of Freedom until we get free from the tyranny of our own passions. Till then we
ourselves are in bondage. How many professed Abolitionist are thus
enslaved!"[26]

For all ardent young men who might not travel to the big city and get a
chance to stay at a Graham boardinghouse, *A Lecture to Young Men* (1834)
provides advice on how to handle freedom. Graham begins by espousing a
methodology that addresses not liberty in a political sense, but the specific
liberties young men take with their genitals: "It is to little purpose that we
are nicely accurate in the theoretical abstractions of political rights, while we
neglect all the practical interests of political truth. . . . I do not say that political science is not to be cultivated; nor that abstract rights are not to be
insisted on. . . . I contend, that it is infinitely better to secure the prosperity
of the State, through the happiness of the people, than to sacrifice both in the
defence of abstract metaphysical rights."[27] Sociopolitical critique, so abstract
as to be unwieldy and impractical, accomplishes little. The body politic needs
embodiment in the adolescent male so that nonrepresentational "abstract
rights" can be made flesh. After all, democracy would seem to demand commitment to what can be represented, not "abstract rights." White male
sexuality—as a representation of political distress—misrepresents the *socius*
as a body, one whose reform depends not on attention to foundational linkages between race and capital, but on private habit. Such misrecognition
truncates systemic analysis by giving critique a self-reliant body, obscuring
the complex connections that sustain domestic slavery.

Democracy as Sexual Threat

In more drastic form, such truncation visited the male body as well. Frustrated by futile attempts to cure a patient's "great constitutional disturbance," Dr. Josiah Crosby reestablished corporeal order by radical means. He communicated to the *Boston Medical and Surgical Journal* his heroic efforts in treating one "Mr. ——," a confirmed masturbator for a decade: "I did not think it advisable to continue the use of ordinary medicines to cure so desperate a disease. Believing the great constitutional disturbance to have been produced and kept up by the severe and repeated shocks given to the brain and nervous system by the seminal emissions, and that removing the testicles would remove the great source of difficulty, I recommended castration." Curtailment of liberty benefits the citizen: "Mr. ——" is now embarked upon "a life of usefulness . . . actively engaged in making arrangements to go into business."[28] Castration reduces the perils of an autonomy that spills many seeds but reaps no harvest by prodding the citizen to enjoy regular, bourgeois pursuits. No longer a profligate in the spermatic economy, "Mr. ——" disburses financial assets rather than squandering physiological ones.

Despite this regeneration through surgical violence, contributors to the *Boston Medical and Surgical Journal* condemned Crosby's treatment, insisting that what was touted as a cure was, in fact, a "mutilation."[29] Yet castration seemed appropriate treatment for other slaves to the "solitary vice"—if indeed they were black slaves. A physician from Fort King, Florida, reported in 1846 the case of a habitual onanist who "not unfrequently operated in this manner eight or nine times in the course of twenty-four hours," so that paralysis and death seemed imminent. Once threatened with castration, however, the patient overcame his addiction. But unlike Crosby's patient, who was successfully reintegrated into family and community, this self-abuser was a slave, making his cure of an entirely different order. While "Mr. ——" enjoyed a generic identity, the slave did not, and only the most insensitive surgeon would confuse two very different political bodies by prescribing the slave's castration for the citizen. Crosby's handling of masturbation runs afoul of white manhood by saddling the citizen with a remedy whose severity appears better suited to persons congenitally sentenced to servitude. Antithetical to the principles of democratic health, castration produces the unwanted side effects of historicizing the body of a New England youth with a type of paternalism encumbering a "negro man placed under his [the doctor's] care."[30]

Viewed against the flood of antimasturbation tracts first emerging in the 1830s, Crosby's error lay in his incorrect inference that a democratic disease should be combated with autocratic surgical methods. In a rare instance when genital mutilation seemed consistent with individual freedom, however, castration was applauded as a citizen's duty. In contrast to the suspect case of "Mr. ——," castrated on his doctor's orders, the *Boston Medical and Surgical Journal* viewed somewhat more optimistically the castration of "H. F." because in this instance the act had been totally self-reliant, inflicted by the masturbator himself:

> All the evils resulting from this unrestrained indulgence, were presented in this truly unhappy man. He had been apprised of the danger which the continued practice would bring upon him, and was sensible that all his trials had their origin in this vice; and yet the propensity had become so strong that he could not resist it. . . . In his intercourse with his friends he was covered with shame and confusion, and seemed to feel conscious that every individual that he met with knew, as well as himself, the height and the depth of his degradation. In this condition, in a fit of desperation, he attempted to emasculate himself, but succeeded in removing one testicle only. After he recovered from the dangerous wound which he inflicted, he began to get better, and after two years he recovered his health and spirits. He has since, at the age of forty-five, *married* a very clever woman, and they live in peace and harmony.[31]

Unlike Crosby's account of his patient, the story of "H. F." documents the self-consciousness of the sufferer, unable to overcome the compulsive humiliation that begets losses of semen, control, and fellowship. If "unrestrained indulgence" demands restraint, if liberty requires a little tyranny as Crosby supposed, then the citizen could decide when and how much was necessary. As "H. F." proved by his rehabilitation and eventual marriage, authority need not be applied with full despotic force. Without recourse to autocratic practices that seemed more suited to the treatment of slaves, democratic sons could be trusted to cure themselves. The body's fate lay in the individual's hands.

The efficacy of such cures corresponded to a young man's willingness to sever himself from civic life. The healthy citizen could do without the polis. This alienation need not be regretted since the white propertied male was presumed to enjoy independence from social and economic complexities.

Impurity came not from the democratic individual, but from democracy itself. Iniquity was known to stalk boardinghouses, gambling dens, and slave plantations, but seemingly more innocuous sites of democratic association such as factories, conversation clubs, and schools bred vice as well. Even the nursery became unsafe once parents opened it up to domestic servants who instructed young masters and mistresses in the mysteries of "self-abuse."

The etiology of masturbation uncovered proof of its nonessential, extraneous character. Legislation decreeing it an offense to teach a person how to masturbate reveals an insistent belief that the origins of "solitary vice" were social.[32] Return to an asocial existence is impossible, but the most basic social grouping—the family—could be protected from incursions. Children who never encounter dissolute servants or fallen schoolmates never have reason to let hands or minds go astray. The solitary vice would never afflict her boys, one moral reformer explained, because she never allowed their chums to spend the night, and the "secret indulgence" would never excite her daughters because a servant from the lower classes would never find employment under her roof.[33] She admitted this household regimen might appear unneighborly, snobbish, even unegalitarian, yet far better to keep a child friendless or a daughter overworked than to "expose them to be instructed in that knowledge which would be a life-long curse."[34] A healthy democracy demanded antidemocratic measures: Sons and daughters could remain free only by rejecting an inherently debased public sphere. It is hardly surprising that this mother urged parents in Emersonian fashion to "teach a useful and valuable lesson to our children of self-reliance."[35]

But as antimasturbation tracts conceded, filtering out profane influences was an insurmountable task in a nation whose devotion to middle-class culture made boarding schools, professional workplaces, and social organizations (such as sewing bees and lyceums) normative settings that replaced the family as the locus of order and interaction. Democracy facilitated contagion: Although socials and clubs reproduced bourgeois values of industriousness, diligence, and self-improvement, they also engendered unpredictable forums where people of different ages, class backgrounds, and tastes mingled. In an era of unprecedented migration of rural youth to urban centers, bachelor guides attempted to supply young clerks and apprentices with surrogate images of patriarchal stability. One such conduct book, Seth Pancoast's *Onanism, Spermatorrhoea* opens with a plate of "The Healthy Couple and Their Child" (Figure 2). This well-attired family represents the surest protection against the solitary vice, their wholesome interaction laced with

Figure 2

❧

The Healthy Couple and Their Child

The contrast between the families in Figures 2 and 3 implies the fear of auto-eroticism as a collective disease in which the sin of the fathers is visited upon generations of future citizens. [From Pancoast, *Onanism, Spermatorrhoea.*]

pedagogical offerings for the unconscious of the (potential) masturbator. The capering child remembers to look back to his parents for approval; the grid-like pattern of the father's trousers implies that order resides in this man's loins; the demure matron holds her husband's umbrella rather than allowing him to handle it: Each of these details marks the bourgeois family as a virtu-ous breeding ground for future citizens. And yet, the close proximity and social interdependence of bodies can also make the family the parent of vice. A second plate, a distorted reproduction of the "healthy couple," supplements the frontispiece, questioning the family's ability to provide collective resis-tance against autoeroticism. Entitled "The Onanists and Their Child" (Figure 3), this portrait displays telltale signs of vice. Sallow and decrepit, each family member has hands turned inward in an unnatural perversion of self-reliance. Hunched shoulders and dependence on canes to support broken-down con-stitutions imply a severe lack of individual mettle. The family portrait documents the social logic of the "solitary vice": Sexual corruption is not self-derived, but springs from uncontrolled pleasures of association passed down to future generations of the republic.

Figure 3

∽

The Onanists and Their Child

Community seems compulsive, intent on democratizing vice. No wonder then that Emerson characterized society in paranoid fashion as a "conspiracy against the manhood of every one of its members."[36] To counteract the threat posed by collectivity, social theorists characterized meetings, associations, and companionship as corrupt supplements to an unmarked, undefiled individualism. If Emerson asked, "Is not a man better than a town?"[37] moral reformers knew why. Virtue lay in a nonsocial existence. Celebrated female health reformer Mary Gove dispensed exactly this prescription, warning women to beware the passions diffused outside the home and avoid the commotion of the public sphere. Although Gove broadened hygienic rhetoric to address women, her argument amounts to a paradoxical ideology in which women best serve democracy by remaining immune to it. Identifying women as equally susceptible to the "solitary vice," she insisted that women could also exercise the appropriate "cure" of self-reliance, a radical gesture that placed women within a male political pathology even as it removed them from public culture by emphasizing the putatively presocial roles of wife and mother.

In *Lectures to Women on Anatomy and Physiology* (1846), Gove described the "solitary vice" as a social disease bred by clamors of an enervating public sphere. The source of genital misery lay in a hypercivilized world that unhinged the self with a bombardment of dangerous stimuli. This "female equivalent to Sylvester Graham," as Stephen Nissenbaum dubs Gove,[38] rhapsodizes about the prelapsarian existence of "the Indians, the lower orders of Irish, and the slaves of the South," who in her estimation live happier, healthier lives because they are sheltered from the pernicious influence of bourgeois democracy. Because neither "primitive" hunters nor "uncivilized" laborers live in an "artificial manner," and because neither are deprived the supposed benefits of drudgery euphemistically recast as "exercise," they remain physiologically free—if not politically so.[39] Immediately after she imagines the virtues of being racially oppressed, Gove sketches the vices of white women whose bodily habits make them "victims of civilization."[40] On the one hand, her argument naturalizes slavery as a presocial formation unconnected to the exploitative systems of "civilization"; on the other, her analysis reconciles white women to social alienation by inveighing against "evils of civic life."[41] If "habits are very enslaving"[42] as a character in Gove's 1849 novel, *Agnes Morris*, says, then for the body politic it is not slavery that is enslaving but the human body itself.

With society to blame for the body's bad habits, racial oppression vanishes only to reappear as the private symptoms of individual illness. With only the self to blame, could the citizen produce a social diagnosis? Consumed with authoring one's own text, could the self write cultural criticism? Autoeroticism made for an autoreferential political subject, cleansed of the economic forces, racial specificities, and historical limitations that constrain and identify blacks as slaves. If, to invoke Thomas Laqueur's simile, the "body is like an actor on stage, ready to take on the roles assigned it by culture," then the ideal American body in the script provided by Graham, Emerson, Gove, and other reformers studiously forgets culture's multiple and constant interpellations.[43]

In his homespun anatomy of the human body, William Alcott unveiled this perfected citizen as a skeleton (Figure 4). Divested of the flesh that endows the self with gender and race, this body lacks all foundation and motivation for involvement in the historical world. Although its pose hearkens back to the antislavery figure of the kneeling slave (Figure 5), this skeleton has no need to clamor for dignity because his sheer anonymity already tokens

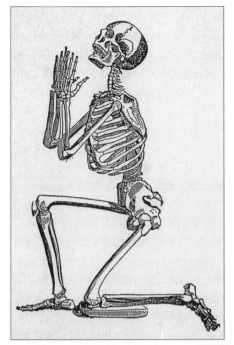 

Figures 4 and 5

❧

The ideal citizen, unlike the slave of northern liberal imagination in Figure 5, has no difficulty achieving disembodiment. [Skeleton. From William Alcott, *The House I Live In; or the Human Body. For the Use of Families and Schools.* 11th edition (Boston: Waitt, Pierce & Co., 1844). The kneeling slave. From Specimens for Modern Printing Types, Cast at the Letter Foundry of the Boston Type and Stereotype Company (Boston: White and Potter, 1845). Stereotype plate. No. 844. 1-5/8" Rare Book and Manuscript Library, Columbia University.]

acceptance in nothing less than the universal: the unmarked whiteness of national citizenry. Appearing in Alcott's *The House I Live In; or the Human Body*, the figure of self-as-skeleton-as-house becomes domesticated as eye sockets are figured as windows, joints as hinges, and bones as pillars. Political significance fades in this domestic body, itself the culmination of the reformist desire to restrict the body's social intercourse. Such a self is not without a specific identity, however; this intense cultural nakedness is the property of white middle-class males.

Political Pleasure

Caught up in the struggle to discover a practical remedy for the peculiar institution, antebellum social critics found that self-reliance promised the
liberation not of the bondsman, but of the slave owner. This ambivalent
politicization of bodily habit suggests the masturbator's ability to represent
both slave and master: In a confusion of legal and physiological constitutionality, Sylvester Graham attributed the especial evil of masturbation to the fact
that "it is a secret and solitary vice, which requires the consent of no second
person,—and therefore the practice has little to prevent its frequency."[44]
With no checks and balances within his constitution, the self's passions tyr-
annize over the individual. The self-reliant individual qua masturbator bears
an uncanny relation to the irresistible autocrat: Self-subjected to physical
stimulus, his body becomes both master and slave. Hygienic understandings
of power and its abuse offer substantial political dividends: The body that is
simultaneously enslaving and enslaved recasts the relation of master and
slave so that it is neither a relation nor a dialectic. Instead it is an insular, privatized system based neither on "consent" nor on national policy.

Physiological concepts—especially in their capacity to individualize corruption as vice—seeped into the language of antislavery reform. In an
early address on slavery, Emerson discussed the body politic as politicized
body, going so far as to employ a common euphemism for masturbation—
"self-indulgence"—to suggest the seductiveness of bondage for the master.
Sympathizing more with slaveholder than slave, Emerson said in November
1837, "For us to keep slaves would be the sum of wickedness, but in the
planter it may indicate only a degree of self-indulgence which we may parallel readily enough nearer home; in attacking him we are demanding of him
a superiority to his conditions which we do not demand of ourselves. He is
to blame, of course, but in the same sense the slave is to blame for allowing
himself to be held as a slave."[45]

Slavery has nothing to do with social relationships; instead it appears as
a matter of individual proclivity. Emerson's stake in equality leads him to
recognize that slaveholder, nonslaveholder, and slave each share common
frailties. Bestowing humanity upon chattel is a radical gesture, but it is also
one that severs the slave from an institutional context. Within this humani-
tarian logic, the slave is only subject to the claims of a common humanity; he
suffers nothing from a race-based economic system and everything from his
own weakness. Self-reliance offers no help to the slave; in fact, it legitimates
continued enslavement.

Emerson's remarks reveal the cross-pollination between antislavery discourse and the regulation of sexuality. Just as moral crusaders spoke of masturbation as a form of slavery, antislavery texts asserted that slavery dangerously eroticized Southern society, bombarding it with harmful stimuli that overexcited the planter class. Enthralled by what Emerson saw as the "love of power, the voluptuousness of holding a human being in his absolute control," the slave owner can liberate himself only by making a steadfast resolution not to pursue such self-gratification.[46] Slaveholding demands the same ideological cure as masturbation: Only an individualist perspective can overcome these kindred vices; only avoidance of systemic contact (and systemic analysis) can grant the individual a body impervious to culture. This logic prompts a distinction between slaveholding and slavery in which the former, because it is constructed as the "disease" of white male bodies, can be treated, while the latter, alluding to a complex economic and racial system, is beyond ideological repair. In contrast to the social transparency that makes the white male body treatable, the institutional particularity of blackness is beyond reform.

"Progress is not for society. Progress belongs to the Individual," wrote Emerson in an early lecture containing many concepts that would become central to "Self-Reliance."[47] Fascination with the individual, mirrored by hygienic concern for the solitary sexual subject, facilitates rejection of a comprehensive outlook. Emerson uses "progress" to renounce a social vision as inconvenient, opting instead to pursue reform privately as a matter of personal fulfillment. The young man in control of his changing body unfolds into the citizen well adjusted to his limited social role in the state: Each refuses to indulge behaviors that would throw consciousness into an interactive public sphere.

Postscript

Sixteen years after the first printing of his *Lecture*, Graham again decried the dangers of "fanatical excitement," except that now his reference was not the human body, but the American union besieged by the 1850 constitutional crisis over slavery.[48] Now leagued with "the most fervent of the Abolitionists," Graham found that his early vocabulary of corporeal virtue and vice extended seamlessly into a critique of national corruption.[49] As a health reformer, he urged "man" to respect the "laws of his constitution" or suffer from "excess"; now in *Letter to the Hon. Daniel Webster* he acts as a social reformer, imploring his nation to uphold the Constitution or undergo the ravages of civil war.[50] Not having to retool his argument is more than convenient: The equivalence between political and hygienic vocabularies accords the nation a corporeal form whose disruptions seemed as atomized as the debilities plaguing the white male body. Reading Daniel Webster's support of the Fugitive Slave Law as a sullying of the Constitution, Graham merely updates his earlier exhortations that young men cherish their physical constitutions. Slavery, like masturbation, is an unnatural practice spawned by "sordid minds" of the South "where the passions prevail over reason."[51] Much as the original nature of a young man's physiological frame is uncorrupted, the textual frame of the nation, in Graham's eyes, was pure in its inception until the slaveholders' lust for power adulterated the compact. Graham's translation of "constitution" from the *Lecture* (1834) to the *Letter* (1850) does not represent an enlarged analytic vision that conjoins the sexual with the political; instead, it reveals the reinscription of national agenda as a private sexual matter.

Equally delicate in nature, both the male constitution and the U.S. Constitution are threatened by powerful stimulants ranging from coffee to sectional disputes. Like masturbation, the unhealthy debate over slavery excites the internal workings of the body politic, a fact that Graham finds confirmed in the vitriolic ejaculations of proslavery politicians. Underlying his 1834 tirade against onanism is an idea of a "reciprocal influence" of the "cephalo-spinal nerves" in which genital self-abuse injures the brain, and in turn, lascivious fantasies dangerously titillate the genitals.[52] With proper self-government, however, the young man can make an ally of "reciprocal influence" and in one stroke tame the "stimulations of semen" as well as the "imaginations upon the mind."[53] Likewise, the weakness of the American republic in 1850 stems from lack of "reciprocal obligation" between North and South to uphold the mutual interests of union.[54] This failure allows sectional passions to run rampant, inducing uncontrolled spasms in a once orderly nation.

In specific terms, "reciprocal obligation" requires the South to "unite with us in establishing, sustaining, and submitting to a national government, by which all further extension of slavery in our country shall be absolutely and for ever prohibited."[55] Exactly as self-government is the key to controlling the "reciprocal influence" between cerebral impulse and genital conduct, only Southerners' moral confrontation of slavery can bring about a healthy sense of "reciprocal obligation" between the states. Conceived not as a social ill, but as an individual sin, slavery can be remedied with the same cure applied to the masturbator—virtuous self-reliance. Graham thus presents "voluntary emancipation" as the only effective cure to civic unrest; any efforts to bend the South to the North's mandates will prove as fruitless as attempts to curb masturbation with autocratic contraptions and surgeries.[56] Only the "spontaneous action of the slaveholders individually" to set blacks free can preserve the fathers' constitution.[57] To be sure, Graham offers a condemnation of slavery; but no analytic vision that critiques the slave *system*, no perspective that exposes slavery's complex foundations in material and institutional praxis, develops in an environment in which reformist action is as "spontaneous" and as individual as masturbation. This nonsystemic, nonsocial criticism performed an invaluable patriotic service by disabling any inquiry that might take an unflinching look at the unmarked white male body's ability to obscure race and cleanse the national body of structural corruption.

Emerson's statement that "it is the age of the first person singular," presents more than an impressionistic assessment of his times. It also registers the prevailing political and sexual idioms of a nation trying to devise a democracy impregnable to excess. Somatic analysis narrowed cultural critique, disabling perspectives that looked at spectrums larger than the body as part of a performative indictment of the superstructure and its support for race slavery. Within this romantic yet ultimately ascetic language little remained for the conception of a more articulated, interconnected subjectivity. Contraction of the nation to the body leaves the public sphere pristine but denuded of complexity, contradiction, and nuance. And not just any physical body would do: The white male sexual body served as the subject of a sterile cultural criticism ironically implemented to free American culture from criticism. The discourse on self-abuse provided spasms of ideological pleasure by legitimating a rhetoric that refused to disabuse the nation of its innocence.

Notes

1. William Bradford, *Of Plymouth Plantation*, in Nina Baym et al., eds., *The Norton Anthology of American Literature*, 4th ed., 2 vols. (New York: Norton, 1994), 1:154.

2. See, for instance, Ronald Walters, *Primers for Prudery: Sexual Advice to Victorian America* (Englewood Cliffs, N.J.: Prentice Hall, 1974); and David Pivar, *Purity Crusade: Sexual Morality & Social Control, 1868–1900* (Westport, Conn.: Greenwood, 1973). Pivar constructs a history of sexuality shrouded in silence: "Until the twentieth century, Americans tended to refrain from public discussion of sex" (3).

3. Michel Foucault, *The History of Sexuality: Volume 1: An Introduction*, trans. Robert Hurley (1978; reprint, New York: Vintage, 1990), 18.

4. Ann Laura Stoler, *Race and the Education of Desire: Foucault's History of Sexuality and the Colonial Order of Things* (Durham, N.C.: Duke University Press, 1995), 6.

5. Nathaniel Hawthorne, *The Scarlet Letter: A Romance* (New York: Penguin, 1983), 203.

6. William Alcott, ed., *The Library of Health and Treatment of the Human Constitution*, 6 vols. (Boston: George W. Light, 1837–42), 4:345.

7. George Calhoun, *Report of the Consulting Surgeon on Spermatorrhea, or Seminal Weakness, Impotence, the Vice of Onanism, Masturbation, or Self-Abuse, and Other Diseases of the Sexual Organs*, in *The Secret Vice Exposed! Some Arguments against Masturbation*, ed. Charles Rosenberg and Carroll Smith-Rosenberg (New York: Arno Press, 1974), 22; R. N. Trall, *Home Treatment for Sexual Diseases. A Practical Treatise on the Nature and Causes of Excessive and Unnatural Sexual Indulgence, the Diseases and Injuries Resulting therefrom, with Their Symptoms and Hydropathic Management* (New York: Fowlers and Wells, 1853), x, 48. The proliferation of antimasturbation literature is well documented in John D'Emilio and Estelle Freedman, *Intimate Matters: A History of Sexuality in America* (New York: Harper and Row, 1988), 71, and Stephen Nissenbaum, *Sex, Diet, and Debility in Jacksonian America: Sylvester Graham and Health Reform* (Westport, Conn.: Greenwood Press, 1980), 26.

8. David Roediger, *The Wages of Whiteness: Race and the Making of the American Working Class* (New York: Verso, 1991), 86.

9. Euphemisms for masturbation are scattered throughout antimasturbation literature. These examples are from Sylvester Graham, *A Lecture to Young Men* (Providence: Weeden and Cory, 1834), 44, 51; Orson Fowler, *Sexual Science; Including Manhood, Womanhood, and Their Mutual Interrelations; Love, Its Laws, Power, Etc.; Selection, or Mutual Adaptation; Married Life Made Happy; Reproduction, and Progenal Endowment, or Paternity, Maternity, Bearing, Nursing, and Rearing Children; Puberty, Girlhood, Etc.; Sexual Ailments Restored, Female Beauty Perpetuated. etc., etc., as Taught by Phrenology* (Philadelphia: National Publishing Company, 1870), 379, 380; William Sweetser, *Mental Hygiene: Or, An Examination of the Intellect and Passions. Designed to Show How They Affect and Are Affected by the Bodily Functions, and Their Influence on Health and Longevity* (New York: George Putnam, 1850), 386; Samuel Gregory, *Facts and Important Information for Young Women on the Subject of Masturbation: With Its Causes, Prevention, and Cure*, in Rosenberg and Smith-Rosenberg, *The Secret Vice Exposed!*, *Library of Health and Treatment*, 14, 62; Alcott, 2:298, 4:343, 5:316, 5:317, 6:106; Trall, *Home Treatment*, 57.

10. Seth Pancoast, *Onanism, Spermatorrhoea, Porneiokalogynomania-pathology. Boyhood's Perils and Manhood's Curse; an Earnest Appeal to the Young of America* (Philadelphia: n. p. 1858), 151.

11. Alcott, *Library of Health and Treatment*, 4:345–46.

12. Masturbation was thought to induce seminal loss, poor complexion, gonorrhea, inflammation of the optic nerve and blindness, epilepsy, impotence, and dulled intellectual capacity. One homeopathic journal stated that five hundred "disorders" could be "traced to the constant practice of the vice alluded to and its kindred vices."

"Masturbation and Its Effect on Health," *The Graham Journal of Health and Longevity* 2 (1838): 19.

13. William Cornell, *The Beacon: Or, a Warning to Young and Old. In Which Is Shown, in the Medical Practice of the Author, How Body and Mind Are Destroyed by Evil Habits; Resulting in Epilepsy, Consumption, Idiocy and Insanity* (Philadelphia: F. Humphrey & Co., 1865), 59–60.

14. Alcott, *Library of Health and Treatment,* 1:160.

15. Emerson, *The Journals and Miscellaneous Notebooks of Ralph Waldo Emerson,* ed. William H. Gilman et al. (Cambridge: Harvard University Press, 1960) 5:484.

16. Quoted in Alcott, *Library of Health and Treatment,* 6:291.

17. Emerson, *Essays and Lectures* (New York: Library of America, 1983), 266.

18. G. J. Barker-Benfield, *The Horrors of the Half-Known Life: Male Attitudes toward Women and Sexuality in Nineteenth-Century America* (New York: Harper & Row, 1976), 165, 171.

19. S. B. Woodward, *Hints for the Young in Relation to the Health of Body and Mind,* in Rosenberg and Smith-Rosenberg, *The Secret Vice Exposed!,* 64.

20. Alcott, *Library of Health and Treatment,* 6:24, 106.

21. Emerson, "The Fugitive Slave Law," *Emerson's Antislavery Writings,* ed. Len Gougeon and Joel Myerson (New Haven: Yale University Press, 1995), 83.

22. Emerson, *Essays and Lectures,* 263.

23. Graham, *Lecture,* 8, 19.

24 Graham, *Lecture,* 14. Ronald Walters documents the popularity of Graham's ideas among abolitionists. See Walters, "Boundaries of Abolitionism," in *Antislavery Reconsidered: New Perspectives on the Abolitionists,* ed. Lewis Perry and Michael Fellman (Baton Rouge: Louisiana State University Press, 1979), 11.

25. Letter of William Tyler to Edward Tyler, quoted in Thomas Le Duc, "Grahamites and Garrisonites," *New York History* 20 (April 1939): 190.

26. *Letters of Theodore Dwight Weld, Angelina Grimké Weld and Sarah Grimké, 1822–1844,* ed. Gilbert Barnes and Dwight Dumond, 2 vols. (New York: D. Appleton-Century, 1834), 2:868.

27. Graham, *Lecture,* 7-8.

28. Josiah Crosby, "Seminal Weakness—Castration," *Boston Medical and Surgical Journal* (9 August 1843): 10–11.

29. *Boston Medical and Surgical Journal* (6 September 1843): 97.

30. Edward L. Baker, "A few cases illustrative of the ill effects of Onanism," *Southern Medical and Surgical Journal* 2 (June 1846): 337.

31. "Effects of Masturbation," *Boston Medical and Surgical Journal* (11 March 1835): 140.

32. Vern L. Bullough and Bonnie Bullough discuss antimasturbation statutes in *Sexual Attitudes: Myths and Realities* (New York: Prometheus Books, 1995), 73.

33. Ellen White, *An Appeal to Mothers. The Great Cause of the Physical, Mental, and Moral Ruin of Many of the Children of Our Time* (1864; reprint, Payson, Ariz.: Leaves-of-Autumn Books, Inc., 1984), 16.

34. White, *An Appeal to Mothers*, 11.

35. White, *An Appeal to Mothers*, 19.

36. Emerson, *Essays and Lectures*, 261.

37. Emerson, *Essays and Lectures*, 282.

38. Nissenbaum, *Sex, Diet, and Debility*, 164.

39. Gove, *Lectures to Women on Anatomy and Physiology. With an Appendix on Water-Cure* (New York: Harper and Brothers, 1846), 174.

40. Gove, *Lectures to Women*, 174.

41. Gove, *Lectures to Women*, 26.

42. Gove, *Agnes Morris; or, the Heroine of Domestic Life* (New York: Harper and Brothers, 1849), 36. See also Emerson's "Divinity School Address" on "our soul-destroying slavery to habit" (*Essays and Lectures*, 89).

43. Thomas Laqueur, *Making Sex: Body and Gender from the Greeks to Freud* (Cambridge: Harvard University Press, 1991), 61.

44. Graham, *Lecture*, 44.

45. James Cabot, *A Memoir of Ralph Waldo Emerson*, 2 vols. (Boston: Houghton Mifflin and Co., 1887), 2:427.

46. Emerson, *Antislavery*, 17. On sexualization of the slaveholding South, see Ronald Walters, "The Erotic South: Civilization and Sexuality in American Abolitionism," *American Quarterly* 25 (May 1973): 177–201.

47. Emerson, *Early Lectures*, 2:176.

48. Graham, *Letter to the Hon. Daniel Webster, on the Compromises of the Constitution* (Northhampton, Mass.: Hopkins, Bridgeman & Co., 1850), 18.

49. Graham, *Letter*, 3.

50. Graham, *Letter*, 14.

51. Graham, *Letter*, 13.

52. Graham, *Lecture*, 40, 19.

53. Graham, *Lecture*, 16.

54. Graham, *Letter*, 8.

55. Graham, *Letter*, 8.

56. Graham, *Letter*, 3.

57. Graham, *Letter*, 8.

The Other Woman's Sphere

Nuns, Prostitutes, and the Medicalization of Middle-Class Domesticity

∾

Tracy Fessenden

The difference between the Puritan woman and her antebellum counterpart, according to *The Scarlet Letter*, is the latter's surer sense of the "impropriety" attaching to her appearance in the public sphere. "The [Puritan] age had not so much refinement, that any sense of impropriety restrained the wearers of petticoat and farthingale from stepping forth into the public ways, and wedging their not insubstantial persons, if occasion were, into the throng [of public life] . . . Morally, as well as materially, there was a coarser fiber in those wives and maidens of old English force and breeding, than in their fair descendants, separated from them by a series of six or seven generations; for, throughout that chain of ancestry, every successive mother has transmitted to her child a fainter bloom, a more delicate and briefer beauty, and a slighter physical frame, if not a character of less force and solidity than her own.[1]

In this setting, the "more lady-like"[2] Hester Prynne, who accepts her own enclosure, would seem to be an evolutionary prodigy, a prototype of the Protestant "true woman" of Hawthorne's own time. Hester's difference from the Puritan women who are her contemporaries is signaled most vibrantly in the novel, however, by her resemblance to two figures who appear to stand well outside of the nineteenth-century Protestant woman's sphere[3]: the prostitute and the nun. Alternately embodying the "brazen hussy" and the "image of Divine Maternity," the "scarlet woman" and the "Sister of Mercy," only Hester among the novel's women is "inclos[ed] . . . in a sphere by herself" and only she discerns the "new truth" that will "establish the whole relation of man and woman on a surer ground." One consequence of that coming revelation, the opening scene in the marketplace implies, will be a more stable gendering of the public and private spaces whose boundaries the coarse and "manlike" Puritan wives enter this novel by overstepping.4

The nun-as-prostitute figure is ubiquitous in Western cultures: In one or another incarnation she inhabits medieval hagiography; the works of Boccacio, Chaucer, Erasmus, Shakespeare, Rabelais, and Diderot; eighteenth-century tracts on No-Popery; Victorian pornography; and contemporary camp. *The Scarlet Letter*'s positioning of the nun-as-prostitute in relation to the nineteenth-century ideology of woman's sphere, however, lends some specific historical salience to this clichéd image. Within the discourses of antebellum Protestantism, the nun-as-whore figures most centrally in the bestselling genre of the convent exposé, most famously the 1836 *Awful Disclosures* of Maria Monk, a self-styled "escaped nun" whose unmasking as a prostitute did not render her story of Catholic depravities less believable to her Protestant supporters. The whore clothed in sanctity also animates sensationalist and hortatory literature on prostitution, as well as writings that, if not explicitly focused on women, give misogynist voice to anti-Catholicism's veil-rending impulse, its desire, in the words of one anti-Catholic writer, to "divest . . . the system that claims to be infallible of some of its more repulsive attire."5 As Jenny Franchot suggests in *Roads to Rome: The Antebellum Protestant Encounter with Catholicism*, the Protestant crusade to expose Catholic forms of life to democratic scrutiny, driven in part by anxieties over changing sex roles and family structures, could be seen as the desire "to expose the Whore of Babylon at the heart of Mother Church."6

As sites for probing the boundaries of private and public spaces, behaviors, and roles, the figures of nun and prostitute both vex and bolster nineteenth-century constructions of legitimate femininity as domestic, maternal, pious, and separate from the workings of the market. The emergence of this discourse of woman's proper sphere marks a reversal in Anglo-American representations of women's sexuality since the seventeenth century: Where Puritan theology typically attributed greater carnality to women than to men, nineteenth-century domestic ideology defined the middle-class Protestant woman by an ennobling absence of sexual feeling. However, as Nancy Cott has argued, the view of women as *more* sexual than men persisted into the nineteenth century, "to be wielded against women manifesting any form of deviance [including, I would add, forms of "deviance" ascribed to racial, class, and other differences] under the reign of passionlessness."7 In conjunction with a transformation that required the sexuality of middle-class Protestant women to be, in effect, *veiled*, nineteenth-century escaped nun's tales and Magdalen narratives, I suggest, emerge as sites for the repositioning—and strategic retrieval—of this abandoned strain of discourse on female sexual "excess."

The Other Woman's Sphere

The arrival of more than three million Catholic immigrants in the middle decades of the nineteenth century reconfigured urban spaces and magnified existing tensions among races, classes, and regions. Skilled craftspeople viewed the immigrants as fodder for industrialists, while factory owners saw them as shiftless and unprofitable. Immigrants threatened industrial and domestic laborers by accepting even the lowest-paying jobs, which until then only free black men and women had been called on to fill. To slave owners, Catholic immigrants were instinctive abolitionists who were unwilling to compete with slave labor; Protestant abolitionists who saw Catholicism as inherently despotic, meanwhile, considered them natural allies of the slave power. The seemingly monolithic structure of Catholicism cast the splintering of Protestant congregations and the arrival of new religious bodies into relief, while Catholicism's celibate vocations appeared to threaten both the family and the workplace as bulwarks of Protestant power.[8] Set against this backdrop, the creation and maintenance of a Protestant woman's sphere in the nineteenth century emerges as part of the larger project of asserting a unified Protestant America in the face of social fragmentation along multiple axes, and then of managing that fragmentation by processing difference through a binary logic of gender.

In reading images of nuns and prostitutes in relation to the ideology of the Protestant woman's sphere, I follow a strand taken up by a number of theorists of Protestant-Catholic encounters in nineteenth-century America: the pervasive cultural representation of Catholicism as feminine, and the attendant imputation, by its detractors, of licentiousness.[9] These characterizations of the Catholic/whore overflow into other genres, not overtly religious in orientation, and they appear to have appealed differently to Protestant women and Protestant men. Middle-class Protestant women, I suggest, negotiated divided allegiances in relation to these discourses, which threatened to undercut the privilege of their identification with Protestantism by associating their femaleness with the destabilizing otherness of Rome. Although Susan Griffin argues that wayward nuns' stories point out "the fundamental weakness of the female self on which the future of American Protestantism rests,"[10] I contend that what these narratives are able to say about "the female self" or about women in general, and the degree to which they are able to homogenize Protestant and Catholic (and other) women, are bound up with their work of distinguishing Protestant and Catholic spaces, subjectivities, and histories— work that often depended on the gendering of Catholicism as female. Protestant women, I suggest, both resisted this homogenization of "woman" and put it to work to serve their own interests.

Behind the Veil

Juxtaposed or hybrid images of nuns and prostitutes appear not only in sala- cious tales of convent escape but also in the more sober attempts of nineteenth-century Protestant women to test the bonds of sisterhood within and across ethnic, class, and religious lines; they figure as well in Protestant and rapidly secularizing discourses of female sexuality. As (at least rhetori- cally) veiled women, the nun and the prostitute typically signal feminized forms of instability, hiddenness, or deception. The veil's submergence of reli- gious, racial, and other distinctions among women, I suggest, served the interests of a similarly uninflected patriarchy, even as it offered Protestant women an imaginative respite from "sincerity" and an occasion for inhabit- ing alternative female identities in potentially subversive ways.[11]

In what I will risk calling a female discourse of gender, middle-class Protestant women's strategic and partial identification with nuns and prosti- tutes enlarges their own "sphere" and, ultimately, their power over women whose religious, ethnic, and class identifications differ from their own. At the same time, what I read as a predominantly male discourse of sex deploys the figures of nun and prostitute to biologize the woman's sphere and so render all women, whatever their claims to social privilege, sexual agency, or spiri- tual autonomy, captives of their female embodiment. By "female discourse of gender" I mean to refer to the strategies of nineteenth-century women who, operating within frameworks of racial, class, and religious privilege, attempted to define "woman" in such a way as to reject biological essentializ- ing, as a means of taking control of their circulation under the broader social conditions of patriarchy. By "male discourse of sex," I refer to the efforts of nineteenth-century men, also operating within frameworks of privilege, to ascribe less politically flexible meanings to femininity as a way to enforce the superiority of a denotatively WASP masculinity, a cultural formation that benefited even the men it excluded on the grounds of race, class, or religion, who by virtue of their maleness could partially share in its privileges, at least within their respective groups.

I am suggesting not that these discourses are strictly divisible along gender lines, but rather that their shared thematics could be put to work by men and women for different purposes.[12] The construction of the middle-class Protestant woman as "passionless," for example, could further women's interest in controlling their fertility even as it reassured men that sexual dominance in marriage was not beyond their power, nor gratification outside of marriage beyond their entitlement. Similarly, the stock image of the nun who drowns or strangles her illegitimate infant—and who might be said at that point to have lost whatever innocence still clings to her conventional depiction as a faithful virgin seduced into taking the veil—plausibly conveyed the radical ambivalence, for middle-class families, of the possibility of reproductive choice. To women terrified of pregnancy, the shocking image of the infanticidal nun could register the moral enormity of the difference between consciously avoiding multiple pregnancies and submitting to their dangers; to others threatened by reproductive freedoms, the same image could pit emancipated women in murderous opposition to the Protestant family as the final bulwark against the corrosive powers of democracy and demographic change.

In either case, the association of the infanticidal nun's power with the Protestant woman proceeds as an instance of what Stephen Greenblatt calls "metaphorical acquisition," a "teasing out [of] latent homologies, similitudes, and systems of likeness" that "depends . . . upon a deliberate distancing or distortion that precedes the disclosure of likeness."[13] Lodging power over motherhood in the brothel-cloistered nun both contained that power and enabled its meanings to be elaborated in ways that Protestant commentators might otherwise have been reluctant to pursue. For Protestant women, in particular, to go behind the veil by speculating on the hidden lives of nuns or prostitutes was also potentially to voice criticisms of institutions that were normally protected from scrutiny, as white male sexual freedom, in Lydia Maria Child's view, was "veil[ed]" by gallantry, or the tensions within middle-class marriages shielded by the "thinnest possible crust of appearances."[14]

The figures of prostitute and nun were ripe for investment with nineteenth-century Protestant anxieties because of their shared liminality within

American social space. From the arrival in America of the first order of Ursuline nuns in the eighteenth century, the relationship of nuns to American public culture was regulated by complex rules of enclosure. Different orders and classes of nuns were defined by the degree of mobility allowed by their vows (simple or solemn) and by the cloistral regulations of their communities. These regulations, objects of intense fascination for Protestant observers, effectively distinguished the nun from other female identities in nineteenth-century America.[15]

The category of prostitute, in contrast, was remarkably labile. A New York statute classified prostitution together with fortune-telling and juggling as forms of disorderly conduct; under that law, any woman walking alone in the street at night could be arrested for prostitution. In occupied New Orleans during the Civil War, a notorious order by General Benjamin Butler declared that any woman who insulted a Union officer "shall be regarded and held liable to be treated as a woman of the town, plying her vocation." Other states' laws charged with "open and gross lewdness" both women who had sex for money and women who had sex outside of marriage. "Self-prostitution" was a common code word for masturbation. Nineteenth-century women and girls deemed guilty of prostitution, under these and other definitions, were among the first to be classified within the nascent discourses of mental illness as "moral imbeciles" or as "feeble-minded," a designation that a Massachusetts school for the retarded used to describe intellectually capable girls who displayed inordinate sexual passion.[16]

If a nun was a woman whose seclusion prompted Protestant demands that convents be opened to public scrutiny,[17] a prostitute was a woman whose too-public behavior called for enclosure, in the form of vice districts, Magdalen asylums, medical quarantine, homes for the retarded, or restraining devices to prevent masturbation. As figures of (differently) precarious containment, I suggest, nuns and prostitutes permitted the articulation by white middle-class men and women of the pressures of a rapidly expanding democracy, providing gendered rhetorical occasions for the imaginative capture, control, and manipulation of social change.

Secrets of the Convent Revealed

The voyeuristic interest of the Protestant convent narrative is evidenced in such revelatory nineteenth-century titles as *Secrets of Nunneries Disclosed, The Veil Lifted, Convent Life Exposed,* and the notorious *Awful Disclosures.* Such narratives typically proceed as tales of seduction (often initiated in the confessional) of a girl by a lecherous priest. Her purity lost, her spiritual vibrancy quenched by deadening ritual, subject to repeated rape and humiliation by the priest(s) whose power over her is absolute, the young woman will give birth to one or more children, preside grimly over their deaths, and, barring her escape and succor by the Protestant Church, live out her days in morbid confinement, mourning the youth she naively dedicated to God. George Bourne sets the scene in *Lorette, or the History of Louise, Daughter of a Canadian Nun, Exhibiting the Interior of Female Convents*: "The interior of a convent is the *sepulchre of goodness*, and the *castle of misery*. Within its unsanctified domain, youth withers; knowledge is extinguished; usefulness is entombed; and religion expires. The life of a Nun is a course of exterior solemn mummery, from which all that is lovely is ejected; and under the vizor dwells everything loathsome and horrible. . . . [T]he chief solicitudes and contrivances consist in their efforts to conceal from the world at large, the secrets which appertain to the dreadful prison."[18]

Often these stories reproduce while repudiating the convent's promise of a seductive counter-domesticity to Protestant women: Only a "Romanizer," says the Protestant author of *Constance Kent and the Confessional*, would fail to guard his daughters from the snares of a "bastard convent," "so softly, so lovingly termed 'a Home.'"[19] Depictions of these Catholic "homes" encoded an issue of immediate concern to white, middle-class Protestants: the stability of marriage and the family as the guarantor of Protestant dominance. According to Lyman Beecher's *A Plea for the West*, for example, the sexual norms of Catholic religious orders were threatening because, on the one hand, they constituted a plot to outpopulate Protestants through seduction and reproduction ("protestant children, with unceasing assiduity, are gathered into Catholic schools . . . so that every family in process of time becomes six"); on the other, they made it impossible to assimilate a celibate clergy within the American political family ("Were they allied to us by family and ties of blood, like the ministry of all other denominations, there would be less to be feared.")[20]

As a displaced story of domestic disappointment, moreover, the captive nun's tale also potentially enabled a minimally relieved assessment (or merely a cathartic rehearsal) of the situation of middle-class Protestant women, whose own desires for spiritually regenerative homes—as suggested by the fictions of Susan Warner, Caroline Lee Hentz, and others—were likewise routinely thwarted by endless chores, dying children, abusive husbands, and nowhere to go. Franchot suggests that for Protestant readers, the carceral drama of the prostituted nun "refashioned the seclusion of women within the domestic sphere as liberty, their subordination to patriarchal authority as voluntary, [and] their sexual repression as 'purity.'"[21] Nevertheless, the story of female purity and spiritual power sacrificed to lecherous men and stultifying institutions was also the Protestant woman's story; the "nun" at the center of these narratives of confinement is revealed to be, in reality, the white slave.

The lives of nuns fascinated nineteenth-century Protestants not only in their imagined privations, however, but also in their improbable freedoms. Elizabeth and Emily Blackwell, the first women medical doctors in America, observed that while "it is common to speak of nuns renouncing the world, the fact is, that members of these sisterhoods have a far more active participation in the interests of life than most of them had before."[22] Protestant leaders of the common school movement spoke with a mixture of envy and disparagement of parochial schools, implying that nuns' achievements as teachers were neither furtive nor negligible. In the antebellum South, nuns openly violated laws against teaching slaves. American nuns also violated the constitutions of their communities by "disguising" themselves in secular dress when the habit and veil, regarded by some Protestants as "meretricious garbs [worn] expressly to ensnare and seduce our citizens," would expose them to verbal and physical abuse.[23] Some American nuns formed uncloistered communities based on the constitutions of St. Vincent de Paul, which provided them with "no cell but a hired room, no cloister but the streets of the city or the wards of hospitals, no enclosure but obedience, no grate but the fear of God, no veil but holy modesty."[24] Because their communities were self-supporting, American nuns not only ran schools and hospitals, occupying positions of power that remained unavailable to secular women, but also worked alongside laboring women and men in factories and as farmhands, all the while escaping the private appropriation of their labor by marriage.

Even where Catholicism was imagined in tyrannical opposition to women's freedoms, the visibility of nuns as capable negotiators of masculine authority within their own traditions cast them as Arminian reformers of an enslaving system. Their entrance into the public sphere also implied a voluntary relationship to the enclosures of convent and veil, freeing these images for use in Protestant women's discourse to signify elective spaces of safety, creative flourishing, and homosocial love. Harriet Beecher Stowe cheerfully nicknamed the parlor of her home "the Presbyterian Nunnery."[25] Elizabeth Blackwell spoke of "becom[ing] a physician, and thus plac[ing] a strong barrier between [herself] and all ordinary marriage," as "tak[ing] the veil."[26] Catharine Beecher, who routinely compared herself to a mother superior or abbess, referred to Protestant single women teachers as "Sisters of Mercy" and based her expanded conception of "motherhood"—which extended even the single woman's influence from home and family to school, hospital, and nation—on the model of convents and their concentric networks of activity and support.[27]

Neither antebellum Protestant women reformers nor their historians, however, have generally been eager to acknowledge Catholic influence on the "feminization" of American religion, on the sororal model of Protestant women's friendship and political alliance, or on the extension of educational opportunities for girls. By about 1820, conversion to Catholicism typically meant trading the privileges of unmarked religious and ethnic identity and implicit commitment to middle-class values for membership in a rapidly expanding, largely immigrant and working-class "minority" population that was increasingly figured as a threat to American institutions.[28] Women unwilling to ally themselves (through conversion or less drastic forms of affiliation) with the enemies of Protestant power typically acknowledged, then distanced themselves from, the Catholic sisters whose salutary example was compromised by their dangerous otherness. Sarah Josepha Hale, editor of the *American Ladies Magazine*, decried the 1834 Ursuline convent burning at Charlestown, Massachusetts, as an "outrage" that "every female heart" must condemn, but her praise for the Charlestown nuns as "models to all instructresses" in that editorial was followed two months later by an editorial on "How to Prevent the Increase of Convents."[29] Catharine Beecher urged Protestant institutions to "employ the piety, education and wealth of American females that is now all but wasted for want of such resources as the Catholic church supplies," if only to protect Protestant women from the alternative of conversion to "a false and slavish faith."[30] At a time when nuns provided the bulk of trained nurses in the Civil War and won public praise from Florence Nightingale, Abraham Lincoln, and Ulysses S. Grant, Catharine Maria Sedgwick invoked a stock image from convent intrigues to elevate the work of single Protestant nurses: "What a different consecration from that of nuns! . . . Surely more acceptable to God is the tending and solacing of sick soldiers than protracted prayers kneeling upon stone floors."[31]

Other Protestant women damned nuns with faint praise. In Harriet Beecher Stowe's 1875 novel *We and Our Neighbors*, "inquisitions" by a Protestant ladies' "Committee of Supervision," "even to the private sleeping apartments" of nuns, force the Sisters of St. Barnabus, an urban order who run a prostitutes' shelter, to abandon their convent for a tenement "not a bit more conventual or medieval than the most commonplace of New York houses." Apparently modeling the nuns' removal on the Charlestown convent riot that Lyman Beecher's anti-Catholic sermons had helped to instigate four decades earlier, Stowe pokes fun at Protestant vigilance by making light of Catholic suffering. Rendered "commonplace" by invasive Protestant assaults, the "sweet," "motherly" nuns are negligible objects of reform, and the novel turns from their harmless "little points of Ritualism" to more dangerous forms of "paganism," namely the sale of liquor. Before leaving the nuns, however, *We and Our Neighbors* installs one of their charges, an Irish prostitute named Maggie, in the home of Protestant Eva, who worries that the sisters' devotion to the poor answers the call of Christ better than her own to her home, "a little paradise of ease and forgetfulness." Resolving to "make [her] home sacred by bringing into it this work of charity," Eva allows Maggie, who had in fact been horribly "bored" by the nuns' chilly piety, to follow her around the house with a "sort of wondering, passionate admiration," picking up the household skills that qualify her for entrance, as Eva's maid, into a rather more narrowly circumscribed version of the Protestant woman's sphere.[32]

Maggie's response to the nuns' efforts on her behalf—she finds them "chilling, "wearing," "dreary"—exactly reproduces the novel's description of her life on the street, reinforcing the sense that the rescue of women from prostitution and the rescue of the former prostitute from the convent in which she has found refuge are parallel missions. A similar dynamic informs Elizabeth Stuart Phelps's 1870 novel of prostitution, *Hedged In*. The novel says little about its protagonist Nixy's stay in a prostitutes' shelter except that she was brought there by a veiled figure and was decently cared for and educated; inexplicably, she runs away and lives in fear of being taken to another "Magdalen 'sylum." Her stay there belongs to a period of her life prior to her rescue under Protestant auspices, a time marked by her involvement with drunks, young mothers who murder their babies, and tambourine players with Italian names. Her rescue installs her, like Stowe's Maggie, in a Protestant home as a servant.

We and Our Neighbors ascribes to the nuns the sterile holiness of the "immaculate Pharisee" whom, the narrator recalls, Jesus pairs with "a fallen woman in one sentence as two debtors, both owing a sum to a creditor, both having nothing to pay,—both freely forgiven by infinite clemency."[33] With less vaunted largesse, "The Strange Woman," one of Henry Ward Beecher's 1844 *Lectures to Young Men*, links the house of prostitution and the "Pharisee's sepulchre" of false modesty: both "clean white, beautiful without, full of dead men's bones within!" Not an explicitly anti-Catholic text, "The Strange Woman" shows how easily the imagery of convent and brothel may be made to cohabit. Entering the strange woman's "house of death" through luxurious gardens concealing labyrinthine chambers, Beecher's Protestant gaze discovers recessed wards of deepening depravity, culminating in the inquisitorial tortures of venereal disease: "the wheel, the rack; the bed of knives, the roasting fire, the brazen room slowly heated, the slivers driven under the nails, the hot pincers,—what are these to the agonies of the last days of licentious vice?"[34]

More Awful Disclosures

Beecher's reformer's interest in hidden female spaces is repeated in the titles of nineteenth-century brothel exposés such as *Female Depravity, or the House of Death*; *The House of Bondage*; *Madam Restell* [a procurer of prostitutes and a rumored abortionist], *An Account of Her Life and Horrible Practices*; *New York Naked*; and *New York in Pieces, by an Experienced Carver*. After midcentury, the urban literature of prostitution increasingly inhabits the structures of the anti-Catholic convent exposé to portray prostitution as a foreign conspiracy involving "French traders," "Jew traders," "Polish Jewesses," and "Italians masquerading under Irish names" who scour American towns for innocent girls to seduce, corrupt, and enslave.[35] In advice books for city-bound young men of the "Arthur in Babylon" genre, the *whore* of Babylon remains the greatest danger to Protestant manhood. Just as convent exposés often depicted nuns as wily seducers, so this literature portrayed the prostitute as "initiat[ing] more young men into these destructive ways, than the most abandoned rakes have debauched virgins during their whole lives."[36] Like the convent exposé as well, however, this depiction was compatible with a view of fallen women as innocent victims beguiled by false promises of luxury, safety, and eternal love.

For middle-class Protestant women the Magdalen's story, like the nun's, offered a displaced critique of Protestant gender norms; as Ruth Rosen suggests, "prostitution came to symbolize the injustices suffered by all women as a result of the sexual double standard."[37] The charter of the Boston Female Moral Reform Society, for example, announced its commitment "to guard our daughters, sisters, and female acquaintances from the delusive arts of corrupt and unprincipled men."[38] In a rejoinder to John R. McDowell's salacious *Magdalen Facts*, the New York Ladies Reform Society affirmed that "no woman ever voluntarily surrendered the blessings of a fair name. The sensitive plant shrinks not more instinctively from the touch, than the nature of woman from defilement."[39]

The view of prostitutes as victims of "unprincipled men," however, veiled the scandal of pleasure and sexual autonomy that the prostitute might also be imagined to represent. More than eight hundred of the two thousand prostitutes who responded to the physician William Sanger's well-publicized 1858 survey explained that they had chosen this life for its freedoms, including, most prominently, the freedom "to gratify the sexual passions."[40] Coverage of the 1835 murder of the New York prostitute Helen Jewett, and the cultural productions it inspired for decades after, portrayed the victim as worldly, surrounded by luxuries, and beloved by close female friends.[41] Protestant middle-class women who organized themselves in their own "Magdalen Societies" may have sought in the objects of their attentions a share in the prostitute's sexual, social, and financial autonomy, real or imagined, that remained unavailable within the ideology of woman's sphere.

Like the industrialization of female sexuality in prostitution, the work of female moral reform societies made visible the uneven distribution of power between men and women and between classes.[42] Speaking in many cases to men whose licentious attitudes they sought to change, women reformers typically treated women in ways that accorded with the logic of men like McDowell or Henry Ward Beecher, who argued that while men may become corrupted, it was women who needed redemption. The Philadelphia Magdalen Society, for example, sought through prayer and domestic training to "be instrumental in recovering to honest rank in life those unhappy females who, in an unguarded hour, have been robbed of their innocence, and sunk into wretchedness and guilt."[43] The Boston Female Moral Reform Society sought to "elevate woman to her proper standing in society without moving her from her 'appropriate sphere,'"[44] but the solutions it and like groups proposed usually reflected their notions not of *woman*'s proper sphere but of the behaviors and freedoms they considered appropriate to the specific population of women targeted for reform. Women served by institutions like the Philadelphia Magdalen Asylum, the New York Houses of Refuge for Women, or the Lancaster Industrial School for Girls were trained to acquire the demeanor and skills that suited them for placement in middle-class Protestant homes as servants, leaving Protestant women free to pursue versions of motherhood and Christian regeneration that could increasingly spill over into extra-domestic spaces.[45]

The Protestant woman's strategic identification with the nun or prostitute to expand her own freedoms, then, depended finally on her ability to differentiate herself from these surrogate captives. In parallel male discourses, however, the worlds of the nun and the prostitute could be annexed to the domestic sphere not to enlarge on its liberties but to intensify its demands. Edward Beecher's *Papal Conspiracy Exposed*, for example, points to the coming "marriage supper of the Lord," when "the nations [shall] know the difference between the harlot of Rome in her meretricious purple and scarlet attire, and the bride, the Lamb's wife, in her fine linen, clean and white, in which she shall be publicly owned and acknowledged by her royal and divine Head." This image combines the Book of Revelation's defeat of the Whore of Babylon with Paul's injunctions to women to be submissive to husbands (1 Cor. 11:3). Beecher would have known that the marriage supper of Christ and his bride was symbolically enacted by Catholic novitiates in ceremonies to which Protestants were often invited; his pitting of harlot against virgin bride allies the Protestant wife with the nun even as it dismisses nuns as "deluded and hopeless victims" and convents as their "prisons."[46]

In liberal reformer Thomas Wentworth Higginson's *Women and Men*, young women "bred in convents" are made the special exemplars of the "shy graces" and "charming sweetness" that signal the "humble and subordinate condition" of women as a class. Higginson asserted that the "source and spring of humility" that naturally "lies deeper" in woman is in fact a particularly "Anglo-Saxon" or "Anglo-American" trait, since the convent-bred French or Italian girl, in contrast to her Protestant counterpart, is likely to become "the artful wife or the intriguing old woman." Lending his support to women's emancipation, Higginson assured his readers that the "more public station" for which the American woman is "destined" need not "mar" her more genuinely nunlike docility and charm.[47]

A later text, written at the height of the white slavery scare, depicts not the nun but the prostitute as Protestantism's "true woman": How much "better" for society, reasoned the author of *The Underworld and Its Women*, "if the Magdalen could be persuaded to become a Madonna and the Madonna, for a time be reasoned out of her frantic motherliness into cultivation of some of the charms of the Magdalen, in order to enamor her husband into love of herself as woman pure and simple. . . . We are dinging the doctrine of home and

motherhood into the ears of our women so continually that they forget they
... as women have a reason to fascinate and charm."[48]

Hedged In

In these examples, both "passionlessness" and "deviance," to invoke Nancy
Cott's terms, are flexibly wielded by male writers against white, middle-
class, Protestant women either to fortify the boundaries of their "sphere" or
to set the course and limits of their emancipation in ways that maintain
their ultimate subjection to white, middle-class, Protestant men. This strategic flexibility becomes especially apparent in discourses that take female
sexuality as their explicit theme. The Bible verse routinely affixed to convent
escape narratives and other anti-Catholic tracts—"Come out of her my people, that ye be not partakers of her sins, and that ye receive not of her
plagues" (Rev. 18:4)—identifies the Catholic "woman" with her sin- and
disease-saturated interiors and with the spaces of her assigned activity. So
too Henry Ward Beecher's encircling wards of pleasure, disease, and death,
whose walls "ooz[e] . . . blood" and whose "stench repels," collapse the
strange woman's house into a malignant image of her womb.[49] The habitual superimpositions of female spaces in these genres reappear in
medicalized discourses that define women by the mysterious interlocking
interiors that connect their bodies, subjectivities, and allotted sphere.

Nineteenth-century gynecology was not unmindful either of nuns or prostitutes, since it was materially enabled, in part, by the prostitutes who
supplied surgeons with cadavers and indigent bodies and the nuns who did
the administrative and nursing work that allowed research to proceed.[50] The
actual presence of these women in hospital wards was often noted. The imaginative presence of horrific, stock narratives about them is audible in an 1855
treatise's warning to readers that "startling and fearful as may be the sight of
streams of blood and clotted gore in various scenes, there are none found
more appalling than in the obstetric chamber."[51]

The pain and violation of actual women enacted (and routinely acknowledged) in the production of these discourses is strangely elided, however, in
the figure of the passionless, spiritual "woman" they yield.[52] With occasional
atmospheric nods to blood-splattered walls and the screams of drugged
women, nineteenth-century obstetric and gynecological discourses by men
defined woman as the pliant captive of her inner spaces. Woman's distinctive
bodily processes, in these representations, make her "mentally, socially, spir-

itually . . . more interior than man"; her mind, by analogy to the "conservative" ovum, is a secure "storehouse filled with instincts, habits, and laws of conduct" that permits by anchoring the roving mobility of the "male mind . . . extending experience over new fields." "A vile lump of animal texture in the inner court of the temple of the body," her uterus is at the same time "the ark that contains the law" of human regeneration and sets "the genus man . . . as it were, in a magic circle, out of whose charmed round it can never stray." Even as "the influence of the ovaries over the mind" conveys her characteristic powers of "artfulness and dissimulation," she remains intuitively aware that she is "still in a manner in bonds" and that "her best rewards for the pains, hazards, and toils of existence are to be found within the narrow circle of her domestic reign."[53]

Typically practicing on prostitutes, indigents, or slave women,[54] gynecological researchers produced a biologized version of woman's sphere that bound the middle-class Protestant woman in enclosures no longer specific to her, since she shared the fact of her anatomy with the drugged, purchased, or dead women who yielded its secrets. At the same time, nineteenth-century medical constructions of femininity remained compatible with a version of woman's sphere that figured the brothel and the convent not as extensions of itself but as its ruinous alternatives. One physician remarked on the trajectory of (dangerously) "independent women": "innocent now, very soon they become kept mistresses, and their descent is afterwards rapid to the conditions of the common courtezan, the street sweeper, the inmate of the hospital, the subject of the dissecting room."[55] Announcing its findings that prostitutes were likely to have worked as factory hands, sales girls, or servants in other women's homes, an 1895 research notice in the *American Medico-Surgery Bulletin* concluded that "public occupations [for women] are dangerous. A woman who works outside the home commits a biological crime against herself and her community."[56] Turning to the conventlike spaces of schoolgirl dormitories and other sororal networks, an 1899 paper on the "Gynecological Consideration for the Sexual Act" charged that women thus segregated by their sex "kiss each other fondly on every occasion," "embrace one another with mutual satisfaction," and "in the course of their fondling" discover and commit certain "cunni-linguistic practices" which leave "the normal sex act" unable "to satisfy" them thereafter.[57]

Unlike the brothel or the convent, then, the biologized woman's sphere admitted no avenue of escape, no outside to the "magic circle" of female reproductivity, whether active, potential, squandered, or perversely defied.

Biologized discourses of woman's sphere, moreover, not only veiled racial, religious, economic, and other differences between women, but also threw the mantle of inevitability over this resolution by allowing the normalization of specifically religious arguments about sexuality to pass for their increasingly welcome disappearance. Even when his experimental subjects were black slaves or Irish prostitutes, the nineteenth-century gynecological researcher typically devoted his labors to the cause of white motherhood and the triumph of a white Protestant population over its nonwhite and immigrant rivals.[58] To the degree that these efforts on behalf of a race-, religion-, and class-specific population required the homogenization of "woman," they extended the ideology of "woman's sphere" to allow nineteenth-century Americans to experience a society increasingly divided by racial, religious, class, and other differences without being conscious of the divisions as anything but "natural"—that is, gendered.

The intricately constructed discourse of woman's sphere, I have suggested, enabled white middle-class Protestant women to extend their power over other women while allowing men to maintain their dominance over women as a class. It allowed Protestant men and women to protect their interests, insofar as they were shared, and to frame the issues that divided them in ways that did not dislodge the hegemony of the white Protestant middle class over other religious, racial, and class formations. This process did not go uncontested, however, and I have no desire to second its vaunted inevitability. Had the nineteenth-century Protestant discourse on sexuality, the family, and the home been effectively naturalized as science, it presumably would not need to be so routinely revived as political speech. That alternative meanings for these terms have managed to flourish at the margins of the normal is thanks in part to the Protestant middle-class women who contended meaningfully with their own divided loyalties in relation to the dominant discourse's other woman. But credit must also go to the renegade nuns, incorrigibly wayward girls, and other women and men who resisted the Protestant reformation of our sex/gender system, even as they fell increasingly under its surveillance.

Notes

I wish to thank Carolyn Allen, John Corrigan, Thomas J. Ferraro, Jenny Franchot, Judith A. Howard, Kathleen Joyce, and Rosemarie Garland Thomson for their encouragement and editorial suggestions.

1. Nathaniel Hawthorne, *The Scarlet Letter*, ed. Ross C. Murfin (Boston: Bedford Books, 1991), 55.

2. Hawthorne, *The Scarlet Letter*, 57.

3. I am aware of the argument from many quarters that there has been no theologically, racially, economically, and politically homogenous culture named American Protestantism at any point in our history, and therefore that the designation of "woman's sphere" as a Protestant construction is imprecise. At the same time, it is clear from their own self-identification as "Protestant" or "Christian" that Presbyterian, Methodist, Congregationalist, and Baptist women, for example, experienced a common religious identity that did not extend to Roman Catholic or non-Christian women. The experiences of women who are empowered or disempowered on the basis of their religious affiliation—whether visible or invisible, whether experienced as chosen, assigned, or innate—are both like and unlike those of women who encounter power in other realms of experience; so too the ways religious difference is inscribed into patriarchy are both like and unlike the ways that racial, class, and sexual differences are so inscribed. But both the similarities and the differences will remain hidden as long as we persist in thinking that religion, unlike race or class or sexuality, remains epiphenomenal in relation to American cultural history or to the experience of gender in wider arenas. The widespread critical unwillingness to engage religion as a category of identity alongside or encoded within race or class also elides the ways that female power, whether represented as belonging to or transcending woman's sphere, has frequently been organized as power *over* (and at the expense of) women whose racial, class, and religious identities set them in ambiguous relation to dominant and implicitly white, middle-class, and Protestant ideologies of womanhood.

4. Hawthorne, *The Scarlet Letter*, 58, 59, 96, 131, 58, 201, 55. In this novel so attuned to the privations of public morality, the "new truth" of the sexes whose "angel and apostle . . . must be a woman . . . lofty, pure, and beautiful" (Hawthorne, 201) would appear to be one in which private and public spheres were less rather than more rigorously segregated. Yet even Hester in her most spectacularly transgressive or ethereal moments seems unable to elude the pressures of archetypal femaleness intricately encoded in nineteenth-century formulations of woman's private sphere. Her characterizations as either prostitute or madonna suggest a frantic shuttling between vigorously imagined alternatives to a conventional femininity that nevertheless continues to close in and assimilate them, leaving the gendered public/private distinction operative in Hawthorne's America intact.

5. Henry Wilkes, preface to *Lorette: Or the History of Louise, Daughter of a Canadian Nun, Exhibiting the Interior of Female Convents*, by George Bourne (Edinburgh: Waugh and Innes, 1836), v.

6. Jenny Franchot, *Roads to Rome: The Antebellum Protestant Encounter with Catholicism* (Berkeley and Los Angeles: University of California Press, 1994), 26.

7. Nancy Cott, "Passionlessness: An Interpretation of Victorian Sexual Ideology, 1790–1850," *Signs: Journal of Women in Culture and Society* 4.2 (1978): 221.

8. On these developments see Ray Billington, *The Protestant Crusade, 1800–1860: A Study in the Origins of American Nativism* (New York: Macmillan, 1938); Thomas T. McAvoy, "The Formation of the Catholic Minority in the United States, 1820–1860," *Review of Politics* 10.1 (1948): 13–34; Eric Lott, *Love and Theft: Blackface Minstrelsy and the American Working Class* (New York: Oxford University Press, 1993); Franchot, *Roads to Rome*; and Noel Ignatiev, *How the Irish Became White* (New York: Routledge, 1995).

9. See Billington, *The Protestant Crusade*; Mary Ewens, *The Role of the Nun in Nineteenth-Century America* (New York: Arno, 1978); and Franchot, *Roads to Rome*. I am particularly influenced by Franchot's argument that "convent exposés . . . intricately voiced Protestant perplexities over the ongoing construction of the 'cult of domesticity'" (120). My thinking about Protestant women's vexed relation to the "whore of Babylon" as an image of female depravity as well as a constellation of sexual, spiritual, and other freedoms is also indebted to Joseph G. Mannard, "Converts in Convents: Protestant Women and the Social Appeal of Catholic Religious Life in Antebellum America," *Records of the American Catholic Historical Society of Philadelphia* 104.1–4 (1993): 79–90; and Deborah Epstein Nord, *Walking the Victorian Streets: Women, Representation, and the City* (Ithaca, N.Y.: Cornell University Press, 1995).

10. Susan Griffin, "Awful Disclosures: Women's Evidence in the Escaped Nun's Tale," *PMLA* 3.1 (1996): 105.

11. The classic study of antebellum Protestantism and the burden of "sincerity" is Karen Halttunen, *Confidence Men and Painted Women: A Study of Middle-Class Culture in America, 1830–1870* (New Haven, Conn.: Yale University Press, 1982).

12. Indeed, it is precisely the slippage between the discourse of "sex" and the discourse of "gender" that makes their terms strategically flexible for those who wield them. The imprecision of any sex/gender distinction may help to account for why (white, Protestant, middle-class) formulations of "woman" pressured even those women they did not describe, why the discourses of "gender" and "sex" I examine construct peripheral women so similarly, and why Protestant women's relation to these constructions of peripheral women are continually vexed by suspicions of too close proximity.

13. Stephen Greenblatt, *Shakespearean Negotiations* (New York: Oxford University Press, 1988), 11.

14. As quoted by Kirk Jeffrey, "Marriage, Career, and Feminine Ideology in Nineteenth-Century America: Reconstructing the Marital Experience of Lydia Maria Child," *Feminist Studies* 2.2–3 (1975): 123.

15. I follow Mary Ewens in using the term "nuns" to include both nuns and sisters. Strictly speaking, nuns are Catholic women who profess "solemn" vows and are cloistered; sisters profess "simple" vows and are less bound by rules of enclosure, although they too may live in convents (Ewens, *The Role of the Nun in Nineteeth-Century America* 333[n5]).

16. The order of General Butler is reprinted in Mary P. Ryan, *Women in Public: Between Banners and Ballots* (Baltimore: Johns Hopkins University Press, 1990), 2.

Statutory definitions of prostitution are also taken from Ryan, 97–102. For sources on female sexuality and mental illness, see Peter L. Tylor, "'Denied the Power to Choose the Good': Sexuality and Mental Defect in American Medical Practice, 1850–1920," *Journal of Social History* 10.4 (1977): 472–89. On the instability of nineteenth-century definitions of prostitution, and the social uses of that instability, see Ruth Rosen, *The Lost Sisterhood: Prostitution in America, 1900–1918* (Baltimore: Johns Hopkins University Press, 1982); Christine Stansell, *City of Women: Sex and Class in New York: 1789–1860* (New York: Knopf, 1986); Timothy Gilfoyle, *City of Eros: New York City, Prostitution, and the Commercialization of Sex, 1790–1920* (New York: W.W. Norton, 1992); Marilyn Wood Hill, *Their Sisters' Keepers: Prostitution in New York City, 1830–1890* (Berkeley and Los Angeles: University of California Press, 1993).

17. See, e.g., Theodore Dwight, *Open Convents: or, Nunneries and Popish Seminaries Dangerous to the Morals, and Degrading to the Character of a Republican Community* (New York: Van Ostrand and Dwight, 1836); Andrew B. Cross, *Young Women in Convents, or Priests' Prisons to Be Protected by Law or the Prisons to Be Broken Up* (Baltimore: Sherwood & Co., 1856).

18. George Bourne, *Lorette, or the History of Louise, Daughter of a Canadian Nun, Exhibiting the Interior of Female Convents* (New York: Wm. A. Mercein, 1834), 124.

19. A Clergyman, *Constance Kent and the Confessional* (London: n.p., 1865), 7.

20. Lyman Beecher, *A Plea for the West* (1835; reprint, New York: Arno, 1977), 117, 135.

21. Franchot, *Roads to Rome*, 120.

22. Elizabeth Blackwell and Emily Blackwell, *Medicine as a Profession for Women* (New York: W. H. Tinson, 1860), 12.

23. *Female Convents: Secrets of Nunneries Disclosed* (New York: Appleton, 1834), 9. On incidents of nuns in habits being verbally and physically abused, see Ewens, 145–61. Such incidents point up the idealism of Hawthorne's depiction of Hester's scarlet letter as having an effect "like the cross on a nun's bosom," enabling her to "walk securely amid all peril" (Hawthorne, 132).

24. Hélène Roderer Bailly de Barberey, *Elizabeth Seton*, trans. Joseph B. Code (New York: Macmillan, 1927), 303.

25. Unsigned note in Harriet Beecher Stowe's hand; as quoted by Joan P. Hedrick, *Harriet Beecher Stowe: A Life* (New York: Oxford University Press, 1994), 85.

26. Elizabeth Blackwell, *Pioneer Work in Opening the Medical Profession to Women* (1895; reprint, New York: Source Book Press, 1970), 28, 32.

27. Katherine Kish Sklar, *Catharine Beecher: A Study in American Domesticity* (New Haven, Conn.: Yale University Press, 1973), 171–72.

28. See Billington, *The Protestant Crusade*, and McAvoy, "The Formation."

29. Sarah Josepha Hale, "The Ursuline Convent," *American Ladies Magazine* 7 (September 1834): 426, 419; "How to Prevent the Increase of Convents," *American Ladies Magazine* 7 (November 1834): 517–521.

30. Quoted in Jeanne Boydston, Mary Kelley, and Anne Margolis, *The Limits of Sisterhood: The Beecher Sisters on Women's Rights and Woman's Sphere* (Chapel Hill: University of North Carolina Press, 1988), 329.

31. Catharine Maria Sedgwick, *Life and Letters*, ed. Mary Dewey (New York: Harper and Bros., 1871), 407–8.

32. Harriet Beecher Stowe, *We and Our Neighbors, or, The Records of an Unfashionable Street* (New York: J. B. Ford and Co., 1875), 222, 225, 221, 440, 244, 245.

33. Stowe, *We and Our Neighbors*, 247.

34. Henry Ward Beecher, *Lectures to Young Men on Various Important Subjects* (1844; reprint, Salem: D. B. Brooks, 1855), 174, 204.

35. Ernest A. Bell, *Fighting the Traffic in Young Girls, or The War on the White Slave Trade* (Chicago: n.p., 1910), 260, 186. The association of prostitution with both religious and national otherness functions would seem to locate the threat of sexual corruption both within (as menacing alien presence) and safely outside the borders of white, Protestant America.

36. *First Annual Report of the Executive Committee of the New York Magdalen Society, Instituted, January 1, 1830* (New York, 1831), 12; as quoted by Keith Melder, "Ladies Bountiful: Organized Women's Benevolence in Early 19th-Century America," *New York History* 48.3 (1967): 244.

37. Rosen, *The Lost Sisterhood*, 8.

38. *Third Annual Report of the Boston Female Moral Reform Society* (1838), 7; as quoted by Melder, "Ladies Bountiful," 245.

39. *Advocate of Moral Reform* 1 (January 1835): 31; as quoted by Robert E. Riegal, "Changing American Attitudes toward Prostitution, 1800–1920," *Journal of the History of Ideas* 29.3 (1968): 441.

40. William W. Sanger, *The History of Prostitution—Its Extent, Causes, and Effects throughout the World* (1858; reprint, New York: The Medical Publishing Company, 1927), 492–93.

41. Patricia Cline Cohen,"The Helen Jewett Murder: Violence, Gender, and Sexual Licentiousness in Antebellum America," *National Women's Studies Association Journal* 2.3 (1990): 374–389. Ruth Rosen observes that the New York Female Benevolent Society "dedicated itself to assisting the 'many sisters in the common tie of humanity, who are fallen,'" and that Lydia Maria Child "emphasized the similarities [between prostitutes and women reformers], each within a 'hair's breadth' of being the other" (Rosen, *The Lost Sisterhood*, 8).

42. I owe this point to Barbara Littlewood and Linda Mahood, "Prostitutes, Magdalenes and Wayward Girls: Dangerous Sexualities of Working Class Women in Victorian Scotland," *Gender & History* 3.2 (1991): 160–75.

43. *The Constitution of the Magdalen Society of Philadelphia* (1909), 3; as quoted by Steven Ruggles, "Fallen Women: The Inmates of the Magdalen Society Asylum of Philadelphia, 1836–1908," *Journal of Social History* 16.4 (1983): 65.

44. *Second Annual Report of the Boston Female Moral Reform Society* (1837), 70; as quoted by Melder, "Ladies Bountiful," 245.

45. On the disciplinary course of fallen womanhood in nineteenth-century America, see, e.g., Barbara M. Brenzel, *Daughters of the State: A Social Portrait of the First Reform School for Girls in North America, 1856–1905* (Cambridge, Mass.: MIT Press, 1983); Ruggles, "Fallen Women," 65–82; Estelle B. Freedman, "Sentiment and Discipline: Women's Prison Experiences in Nineteenth-Century America," *Prologue* 16.4 (1984) 249–59; Mimi Abramovitz, "The Family Ethic: The Female Pauper and Public Aid, Pre-1900," *Social Services Review* 59.1 (1985): 121–35.

46. Edward Beecher, *The Papal Conspiracy Exposed* (1855; reprint, New York: Arno, 1977), 396, 418; on convent initiation ceremonies see Ewens, *The Role of the Nun*, 174–76.

47. Thomas Wentworth Higginson, *Women and Men* (New York: Harper and Brothers, 1888), 306, 309, 307, 310.

48. Paul Karishka, *The Underworld and Its Women* (New York: Roger Brothers Publishing, 1910), 13.

49. Henry Ward Beecher, *Lectures to Young Men*, 207, 203.

50. On nuns as caregivers and prostitutes as experimental subjects in nineteenth-century American hospital wards see G. J. Barker-Benfield, *The Horrors of the Half-Known Life: Male Attitudes toward Women and Sexuality in Nineteenth-Century America* (New York: Harper & Row, 1976); Vern L. Bullough and Bonnie Bullough, *The Care of the Sick: The Emergence of Modern Nursing* (New York: Prodist, 1978); Janet L. Bryant and Kathleen Byrne Colling, "Broken Wills and Tender Hearts: Religious Ideology and the Trained Nurse of the Nineteenth Century," in *Florence Nightingale and Her Era: A Collection of New Scholarship*, ed. Vern L Bullough, Bonnie Bullough, and Marietta P. Stanton (New York: Garland, 1990), 153–67; Jean Richardson, "Sisterhood Is Powerful: Sister-Nurses Confront the Modernization of Nursing," in Bullough, Bullough, and Stanton, *Florence Nightingale*, 261–73.

51. Augustus Kinsley Gardner, "Treatise on Uterine Haemorrage," *American Medical Monthly* (June 1855), 1; as quoted by Barker-Benfield, 281.

52. On the nineteenth-century gynecological surgery as a chamber of horrors see Ann Douglas Wood, "The 'Fashionable Diseases': Women's Complaints and Their Treatments in Nineteenth-Century America," *Journal of Interdisciplinary History* 4 (1973): 25–52; Barker-Benfield, *The Horrors*; Barbara Ehrenreich and Dierdre English, *For Her Own Good: 150 Years of the Experts' Advice to Women* (Garden City, N.Y.: Anchor Press, 1979).

53. William H. Holcombe, *The Sexes Here and Hereafter* (Philadelphia: J.B. Lippincott, 1869), 201–2; W. K. Brooks, "The Condition of Women from a Zoölogical Point of View," *Popular Science Monthly* 15 (1879): 150–54; Charles D. Meigs, *Woman, Her Diseases and Remedies; A Series of Lectures to His Class*, 2d ed. (Philadelphia: Lea and Blanchard, 1851), 48; W. W. Bliss, *Woman and Her Thirty-Years' Pilgrimage* (Boston: B. B. Russell, 1870), 96; Meigs, *Woman*, 51.

54. See Barker-Benfield, *The Horrors,* 96–101.

55. Augustus Kinsley Gardner, as quoted by Barker-Benfield, *The Horrors,* 291–92.

56. As quoted by Hill, *Their Sister's Keepers,* 67.

57. Denslow Lewis, *The Gynecological Consideration for the Sexual Act* (1899; reprint, Weston, Mass.: M+S Press, 1970), 13.

58. See Carroll Smith-Rosenberg and Charles Rosenberg, "The Female Animal: Medical and Biological Views of Woman and Her Role in Nineteenth-Century America," *Journal of American History* 60 (1973): 332–56.

Christian Maidens and Heathen Monks

Oratorical Seduction
at the 1893 World's
Parliament of Religions

༄

Carrie Tirado Bramen

> *I thought th' Fair was mixin' an' th' Midway made me crawl,*
> *But th' Parl'ment of Religions was th' mixin'est of all!*
>
> *I see th' Turks agoing round th' Midway in th' Fair,*
> *But our minister reproved me when he seen me peep in thair,*
> *"Defilin' place" he called it, an' th' Turk "a child of sin"*
> *But th' Parl'ment of Religions took all them heathen in.*

—Minnie Andrews Snell,
"Aunt Hannah on the
Parliament of Religions" (1893)

Held in the Hall of Columbus on Chicago's Michigan Avenue in September 1893, the World's Parliament of Religions, an auxiliary event at the 1893 Columbian Exposition, attracted a total of almost 150,000 spectators who came over a two-week period to hear nearly two hundred speakers representing twelve world religions. Many observers and participants, including the fair's chief of construction Daniel Burnham, confidently predicted that in a hundred years the fair would be forgotten, while the parliament would long be remembered. The event's chairman, John Henry Barrows, a Presbyterian minister and professor of religion at the University of Chicago, claimed that "while the fair was no novelty, the parliament was unique and unexampled."[1] As the most heavily attended of all the fair's twenty supplementary congresses, the parliament was the first of its kind to invite participants from all over the globe to take part in an interreligious forum that was open to the general public. For the majority of audience members, who were overwhelmingly middle-class and Protestant, the parliament marked their first encounter with representatives of Asian religions, or what were then referred to as "ethnic religions." Despite the novelty and popularity of this international congress, Burnham was wrong to predict that the parliament would be remembered long after the fair was forgotten. Over a century later, the fair has become a favorite topic of historians and literary scholars, while the parliament, except for the work of a few historians of religion, has fallen into relative obscurity at a time of increased scholarly interest in multiculturalism.

One reason for the popularity of the fair and the neglect of the parliament is suggested in Aunt Hannah's use of "mixin'," a term that refers not only to people of doubtful character, but also more generally to a muddled and confusing situation. Where the fair's Midway Plaisance was "mixin'," the parliament was "mixin'est." The distinction implies that the less "mixin'" fair offered a more coherent arrangement of diverse cultures, one that followed evolutionary lines portraying humanity in its most "civilized" stages down almost to its animalistic origins. The milelong strip of land, which the *Chicago Tribune* labeled the "Royal Road of Gaiety," consisted of a populist display of discrete ethnographic exhibitions of nonwhite people who performed their "native" customs in a nondialogic manner. Such an arrangement told a linear narrative that reinforced Victorian America's longstanding racial and cultural prejudices. This arrangement not only reiterated an evolutionary understanding of "progress," but also relied on an imperial mode of seeing, which Edward Said has described as "the vision of Orient as spectacle."[2] The fair, and more specifically the Midway Plaisance, has become a popular chronotope of contemporary study precisely because it exhibits the conventional power dynamics of Orientalist performance. The Occidental gaze managed the Oriental "other" through a constellation of disciplinary practices that portrayed Asianness as an ethnographic prototype of backwardness.

The parliament, by contrast, was a far more unstable affair, one that could not easily be reduced to an Orientalist spectacle. Rather than silently performing "native" customs along the Midway, Asian representatives directly addressed the largely Christian audience—and not in an unfamiliar tongue that was then translated, but in English. Many of the Asian orators spoke English fluently, a point that was frequently noted in private and public accounts of the parliament. Of Swami Vivekananda, a popular Hindu speaker from Calcutta, the *Chicago Advocate* wrote: "His knowledge of English is as though it were his other tongue." Regarding an equally popular orator, Dharmapala, a Buddhist from Ceylon, the *Dubuque (Iowa) Times* noted that his "peroration was as pretty a thing as a Chicago audience ever heard."[3] Vivekananda and Dharmapala were also highly conversant in Christian doctrine, able to draw conceptual parallels between Hindu and Buddhist philosophy and biblical parables. During one of his speeches at the parliament, Dharmapala, who was educated in Christian missionary schools, described his leather-bound Bible as "falling apart from constant use." They were colonial mimics gone awry, able to use their knowledge of the imperial religion to describe its failings in mellifluous prose. Dharmapala, for example, highlighted the contradiction between Christian charity and the slaughter of animals. He declared the "great slaughter-houses in Chicago . . . a disgrace to civilization and to the world," explaining that a "religion which allows such practices the people of the East cannot understand." Swami Vivekananda similarly underscored Christian hypocrisy when he addressed his audience directly: "You Christians, who are so fond of sending out missionaries to save the soul of the heathen—why do you not try to save their bodies from starvation?"[4] Their linguistic and cultural fluency was a source of oratorical power, which inspired religious doubt among many earnest attendees such as Aunt Hannah, the archetypal Hoosier.[5]

Because the parliament was characterized by the openness of the spoken word and the unpredictable nature of the relation between speaker and audience, the critical paradigms used to analyze the fair are not readily transferable to the parliament. If the fair illustrates the Victorian preoccupation with otherness as order, classification, and discipline, the parliament typifies the equally Victorian concept of otherness as disorganization, as messy and contradictory attempts to assemble the heterogeneous. Although its Protestant organizers attempted to display the religions represented at the parliament in a discrete "side-by-side" manner, the actual event was a far more disorderly affair. The parliament had a distinctively carnivalesque atmosphere, with speakers running between the Hall of Columbus and the adjacent Hall of Washington to deliver and redeliver their papers to overflow crowds. At times, speakers did not even show up, especially for the afternoon sessions, and the organizers were forced to gather whomever they could for an impromptu speech. Some observers described it as "bedlam" and "babel."

Occurring at the height of imperialism, the event was an unmanageable encounter between dominant and subordinate religions and races within a hall filled with over four thousand people. Within this dynamic space, where the audience frequently interrupted speeches with boos and cheers, the minority presence of the Asian delegates stole the show, their "colorful" robes overshadowing, literally and figuratively, the black raiment of the Christian clergy. Speakers such as Anagarika Dharmapala and Swami Vivekananda became instant celebrities, pursued by largely female fans and soon lecturing across the country. Matthew Trumbull, a labor organizer in Chicago, sardonically noted that the "heathen carried away the prizes of most value, while the agnostic and unbelievers cheered." Charles Little, a Methodist speaker at the event, observed a similar dynamic in more generous terms: "[P]eople expected pagans. And pagans, they thought, were ignorant and impotent of mind, with no reasons for their worship and no brains in their theology. To them the Parliament was a stunning revelation." The "wise men of the East," according to another attendee, provided "a surprise to the whole Occidental world."[6]

This point was not lost on the Asian representatives. In an 1897 interview, Swami Vivekananda said, "The Parliament of Religions, as it seems to me, was intended for a 'heathen show' before the world; but it turned out that the heathens had the upper hand, and made it a 'Christian show' all round." Virchand Gandhi, a Jain delegate from India, wrote in the *Arena* that "at least a third and sometimes two-thirds of the great audience of Columbus Hall would make a rush for the exits when a fine orator from India had closed his speech."[7] By moving from the margins to the center, the Asian representatives altered the Christian logic of the event, transforming a potentially Orientalist spectacle into an anticolonial critique. This shift from the margins to the center recalls William James's pluralistic philosophy, itself partly the result of his engagement with the teachings of Dharmapala and Swami Vivekananda, both of whom James met years later. "The centre [of consciousness]," wrote James, "works in one way while the margins work in another, and presently overpower the centre and are central themselves."[8] By becoming central, the Asian delegates de-Orientalized the parliamentary space by giving it a content firmly situated in the exigencies of the colonial world. This oratorical coup disrupted the conventional relations between West and East, the metropolis and the periphery, the monumental and imperializing Columbian Exposition and the "heathen" religious sideshow.

This colonial reversal also included a sexual element that manifested itself in the oratorical relations between the Asian speakers and the largely Christian female audience. Protestant constructions of the Parliament's sexual dynamics—Asian ascetics seducing Christian women—both reverse the conventional valences of Orientalist eroticism (where the exotic "other" is typically female or feminized) and extend to Asian religions the logic of anti-Catholic narratives earlier in the century, in which Protestant women are seduced by allegedly ascetic and subtly Orientalized Catholic priests. I will focus primarily on the two most charismatic speakers at the event, Swami Vivekananda and Dharmapala, who were described as "the most impressive figures of the Parliament."9 As media reports and personal testimony make clear, their popular appeal was registered mainly by white Christian women. "Great crowds of people," one journalist noted, "the most of whom were women, pressed around the doors leading to the Hall of Columbus an hour before the time stated for opening the afternoon session, for it had been announced that Swami Vivekananda, the popular Hindoo monk who looks so much like McCullough's Othello, was to speak."

Like his Shakespearean counterpart's, Swami Vivekananda's erotic allure crossed racial borders. Cornelia Conger, the granddaughter of Swami Vivekananda's official hosts during the parliament, recounted that he was "such a dynamic and attractive personality that many women were quite swept away by him and made every effort by flattery to gain his interest."10 Vivekananda was not the only Asian delegate whose popularity was based largely on female adoration. Dharmapala, whom the Swami pejoratively described as an "ignoramus," was also cast as an oratorical seducer. The *St. Louis Observer* sexualized Dharmapala's rhetorical style by focusing less on his words than on his bodily inflections: "his black, curly locks thrown back from his broad brow, his keen, clear eye fixed upon the audience, his long brown fingers emphasizing the utterances of his vibrant voice." His popularity with women was seen as the logical outcome of his seductive rhetorical manner. One parliament observer noted that Dharmapala "ungrudgingly shook hands with the many hundred Christian women who thronged about him for that purpose, and wrote his name in their autograph albums, and on their fans: very wise actions that will tend to decrease the contributions to the missionary funds the coming Christmas, and will also make the Christian maiden less shy of a Buddhist lover."11 The oratorical power of the Asian delegates was portrayed as a form of interracial seduction. (Figure 1)

The continuities and reversals of Protestant conventions for representing religious otherness exhibited at the parliament came to the fore in oratorical displays of what I call the "heathen's jeremiad." As a reworking of Sacvan Bercovitch's notion of the jeremiad, a way of reconstituting a Christian community through reproach, the heathen's jeremiad mimed and reversed the

Figure 1

༄

Eastern delegates seated on the platform of the parliament (*from left to right*):
Virchand Gandhi, Anagarika Dharmapala, and Swami Vivekananda. [Source: Swami
Chetanananda, *Vivekananda: East Meets West* (St. Louis: Vedanta Society of St. Louis,
1995), p. 62.]

prototypical Puritan genre by calling Protestants to confront the limitations
of their allegedly tolerant faith. Where the Puritan jeremiad aimed to rescue a
religiously uniform community from the threat of spiritual declension, the
heathen's jeremiad imagined new forms of alliance based on a shared opposition to imperial practices such as Christian missionary work. Swami
Vivekananda, for instance, railed against Christian missionaries in India for
offering words rather than bread during a series of famines: "It is an insult to
a starving man to teach him metaphysics." Such critiques of Christian
hypocrisy found a particularly sympathetic ear among the Christian women
in the audience. Rather than produce defensiveness, his anticolonial diatribes
cultivated affection. One newspaper observed that the Swami was "daily beset
by hundreds of women who almost fought with each other for a chance to get
near him, and shake his hand."[12] The popularity of the Asian speakers cre-

ated a highly sexualized "contact zone" that destabilized the colonial relations between East and West, including the Protestant modes of organization that structured the event.

The Heathen's Jeremiad

> I listened to th' Buddhist, in his robes of shinin' white,
> As he told how like to Christ's thair lives, while ours was not—a mite,
> 'Tel I felt, to lead a Christian life, a Buddhist I must be,
> An' th' Parl'ment of Religions brought religious doubt to me.
>
>   —"Aunt Hannah at the Parliament of Religions"

Through its format of individual speeches, the parliament typified a particularly Protestant mode of organization that underscored the "distinctive truths of each religion." This format suppressed the relational character of religious thought and instead promoted a reified view of each discrete creed. Like the Methodist metaphor of Christian union, where each denomination signifies a separate string of the harp, the parliament organized the different faiths so that each speaker represented a distinct theology. Even when the speakers in the second half of the event were asked to lecture on the future of religion and to evaluate their faith in relation to others, the information was still conveyed through individual presentations with little or no room for dialogue. Barrows, in his opening remarks at the parliament, sounded like a referee as he lectured the speakers on sportsmanlike conduct: "We are met in a great conference, men and women of different minds, where the speakers will not be ambitious for short-lived, verbal victories over others, where gentleness, courtesy, wisdom and moderation will prevail far more than heated argumentation." This caveat was reiterated by the president of the Auxiliary Congress, Charles Frank Bonney, who had claimed only moments earlier that "each system of Religion stands by itself in its own perfect integrity, uncompromised, in any degree, by its relation to any other."[13]

To reinforce further the distinctiveness of each religion, the organizing committee arranged for "separate and independent" denominational congresses to concur with the parliament, with the aim of more fully describing "their doctrines and the service they have rendered to mankind." At least one observer of the period criticized the parliament for structuring the conference around individual presentations rather than interfaith discussions: "This cosmopolitan assembly was not strictly a parliament, because extemporaneous debate was absent. It was rather a World's Fair of theological exhibits with a sort of Midway Plaisance attachment for the *bric a brac* of creeds." Reflecting on the parliament, Crawford Toy believed that this arrangement was the source of the parliament's success: "It was not intended to be a scientific gathering, but rather a friendly meeting for the exhibition of different religious ideas side by side."[14] The "side-by-side" arrangement strategically preserved not only the uniqueness of American Protestantism, but also the distinctiveness of the "Oriental Other." What the organizers did not anticipate was that the powerful East-West bond produced by the popularity of the Asian speakers, especially among the largely female audience, would dislodge the tidy arrangement of religious cultures they had sought to enforce.

Paul Carus, a participant at the parliament and a founder of the Open Court Press (which soon became a major vehicle for bringing Eastern texts to Anglophone readers), observed in his reflections on the parliament that although "discussion had been excluded from the programme so as to avoid friction, it could not be entirely controlled."[15] The "side-by-side" model that the Protestant organizers tried to maintain was easily thrown into disarray. One evening, for example, Dharmapala went far beyond his allotted time, and the next morning's schedule was adjusted so that he could finish his lengthy lecture on the Vedanta philosophy. Swami Vivekananda, whom the *New York Times* dubbed "the greatest figure in the Parliament of Religions," gave an impromptu talk the first afternoon, which soon resulted in a mandate for ten more appearances. Not only did the charismatic presence of these speakers result in schedule changes, but their very presence was perceived by some as "propaganda" that could potentially convert the Christian audience in a threatening process of reversed assimilation. The *St. Louis Observer* noted that Dharmapala "looked the very image of a propagandist, and one trembled to know that such a figure stood at the head of the movement to consolidate all the disciples of Buddha and to spread 'the light of Asia' throughout the civilized world." Vivekananda claimed to have converted nearly four thousand Americans to Hinduism during his stay. The *Indian Mirror* reported that the "tide of conversion seemed to have rolled back from the East to the West—the tables were completely turned."[16] Not only did such figures as Vivekananda and Dharmapala unsettle the side-by-side arrangement of the meeting's format, they also threatened to woo Christian women away from their husband's sides through the power of oratorical seduction.

Intriguingly, the Asian delegates managed to seduce their Protestant audience by vociferously attacking Christianity. The harsher the Asian jeer, the more vigorous the Christian cheer. When Protap Chandra Majumdar, the author of *The Oriental Christ* (a book that was especially popular among Boston Unitarians), charged that the Protestant preoccupation with activity and work left "little time to consider the great questions of regeneration, of personal sanctification, of truth and judgment and of acceptance before God," the audience broke into loud applause. Dharmapala's criticism of Christian missionaries as "intolerant" and "selfish"[17] was greeted not with defensiveness, but with tolerance and even warmth. The *Chicago Tribune* referred to the third day of the parliament, when Asian speakers criticized missionary practices in the East, as the "greatest day so far of the parliament," coining it "Oriental day."[18]

Christian tolerance thus mediated the conflictual words from the East, not only to evade addressing critiques of missionary work, but also to demonstrate the superiority of Christianity through displays of its benevolence. Christianity requires dissent, opposition, and criticism in order to highlight its own tolerance. For a religion that relies on persuasion as a mode of conversion, tolerance is a way of persuading through generosity: The heathen subject unmoved by doctrine might yet be converted through kindness. Tolerance also offers a strategy for cohering the different segments of the Protestant community through a shared belief in the value of Christian charity. At the Parliament of Religions, Christian tolerance united the mainly Protestant audience, but it also established a bond of sympathy between the audience and the Asian speakers on the stage. That this bond of sympathy should be expressed most intensely when the Asian speakers were at their most vituperative illustrates the lengths to which liberal Christianity would go to embrace opposition in order to preserve its own sense of specialness.

This display of tolerance confused a number of the Asian representatives, especially the Japanese Buddhist layman Hirai Kinzo. The only Buddhist representative from Japan who was fluent in English, Hirai arrived in Chicago with what he knew would be a highly controversial speech entitled "The Real Position of Japan toward Christianity." Barrows, forewarned, even considered preventing Hirai from presenting his paper. Undeterred, Hirai vilified Christian hypocrisy, racism, and imperialism, listing one offense after another and concluding by proudly declaring himself a "heathen":

> When some years ago a Japanese was not allowed to enter a
> university on the Pacific coast of America because of his being of

a different race; when a few months ago the school board in San
Francisco enacted a regulation that no Japanese should be
allowed to enter the public school there; when last year the
Japanese were driven out wholesale from one of the territories of
the United States; when our business men in San Francisco were
compelled by some union not to employ the Japanese assistants
or laborers, but the Americans; when there are some in the same
city who speak on the platform against those of us who are
already here; when there are many men who go in procession
hoisting lanterns marked "Japs must go." . . . If such be the
Christian ethics—well, we are perfectly satisfied to be heathen.[19]

Hirai's presentation received overwhelming approval from the four thousand Americans who had gathered to hear him speak in the Hall of
Columbus. The *Chicago Herald* reported that the "loud applause" and "a thousand cries of 'Shame!'" followed his litany of "the wrongs . . . of false
Christianity." At the conclusion of Hirai's speech, "Dr. Barrows grasped his
hand, and the Rev. Lloyd Jones threw his arms around his neck, while the
audience cheered vociferously and waved hats and handkerchiefs in an
excess of enthusiasm."[20] Hirai was shocked at this response, having expected
to be "torn from the platform" before finishing his address. But the "excess of
enthusiasm" also persuaded Hirai to return to Japan as a "Christian." In an
article written a year after the event, John Henry Barrows reports what Hirai
had told him before embarking for Japan: "I go back a Christian, by which I
mean that Christianity is a religion which I shall be glad to see established in
Japan. Only let the Christian missionaries not interfere with our national
usages and patriotic holidays. I have been delighted with America and especially with its tolerance."[21] Even the most embittered and stubbornly
"heathen" opponents of Christianity, Hirai's example seemed to say, could
still be shown the light through a handshake and a hug.

According to Bercovitch, the jeremiad as a public mode of exhortation was
"designed to join social criticism to spiritual renewal, public to private identity, the shifting 'signs of the times' to certain traditional metaphors, themes,
and symbols."[22] In this period of growing secularization and weakening
Christian unity, it seems only appropriate that the jeremiad should surface
during the parliament as a way to make sense of these shifting "signs of the
times." That the figure of Jeremiah should be an "outsider," and particularly
a non-Christian, shows the extent to which the Christian community was
refashioning itself to be more inclusive, to be the common ground upon

which a global community would develop. The jeremiad, as a mode of social control, was a way of including the outsider, even the self-confessed "heathen," as already part of the Christian community. As James Ketelaar points out, "the invited 'others' of the Orient were *by their very participation* already constituted by the parliament as representatives who desired to be *included*."[23] The heathen's jeremiad, therefore, was a way for a modernized Christianity to embrace its own internal denominational variety as well as to domesticate religious diversity at an international level.

Celibate Seduction

If Eastern criticisms of Christianity offered some listeners an occasion for the exercise of Christian tolerance, other listeners were moved to religious doubt. For still others, the heathen's jeremiad inspired passion, as the boundaries distinguishing the speaker from the audience were not only transgressed vocally with shouts of "Shame!" but even physically, when women from the audience climbed over chairs and tables to pay their compliments to Shibata Reiichi, the Japanese "high priest" of Shintoism. The Shinto priest embraced and kissed "three Caucasian ladies," an event that marked the second significant occurrence of "Oriental day."[24] The parliament's organizing principle, unity-in-discreteness, was becoming indiscreet as Victorian ladies not only leapt to the platform to embrace the Japanese speaker, but also crowded such charismatic figures as Dharmapala and Swami Vivekananda, asking them to autograph their fans. As the congress progressed, the arrangement of cultures into discrete clusters began to disperse, and the Protestant models of cultural contact became increasingly irrelevant.

In recollecting their first impressions of Swami Vivekananda at the parliament, American women explicitly connected his oratorical power with sexual appeal. According to Mrs. S. K. (Roxie) Blodgett, "When that young man got up and said, 'Sisters and Brothers of America,' seven thousand people rose to their feet as a tribute to something they knew not what. When it was over I saw scores of women walking over the benches to get nearer to him, and I said to myself, 'Well, my lad, if you can resist that onslaught you are indeed a God!'" When Mrs. Lyon, who was Vivekananda's official host during the parliament, expressed concern that he may find himself in an uncomfortable situation, he exclaimed, "You dear American mother of mine . . . I am used to temptation, and you need not fear for me!"[25] Although the majority of the Asian representatives were celibate monks, called *sannyasi* in Bengali, few advertised their celibacy with such candor and aplomb as Swami Vivekananda. His celibacy was of particular interest to American audiences who were fascinated that a celibate "heathen" could become the locus of female attention while at the same time exhibiting such self-control in resisting their charm. "'Why should I marry,' was his abrupt response to a comment on all he had renounced in becoming a monk, 'when I see in every woman only the divine Mother?' "[26] In letters and lectures, the Swami commonly referred to his female friends and followers in strictly familial terms as "mother" and "sister." Of Roxie Blodgett, whose Los Angeles home he would visit in 1899, he wrote, "very motherly."[27]

In Vivekananda's case, however, his proclamations of celibacy actually contributed to his sexual mystique. Constructing himself as an erotic ascetic on the model of his favorite god Shiva (the Hindu god of self-control), Vivekananda challenged the colonial image of the effeminate Bengali by producing an alternative masculinity based on self-mastery. Asceticism, for Vivekananda, was a way to remasculinize the colonized male as physically virile and spiritually potent at a time when Eastern religions were dismissed in the U.S. press as "effete religious mysticism."[28] The charismatic performances at the parliament were not only attempts to convert Christians into "heathens"—to reverse the tide, in other words, of colonial influence—but also to project an image of Eastern masculinity that challenged both Western manliness and its necessary obverse, Asian effeminacy. Vivekananda's attempt to make the celibate monk manly can be understood as part of a much larger intervention into what Mrinalini Sinha has called "colonial masculinity," a late nineteenth-century formation that emerged not only out of the colonial relations between India and Britain but also among the colonial elite of Indian society.[29] (Figure 2)

Born into an aristocratic Bengali household in Calcutta, Narendranth Dutta (later Swami Vivekananda) was Western-educated and a student of colonial reason. His turn to the teachings of Ramakrishna Paramhansa was the result of his family's financial crisis after the death of his father as well as a more general response to concerns about Western assimilation. As Ramakrishna's biographer Sarandananda has pointed out, Ramakrishna's teachings brought Anglicized Bengalis, such as Vivekananda, back into the "Hindu spiritual-fold."[30] This reconversion of Westernized Indians into Hindu subjects constituted a program of *indigenismo* that proved an important counter to colonial rule.

Figure 2

◠

A poster of Swami
Vivekananda from the 1893
Chicago World's Fair.
[Source: Swami
Chetanananda, *Vivekananda:
East Meets West* (St. Louis:
Vedanta Society of St. Louis,
1995), p. 62.]

Compared to his guru, Vivekananda understood Hinduization as a far
more eclectic process that combined Eastern spiritualism with Western masculinity in an attempt to change the image of the effeminate *babu*. "You will
be nearer to God through football," he once said, "than through the *Bhagwad
Gita*." Vivekananda's work at the parliament must be seen as part of this
larger mission of promoting a modern form of Hindu nationalism that was
based on what he called "man-making." As Partha Chatterjee has argued,
Vivekananda combined Hinduism with nationalism in a "call to viriliza-
tion."[31] This mission challenged the gendering of colonial rule through a
religious discourse that remasculinized Bengali men in terms that did not
merely mimic the manliness of the Christian West, but appropriated "indige-
nous" models. To do this, Vivekananda used a discourse of sexuality based on
the Hindu practice of *brahmachary*, an understanding of celibacy as a means
of self-control and virility.

At the parliament, Western women contributed to this image of the erotic ascetic through their adoration. As Parama Roy has argued in *Indian Traffic*, Vivekananda's program for reimagining Hindu masculinity depended on the figure of the Western woman. Vivekananda needed the West, and especially white women, for his "validation as nationalist, masculine, heterosexual": "[I]t is her very (racial) difference that guarantees Vivekananda's, and paradigmatically, the Indian male's Indianness and masculinity." For Roy, Vivekananda's masculinity is fundamentally heterosexual, directed toward a specific object choice, namely Western women. "To be (properly) masculine," writes Roy, "was to be heterosexual."[32]

Although I agree with Roy that the parliament's audience of white Western women played a vital role in remasculinizing the Hindu man, what Roy's emphasis on Vivekananda's "masculine heterosexuality" does not address is the significance of his celibacy. Indeed, Vivekananda's performance of masculinity at the parliament was not entirely or even primarily heterosexual. To represent "masculine heterosexuality" would be a mimicry of Western manliness. Vivekananda was not about to claim for Indian men the stereotype of Western manhood: a desiring male subject who spends rather than retains his semen. He imagined instead a radically different spermatic economy, one that viewed celibacy as the precondition of true manhood where nondesire replaced desire. As an (a)sexual corollary to his anticolonial jeremiad, Swami Vivekananda appropriated the Hindu tradition of celibacy to define an anticolonial masculinity. His oratorical style and his sexual practice complemented each other in a double-edged strategy that rebuked the West through nonidentification. He remained the resilient "heathen" who refused to be converted to Western ways, whether by worshiping a Christian God or by romancing white American women.

The Asian Ascetic Encounters the New Woman

The encounter between ascetic monks and Christian maidens created a transnational chronotope where the "new man" of the East met the "new woman" of the West. The nondesiring anticolonial man established, and indeed depended upon, nascent relations with the neo-desiring woman, who abandoned Victorian protocol in order to assert her sexual and social independence. The majority of the Swami's female fans belonged to this group: highly educated and independent women from the upper-middle and aristocratic classes who were enjoying newfound freedoms ranging from professional careers to sexual and spiritual self-fulfillment.³³ Such a pairing at first seems highly unlikely: What could a celibate swami provide a class of women who were just beginning to articulate social and sexual desires? And, conversely, wouldn't the New Woman be a source of further colonial emasculation?

Swami Vivekananda's response to his women supporters was ambivalent, oscillating between admiration and repulsion, gratitude and repugnance. Soon after his arrival in America for the parliament, Vivekananda wrote a fellow monk in India that "there are no women in the whole world comparable" to the American. "How pure, free, self-reliant, and kind they are! . . . Good God! When I see them, bang! I am at wit's end!" American women invited Swami Vivekananda into their homes, providing him with comfortable accommodations, food, and company. Soon after his arrival, they supported his talents as a public speaker and cultivated his image as a celebrity, acting as his public relations agents. They also provided tremendous financial support throughout his brief life (he died in 1902), supporting his travels throughout the United States and Europe, and supporting the Ramakrishna Order in India. "American women!" he wrote, "A hundred lives would not be sufficient to pay my deep debt of gratitude to you!"³⁴

But Vivekananda also expressed a certain repugnance toward the New Woman, even directing the "heathen's jeremiad" specifically toward her. At a reception during the parliament in the Woman's Building, the Swami declared that "the Hindu women are very spiritual and very religious, perhaps *more so than any other* women in the world." The following year in Detroit, where it was rumored that he was having liaisons with local society women, he challenged the audience to show him "a dozen spiritual women in America."³⁵ Although "[n]ice dress, wealth, brilliant society, operas, novels" were available to American women, "[t]here should also be spirituality, but that side is *entirely absent* from Christian countries. They live in India."³⁶ Of Boston, he declared that "there the women are all faddists, all fickle, merely bent on following something new and strange."

His ambivalence toward the New Woman was in part a response to being treated as a "curio from India," an exotic specimen whom one showed off to her society friends. It was also a response to his own internalized notions of imperial beauty, what biographer Narasingha Sil has called "his obsession with fair skin." In a confidential letter to a Bengali friend, he wrote that "the American women are very beautiful" and that by contrast, "even the prettiest woman of our country will look like a black owl there." Vivekananda's attitude toward the women who followed and supported him was a mixture of admiration and contempt. He was also contemptuous of the "lustful" woman, where lust was synonymous with whiteness and Westernness. Like his guru Ramakrishna, Vivekananda's asceticism was based in part on what Sil has called "the misogynist phobia of a sexual female."[37] His celibacy was the condition from which he glorified women and denounced them, especially the sexualized woman who was perceived as a threat to *brahmachary*, the basis of his Bengali masculinity.

Celibacy was a means not of diffusing the sexual dynamic between the monk and the sexualized Western woman, but of channeling it toward ends that would ultimately give the monk a degree of international visibility, credibility, and financial backing. This relation of nonreciprocity actually empowered the celibate, since he could control not only his own desire but also the desire of others. Vivekananda was well aware, moreover, of the seductive power of his oratorical performances, remarking in one letter to a friend in India that American "sluts and studs" *(magi minsegulo)* used to be sexually aroused after hearing his lectures. After one lecture, a woman stood up and said: "'Swami! You are my Romeo and I am your Desdemona!' The Swami said quickly, 'Madam, you'd better brush up your Shakespeare.'"[38] One biography of Vivekananda reports that "Western women were sometimes so fascinated by the Swami's personality that some actually proposed marriage to him. One such, an heiress to a fortune, said, 'Swami, I offer myself and all my riches at your feet!' His reply was, 'Madam, I am a *sannyasin;* what is marriage to me! To me all women are as my mother!'"[39]

This anecdote illustrates the interdependent relation between the desiring New Woman and the nondesiring ascetic. The assertion of the former finds a safe and nonthreatening outlet through the refusal of the latter. To be sure, this reversal of the conventional proposal—the woman is the one proposing—borders on effeminizing the Asian male, of continuing the orientalist stereotype of the emasculated Bengali by putting the Asian man in the passive position. But the celibacy of the Asian monk also affirms the agency of the colonial subject in his refusal to marry. The New Woman's assertiveness—in publicly proposing to the Hindu monk—produces his desirability, which in turn provides an occasion for the celibate Hindu to assert his manliness by refusing her advances. Her infatuation creates his authority as a level-headed, rational subject. Thanks to his female audience, he can cast himself as desirable but not desiring. The metropolitan woman needs him, but he is autonomous—a sovereign self asserting his independence at the height of the colonial era. Despite his material dependence on wealthy American women, his public rejection of their sexual overtures allowed him to perform his masculinity as an anticolonial spectacle of celibate self-determination.

What did the New Woman gain from this relationship? She was able to express publicly her desires without concern for the consequences. She could declare her affections, in other words, without worrying about becoming a wife. He could remain celibate, and she could remain single. They made an ideal couple.[40] In the oratorical encounter between the Asian monk and Christian women, imperialism, race, sexuality and gender intersected and clashed in ways that cannot be simply reduced to either Orientalism on the part of the white women or misogyny on the part of Swami Vivekananda.[41] Although both factors played a role in how the accomplished rhetorician and the eager audience interacted within the lecture hall and outside its doors, the sexual dynamics that informed this relationship also created a space of mutual autonomy. One could be heterosocial without necessarily being heterosexual, a distinction that allowed each party, and the New Women in particular, to use their relationship as a way to explore the limits of Protestant orthodoxy.

In its most generous light, the Swami's alleged celibacy created a safe space for women as intellectuals to rethink the faith of their fathers. Martha Brown Fincke recollected her experience of meeting Vivekananda when she was a freshman at Mt. Holyoke in November 1893.[42] During his talk at the women's college, Vivekananda was challenged by the "champions of Christianity," male Protestant professors and local ministers who tried to upstage him by referring to biblical passages, European philosophers, and Western poets. "How could one expect a Hindu from far-off India," asks Fincke, "to hold his own with these, master though he might be of his own learning?" What most impressed Fincke was that the Swami replied to his Christian critics by demonstrating that he was a master of both Western and Eastern intellectual traditions. He, too, quoted from the Bible, from English thinkers on religion, and from obscure passages in Wordsworth and Thomas Gray. For the young Fincke, Vivekananda "personified Power": "Power can awe even when it does not force agreement."[43] After the talk, Fincke spoke with Vivekananda about the violent metaphors of Christianity, such as the "blood of Christ," which both found especially abhorrent. He encouraged her to learn Sanskrit, and to read the Vedas, the holy texts of Hinduism, which she eventually did, albeit in translation.

As Fincke's experience demonstrates, Christian women were more receptive than their male counterparts to the words of the Asian speakers. They responded with curiosity rather than defensiveness in exploring different faiths to find what Fincke called the "freedom of the spirit." The popularity of the Asian speakers was a result of multiple factors ranging from exotic infatuation to intellectual curiosity. What unites these factors is a common frustration with the orthodoxies of Protestantism that the New Woman of the 1890s found particularly stifling. The audience's vocal cheers during the "heathen's jeremiad," which were frequently followed by loud applause and handkerchief waving, were signs not only of Christian tolerance but also of an internal, gendered challenge within liberal Protestantism, with women largely determining the general sentiment toward the Eastern "other." The same identification that Mary Fincke forged with Vivekananda at Mt. Holyoke, when she silently rooted for the Swami to "triumph" over the "champions of Christianity," surfaced vocally and loudly at the Parliament of Religions, when Protestant women, in particular, welcomed the rebuking words of the Eastern delegates. Anticolonialism intersected with antipatriarchal sentiments in an East-West bond that was at times mutually enhancing and at other times destabilizing. Such a transnational bond provides a useful context to study the intersections and divergences of colonial masculinity and metropolitan feminism.

Notes

I am grateful to David Schmid, Gil Harris, and Margaret Pappano for their helpful suggestions.

1. John Henry Barrows, "Results of the Parliament of Religions," *The Forum* 18 (September 1894): 54–67. Reprinted in Eric J. Ziolkowski, ed., *A Museum of Faiths* (Atlanta, Ga.: Scholars Press, 1993), 131–47.

2. Edward Said, *Orientalism* (1978; reprint, London: Penguin, 1985), 158.

3. The quotation from the *Chicago Advocate* is taken from Swami Chetanananda, *Vivekananda: East Meets West* (St. Louis: Vedanta Society of St. Louis, 1995). 59. The *Dubuque (Iowa) Times* is cited from Mary Louise Burke, *Swami Vivekananda in America, New Discoveries* (Calcutta, India: Advaita Ashrama, 1963), 75.

4. Anagarika Dharmapala, *Return to Righteousness: A Collection of Speeches, Essays and Letters of Anagarika Dharmapala*, ed. Ananda Guruge (Ceylon: Ministry of Education and Cultural Affairs, 1965), 681–82; Dharmapala's reference to the slaughter of animals is cited from the *Chicago Tribune*, 23 September 1893, 2; Swami Vivekananda, *Selections from Swami Vivekananda* (Calcutta, India: Advaita Ashrama, 1963), 21.

5. "Aunt Hannah" was the creation of Minnie Andrews Snell, whose poem, "Aunt

Hannah at the Parliament of Religions" appeared in Paul Carus's journal *The Open Court* (12 October 1893.)

6. Trumbull is quoted from Richard Hughes Seager, *The World's Parliament of Religions* (Bloomington: Indiana University Press, 1995), 146. Charles Little, "The Parliament of Religions," *Methodist Review* 76 (March 1894): 211; Mary Atwater Neely, "Opinion," in *Neely's History of the Parliament of Religions and Religious Congresses of the World's Columbian Exposition*, ed. Walter R. Houghton (Chicago: F. T. Neely, 1893), 973.

7. Pravrajika Prabuddaprana, "Chicago and Its Impact: Swami Vivekananda's Influences on American Religion and Philosophy," in *Swami Vivekananda: A Hundred Years since Chicago*, ed. R. K. Dasgupta (Belur, India: Ramakrishna Math and Ramakrishna Mission, 1994), 131. Virchand Gandhi is quoted from Burke, *Swami Vivekananda in America*, 68.

8. William James, *A Pluralistic Universe.* (1908), in *William James: Writings, 1902–1910*, ed. Bruce Kuklick (New York: Library of America, 1987), 761. The ideas of both Dharmapala and Vivekananda influenced James's work at the turn of the century. In 1903, James invited Dharmapala to lecture on Buddhism to his advanced students in psychology at Harvard. After the lecture James jumped up from his seat and declared: "This is the psychology everybody will be studying twenty-five years from now." See Dharmapala's account of this encounter in *Return to Righteousness*, 681. In *Varieties of Religious Experience*, James refers to Vivekananda's lectures on yoga and the Vedanta philosophy from the 1890s. For more on the relation between the Swami and James, see Dasgupta, *Swami Vivekananda, a Hundred Years since Chicago*, 135–39. For a more elaborate discussion of Jamesian pluralism and Dharmapala's Buddhism, see my book, *The Uses of Variety: Modern Americanism and the Quest for National Distinctiveness* (Cambridge, Mass.: Harvard University Press, 2000), ch. 6.

9. See Burke, *Swami Vivekananda in America*, 85. For biographical information on Vivekananda and Dharmapala with a specific emphasis on their sudden fame at the Parliament, see Ziolkowski, *A Museum of Faiths*, esp. 219–51. The legacy of Vivekananda continues to inform the Arts Institute in Chicago with the segment of Michigan Avenue immediately in front of the Institute aptly called "The Honorary Swami Vivekananda Way."

10. Satish K. Kapoor, *Cultural Contact and Fusion: Swami Vivekananda and the West* (Jalandhar, India: ABS Publications, 1987), 55. See also Richard Hughes Seager, *The Dawn of Religious Pluralism: Voices from the World's Parliament of Religions, 1893* (La Salle, Ill.: Open Court, 1993). Cornelia Conger is quoted from *Reminiscences of Swami Vivekananda by His Eastern and Western Admirers* (Calcutta, India: Advaita Ashrama, 1983), 131.

11. For descriptions of Dharmapala's oratorical style, see *The World's Parliament of Religions* (cited hereafter as *WPR*), ed. John Henry Barrows, vol. 1 (Chicago: The Parliament Publishing Company, 1893), 95. Rick Fields, *How the Swans Came to the Lake* (Boulder, Col.: Shambhala, 1981), 130.

12. Vivekananda, *Selections from Swami Vivekananda*, 21. *The Life of Swami*

Vivekananda by His Eastern and Western Disciples, vol. 1 (Calcutta, India: Advaita Ashrama, 1979), 428.

13. Barrows, *WPR* I:75; Bonney, *WPR* I:72.

14. Charles Carroll Bonney, address of "The World's Congress Auxiliary," in *WPR* I:68a; M. M. Trumbull, "The Parliament of Religions," *The Monist* 4 (April 1894): 334; Crawford Toy, "The Parliament of Religions," *The New World* 2 (December 1893): 737.

15. Paul Carus, "The Dawn of a New Religious Era," *Forum* (November 1893): 388.

16. Seager, *WPR*, 110; Harold French, *The Swan's Wide Waters* (Port Washington, N.Y.: Kennikat Press, 1974), 69.

17. P. C. Majumdar, "The Principle of the Brahmo-Somaj" in *The World's Congress of Religions*, ed. J. W. Hanson (Chicago: Union Publishing House, 1894), 431; Dharmapala, "Criticism and Discussion of Missionary Methods," *WPR* II:1093.

18. *Chicago Tribune*, 14 September 1893, 9.

19. Hirai Ryuge Kinzo, "The Real Position of Japan toward Christianity," *WPR* I:448–49.

20. *Chicago Daily Times*, 14 September 1893, 1. Quoted in Fields, 124–25.

21. Barrows, "Results" in Ziolkowski, *A Museum of Faiths*, 141.

22. Sacvan Bercovitch, *The American Jeremiad* (Madison: University of Wisconsin Press, 1978), xi.

23. James Ketelaar, "The Reconvening of Babel," in Ziolkowski, *A Museum of Faiths*, 274.

24. *Chicago Tribune*, 14 September 1893, 9. For more on this incident, see Ketelaar, "The Reconvening of Babel," 276–77. The sexual resonance of the act was immediately placated through familial references. "Upon the right cheek of each," wrote the *Tribune*, "he imprinted the chaste kiss of religious brotherhood."

25. *The Life of Swami Vivekananda*, vol. 1, 418. Mrs. Lyon is quoted from *Reminiscences of Swami Vivekananda*, 135.

26. *Boston Evening Transcript*, 23 September 1893, 1–3. See also *The Life of Swami Vivekananda*.

27. *The Complete Works of Swami Vivekananda*, vol. VIII (Calcutta, India: Advaita Ashrama, 1977), 488.

28. *Chicago Tribune*, 28 September 1893, 2.

29. Mrinalini Sinha, *Colonial Masculinity: The 'Manly Englishman' and the 'Effeminate Bengali' in the Late Nineteenth Century* (Manchester, U.K.: University of Manchester Press, 1995).

30. For a discussion of Ramakrishna's impact on his disciple Swami Vivekananda, see Parama Roy, *Indian Traffic: Identities in Question in Colonial and Postcolonial India* (Berkeley and Los Angeles: University of California Press, 1998), ch. 4. I am grateful to my colleague Danny Hack for bringing this book to my attention.

31. Vivekananda quoted from Sinha, 21. Partha Chatterjee, "A Religion of Urban Domesticity: Sri Ramakrishna and the Calcutta Middle Class," in *Subaltern Studies VII: Writings on South Asian History and Society*, ed. P. Chatterjee and G. Pandey (Delhi, India: Oxford University Press, 1992), as cited in Roy, *Indian Traffic*, 107. For biographies of Vivekananda that continue to celebrate his masculinity, see T. S. Avinashilingam, *Make Me a Man: Message of Swami Vivekananda* (Coimbatore, India: Sri Ramakrishna Mission Vidyalaya, 1989); Hansraj Rahbar, *Vivekananda: The Warrior Saint* (New Delhi: Farsight Publications and Distributors, 1995).

32. Parama Roy, *Indian Traffic*, 121–22, 111. Roy's book offers the first critical analysis of the relationship between Western women and Swami Vivekananda. For a biographical overview of his women disciples, which includes their reminiscences, see *Western Women in the Footsteps of Swami Vivekananda*, ed. Pravrajika Atmaprana (New Delhi, India: Ramakrishna Sarada Mission, 1995).

33. On the New Woman, see Carroll Smith-Rosenberg, *Disorderly Conduct: Visions of Gender in Victorian America* (New York: Knopf, 1985); Sally Ledger, "The New Woman and the Crisis of Victorianism," in *Cultural Politics at the Fin-de-siècle*, eds. Sally Ledger and Scott McCracken (Cambridge: Cambridge University Press, 1995), 22–44; Linda Dowling, "The Decadent and the New Woman in the 1890s," *Nineteenth-Century Fiction* 33 (1979): 434–53.

34. Narasingha P. Sil, *Swami Vivekananda, A Reassessment* (Selinsgrove, Pa.: Susquehanna University Press, 1997), 115–16. In contrast to the vast majority of biographical works on Vivekananda, which were written by "disciples" and "admirers" within the Ramakrishna Order, Sil's biography offers the most critical interpretation of Vivekananda's life, including passages of letters and speeches that have not appeared elsewhere.

35. During his stay in the United States, there were sporadic rumors that Swami Vivekananda's chastity was in question. One includes his alleged indiscretions with women during his stay in Detroit. Prior to this, however, P. C. Mazumdar returned to Calcutta preaching that Vivekananda was leading a life of debauchery and decadence. In a letter to his friend Mary Hale in 1894, Vivekananda mocked accusations that he was "committing every sin under the sun in America—especially 'unchastity' of the most degraded type!!!" See Sil, *Swami Vivekananda, A Reassessment*, 126; and *The Life of Swami Vivekananda*, vol. 1, 482.

36. Sil, *Swami Vivekananda, A Reassessment*, 116–17.

37. Sil, *Swami Vivekananda, A Reassessment*, 123, 125.

38. Sil, *Swami Vivekananda, A Reassessment*, 117. Swami Nikhilananda, *Vivekananda, A Biography* (New York: Ramakrishna Vivekananda Center, 1953), 89.

39. *The Life of Swami Vivekananda*, vol. 1, 446.

40. Not all women who attended Swami's jeremiads felt this way. After one lecture in Pasadena in 1900, when Vivekananda contrasted the purity of Indian women with the lustful nature of American women, a lady in the audience said to his secretary,

Mrs. Alice Hansbrough, who was quickly escorting the Swami out of the room: "You little fool! Don't you know he hates you?" (Sil, 117).

41. On a number of occasions, both publicly and privately, Vivekananda spoke of the difficult conditions of Indian women. According to his biographer Nilchilananda, he recalled "the tragic circumstances under which one of his own sisters had committed suicide. He often thought that the misery of India was largely due to the ill-treatment the Hindus meted out to their womenfolk" (74). Part of the money he raised during his speaking tour was sent to a foundation for Hindu widows.

42. *Reminiscences of Swami Vivekananda,* 147–53. Forty-two years after her first and only meeting with Vivekananda at Mt. Holyoke, Fincke traveled to Calcutta as a "pilgrim" to bow her head at the tomb of Swami Vivekananda.

43. *Reminiscences,* 150–51.

Americanization of a "Queer Fellow"

Performing Jewishness and Sexuality in Abraham Cahan's *The Rise of David Levinsky*, with a Footnote on the (Monica) Lewinsky'ed Nation

∽

Magdalena J. Zaborowska

> *The president's men ... attempt relentlessly to portray their opposition as bigoted and intolerant fanatics. ... At the same time they offer a temptation to their supporters: the temptation to see themselves as realists, worldly-wise, sophisticated: in a word,* European. *That temptation should be resisted by the rest of us. In America, morality is central to our politics and attitudes in a way that is not the case in Europe, and precisely this moral streak is what is best about us. ... Europeans may have something to teach us about, say, wine or haute couture. But on the matter of morality in politics, America has much to teach Europe.*
>
> —William J. Bennett,
> *The Death of Outrage:*
> *Bill Clinton and the Assault on American Ideals*

An Immigrant Tragedy in the Promised Land

The narrative of David Levinsky's acculturation in Abraham Cahan's 1917 novel, *The Rise of David Levinsky*, is framed by its first-person protagonist/ narrator's reflections about the somewhat ambivalent effects of his Americanization. The book opens with Levinsky's contemplation of his truly

American "metamorphosis" from a poor East European Jewish peddler into a millionaire, which "strike[s] him as nothing short of a miracle."[1] It closes, over five hundred pages later, with an acknowledgment that he sometimes feels "overwhelmed by a sense of [his] success and ease" (525). Levinsky tells his story after his struggles are over, when he is middle-aged, has everything money can buy, and finally has leisure to analyze and ponder his condition in depth. Cahan's narrative thus gives the reader access to two versions of his protagonist in the historical and social context of the late 1890s and early 1900s: The first is Levinsky the character—the relatively innocent greenhorn striving to become an American; the second is Levinsky the narrator—the more insightful and mature persona who has made it and now reconstructs his life in the past in an effort to make sense of his identity in the present. This preoccupation with two distinct incarnations of the main character—Levinsky before and after acculturation—and the employment of the rags-to-riches narrative of male economic success indeed make Cahan's text, in Jules Chametzky's words, "a classic of American literature."

Despite its being so, or perhaps because it *is* a truly *American* classic, Cahan's novel also probes and reveals the mixed blessings and paradoxes of Americanization. As Chametzky, Sam B. Girgus, and more recently, Donald Weber point out, Levinsky is an ambivalent character, a "grotesque perversion of the American Dream," and a "Diaspora Man," engaged in a "sad narrative of unfulfillment."[2] Although he often boasts about the fantastic coup that made him "worth more than two million dollars" as "one of the two or three leading men in the cloak-and-suit trade," he often gives in to feelings of loss and confusion about his identity. As if to undermine the miracle of his transformation into the "new Man, the American," he states on the very first page of the novel that "my inner identity . . . impresses me as being precisely the same as it was thirty or forty years ago" (3). "There are cases when success is a tragedy," he also says in the last chapter, where he complains about his inability to break away from his past, to forget his Old World, Polish-Russian-Jewish self and immerse himself fully in America: "I can never forget the days of my misery. I cannot escape from my old self. My past and my present do not comport well. David, the poor lad swinging over a Talmud volume at the Preacher's Synagogue, seems to have more in common with *my inner identity* than David Levinsky, the well-known cloak-manufacturer" (530).

Instead of transforming him into a happy American—or a "melted" ethnic—Levinsky's superficially successful acculturation results in a deep identity split that complicates and subverts the clichéd readings of Cahan's novel as a classic immigrant narrative. Levinsky's post-Americanization subjectivity, what he calls his "inner identity," seems suspended and constructed between the binarized selves he refers to in the third person—the "poor lad swinging over a Talmud volume at the Preacher's Synagogue" in the Old World and "the well-known cloak-manufacturer" in the New. The images of these two David Levinskys bracketing Cahan's narrative are mutually exclusive and viewed as deeply problematic by the narrator. When the memories of the Old World and his oppressive "old self" overwhelm him, Levinsky feels that "[his] present station, power, the amount of worldly happiness at [his] command . . . seem to be devoid of significance" (3). Thus he perceives himself as devoid of stable subjectivity, as undefinable and unanchored. He is fragmented into his mysterious, "insignificant" "inner identity" that resists Americanization—or his past incarnation as an Old World Talmud scholar from Antomir—and his recently acquired facade as a successful American businessman.

In this essay, I explore the reasons for and the significance of this identity fragmentation in Cahan's protagonist and argue that it results from Levinsky's failure to be successfully Americanized as a Jew and as a male who is rejected by the dominant culture. Levinsky's inability to achieve coherent subjectivity after his acculturation illustrates a profound crossbreeding of the narrative models available to Cahan in early twentieth-century America with what Diana Fuss calls "the social and discursive formations" of identity.3 My close reading of Cahan's novel reveals that both Levinsky the character and Levinsky the narrator are products and victims of late nineteenth- and early twentieth-century immigrant identity politics in the United States, which dictate appropriate narrative models for immigrant stories like Levinsky's, stigmatize him as an ethnic for his Jewishness, and reject him for his ambivalent sexuality in order to write the master narrative of American consensus.4 Basing my approach on Sander Gilman's theories of Jewishness and the body and on Judith Butler's and Diana Fuss's theories of gender as performance, and identity as marginalizing difference, I argue that Cahan's narrative reflects and explores American culture's desire to marginalize ethnic males by "feminizing" them, transforming their alien bodies and sexual conduct into a threat against the middle-class, white Anglo-Saxon Protestant heterosexual hegemony. Long before literary criticism theorizes these issues, *The Rise of David Levinsky*, I suggest, actually reveals and explores the complex ways in which ethnicity is shaped by specific performances of gender and sexuality.

I end the essay with a "footnote" on the so-called "Lewinsky Affair," which I see as affirming the persistence of such performances during the millennial resurgence of Puritan rhetoric and anti-immigration sentiments. Just as David Levinsky fails in his Americanization, his near-namesake, Monica Lewinsky, seems to triumph, albeit for very different reasons, in her self-making as an *un*-American, sexual, Jewish woman who defies both the "president's men" and their more puritanical opponents. The ambivalent "oral history" and public discourses surrounding this recent national scandal echo the racialized, sexualized, and gendered notions that permeate the exclusionary model of Americanization in Cahan's novel. Almost a century after the fictional time frame of David Levinsky's immigrant plight, the "Lewinsky Affair" invites a sexualized and racialized jeremiad whose roots can be found in the Puritan ideals of representative individualism.

Narrating Acculturation as Heterosexualization

Despite the foreshadowing in its title, Cahan's novel, like its inspiration, William Dean Howell's *The Rise of Silas Lapham*, explores the ironies and self-destructiveness of its protagonist's "rise" to the pinnacle of capitalist prosperity. However, Cahan's text concentrates more openly on constructing its main character's identity split through the rites of gender and sexuality that Levinsky has to perform between the Old and the New Worlds. As a lower-class Jewish immigrant who can succeed only on the dominant culture's terms, Levinsky has to abandon the familiar milieu of Talmud scholars and the intellectual and moral values they represent and exchange the comfortable practices of Orthodox Judaism for a dramatically new way of living and thinking, for the quasi-religion of American capitalism, which demands a whole new cultural identity. Therefore, he not only crosses from one patriarchal culture into another, but he also has to negotiate two diametrically different versions of spirituality, masculinity, and homosociality. These negotiations interestingly prompt Levinsky to chart his transition into America in economic and sexual terms, as his rags-to-riches narrative unfolds simultaneously with his sexual history.

Although a virgin, only tempted to "think" of sex by Satan in the Old World, Levinsky is a perceptive greenhorn in the New World, where he identifies successful Americanization with heterosexual machismo. While beginning his business ventures as a struggling peddler of "dry goods," he is also getting his sexual education from other vendors on the Lower East Side, the more experienced Jewish men who "were addicted to obscene storytelling . . . never tired of composing smutty puns . . . [or] hinting, with merry bravado, at . . . illicit successes with Gentile women" (115). Levinsky is "scandalized beyond words" by these men, especially by their verbal abuse and harassment of the women customers on whom they rely for their livelihood, thus linking money, merchandise, and sex in a transaction that produces and defines (Jewish) manhood as a misogynist and lewd performance in the public sphere (123).

Unable to reject or resist this model of ethnic masculinity young Levinsky pretends to be a quiet accomplice of his elder fellow vendors and learns quickly the rules of performance that a marginal bystander needs to embrace to appear one of the group. His teachers enjoy his complicity and derive self-esteem from it: "Look at Levinsky standing there quiet as a kitten. . . . One would think that he is so innocent he doesn't know how to count two. Shy young fellows are the worst devils in the world" (124). Never revealing that he is an outsider to this discourse and not a "man enough," Levinsky pretends to be sexually experienced and soon translates the gender and sexual roles that his peers "invent" for him into action. When he announces the loss of his chastity in curiously "feminine" terms—"the last thread snapped"—he connects it with severing the last ties to his Old World innocence and thus also with becoming an American. Yet his sexual initiation spells loss of control over and absence of any anchored identity, as Levinsky becomes more ambivalent, confused, and fragmented as an acolyte of Americanism who has discovered the secret of knowledge in the Garden of Eden: "Intoxicated by the novelty of yielding to Satan, I gave him a free hand and the result was months of debauchery and self-disgust. The underworld women I met, the humdrum filth of their life, and their matter-of-fact, business-like attitude toward it never ceased to shock and repel me. I never left a creature of this kind without abominating her and myself, yet I would soon, sometimes during the very same evening, call on her again or on some other woman of her class" (125).

Interestingly, although himself a performer of the roles picked up among his ethnic peers, he sees the prostitutes as bad actors performing in the capitalist theater of market economy and projects his self-hatred onto them: "[T]hey failed to deceive me." Levinsky critiques their masquerades of "love" for sale, and then proceeds to identify their failure with his own as a businessman: "I knew they lied and shammed to me just as I did to my customers, and their insincerities were only another source of repugnance to me. But I frequented them in spite of it all, and *in spite of myself*" (125). Distancing the illicit sexual exploits that define and establish his Jewish manhood in the New World from "his inner identity," Levinsky illustrates Fuss's concept of "identity as difference": "To the extent that identity always contains the specter of non-identity within it, the subject is always divided and identity is always purchased at the price of the exclusion of the Other, the repression or repudiation of non-identity."[5]

But New World homosocial relations are determined by and designed to uphold compulsory heterosexuality that is encoded as white and Protestant. Although Levinsky acquiesces in the dominant scenario of masculinity, he realizes that, as a Jew, he fails to attain such a cultural identity and is thus prohibited from entering the mainstream. His failure is especially marked in the social and historical context of the late nineteenth- and early twentieth-century United States, which was dominated by racist theories of eugenics and anti-immigrant legislation that restricted Jewish and other minorities' civil rights.[6] As Butler argues in response to Michel Foucault's theory of identity, "prohibitions produce identity . . . along the culturally intelligible grids of an idealized and compulsory sexuality."[7] As those who embody prohibitions, Jews serve as the perfect "other" for the heterosexual ethos of masculine Americanization.

Leonard Dinnerstein explains that anti-Semitism in the early twentieth-century United States "was part and parcel of . . . expressions of hostility toward the foreigner and the outcast," and that Jews were seen as "allegedly favor[ing] alcoholism, spread[ing] pornography, [and] subvert[ing] Christian principles."[8] Constructing Jews as a threat to the social order and morality—they "would . . . take over American government and society if allowed to do so"—goes hand in hand with designating their bodies and sexuality as abnormal and perverse. In *The Jew's Body*, Sander Gilman suggests that the Jew was perceived as "the surrogate for all marginalized males . . . who can be the source of [sexual] corruption."[9] Although the gender designation of the Jewish body is masculine, Gilman argues, its cultural representations focus on its "feminine" nature by, for example, linking Jews and prostitutes as "outsiders whose sexual images represent all of the dangers felt to be inherent in human sexuality" and who "have but one interest, the conversion of sex into money or money into sex."[10] Moreover, in being viewed as sexual polluters with diseased bodies, Jewish males are also linked with homosexuality; in the medical and psychoanalytic discourse, the body of the

Jew, and especially of the Eastern Jew, is often seen as "interchangeable with the body of the gay man—physically different, exotic, feminine."[11]

Read in the context of such constructions of Jewishness, Levinsky appears marginalized in ways similar to Jewish females' marginalization at that time, despite his "macho" economic feat. Being dependent on WASP men's power and support in business, he learns that he has to abandon his "race" and excel in the native performance of "white" economic prowess in order to *be like* "true Americans," although he can never *become* them. As a feminized male, he has to turn his Jewishness and sexuality into Fuss's "non-identity," to participate, as it were, in his own self-annihilation in the anti-Semitic New World. His participation in what Butler calls "the public regulation of fantasy through the surface politics of the body" is, then, a multilayered, gendered performance of acculturation doomed to fail.[12]

The realization that he is a sexually suspect and unacceptable ethnic informs Levinsky's ironic comments about the sexualization of his economic success: "I pictured civilization as a harlot with cheeks, lips, and eyelashes of artificial beauty. I imagined mountains of powder and paint, a deafening chorus of affected laughter, a huge heart, as large as a city, full of falsehood and mischief" (380). He identifies Americanism with images of the goddess Fortuna, who seems to have stepped down from one of the cosmetics advertisements of that time: "Success! It was the almighty goddess of the hour. Thousands of new fortunes were advertising her gaudy splendors. Newspapers, magazines, and public speeches were full of her glory, and he who found favor in her eyes found favor in the eyes of *man*" (445). As Levinsky has learned from his performances with prostitutes and from "prostituting" his capitalist machismo in the land of plenty, a newcomer's rites of entrance into America, his acceptance or rejection there, are warranted by "winning the favor" of the "bitch goddess"— that is, by gaining the approval of the American *"man"* for a successful performance of metaphorical rites of heterosexual romance.

Levinsky's ironic construction of economic success as "making out" with Fortuna-America[13] elicits his necessity to excel in the realm of idealized, nuclear-family, compulsory heterosexuality. His failure to do so means that he can never be American enough; that, as a Jew, he will remain marginalized and feminized as the necessary other for the dominant culture. Levinsky the narrator realizes that his inability to enter this culture through the marriage narrative, despite having become the most desirable catch in Jewish New York, proves again that there is something "wrong," not simply with his gender, but with his sexuality (526).[14]

Queer Moments

Levinsky's overperformance of heterosexualized acculturation repudiates and represses, turns into "non-identity," his Old World Talmud scholar innocence, chastity, and boyishness that his Jewish elders ridicule early on in the novel. He has to erase the homoerotic bonds he has had with his Preacher's Synagogue peers and teachers in Antomir—Reb Sender, whom he "loved passionately" (32) and Naphtali, whose "scrupulous tidiness," "girl-like squeamishness," and "ardent singsong" he "thought fascinating" and whom he missed "as [he] would a sweetheart" (35–36). He learns to hide his "inner identity" and the desires of "a queer fellow" and engages instead in producing himself as the only acceptable male in the culture of New World homosociality—the heterosexual. Levinsky is clearly self-conscious and ashamed of his transformation under the eyes of men who dictate and perpetuate this narrative—he feels "like one stripped in public" when his fellow vendors compliment him on his good looks (116). Yet his mature narrative persona—the fragmented and fluid nonsubject the novel ends with—has clearly survived the heterosexist rituals of Americanization and recognizes the paradoxes of gender and sexuality inherent in this process.

This ability to read through his performance enables Levinsky the narrator to salvage *some* of the "queerness" that relates to his "otherworldly" eroticism, sexualities, and desires that are so alien to the WASP descendants of the Puritans. His discovery that a person is not a stable concept but a fluid process finds him "everlastingly revising [his] views of people, including [his] own self" (350). He also revises the effects of his acculturation performance, which although designed to erase all "queerness" while producing Americanness, did not entirely exclude the possibility of "queer" survival, opportunities, and relationships amid the exclusionary politics of dominant identity production. As Levinsky admits, among the "astonishing discrepancies" in "topsy-turvy" America, "the average man or woman was full of all sorts of false notions" (128).

The ways Levinsky the narrator presents his own "notions" concerning his relationships with men and his ambivalent conquests of women suggest and even compel "queer" readings of Cahan's novel. He talks about his male friends in the eroticized language of love and romance. When crossing to the New World, he befriends a tailor, Gitelson, who "cling[s] to him like a lover" (87–88) and with whom he celebrates their "ship brotherhood" twenty-five years later as if it were a "love-tryst" (514). When he becomes infatuated with Jake Mindels, he "adores him" for his "too soft and too blue" eyes, his blushes, and his virginity ("a regular bride-to-be"), which he discovers when they both become the "lovelorn slaves" of a diva in a Jewish theater (158–61). He compares another friend, his elder benefactor Meyer Nodelman, to "a girl of sixteen" and cherishes their moments of sexual confession, yet he is unable to use similar language in his descriptions of women and be spontaneous in his relationships with them. While attempting to find a wife, Levinsky either chooses an object impossible to conquer and thus sabotages any marriage narrative, as he does with Anna Tevkin, or withdraws at the last moment repulsed and turned off, as he does with Fanny Kaplan. Moreover, he acknowledges and despises his heterosexual performances as fake and troubling: When proposing to Anna he watches himself like an actor ("That's it. . . . I am speaking like a man of a firm purpose [496]); he is "somewhat bored" while listening to a confession of love from Dora, a married woman whose "moral downfall" he succeeds in inducing after an elaborate courtship that reveals to him that conventional "love" is "a blend of animal selfishness and spiritual sublimity" (280, 279).

Although necessarily embroiled with the homophobic discourses he was constructed by and could not help internalizing (much like Cahan himself, perhaps; not to get into his supposed anti-Semitism or self-hatred), Levinsky the older man is able to author and revise himself beyond the exclusionary Americanization by preserving the "queer moments" of his tale.[15] Reading into these moments, we can glimpse other sexualities in Cahan's text, through which the protagonist is unable to constitute himself fully, but which remain in the realm of possibility and thus help him vocalize his "queer" otherness.

By emphasizing this "queer," almost tragic, dimension of Cahan's otherwise often unsympathetic character (he is a class enemy to the author and often a convincingly disgusting sexist capitalist chauvinist), we can read *The Rise of David Levinsky* as illustrating the ways that sexuality and gender are used to marginalize immigrants in America. Even though on the surface these immigrants may have been allowed to partake of all the happiness and glitter of economic success implicit in the American Dream, like Levinsky, they will always remain "victim[s] of [sexual] circumstances." Although he makes it out big with goddess Fortuna, Levinsky ends up as a rather sterile character sexually, one who has exhausted all his manly prowess while breeding money and thus cannot become one of the "Fathers" (523).

Cahan's novel exploits the rags-to-riches narrative of male economic success by constructing the story of a peddler transformed into a millionaire, yet it simultaneously debunks such a vision of success by having this story told by a "queer" character who loses his sense of self as a result of this transformation and who is "devoid of significance" because he is constructed as a failed ethnic and an unfulfilled American. While it is clear that immigrant acculturation is gendered, I hope that I've also demonstrated that it is sexualized. In the dynamic in which Levinsky finds himself, he becomes and remains a "queer" to the extent that he cannot/does not—because of his Jewishness—become a true American, a WASP, a hetero, a married man.

His Fall/Her Rise/Our Problem:
A Footnote on Monica Lewinsky's Queering of the Nation[16]

The Rise of David Levinsky reveals early twentieth-century American nationhood working as a tool of "normalization" through assimilated sexuality and ethnicity. Cahan's protagonist fails in his acculturation rather tragically, but his failure is individual and does not disturb the social order that represses him, even as it allows for the "queer" moments in his story. In contrast, the sex scandal that almost brought down William Jefferson Clinton's presidency in the wake of the so-called "Lewinsky Affair" in 1998 and 1999, ends with a young, "fallen" Jewish woman's paradoxical rise to public prominence. Lewinsky's rise points to a major shift in how the majority of Americans view sex, privacy, and erotic transgression at the millennial juncture. Against David Levinsky's story, "Monica's Story"—to pun the title of Andrew Morton's book[17]—can be seen as a curious flip side to the narrative of Americanization given in Cahan's novel. It shows that the exclusionary notions of ethnicity, sex, and sexuality that have been very narrowly proscribed in this culture ever since the time of the Puritans no longer define, and perhaps never have defined fully, the collective dimensions of what counts as an American.

What I would like to glimpse in this footnote is not so much the sordid details of the scandal, by now obsessively rehearsed, but rather the imprints it has left on American culture in the wake of Monica Lewinsky's plight as the "most humiliated woman in the world."[18] The Lewinsky-Clinton scandal and its pornographic narration, authored and exhibitionistically paraded by the Independent Counsel Kenneth Starr, triggered a revival of jeremiadlike rhetoric of national crisis that hearkens back to Puritan concepts of representative individualism and collective responsibility for the public disclosure, punishment, and forgiveness of sins. I want to argue that this revival of the

Puritan narrative of transgression, repentance, and redemption in the public discourse, which largely centered on the president as the symbol of the nation, can be seen as disrupted by a "queering" narrative of sorts, one that has irrevocably impacted sexual mores and sexual symbologies[19] in American culture. In this narrative, Monica Lewinsky's simultaneous misogynist and anti-Semitic victimization by the media—her *de*-Americanization as an ethnic, "witch," or "modern woman"—goes hand in hand with her rise to prominence as a popular icon of rebellious, status-quo-defying female sexuality that transcends national borders.

The New American Jeremiad

When the Clinton-Lewinsky sex scandal broke out all over the American media, and soon after all over the globe, it was followed by a vigorous resurgence of both neo-Puritan and anti-Puritan rhetoric. Apocalyptic voices cried fire and brimstone and the annihilation of the nation's sacred principles, while those denouncing the Starr investigation saw it as unconstitutional and signifying an ugly rebirth of Puritanism's "punitive lusts and its theocratic visions."[20] For my purposes of contextualizing the national conflict about the earthly symbologies of sex embodied by Monica Lewinsky, I glimpse only a few major examples in the vast ocean of publications.

The printed version of the Starr report is accompanied by the "Analysis by the Staff of the *Washington Post*," which includes cracks at Clinton's confession as a "full Swaggart" (linking the father of the nation's Oval Office performances to televangelism), reactions of "average Americans" to the release of the raunchy report on the Internet, and even an attempt to read it as though it were a nineteenth-century novel.[21] The fallen woman, Monica Lewinsky, is present in the eighteenth-century-like title of the volume as an event rather than a person—"the Lewinsky Affair"—while at the same time being stripped bare, tortured, and probed like a cadaver inside the documentary text whose persecutory zeal echoes Cotton Mather's *Wonders of the Invisible World*.

Monica's Story, an as-told-to account by a British writer, Andrew Morton, blames "modern moral America" for victimizing and "criminalizing" Lewinsky for what many women were persecuted for centuries earlier: being "female, young, confident . . . at ease with her sexuality."[22] Alan M. Dershowitz's *Sexual McCarthyism: Clinton, Starr, and the Emerging Constitutional Crisis* decries the investigation as a direct attack on American democracy and a revival of the Cold War witch-hunts while proclaiming that, ever since the time of the country's morally dubious Founding Fathers, "sex *is* politics and politics *is* sex, and never the twain shall be parted."[23] In a book carefully avoiding any references to specific sexual acts and loaded with jeremiad rhetoric, *In the Eye of the Storm: A Pastor to the President Speaks Out,* J. Philip Wogaman preaches that the president's sin is a sign of national crisis, and he urges all Americans to take collective responsibility for his "sex addiction" and repentance. This "struggle by the nation to define its soul" provides also the last chance to embrace compulsory married heterosexuality: "One does not have to be moralistic or self-righteous to see that monogamous, committed love is the best setting for sexual activity, and that there are moral risks in looser behavior."[24]

What these texts suggest most interestingly is that the rhetoric of the Puritan jeremiad as a vehicle for national soul-searching and sex-policing has not changed much since Jonathan Edwards.[25] As Patricia Roberts-Miller points out, "the recurrence in Jeremiads of the theme of sexual incontinence . . . and the frequency of prosecution for sexual crimes," indicate that "the Puritans were well aware of the pleasures of the flesh." Yet she cautions against overtly simplistic readings of their hypocritical distaste for the matters of "this world" in her analysis of Anne Bradstreet's work: "It is, in essence, our determination to see the Puritans as monologic that creates the expectation that describing the flesh as dangerous is necessarily the same perception as damning it as sinful."[26] I agree with Roberts-Miller that at the root of the problem not only with the Puritan ambivalence about sex but also with the Clinton-Lewinsky scandal is a profound conflict[27] about the very meanings of sex and sexuality in a culture that has not been able to accept the latter as a free, private, normal, and integral part of every individual. As E. L. Doctorow decries, in America, "one of the abiding shames of the Calvinist mind is that only a Son of God can be conceived without animal intercourse."[28] And yet, the ways in which that mind has constructed and responded to Monica Lewinsky's representations in the public discourse seem to indicate that the sexualized Puritan crossbreedings of religion and national identity have been both profoundly recalled and irrevocably disrupted at the millennial moment.

Who Is "That Woman"?

When a contributing editor to the *Jewish Journal of Los Angeles* asked the question—"Who Is Monica Lewinsky?"—the issue at hand was not so much the well-known "twenty-year-old former White House intern" herself as it was her ethnicity as a Jewish woman and the fact that it had seemed irrelevant to the general public.[29] The knowledge that she was "one of us" was important to the Jewish community, some of whom knew that Lewinsky's family belonged to Sinai Temple in West Los Angeles and were second-generation immigrants. And yet, the editorial in the same issue of the *Jewish Journal of Los Angeles* praised the *New York Times* for *not* once mentioning Lewinsky's Jewishness in its biographical sketch of the young woman. This omission allegedly signified the long-awaited disappearance of the old-time ethnic labeling and racial stereotyping—"for many Americans, [she] is just another young woman from a privileged, upper-middle-class family."[30]

But this dual perspective on Monica Lewinsky as *both* an ethnic and a representative national—"a member of the tribe"[31] and an "average American" —impacted the popular oral history and the media accounts surrounding the scandal in ambivalent ways. The Monica Lewinsky of the majority of these stories was seemingly nonethnic but was nevertheless branded for her unapologetic sexuality, for being a spoiled child of her socioeconomic class, for "wanting it all," like so many women of her generation.[32] Despite the hopeful claims of the *JJLA* that "those days of the old anti-Semitic canard about the Jewish Temptress"[33] were over, it is possible to see that Lewinsky's Jewishness was in fact present, though not named, in many of the jokes and commentaries about her class and sex life that made her look "alien" and "foreign" to the mainstream heterosexist (family) values of white America. During a time of renewed anti-immigration sentiments, a "white male crisis," and repeated calls to protect the "white minority" by bigoted southern politicians, Monica Lewinsky's portrait seems to have been painted as a fin-de-siècle rendition of the one created almost a century earlier by Jewish immigrant women writers.

Like the heroines of Anzia Yezierska's and Mary Antin's stories and novels,[34] who felt misunderstood and rejected by the dominant WASP culture, Lewinsky is seen as a compilation of excesses characteristic of centuries-old anti-Semitic and misogynist stereotypes—the "Oriental," the "Jewess," and more recently, the "Jewish American Princess." She eats too much, talks too much, spends too much money, demands too much from men, and obviously has too much sex.[35] Andrew Morton points out that her "saga has spotlighted the underlying misogyny that still permeates American life. . . . Clinton the adulterer is a forgiven man; Monica Lewinsky the temptress is a scorned woman, derided by feminists and conservatives alike. . . . What is far worse, however, she has committed the greatest sin of all: she is overweight. . . . [H]er increased size is a sign of her moral laxity or divine punishment.³⁶

In sketching an ironic portrait of the scandal as a Molière comedy, Elizabeth Hardwick calls Lewinsky an "aggressive, a rouge-lipped exhibitionist," a "fast number," a "Niobe" with a weight problem, a "cataract of expressiveness," and a woman displaying the nuance and smarts of an "oyster" or, at best, a "coyote."³⁷ Hardwick's irony may be meant to cross that fine line between wit and offense. She likens Morton's book to *The Scarlet Letter*, in which the new (Jewish) Hester wears her "A" proudly and spills the beans in "a vertiginous accounting of bantering baby talk mixed with . . . extraordinary bordello reminiscences." Like many others, this critic links Lewinsky's weight to her sexuality: "Anyone who has lived in a town or small city can remember that fat girls 'put out' when they got a chance." As if in response to that insight, Jane Mayer sees the young woman's so-called "social forwardness . . . [her] desire to put herself where the action was" as resulting from *sex* therapy aiming at female "*self*-actualization."³⁸ This portrait of Lewinsky's "self" *as* sex, or vice versa, is so omnipresent—her body, insecurities and complexes, clothing and lipstick so familiar—that David Remnick likens her to "La Gioconda": "In Monica we have taken to seeing anything or anyone we care to. . . . She is everywhere. She suits all interpretations. She is featured in everything from law journals to porn zines. She has given rise to a cable industry."³⁹ No wonder that her caricature by David Levine, a hybrid of her and Clinton's faces sporting a cigar, is now featured on the web site of the *New York Review of Books*.

That this omnipresent female icon has a centuries-old stereotype of the overweight and oversexed Jewish female as its inspiration is confirmed in the series of commentaries that Marlene Marks wrote for the *Jewish Journal of Los Angeles*.⁴⁰ In a statement that seems to echo Pastor Wogaman's call for the nation to take responsibility for the sins of one of its members, Marks claims that Lewinsky's whole ethnic community has been scarred by her behavior and her victimization by the president and the media: "[T]he character and lack of judgment of that Jewish woman is our business."⁴¹ That is so, Marks suggests, because in the eyes of the nation Lewinsky is a product and, in a sense, a grotesque symbol of Jewish women's gendered history and their sexual anxiety, one akin to the likes of Paula Jones and Gennifer Flowers: "Jewish trailer trash. White House trouble, with a good manicure and big hair."⁴²

Marks implies that Lewinsky is not only a dangerous possible influence on the younger generation of women—both Jews and non-Jews—but also that the generation of these women's mothers may have taken their own sexual freedom too much for granted as they rebelled against America's "straight-laced Puritanism."[43] What may lurk behind Marks's comments, too, is that Monica Lewinsky is a Jewish woman who became a dangerous national icon due to her "authentic" performances of alien ethnicity and sexuality—the traits that she was supposed to have overcome as an assimilated, third-generation immigrant. Her very survival of the whole ordeal brands her as foreign, as un-American, an immoral European according to William J. Bennett, and thus threatening to her native beholders. Her unsanctioned, "unnatural" sexuality and carnal knowledge/know-how—oral sex and (phone) masturbation—have the power to bring down the father of the nation, who, as history teaches, is only supposed to engage in the publicly sanctioned, reproductive kind of sex.[44]

But in the surprising denouement to this latest topsy-turvy American narrative of seduction and betrayal, it is the victim, the witch, and the persecuted ethnic mistress-masturbator who wins. Joan Didion explains that, in the end, "Americans . . . favor[ed] the person who had engaged in a common sexual act over the person who had elicited the details of that act as evidence for a public stoning."[45] With the rise of Monica Lewinsky, and the surge of public and international sympathy for her, her paradoxical de-Americanization and de-"naturalization" became signs of attractiveness. Her successful European tour and the popularity she gained at the end of her ordeal, particularly among sexual minorities, confirmed a paradoxical outcome of the Puritan crusade against her as a symbol of America's emerging new sexuality. Although being a "queer" *and* an American may still be as impossible an oxymoron to live by as "resident alien," Monica's narrative has definitely "queered" the nation, if not "Lewinsky'ed" it, with a whole new sexual symbology.[46]

It is also on this new terrain of alien and "queer" sexuality signifying new Americanisms—"where the term 'queer' is to be a site of collective contestation, the point of departure for a set of historical reflections and future imaginings"[47]—that Monica Lewinsky and Cahan's David Levinsky meet again. And their meeting can serve as an explanation of the rather "queer" outcome of Kenneth Starr's consummate chastity crusade. In fact, David Levinsky cites an earlier version of the Monica Lewinsky we all know, or think we know, upon a visit to Florida: "Once, in Florida, I thought I was falling in love with a rich Jewish girl whose face had a bashful expression of a peculiar type. There are different sorts of bashfulness. This girl had the bashfulness of sin, as I put it to myself. She looked as if her mind harbored illicit thoughts which she was trying to conceal. Her blushes seemed to be full of sex and her eyes full of secrets. She was not a pretty girl at all, but her 'guilty look' disturbed me as long as we were stopping in the same place" (527).

Caught in the performance of heterosexist WASP masculinity, David Levinsky seems to act out the desires of the culture that will later condemn Monica Lewinsky. He is attracted to this woman's Orientalized, ethnic sexuality and is profoundly disturbed by its "sinful" appeal. Like the Judeo-Christian paradox of femininity first embodied in Eve/Mary, the nameless young woman in Cahan's novel is both bashful and sinful, virginal and sluttish, pure and repulsive. And like Monica Lewinsky, the oversexed Jewish female from Cahan's novel reveals much more as an embodiment of American sexual symbologies as functions of ambivalent national identity than about Jewish womanhood. This can be seen in the way Cahan's protagonist links his simultaneous desire for her with his self-disgust *and* with her "guilty look."

Here, it is productive to ask a few questions. Of what exactly is this young woman really "guilty"? Premature knowledge of sex and her own seductive powers? Mind reading that reveals to her David's/Clinton's sexual frustration, and thus makes *her* responsible for his/their transgression? Could she be the "masturbating girl," the phone sex offender—that "proto-form of modern sexual identity itself," as Eve Kosofsky Sedgwick puts it?[48] Or is she perhaps seen and represented *as* guilty and ashamed precisely for being all these things, for providing an unapologetic mirror for American sex paradoxes, in short, for her unassimilable, "queer" ethnic sexuality?

As Sander Gilman argues, and as Anzia Yezierska illustrated poignantly in her novel *Salome of the Tenements* (1923),[49] the Jewish woman the late-nineteenth- and early-twentieth-century American culture represents is both the oversexed seductress Salome and the modern, liberated, New Woman: a "blue stocking" whose emancipated sexuality, like the diseases commonly associated with the Jewish body, threatens both white masculinity and a social order based on Christian/Protestant family values.[50] David Levinsky's ambivalent feelings about the nameless young woman can, then, be contextualized in the discourses of sexual, class, religious, racial, and ethnic difference signified as abnormality and sickness—and commonly associated not only with Jews but also with all dark-skinned people, and with some Eastern Europeans, ever since the entrance of eugenics into Western "science."[51]

The fissured image of contaminating ethnic female sexuality in Cahan's novel serves as a screen onto which the voyeuristic protagonist projects his own sexual split. In Monica Lewinsky, it is a reflection of America's most basic ambivalences—if not its *dis-ease*—about any post-Puritan sexuality that threatens, but also serves as the necessary other(s) to, the WASP male reproductive heterosexuality that embodies the national norm.[52] Monica Lewinsky's survival of her "story," then, including her soft landing in the lap of Goddess Fortuna with the publication of Morton's book and international media opportunities, demonstrate that the very rigid notions of American "sex" that meant to destroy her in fact helped to launch her as a paradoxical symbol of the new, post-Puritan America.[53]

It is this ambivalent image of Monica Lewinsky that makes it possible at last to imagine that other woman—the mute erotic object of David Levinsky's gaze—staring back and refusing to be guilty of anybody else's sexual frustrations. As Sander Gilman reminds us, "bodies have a way of being seen again and again in the past, and identity—whether that of Jews, blacks or Hispanics or women—always has to perform a perilous balancing act between self and Other."[54] Ever since the time of Anne Hutchinson and her fictionalized portrait in Nathaniel Hawthorne's *The Scarlet Letter*, Puritan America has despised and persecuted women for being too outspoken and too sexual, and thus has kept them outside of the national consensus. Monica Lewinsky's campy celebrity has proven that the old narratives can be "queered," that the concept of national identity at the fin-de-siècle no longer has to burn with a still-hot Puritan imprint, even though, in many ways, that very imprint has made her "queering" possible. Monica Lewinsky has been described as "the woman of secrets who no longer has any." Her "eyes are not windows, but mirrors, and what we see in them is awful."[55] Could "that woman" really be us? Could Monica Lewinsky's mirror eyes really reflect back to us a new America that is finally coming to terms with its ambivalent history of sexuality? If so, then, in a perversely Puritanlike twist of rhetoric, the "awful" *is* good.

Notes

1. Abraham Cahan, *The Rise of David Levinsky* (New York: Penguin, 1993), 3. Hereafter cited parenthetically in the text.

2. Jules Chametzky, *From the Ghetto: The Fiction of Abraham Cahan* (Amherst: University of Massachusetts Press, 1977), 137; Sam B. Girgus, *The New Covenant: Jewish Writers and the American Idea* (Chapel Hill: University of North Carolina Press, 1984), 74; Donald Weber, "Outsiders and Greenhorns: Christopher Newman in the Old World, David Levinsky in the New," *American Literature* 67 (1995): 738, 740. See

also Sanford E. Maurovitz, *Abraham Cahan* (New York: Twayne, 1996); Eric Homberger, "Some Uses for Jewish Ambivalence: Abraham Cahan and Michael Gold," *Between "Race" and Culture: Representations of "the Jew" in English and American Literature* (Stanford: Stanford University Press, 1996); Philip Barrish, "'The Genuine Article': Ethnicity, Capital, and *The Rise of David Levinsky*," *American Literary History* (winter 1993): 643–62; Bernard Weinstein, "Cahan's David Levinsky: An Inner Profile," *MELUS* (fall 1983): 47–53; David Engel, "The 'Discrepancies of the Modern: Towards a Revaluation of Abraham Cahan's *The Rise of David Levinsky*," *Studies in American Jewish Literature* 2 (1982): 36–60.

3. Diana Fuss, *Essentially Speaking: Feminism, Nature, and Difference* (New York: Routledge, 1989), 109.

4. Sacvan Bercovitch analyzes the "ideology of American consensus" in an essay that grounds it in the Puritan errand in the New World—the "mission in the wilderness." Sacvan Bercovitch, "The Rites of Assent: Rhetoric, Ritual, and the Ideology of American Consensus," in Sam B. Girgus, ed., *The American Self: Myth, Ideology, and Popular Culture* (Albuquerque: University of New Mexico Press, 1981), 5–42.

5. Fuss, *Essentially Speaking*, 103.

6. Leonard Dinnerstein, "Anti-Semitism in Crisis Times in the U.S.: The 1920s and 1930s," in Sander L. Gilman and Steven T. Katz, eds., *Anti-Semitism in Times of Crisis* (New York: New York University Press, 1991), 213–18.

7. Judith Butler, *Gender Trouble: Feminism and the Subversion of Identity* (New York: Routledge, 1990), 135.

8. Dinnerstein, "Anti-Semitism," 213, 216.

9. Sander Gilman, *The Jew's Body* (New York: Routledge, 1991), 123.

10. Gilman, *The Jew's Body*, 4–5, 120–22.

11. Gilman discusses instances of textual intersections of Jewishness and homosexuality in Freud, Proust, and Otto Weininger on pages 83 and 196, 126–27, and 133, respectively.

12. Butler, *Gender Trouble*, 136.

13. America as Fortuna in Cahan's novel is the opposite of the figure of Columbia or Liberty, who symbolized "prostitution's opposite, political and moral purity, though symbolically still expressed through the terms of sexuality," as Dana D. Nelson claims in *National Manhood: Capitalist Citizenship and the Imagined Fraternity of White Men* (Durham, N.C.: Duke University Press, 1998), 35.

14. This argument can be usefully read in the context of Eve K. Sedgwick's theory of "homosexual panic" which, as she explains, "became the normal condition of male heterosexual entitlement." Eve Kosofsky Sedgwick, Epistemology of the Closet (Berkeley: University of California Press, 1990), 185. However, as in many other critiques of sexual identity, ethnic and racialized dimensions of it are not very visible in Sedgwick's model.

15. I use the term "queer" in these pages much in the same way Sedgwick does: as "multiply transitive" and "representing an immemorial current" that is "as antisepa-

ratist as it is antiassimilationist." Although my usage gains new dimensions in its contextualization in the discourses of immigration, race, and ethnicity, Sedgwick's definition works well. "*Queer* can refer to: the open mesh of possibilities, gaps, overlaps, dissonances and resonances, lapses and excesses of meaning when the constituent elements of anyone's gender, of anyone's sexuality aren't made (or *can't* be made) to signify monolithically." Eve Kosofsky Sedgwick, *Tendencies* (Durham, N.C.: Duke University Press, 1993), xii, 8. See also her claim that some recent work "spins the term outward along dimensions that can't be subsumed under gender and sexuality at all: the ways that race, ethnicity, postcolonial nationality criss-cross with these *and other* identity-constituting, identity-fracturing discourses" (*Tendencies*, 9). I demonstrate that the discourses of sexuality and nationality, race, and ethnicity are in fact inseparable and mutually penetrable.

16. The term "queering" refers to what Judith Butler identifies as "a discursive site," a "signal" linked to an inquiry into the historical *"formation* of homosexualities." She also stresses the term's "deformative and misappropriative power" to challenge and complicate existing identity categories. Judith Butler, *Bodies that Matter: On the Discursive Limits of Sex* (New York: Routledge, 1993), 229–30. I want to thank Miriyam Glazer, Nick Radel, Tracy Fessenden, and Colleen Smith for their valuable insights concerning the "Lewinsky Affair," which helped me to see its relevance to my project on Cahan's novel. I am also grateful for Nick Radel's suggestions during the drafting phase of the part dealing with Cahan's novel.

17. Andrew Morton, *Monica's Story* (New York: St. Martin's Paperbacks, 1999).

18. Morton, *Monica's Story*, 340.

19. I am borrowing this term from Sacvan Bercovitch's *The Office of the Scarlet Letter* (Baltimore and London: Johns Hopkins University Press, 1991). While discussing American culture's self-revelations in Hawthorne's novel, Bercovitch defines "cultural symbology" as the "system of symbolic meanings that encompasses text and context alike, simultaneously nourishing the imagination and marking its boundaries. . . . A highly volatile system . . . [that] at once denies aesthetic autonomy and highlights the difference between aesthetics and the political or institutional forms usually associated with ideology. It also reminds us that aesthetic representations are inescapably political, just as literature necessarily assumes an institutional form" (xvii).

20. E. L. Doctorow, "Has Starr Humiliated Us All?" *New Yorker*, (12 October 1998), 50. See also John Stachniewski, *The Persecutory Imagination: English Puritanism and the Literature of Religious Despair* (Oxford: Clarendon Press, 1991) for an account of the "mirroring of puritan theology and domestic social history." Stachniewski emphasizes what Lawrence Stone calls "the reinforcement of patriarchy" in English and American Puritanism. It is interesting to note the link between "Calvin's stipulation of the death penalty (never implemented in Calvin's Geneva, but made legislatively operative in Connecticut and Massachusetts in the 1640s) for disobedience to parents" (79–80) and the ways Clinton's sin was constructed as a crime against his heavenly Father. At the same time, Clinton the sinner was seen as a "child of God," and his public redemption came in the wake of forgiveness he received from the reli-

gious "fathers" of the nation during the prayer breakfast on Sept. 11, 1998. (For more details see Wogaman below.) Toni Morrison's take on Clinton as the first "black" president adds an interesting twist to this reading (Toni Morrison, "Talk of the Town," *New Yorker*, 5 October 1998, 31–32).

21. John F. Harris, "For Clinton, a Day to Atone but Not Retreat. At Prayer Breakfast, President Apologizes and Pledges Legal Defense. White House Issues Apologies, Gets Defensive," *The Starr Report: The Findings of Independent Counsel Kenneth W. Starr on President Clinton and the Lewinsky Affair* (New York: Public Affairs, 1998), XXII; Joel Achenbach, "Dreary Prose, Silly Plot. Can't Put It Down," *The Starr Report* XLV–XLVIII. See also Cynthia Ozick, "Comments on the Topic," *New Yorker* (12 October 1998), 32; Adam Gopnick, "American Studies," *New Yorker* (28 September 1998), 39–40, 42.

22. Morton, *Monica's Story*, 340. See also Doctorow's reference to the Salem witch trials in *New Yorker*, 12 October 1998, 30; and Rebecca Mead, "Who Really Exploited Monica Lewinsky?" *New Yorker*, 28 September 1998, 29, which calls Starr's report "sexual abuse."

23. Alan M. Dershowitz, *Sexual McCarthyism: Clinton, Starr, and the Emerging Constitutional Crisis* (New York: Basic Books, 1998), 210.

24. J. Philip Wogaman, *In the Eye of the Storm: A Pastor to the President Speaks Out* (Louisville: Westminster John Knox Press, 1998), 63.

25. It is beyond the scope of this study to peruse the many titles that deal with the history and practice of the Puritan jeremiad. My main inspirations, however, have been Sacvan Bercovitch, *The American Jeremiad* (Madison: University of Wisconsin Press, 1978), and Emory Elliott, *Power and the Pulpit in Puritan New England* (Princeton: Princeton University Press, 1974).

26. Patricia Roberts-Miller, *Voices in the Wilderness: Public Discourse and the Paradox of Puritan Rhetoric* (Tuscaloosa and London: University of Alabama Press, 1999), 139–40.

27. Like many scholars before her, Roberts-Miller stresses the "centrality of conflict in Calvinistic notions of piety [which] is indicated in Calvin's definition of genuine religion: 'confidence in God coupled with serious fear' (*Institutes* 1:42)." She sees this definition as a "perfect instance of Puritanism" (140).

28. Doctorow, "Has Starr Humiliated Us All?" 29.

29. Tom Tugend, "Who Is Monica Lewinsky? In an Interview with an Israel Newspaper, Her Lawyer Provides Some Answers," *Jewish Journal* online, 30 January 1998; www.jewishjournal.com.

30. Gene Lichtenstein, "Did You Know Monica Lewinsky Was Jewish?" *Jewish Journal* online, 30 January 30 1998; www.jewishjournal.com.

31. Lichtenstein, "Did You Know?"

32. For a historical overview of post–World War II Jewish feminism, see Sylvia Barack Fishman, *A Breath of Life: Feminism in the American Jewish Community* (New

York: The Free Press, 1993), and especially her chapter, "Broadening Sexual and Gender Roles," 95–120.

33. Lichtenstein, "Did You Know?"

34. See Magdalena J. Zaborowska, *How We Found America: Reading Gender through East European Immigrant Narratives* (Chapel Hill: University of North Carolina Press, 1995). For a recent study of Jewish female immigrant experience see also Riv-Ellen Prell, *Fighting to Become Americans: Jews, Gender, and the Anxiety of Assimilation* (Boston: Beacon Press, 1999). Fishman's *A Breath of Life* and Wendy Shalit's *A Return to Modesty: Discovering the Lost Virtue* (New York: The Free Press, 1999) are useful for studying the often contradictory views on Jewish women's role in the community.

35. For a history and analysis of the JAP stereotype, see Prell's chapter, "The Jewish-American Princess: Detachable Ethnicity, Gender Ambiguity and Middle-Class Anxiety" in *Fighting to Become Americans*, 177–208. Prell describes the "JAP's qualities as evocative of earlier intra-ethnic and racist stereotypes . . . the Jewish woman's large Oriental body . . . need to exercise and diet . . . demands for adornment . . . her use of male wealth (193)." See also Joyce Antler, ed., *Talking Back: Images of Jewish Women in American Popular Culture* (Hanover and London: Brandeis University Press, 1998), and Miriam Peskowitz and Laura Levitt, eds., *Judaism since Gender* (New York and London: Routledge, 1997), especially Ann Pellegrini, "Interarticulations: Gender, Race, and the Jewish Woman Question" (49–55) and Amy-Jill Levine, "A Jewess, More and/or Less" (149–57).

36. Morton, *Monica's Story*, 340.

37. Elizabeth Hardwick, "Head over Heels," *New York Review of Books*, 22 April 1999, 6–8.

38. Jane Mayer, "The Love Doctor Who Counselled [sic] Monica Lewinsky," *New Yorker*, 12 October 1998, 30–31. See also Michael Wolff, "Judith's Untold Story," *New York Magazine*, 5 April 1999, 18–19, 111, in which Lewinsky is called a "troublemaker" and "media savant" (111); Walter Kirn, "Lewinsky in Oz," *New York Magazine*, 22 March 1999, 102–3, which likens her to Dorothy, that all-American innocent; Maer Roshan, "Oh, Barbara! Your Dignity!" *New York Magazine*, 15 March 1999, 16, where she and Barbara Walters are called "princesses."

39. David Remnick, "Our Woman of Secrets," *New Yorker*, 8 February 1999, 24.

40. Marlene Adler Marks, "The Daughter," *Jewish Journal* online, 30 January 1998; "Clinton's Confession," *Jewish Journal* online, 21 August 1998; "The Lewinsky/Lieberman Equation," *Jewish Journal* online, 2 October 1998; "Monica's Moment and Mine," *Jewish Journal* online, 12 February 1999, all at www.jewishjournal.com.

41. Marks, "The Daughter."

42. Marks, "Monica's Moment."

43. For a survey of a more recent resurgence of this sentiment see Eric Alterman, "Blowjobs and Snow Jobs," *The Nation*, 20 December 1999, 10, which comments on

the widespread fascination of national and local press with the kind of "queer" sex that is still illegal in some states, e.g.,"Parents are alarmed by an unsettling new fad in middle school: oral sex."

44. Another argument that could be made here is that the incestuous predator, ball-cutting Lewinsky has in fact "emasculated"/eaten her President/Father who symbolizes the virility and unquestionable white hetero-masculine health of the nation.

45. Joan Didion, "Clinton Agonistes," *New York Review of Books*, 22 October 1998, 20.

46. This is also an interesting instance where we could look into the oxymorons used to describe the Puritan experience of faith. Roberts-Miller recalls Jonathan Edwards's "warring contradictions" (140–41).

47. Butler, *Bodies that Matter*, 228.

48. Eve Kosofsky Sedgwick, "Jane Austen and the Masturbating Girl," *Tendencies* 109–29; 118.

49. For a reading of this novel, see Zaborowska, *How We Found America*, 139–47.

50. Sander Gilman, "Salome, Syphilis, Sarah Bernhardt and the 'Modern Jewess'," *The German Quarterly* 66.2 (spring 1993): 195–211; Anzia Yezierska, *Salome of the Tenements* (New York: Boni & Liveright, 1923). See also Gilman, *The Visibility of the Jew in Diaspora: Body Imagery and Its Cultural Context*, The B. G. Rudolph Lectures in Judaic Studies (Syracuse University, May 1992), 4–5.

51. See Gilman, *The Visibility of the Jew*, 4–7, where he demonstrates an interesting racialized connection among Poles, Jews, and African-Americans.

52. I realize that "ethnic female sexuality" is a much larger construct, one that arguably includes all "nonwhite" (or not-quite-"white") women, and that the "un-sanctioned sexualities" is an even wider one. I narrow my discussion and terminology in the interest of this argument's conciseness and its relevance to the context of Cahan's work.

53. See Michael Wolff, "Brand Monica," *New York Magazine*, 1 March 1999, 20–21: "She was supposed to be branded by the media maelstrom—slut, victim, valley girl. Instead, she became one the major brand names of our time" (20).

54. Gilman, *The Jew's Body*, 243.

55. Remnick, "Our Woman of Secrets," 24.

Desert
of the Heart
Jane Rule's
Puritan Outing

༽

Margaret Soenser Breen

Jane Rule's classic lesbian coming-out/conversion novel *Desert of the Heart* invites us to consider the contiguity of lesbian, gay, and queer literature with Puritan texts, specifically with the key Puritan narrative *The Pilgrim's Progress*, commonly acknowledged as a source text for the English as well as Anglo-American realist novel. By framing this literary analysis within lesbian, gay, and queer discussions of religious fundamentalism, I wish to underscore the necessarily political dislocations that occur when gay and lesbian and queer writers deploy Puritan spiritual and literary trajectories. While fundamentalist Christian groups within a contemporary North American sociopolitical context may define themselves in opposition to lesbians, gay men, and queers—in part by invoking Puritan traditions—lesbian, gay, and queer writers often utilize traditional Puritan formulations of spiritual doubt, uncertainty, and faith in their explorations of, for example, homophobia, heterosexism, coming out, and sexual desire. Such productions are inevitably disruptive, transformative, political. They exact their own sexual regulation, while at the same time interrogating older, Puritan constructions. In the case of *Desert of the Heart*, lesbian protagonists Ann and Evelyn are *sanctioned*—at once morally damned and narratologically blessed—by Bunyan's narrative of spiritual progress.

I began writing this essay by looking at a picture postcard of Provincetown, Massachusetts. The postcard, which I keep in my car so that I have it with me as I travel, displays a tower erected in honor of the *Mayflower* Pilgrims who came to North America in search of religious toleration. They first ventured ashore in Provincetown in November 1620 before sailing to Plymouth at the end of that year. If, geographically speaking, the two places are proximate, allegorically speaking they seem worlds apart: Plymouth is the site of the first permanent English settlement in New England; Provincetown is an artist's colony at the tip of Cape Cod, a haven of permission and promise for gay men, lesbians, and bisexual and transgendered people in North America. One might, then, read the postcard as an iconic tribute to the oxymoronic, to those bifurcated meanings of "sanction," blessing and prohibition. What, after all, could a group of seventeenth-century religious dissidents have to do with a set of twentieth- and twenty-first-century sexual deviants? Particularly from the vantage point of contemporary U.S. politics, in which the religious right so often highlights its opposition to queers of all gendered and sexual positionalities, one might well wonder what, aside from a flaccid trumpeting of assimilationist desire,[1] could be the purpose of imagining a historical common ground for Puritans and queers?

The question intrigues many lesbian, gay, and queer writers. Mab Segrest begins her essay "I Lead Two Lives: Confessions of a Closet Baptist": "I lead a double life. By day, I'm a relatively mild mannered English teacher at a southern Baptist college. By night . . . I am a lesbian writer and editor. . . . My employers do not know about my other life. When they find out, I assume I will be fired, maybe prayed to death. For the past four years, my life has moved rapidly in opposite directions."[2] This passage may well seem at odds with Segrest's self-identification as a "closet Baptist." Closeting occurs within the context of her church affiliation, yet it is Segrest's lesbianism, not her Baptism, that is most immediately under sanction. Segrest is only a "closet Baptist" insofar as she is a closet lesbian. For a community of lesbian readers, by comparison, she confesses or outs her religious affiliation.

Driven by Baptism and lesbianism, Segrest may well have been moving "in opposite directions," but her rhetorical strategy suggests something more. How opposite are these directions after all; or, more pointedly, whose political interests does this opposition serve? In Segrest's essay, as throughout lesbian and gay literature, the coming-out narrative bears remarkable similarity and is indeed indebted to the spiritual progress narrative, which, as Barry Qualls has demonstrated, offers a powerful literary formula for conveying "truth."[3] Both narratives foreground the individual's conviction in "truth," even at the cost of penetrating social loss. What, then, could be the point of recognizing a commonality between fundamentalist religious belief and lesbian/bisexual/gay experience?

Simply put, it is to understand completely, profoundly, that no subject position—certainly not a Puritan one—is "pure," inviolable, but is rather, in Jane Rule's terms, "mixed":4 It will have its connections with and incursions into other positions.5 In this particular historical moment, when some of the most vitriolic examples of homophobia have been fueled by fundamentalist rhetoric, it is perhaps surprising but nonetheless imperative to underscore the dynamic relation between Puritan narratives and gay and lesbian litera-ture. For myself, a repatriated American ex-patriot for whom "home" has always signified Austria and Germany—countries whose histories of intoler-ance for various forms of human expression haunt my lesbian reality of cultural exile—I find that my thoughts are never far from Bunyan's City of Destruction. Puritan narratives such as *The Pilgrim's Progress* have proven powerful testimonies to the resilience of a religious minority under attack. Their narrative patterns and paradigms are themselves lessons well worth noting for any oppressed social group.

Both queers and fundamentalists have been shaped by histories of social oppression. As both Segrest's words and the Provincetown monument sug-gest, their histories are at once separate and linked, potentially at odds and potentially mutually empowering. To recognize this is to begin to dismantle the binarisms that currently structure the religious right's homophobia, and so, in turn, to strive toward the "shared understanding" that Shane Phelan considers in her introduction to *Playing with Fire: Queer Politics and Queer Theory*: "We should be working to forge links between movements against oppressions. Such linkages do not require appeals to something in our being; rather they are premised on a shared understanding of social space and power."6

For queers and religious fundamentalists, the potential for a "shared understanding" resides in shared experiences of social intolerance. As Michael Warner puts it in "Tongues Untied: Memoirs of a Pentecostal Boy-hood," "What queers often forget, jeopardized as we are by resurgent fundamentalisms in the United States, is that fundamentalists . . . too con-sider themselves an oppressed minority. In their view the dominant culture is one of a worldliness they have rejected, and bucking that trend comes, in some very real ways, with social stigmatization."7

Both queers and fundamentalists flout the status quo and, in so doing, both are socially stigmatized. Warner continues, "Religion makes available a language of ecstasy, a horizon of significance within which transgressions against the normal order of the world and the boundaries of the self *can be seen as good things*."8 Religion, in other words, may itself be understood as

queer, where "queer" addresses the social margins, the places where the outcast is simultaneously stigmatized and vitalized by her/his outsider status.

The gay poet Mark Doty makes a similar point. He imagines his ancestor
Edward Dotey, a passenger on the *Mayflower*, less as a devout believer than as
a social opportunist, a figure more in line with the derogatory stereotype of
the self-indulgent homosexual than with that of the self-eradicating Puritan
ascetic:

> Edward Dotey himself is a bit of a problem. . . . [I]t appears that the
> young man from London sold himself into indentured servitude
> to escape some fate worse than seven years without liberty in a
> relatively unknown and certainly inhospitable country . . .
>   Once settled in Plymouth, he distinguished himself by fighting
> the first duel on American soil. . . . He filed America's first
> lawsuit. He seems to have been more or less run out of the
> colony. . . . He left behind a wealth of copper pots and iron
> implements, and a nasty reputation.9

Some 350 years after his ancestor's death, the poet muses, "What would my
Pilgrim forefather make of [Provincetown]? It's too easy to suppose that he
would find in the town which has evolved upon his wooded shore a kind of
Babylon. He was himself an outsider. . . . [The Puritans] were . . .contentious
and embattled, both in a threatening England and an even more uncertain
America. We have more in common with their tremendous doubts, with
their fear in the face of an unknown future, than with whatever certainties
they may have claimed."10 The commonality that Doty finds between himself
and his ancestor resides in a shared epistemological stance: the capacity to
dwell in a place of uncertainty or queerness, a space that Puritan writers so
often denominate a "wilderness" or "desert."11

Doty's memoir *Heaven's Coast*, of which the above passages are excerpts,
takes up the cadences and formulations of Puritan meditation. If Michael
Warner performs a queer reading of fundamentalism, Doty offers something
of the inverse: For Doty, the recognition of one's queerness entails "the difficult, frustrating work of living on that dizzying live edge between affirmation
and despair."12 Doty's flaming introspection here—that "dizzying live
edge"—recalls conventional Puritan formulations of spiritual uncertainty.
That shuttling back and forth between hope and despair, the characteristic
posture of spiritual pilgrimage, is perhaps most powerfully rendered by John
Bunyan in the figure of Christian, the hero of *The Pilgrim's Progress*. For Doty,

the posture of Puritan-sanctioned travail embodies queerness's doubled experience of empowerment and estrangement.

Doty's writing here, as well as Segrest's and Warner's, bears out my own experience. Pilgrim monuments, material and metaphoric, populate my familial, political, and sexual landscapes. Within the context of literary criticism, these monuments make me want to understand how gay, lesbian, and queer writers, whose aesthetic and political visions are quite distinct,[13] can provide compelling, dignified critiques of religious systems—critiques whose rhythms, tropes, and narratives are indebted for their power to the very traditions they subvert. Relatively little scholarship has addressed these crucial intersections between Puritanism, especially its narrative patterns, and literary explorations of queer and lesbian-feminist epistemologies. I wish, then, to discompose proprietary religious appropriations of Puritan discourse, discourse that appears again and again in the literary and theoretical works of gay, lesbian, and queer writers.

My most immediate subject is realist writer Jane Rule's *Desert of the Heart*, which I read as a lesbian revision of Bunyan's *The Pilgrim's Progress*. Rule's novel offers not only an explicit critique of *The Pilgrim's Progress*'s representation of female *Bildung*, but, largely by retrieving Bunyan's paradigms of progress, also effects a cautionary allegory for Anglo-American culture's constructions of gender, genre, and sexuality. Being both a lesbian novel and a coming-out narrative, Rule's work is a latter-day pilgrim's progress that subverts the tradition of realist literature shaped by Bunyan, Milton, and the Bible.[14] As Gillian Spraggs observes in her own essay on *Desert of the Heart*, this tradition is committed to "presenting images and narratives of human existence . . . that . . . impress with a conviction of 'truth.' "[15] In Rule's novel, though, this endeavor to represent truth proves to be a "vanity of vanities."

Published in 1964, its action set in 1958, *Desert of the Heart* evinces what Rule, in a 1976 interview with Geoffrey Hancock, termed her "deep mistrust of any system as an answer."[16] The literary "system" that she mistrusts (yet nonetheless sustains) in *Desert of the Heart* is the Bunyanesque tradition of realism, whose investment in truth telling has historically effaced the "truth" of lesbian love. From their first encounter, *Desert of the Heart*'s two heroines, Evelyn and Ann, recognize that they are each the other's double. If the two women belong to the same literary family, which alternately types women as embodiments of seduction and puerility—embedded in the name "Evelyn" is "Eve," and Ann's last name is "Childs"—such definitions of femininity cannot adequately describe or contain either of them. Nor can the mother-daughter paradigm, also suggested by their names and age difference (which ironically links them to Bunyan's pairing of female pilgrims Christiana and Mercy), account for their attraction. Punctuating her initial meeting with Ann with the e.e. cummings line " 'Hello is what a mirror says,' " Evelyn remarks, "There was no family resemblance. . . . It was rather an impression which, when analyzed, seemed to have no firm basis. Ann's face was . . . a memory not a likeness."[17]

The mirror the two women hold up to each other recalls the two-way mirror that, in part 2 of *The Pilgrim's Progress*, daughter-in-law Mercy asks Christiana to bring her: "There is a looking-glass . . . off of which I cannot take my mind; if therefore I have it not, I think I shall miscarry."[18] The margin glosses the mirror as the "word of God," and the narrator continues, "Now the glass was one of a thousand. It would present *a man* one way, with *his* own feature exactly, and turn it but another way, and it would show one the very face and similitude of the Prince of pilgrims himself."[19] If the two-way mirror recalls the central mystery of Christianity that Christ is both God and man, it also reflects the female believer's mediated position within the church. Unlike man, whose identification with Christ is possible on both the personal and abstract levels, woman attains only an abstract relation. So Mercy fears that without the mirror, she will "miscarry"—both physically and spiritually. Thus the mirror images the sexual politics of Bunyan's Puritanism. Neither Christiana nor Mercy may guide herself or the other, even though the two women are traveling, "progressing," together. The male mediation that formalizes the female pilgrim's identification with God and man obscures the immediacy of the women's bond.

By comparison, the basis for Evelyn's identification with Ann, fifteen years her junior, is the recognition that male mediation leaves the heroine estranged from herself. Ann and Evelyn may initially read their relationship in terms of the mother-daughter paradigm, but that equation proves, as Ann says in another context, a transitory one. Lesbian *Bildung* in *Desert of the Heart* disrupts Bunyan's construction of female subjectivity as an aural and biological receptacle for male authority.[20] So Evelyn, aware of her attraction to Ann, traces a singsong formulation of female progress: "If there is no face in the mirror, marry. If there is no shadow on the ground, have a child. These are the conventions. . . . But there is a face. There is a shadow" (128). In so doing Evelyn identifies what Marilyn Farwell has called a key feature of lesbian narrative, the "shadow plot, [which] is absorbed into the dominant plot structure yet challenges the very structure it inhabits because it refuses to be controlled

by the old pattern."[21] Reading her attraction against Bunyanesque convention, Evelyn recognizes in Ann "an alien otherness"; Ann's queerness
corresponds to Evelyn's own "case of mistaken identity" (128).

Lesbianism restores self-visibility to Evelyn and locates her vitality in the
continual reexamination of conventional images of womanhood: "It was curious that, at the very time she was giving up all the external images of
womanhood, Evelyn should become increasingly aware of her own femininity. . . . She was finding in the miracle of her particular fall, that she was, by
nature, a woman. And what a lovely thing it was to be, a woman" (174–75).
With her lesbian "fall," Evelyn finds in Ann a reflection of her own dissocia-
tion from hetero-normative convention. Both women are literary and cultural
exiles; in contrast to the sexual politics of Bunyan's allegory, no male guides,
with their histories and words, determine their progress.

Jane Rule has herself indicated the importance of Protestant spiritual texts
for understanding Evelyn's and Ann's *Bildung*. In a 1976 interview, she
speaks of Anglo-American literature's (and specifically her own) Protestant
inheritance: "Our literature is full of it. The very cadences of our language are
given to us in ritual form. Or were given to me anyway. The language is just
there and the rhythms are very deep. . . . I think a lot that shocks me about the
world we live in is rooted in Christian teaching. . . . And I think embedded in
that mythology is what terrifies me most about the values of our culture. So
it's very, negatively important."[22]

Rule cites seventeenth-century English literature "as the most influential
literary period"[23] for her; in *Desert of the Heart* she makes explicit reference
to *The Pilgrim's Progress*. She fashions lesbian *Bildung* as a pilgrimage. In so
doing she not only calls attention to the ubiquity of Bunyan's narrative paradigm within Anglo-American realism, but also figures the lesbian as the
metapilgrim of that paradigm. The lesbian is a metapilgrim because she
undergoes her progress apart from male mediation; she is an exile from the
very construct engaged to represent exiles, a construct which Rule in turn
renews by figuring Ann's and Evelyn's development (and orientation) as a
wandering in the desert. "As I walked through the wilderness of this world
. . . I dreamed a dream,"[24] begins the narrator of *The Pilgrim's Progress*. It is
a wilderness, geographical as well as epistemological, that the heroines of
Desert of the Heart inhabit.

Desert of the Heart takes up the conventionalizing of faith, its transformation into a semiotic system whose purpose is, above all, its own circulation.
Reno, Nevada, home to gambling casinos and divorce courts, explicitly recalls

Bunyan's city of spiritual waste, Vanity Fair. For Evelyn Hall, who has come for a divorce, and for Ann Childs, who works in a casino, Reno insists on the conspicuous consumption of religion, the market calculation of salvation in terms of profit, loss, and utility.

Juxtaposing this world is the landscape of pilgrimage that Ann and Evelyn as lovers inhabit. They retrieve pilgrimage, the conventional Christian figure for spiritual development, as a figure for their coming out, even as that coming out takes place within Reno and its surrounding desert. Because she houses the women's unconventional relationship within the city of outworn convention, Rule undertakes what Marilyn Schuster calls a "strategy of subtle subversion: social and literary conventions are put to the service of their own destruction."[25] Lesbianism may risk indictment in its association with Vanity Fair; yet, rooted in Puritan spiritual narratives, the "truth-telling" patterns of English realism that place the love story in Vanity Fair do so even more. Evelyn and Ann's pilgrimage is not quite the "enabling escape" that for Catharine Stimpson enacts the "lesbian's rebellion against social stigma and self-contempt."[26] Rather it engenders a brave encampment in the "desert of the heart," where the impossibility of obtaining spiritual comfort generates the desire for emotional self-sufficiency.

Rule's scrutiny of the Puritan narrative conventions that inform realist narration is apparent from the opening of the novel:

> Conventions, like clichés, have a way of surviving their own usefulness. They are then excused or defended as the idioms of living. For everyone, foreign by birth or by nature, convention is a mark of fluency. That is why, for any woman, marriage is the idiom of life. And she does not give it up out of scorn or indifference but only when she is forced to admit that she has never been able to pronounce it properly and has committed continually its grossest grammatical errors. For such a woman marriage remains a foreign tongue, an alien landscape, and, since she cannot become naturalized, she finally chooses voluntary exile.
>
> Evelyn Hall had been married for sixteen years before she admitted to herself that she was such a woman. (1)

The definition of marriage as a "convention" draws attention to both the social plots that constrain women and the patterns of spiritual narrative that help figure the novel as a literary form: Conventionally speaking, both the novel's and women's stories are predicated upon and resolved through marriage.

Rule's opening, then, critiques conventional constructions of female progress. These share a common cultural repository in spiritual narratives, which cast the anticipated union with God as a marriage feast: The believer becomes bride to Christ's bridegroom. Whether or not this figuration sets a compelling precedent for gay marriage, marriage for the female pilgrim is not simply the end point but also the precondition of her travel. *The Pilgrim's Progress* for instance, is divided into two parts. The first chronicles the pilgrimage of Christian to the Celestial City and the second narrates the parallel journey of Christiana, his wife. Framed as it ultimately is as Christiana's reunion with a husband, part two reveals the overlap between social convention and spiritual narration. In Bunyan's work, Christiana's spiritual consummation and reunion with the husband who has gone before her merge to direct her progress. But if Bunyan insists that Christiana is at home with marriage, Rule asks whether marriage is at home with the heroine of novels. For Evelyn Hall, even though she retains the title "Mrs." and her husband's surname after she has left him, it is not. The modifiers "foreign," "alien," and "exile" place her in a Bunyanesque tradition that she immediately problematizes.

For Evelyn, as for Christiana, marriage may be "the idiom of life"; Evelyn, however, possesses an interpretive capacity prohibited to her spiritual foremother that allows her to reenvision marriage as "the long detour" (173) and to inhabit instead a love story predicated upon divorce. In so doing, Evelyn both reenacts the break from family and community that marks the beginning of Christian's progress and rejects the end point of that progress: the arrival in the Celestial City, whose symmetric counterpointing of Christian's initial rupture with marriage in turn propels Christiana on her travel. Freeing her from the interpretive zealotry of male guides, who in Christiana's case equate progress with marriage itself, Evelyn's coming out instead insists on lesbianism's illegibility within a conventional scheme of female development.

If, on the surface, Evelyn resembles Christiana, her very ability to read and reproduce the signs of wifely good undermines her marriage. Like Christiana, the newly wed Evelyn inhabits a world ostensibly directed in absentia by her warrior husband. With George fighting in World War II, Evelyn concludes, "I'll teach. I'll write. I'll make a world for [him]" (125). "Mak[ing] a world," however, effectually marks the difference between Evelyn and Christiana.

Evelyn shares both Christiana's sexual burden and pilgrim Christian's burden of interpretation.[27] Christiana's passive surrender of her sexuality to male

dominion, together with her sustained awareness of her husband's pilgrimage
as the narrative paradigm that shapes, even enacts, her own life, legitimizes
her progress as an extension of his. She is not a reader but rather a vessel of and
audience to her own history. By comparison, Evelyn, initially, is a reader who
subscribes to conventionally gendered texts. As an active reader who reproduces the signs of femininity, however, she finds that she inevitably defies
them. Once husband George returns home, Evelyn tells herself that "there
were a hundred . . . conventions through which she could prove she was a
woman" (127). Yet her role as a professor, as a semiotic rather than biological
mother, threatens George. He suffers one nervous breakdown after another,
and doctor and minister alike counsel divorce. In sum, Evelyn's profession, in
contrast to Christiana's submission, leaves her "carry[ing] the mark of a
strong, intelligent woman like the brand of Cain on her forehead" (52). Where
"'strong, intelligent woman' is a prefeminist code for lesbian," and where the
"brand of Cain" aligns Evelyn with Stephen Gordon, the lesbian hero of Radclyffe Hall's The Well of Loneliness (1928),[28] Evelyn is left far too able an
interpreter of convention ever to embody convention in her own choices.

Evelyn's flight to Reno initially seems to reverse Bunyan's paradigm of pilgrimage, the journey from the City of Destruction to the Celestial City. Evelyn
is from the Bay area, which Reno inhabitants consider "a promised land . . . a
promised sea" (84); Evelyn identifies Reno, in turn, as a modern-day Vanity
Fair, a comparison suggested by her visit to a casino. There she encounters a
man dressed as a minister, who quotes Bunyan. Specifically, he quotes Faithful, Christian's traveling companion in Pilgrim's Progress:

> "There can be no divine faith without the divine revelation of the
> will of God! Therefore, whatever is thrust into the worship of God
> that is not agreeable to divine revelation, cannot be done but by
> human faith, which faith is not profit to eternal life!"
> " . . . This is Vanity Fair. Who judges me but Hate-good? Who
> are you, all of you, but Malice, Live-loose, Love-lust, Hate-light . . . "
> Vanity Fair. Of course, she had heard it all before. He was quot-
> ing Faithful's final speech in Pilgrim's Progress. . . . Crackpot the
> old man might be, but he knew his Bunyan. . . . Evelyn heard him
> shout just before the elevator doors closed behind him: "I buy the
> truth!" (195–96)[29]

Whether the man is mad or, in fact, an overzealous cleric, whether the city is
an actual, latter-day Vanity Fair or a glitzy parody of it is not the point; the

ineluctability of such debate is. Reno and the heckler occupy the same imaginative context, wherein the parting quote, "I buy the truth," is not a statement
of spiritual essentialism but of the conspicuous consumption of Christian
paradigms. In his doubled role as moral critic and allegorical figure, the
would-be minister elicits Evelyn's awareness of Reno's marketing of itself as
a city of destruction.

But if Reno maps out Evelyn's spiritual desertion, it also enables her to
meet Ann Childs, who is quick to point out that the world of Christian pro-
priety and the moral wasteland of Reno are inextricably linked, the former
indeed sanctioning the existence of the latter. Her descriptions of Reno play
on the conventional oppositions between the "well-watered plains of the
Lord" (145) and Sodom and Gomorrah, and in so doing recall how in Genesis 13:10—"the plain of Jordan . . . was well watered every where, before the
Lord destroyed Sodom and Gomorrah, even as the garden of the Lord"—
those places are one and the same. For Ann, "Every place is a Sodom and a
Gomorrah. . . . The faithful say the plain was well watered, even as the Garden of the Lord, before he destroyed the cities. I don't believe it. There
never was any water here, not fresh water" (112). Skeptical of the distinction between desert and garden as landscapes of damnation and salvation,
Ann sees Reno as an ontological supermarket along the straight and narrow road, where the best buys remain cultural complacency and moral
smugness: "They were perfectly ordinary people coming from all parts of
the country into the evil desert . . . perfectly ordinary people, free at last to
be fearful, malicious, greedy. Then home they'd go to the good, well-
watered plains of the Lord to tell what they had seen, the coarse women,
the obsessed men, the deserted children, never guessing that these pic-
turesque inhabitants were tourists like themselves" (145). Its clubs
supplying the church with "both the money to be spent and the souls to be
saved," Reno is, for Ann, "a perfect kingdom, based on nothing but the
flaws in human nature" (200–1). As such it is itself a parodic allegory of
spiritual pilgrimage.

Whether a latter-day Sodom, Vanity Fair, or a city of destruction whose
alter ego is a celestial city, Reno builds its success on the commercialization
of the spiritual landscape. Casino life, in particular, ironizes the female pilgrim's progress as a narrative system responding not to individual
development but to the maintenance of its own "free" economy. At Frank's
Club, where Ann works, the security system's two-way mirrors parody Bunyan's objective correlative of female progress. The ceilings of the club are

lined with mirrors, which promote employee honesty (or, at least, the images of honesty). Looking at one of these, Ann sees "her own face separated from her . . . made smaller. What a device of conscience the mirror was, for behind it, at any time, might be the unknown face of a security officer, watchful, judging; yet you could not see it. You could not get past your own minimized reflection" (27). That reflection locates Ann within a system of surveillance, at once gendered and parodic, that reduces the importance of her actions in relation to herself. Like Christiana and traveling companion Mercy, who requests the two-way mirror, Ann is overseen by male superiors, her behavior subject to their approval. "What a device of conscience that mirror was" (27), Ann muses. Yet the club has despiritualized conscience. Behind the glass is not God, but rather the managers of the casino's interests.

Frank's Club offers employees and visitors alike a parodic city of God, dominated by commercial images of female sexuality that traffic in (and prostitute) Bunyan's representation of the female pilgrim. So one woman cum wayfarer treks ninety miles across the desert for her job as a change apron. Strapped to her belly, the fifty-pound apron itself reminds Ann of "a fetus in its seventh month" (101), and so links Ann to Bunyan's Christiana, whose ineluctable burden is her sex, or the travail of childbearing.

Within Rule's critique of Bunyan, the change apron is, in fact, a gender-marked and heterosexually informed burden that collapses economic and sexual realms together by exposing the interdependence of Bunyan's opposing figures for female sexuality. The apron not only parodies the female pilgrim's sexuality, legitimized through marriage, but also recalls the purse of Christiana's spiritual foil, Madam Bubble, where "purse" is both the lap in which men lay their heads *and* the pouch whose contents she constantly fingers. "Mistress" of "this vain world,"[30] Madam Bubble, as her name suggests, mirrors the ubiquity of Vanity Fair. In Madam Bubble, metaphors of female heterosexual and economic bondage (yet, also, potential self-sufficiency and self-pleasuring) coincide. In the case of the change apron, Frank's Club allows the signs of the female pilgrim and those of the prostitute free exchange.

Like Evelyn, Ann is a critical reader of the context she inhabits. She remains removed from her coworkers, even from her lovers, Silver and Bill, whose names reflect the ubiquity of the marketplace. Tellingly, Ann's nickname is "Little Fish." "Little Fish" inscribes her within a Christian romance, where Evelyn is the fisher of [wo]men who "hook and land" her (148). "Little fish" is also Virginia Woolf's term in *A Room of One's Own* for the woman's thought that, meeting prohibition rather than nurture, darts into hiding. Within the market economy, Ann is a threshold of female consciousness, a thought only acknowledgeable in those cartoons that she draws in her spare time and refuses to sell. These sketches are designed for Ann's own private instruction, introspection; they constitute the *Bilder* of an alternative *Bildung*.

Speaking of the primacy that Christian thought accords productivity, economic as well as sexual, Rule observes of her own writing: "What interests me is watching people detached from all those requirements, figuring out ways to build a human community that is satisfying and nourishing to them."[31] In *Desert of the Heart* the most salient metaphors are those of barrenness, which define nourishment not in terms of reproduction but in terms of self-preservation. So the desert and an alkaline lake provide the backdrop for Evelyn and Ann's romance. Where fertility demands appropriation, Evelyn and Ann's landscape remains a sterile, inviolable one, a wilderness that resists cultivation, that is itself self-sustaining. So Evelyn considers the stillness of Pyramid Lake: "It was no wonder that a Christian God had not been at home here. It would take many animistic gods of men less confident of their own dominant spirit to describe the powers of this world" (183). This "dead sea" does not, however, entirely escape sexual regulation—at one point a National Guard helicopter hovers over the two women. Yet one might also say that such policing, with which Evelyn associates the endurance of Christian faith, remains a suspended possibility, in relation to which Evelyn can maintain a critical distance.

So, too, while Evelyn may initially put off Ann's lovemaking by paraphrasing the Episcopal Church's General Confession—"I live in the desert of the heart" (118)—the younger woman directs her attention toward the figurative richness of the actual desert:

> As they dropped over the crest of a hill, the rain stopped and
> before them was a valley of brilliant, burning sunlight, arched
> with rainbows, edged with lightning.
>   "This is the desert of the heart," Ann said quietly. (120)

Ann inverts the Protestant metaphor for spiritual desolation: Complete with rainbows reminiscent of the one that seals the covenant between God and man in Genesis 9, the desert momentarily becomes a promised land. The desert is the landscape of self-address, the borderland that remains for the exile from convention after the possibility of defining oneself in terms of Christian allegory has been swept away.

This is not to say that Ann and Evelyn do not retain their particular relation—the one's resistance, the other's adherence—to spiritual narrative
conventions. The novel's ending, in which each woman reasserts her respective fear of salvation and damnation, implies that they do. But the
universalizing structures of experience that Puritanism provides break down
through the women's continual (re)reading of them. As Tamsin Wilton
observes, "Lesbian criticism constructs a specifically textual 'lesbian' . . .
whose political importance derives from her disruptive and disobdient presence within/against the master narrative of heteropatriarchy."[32]

In effect, Rule's Puritan outing outs *The Pilgrim's Progress*; *Desert of the
Heart* bewilders Bunyan's semiotic system. His allegory only offers a cryp-
togram for Ann and Evelyn's love. Much as Bunyan's narrator walks
"through the wilderness of this world"[33] in order to dream of pilgrim's
progress, Evelyn walks into the desert in order to struggle with the thought of
love. But in doing so, she splits his paradigm in two—she is a pilgrim without
Bunyan's interpretive ground for her lesbianism and so is a pilgrim without a
conventionally recognizable progress:

> Evelyn had walked half a mile into her own vision of the desert
> before she turned and looked back at the curiously regular edge
> of town she had left; "When they were got out of the wilderness,
> they presently saw a town . . . " And Faithful was tried there and
> died there, but for defending his convictions, not for giving them
> up. If he'd surrendered divine faith to human faith, he would not
> have been killed; nor would he have escaped, however. He would
> have stayed.
>
> Evelyn began to walk slowly back the way she had come,
> neither Faithful nor Christian. There is no allegory any longer,
> not even the allegory of love. I do not believe. Even seeing and
> feeling, in fact, what I do not believe, I do not believe. It's a blind
> faith, human faith, hybrid faith of jackass and mare. That's the
> only faith that I have. I cannot die of that. I can only live with it,
> damned or not. (223–24)

In the desert outside Reno, Evelyn is reminded of pilgrims Christian and
Faithful entering Vanity Fair, only to find that she cannot equate their
progress through it with her continuous wandering within it.

In the "Apology" to part 1 of *The Pilgrim's Progress*, Bunyan invites his readers alternately to lose and find themselves in his work:

Would'st read thyself, and read thou know'st not what
And yet know whether thou art blest or not,
By reading the same lines? O then come hither,
And lay my book, thy head and heart together.34

He seeks to inscribe his readers' understanding of selfhood in his writing. As
Michael Warner notes, "the notion of having a rupture with your self and the
notion of narrated personal coherence are Protestant conventions . . . [which]
offer you a new and perpetual personality."35

In Rule's novel, however, no such personality proves forthcoming. Where
human experience does not lay claim to universality, the link between human
and divine faith remains tentatively lodged within the amazing illegible landscape of "the desert of the heart." Together, Evelyn and Ann constitute a
"cryptic cartoon" (244). And not because of any lack of interpretive capacity
that, as in Christiana's case, can be filled by male mediation. Here it is Bunyan's allegory in its repressive regulation of female sexuality that fails the
female pilgrim, not vice versa. If Evelyn's faith in lesbianism is "blind" and
"hybrid" (and, by extension, sterile), it is because there is no possibility for a
"straight" correspondence between lesbian experience and *The Pilgrim's
Progress*'s narrative paradigms.

Neither is there a correspondence between Christian belief and queer
experience, for that matter: Evelyn's and Ann's narrative stances are not
anomalous in gay and lesbian literature. At the end of Doty's poem "Homo
Will Not Inherit" the speaker assures us,

I'm not ashamed
to love Babylon's scrawl. How could I be?
It's written on my face as much as on
these walls. This city's inescapable,

gorgeous and on fire. I have my kingdom.36

In this parodic beatitude, the speaker finds his salvation in the conventional
signs of damnation: Babylon is in drag, performing kingdom come. The
poem blurs the signs of the sacred and the sinful together; they produce an
enchantingly camp city of God that offers a literary rejoinder to the moral
condemnation of sexual pleasure.

Importantly, Rule's own rejoinder, her insistence on Evelyn's and Ann's
inscrutable narrative positions within Vanity Fair, does not allow for a facile
dismissal of Bunyan, any more than the novel's ending, in which the lovers

walk together toward their reflection in the glass doors of the courthouse where Evelyn's divorce has just been granted, can be read as a utopian conclusion. In both cases, the possibility for cultural and literary policing remains very real (and realistic) indeed. Positioned at the outset of Rule's publishing career, *Desert of the Heart* underscores the limited, self-eradicating plots that a Christian- (and particularly a Puritan-) inflected literary tradition affords protagonists who resist the regulation of their sexuality.

Yet even so, the novel speaks to Bunyan's regenerative potential, for, like *The Pilgrim's Progress, Desert of the Heart* is a narrative of dissent. As is the case with so many lesbian, gay, and queer texts, Rule's novel explores, remaps, and suspends Puritan narrative paradigms in the name of social justice and of sexual freedom. In effect, the novel "purifies" or radicalizes realism's religious heritage: The novel identifies Bunyan as the politically inspired figure behind its own critique of the status quo. Evelyn and Ann's love story is a lesbian pilgrim's progress, an extravagant reminder of and cautionary tribute to Bunyan's persistent literary and political importance for an Anglo-American cultural imagination committed to the possibility that the world can be made new.

Notes

This essay is for Janice L. Robes.

1. For a discussion of assimilationism, see Michael Warner, "Media Gays: A New Stone Wall," *The Nation*, 14 July 1997, 15–19. See also *Harvard Gay and Lesbian Review* 2 (Spring 1998), which is devoted to the "sex wars."

2. Mab Segrest, "I Lead Two Lives: Confessions of a Closet Baptist," in *The New Lesbian Studies into the Twenty-First Century*, ed. Bonnie Zimmerman and Toni McNaron. (New York: The Feminist Press at the City University of New York, 1996), 12.

3. Barry Qualls, *The Secular Pilgrims of Victorian Fiction* (Cambridge: Cambridge University Press, 1983). Speaking of *The Pilgrim's Progress*'s importance for nineteenth-century British fiction, Qualls writes, "that tradition of writing represented by Bunyan . . . seemed to provide the only certain way towards positing and insuring lasting human values in an age where the pilgrim's query 'Where is truth?' found a hundred answers and none" (13–14).

4. Rule uses the word "mixed" at the outset of *Fiction and Other Truths: A Film about Jane Rule*, dir. Lynne Fernie and Aerlyn Weissman, A Great Jane Production, 1994.

5. Even as they themselves searched for religious toleration, the Puritans, of course, were notoriously intolerant of various other groups, perhaps most notably the Native Americans whom they first encountered in the New World.

6. Shane Phelan, introduction to *Playing with Fire: Queer Politics, Queer Theories*, ed. Shane Phelan (London: Routledge, 1997), 4.

7. Michael Warner, "Tongues Untied: Memoirs of a Pentecostal Boyhood," in *The Material Queer: A LesBiGay Cultural Studies Reader*, ed. Donald Morton (New York: Westview Press, 1996), 44.

8. Warner, "Tongues Untied," 43.

9. Mark Doty, *Heaven's Coast: A Memoir* (New York: HarperCollins, 1996), 176–77.

10. Doty, *Heaven's Coast*, 158.

11. See Sacvan Bercovitch, *The Puritan Origins of the American Self* (New Haven: Yale University Press, 1975): "The New Englander, then, had the failure of European Protestantism behind him and before him, as his refuge, what he called 'wilderness' and 'desert.' The terms speak for themselves of his fear" (102).

12. Doty, *Heaven's Coast*, 158.

13. For discussions of the distinctions between lesbian feminism and queer theory see, for example, Marilyn Farwell, *Heterosexual Plots and Lesbian Narratives* (New York: New York University Press, 1996), and Zimmerman and McNaron, eds., *Lesbian Studies into the Twenty-First Century*, xiii–xix.

14. See Qualls, *The Secular Pilgrims*, 12.

15. Gillian Spraggs, "Hell and the Mirror: A Reading of *Desert of the Heart*," *New Lesbian Criticism: Literary and Cultural Readings*, ed. Sally Munt (New York: Columbia University Press, 1992), 115–31, 116.

16. Geoffrey Hancock, "An Interview with Jane Rule," *Canadian Fiction Magazine* 23 (August 1976): 57–112, 65.

17. Jane Rule, *Desert of the Heart* (London: Pandora, 1986), 6. Further citations are given in the text.

18. John Bunyan, *The Pilgrim's Progress* (Harmondsworth: Penguin, 1984), 345.

19. Bunyan, *The Pilgrim's Progress*, 345; emphasis added.

20. See Margaret Soenser Breen, "Christiana's Rudeness: Spiritual Authority in *The Pilgrim's Progress*," *Bunyan Studies* 7 (1997): 96–109; and "The Sexed Pilgrim's Progress," *SEL* 32.3 (summer 1992): 443–60.

21. Farwell, *Heterosexual Plots and Lesbian Narratives*, 129.

22. Hancock, "An Interview with Jane Rule," 65.

23. Hancock, "An Interview with Jane Rule," 65.

24. Bunyan, *The Pilgrim's Progress*, 39.

25. Marilyn Schuster, "Strategies for Survival: The Subtle Subversion of Jane Rule," *Feminist Studies* 7.3 (1981): 431–450, 433.

26. Catharine Stimpson, "Zero Degree Deviancy: The Lesbian Novel in English," *Writing and Sexual Difference*, ed. Elizabeth Abel (Chicago: University of Chicago Press, 1982), 244.

27. I am drawing on Dayton Haskin's analysis of Christian's and Christiana's burdens. See "The Burden of Interpretation in *The Pilgrim's Progress*," *Studies in Philology* 79.3 (summer 1982): 256–78.

28. The surname "Hall," which, as Bonnie Zimmerman has pointed out, recalls Radclyffe Hall, writer of the lesbian classic *Well of Loneliness*, itself encodes Evelyn's outcast status. See Bonnie Zimmerman, *The Safe Sea of Women: Lesbian Fiction, 1969–1989* (Boston: Beacon, 1990), 46.

29. The quotations that Rule incorporates here may be found in Bunyan, *The Pilgrim's Progress*, 132, 126.

30. Bunyan, *The Pilgrim's Progress*, 361.

31. Hancock, "An Interview with Jane Rule," 98.

32. Tamsin Wilton, *Lesbian Studies: Setting an Agenda* (New York and London: Routledge, 1996), 133.

33. Bunyan, *The Pilgrim's Progress*, 39.

34. Bunyan, *The Pilgrim's Progress*, 37.

35. Warner, "Tongues Untied," 44–45.

36. Doty, "Homo Will Not Inherit," *Atlantis* (New York: HarperCollins, 1995), 76–79, lines 96–100.

Sinners in the Hands of an Angry Gardner

Robert A. Morace

❦

Although John Gardner has attracted a great deal of critical attention since his death in 1982—fifteen books in just eighteen years, and at least five others in progress—surprisingly little has appeared on the three interrelated areas that are the subject of this essay. One is his narrative treatment of sex. Another is the way his Presbyterian upbringing manifests itself in his work and connects him to the American Puritan tradition. The third is Gardner's highly personal but also disturbingly puritanical treatment of human bodies in his work, both as physical objects and as metaphorical constructs. Gardner's writings—the criticism as well as the fiction—reveal a deep-seated preoccupation with sin and guilt rooted in the Calvinist obsession with individual worthiness for salvation. Reading biographically through his Presbyterian upbringing and the accidental death in childhood of his younger brother, we can see that Gardner displaced the self-loathing these engendered onto his writing, most notably in its preoccupation with adolescent sexuality and physically disabled figures. More even than his individual psychology, the Puritan elements of Gardner's background and imagination shaped *On Moral Fiction* into a version of what Sacvan Bercovitch calls "the American jeremiad." *On Moral Fiction* adopts this Puritan rhetorical form to argue for a morally uncontaminated national literature in a way that resonates deeply with larger American rituals of casting out the impure or un-American. Thus, the grotesque body of Gardner's fiction is not celebratory and liberating, as it is in Bakhtin.[1] Rather, it is a caricature of carnality that must be controlled, and it can be linked with broader attempts to police

cultural production (such as recent efforts to ban the *Harry Potter* books from
schools, for example, or to discipline and punish the Brooklyn Museum of
Art for its *Sensation* exhibit). Seen in the context of America's shift to the
right in the last quarter of the twentieth century, *On Moral Fiction* demonstrates how Puritan theological forms continue to shape American thinking,
in part through their contribution to larger structures of social and bodily surveillance.

One can well understand why Gardner's most sympathetic critics have
shied away from the treatment of sexuality in his fiction. Although his second
wife, the poet Liz Rosenberg, once jokingly pointed out that sex was about the
only thing for which Gardner was willing to leave his writing,[2] Gardner's narrative handling of sexual relationships in general and scenes of sexual
intimacy in particular is embarrassingly bad. It is so bad, in fact, as to suggest
the same degree of discomfort, even distaste, on his part that Jay Corbie, one
of his earliest and youngest protagonists, experiences near the end of Gardner's 1958 University of Iowa dissertation-novel, "The Old Men." Still
wracked by guilt in connection with an older brother's suicide some years
before, Jay visits Ginger Ghoki in the hospital, where she is recovering from
injuries she inflicted on herself as punishment for her own sexual longings.
Perversely, even self-destructively, this daughter of an obsessively strict Jeho-
vah's Witness (one of several such figures in Gardner's fiction) tells her
rather courtly, certainly repressed, would-be suitor, "Someday I'll let you look
at me, or do anything you want." Jay's reaction to Ginger's offer sets the stage
for Gardner's subsequent handling of sexuality in his work. "Jay had felt sick,
had wanted to take her in his arms, cry over her as over a hurt child, yet had
recoiled, too, as from a cripple or an obscene old woman."[3] Gardner's treatment of sexuality is most successful when least apparent, when it is alluded
to rather than described outright, when it either occurs offstage (or off-page),
or can be chastely assumed not to occur at all (as in the case of Henry and Cal-
lie in *Nickel Mountain*). On the page, Gardner's depiction of sexual
relationships and intimacy is clumsy at best, adolescent at worst; Grendel, for
example, alternates between platonic puppy love for Hrothgar's young and
beautiful wife, Wealtheow, and thoughts of "cooking the ugly hole between
her legs" and "squeez[ing] out her feces between my fists."[4] It is, however, an
ineptness I believe integral to an art that critics have approvingly described as
vaguely "religious."

In describing his work as religious, these critics are not referring to Gardner's actual religious background. Most assume that all Gardner "retained

from his Presbyterian upbringing" was a watered-down version of "the doctrine of grace," namely "That no man can win by his own efforts alone."⁵ But
such an acceptably modern and soothingly secular assessment of the
(benign) role religion played in his youth is at odds with the recollections of
Gardner's two most successful writing students. Raymond Carver recalled
that the Gardner he had known in the late 1950s had looked more like a minister or an FBI agent than an author,⁶ least of all the author of the fiction that
Charles Johnson has approvingly described as "unabashedly Protestant."⁷
The Protestant underpinnings of Gardner's fiction can be defined more narrowly, however. As Samuel Coale has explained, Gardner's fiction belongs to
the American romance tradition, a genre largely defined by the Manichean
dualisms that result from the "clash" of pastoral and Calvinist myths.⁸ However, not even Coale's illuminating analysis of the dark recesses of Gardner's
romancer's imagination quite gets at some of the less savory aspects of his
Puritan mind. Bo Ekelund takes a step in the right direction in his important
sociological reading of Gardner's "literary project." The Presbyterian values
that were "a more or less integral part of Gardner's habitus" were transformed, Ekelund contends, "into something more and more generalized and
rarefied . . . that [would not leave Gardner] open to charges of naivety or lack
of sophistication."⁹ It is precisely Gardner's religious vision at its most generalized and rarefied—which is to say, at its furthest remove from its
embarrassingly unsophisticated origin in the rural Presbyterianism of "the
burned over district" of western New York, but with its ties to the Sunday sermons of Gardner's father, a lay preacher, still intact—that has appealed to
critics drawn to his vaguely spiritualized, seemingly nonsectarian "dream of
peace"¹⁰ and "world of order and light."¹¹

Ronald Nutter offers a different take on the familiar theme of Gardner's
essentially, if vaguely, religious vision by reading the fiction in light of Robert
J. Lifton's study of survivors. In doing so, he emphasizes an important biographical fact that the sociologically, rather than psychologically, inclined
Ekelund downplays to the point of dismissing altogether. This is the death of
Gardner's younger brother Gilbert in an accident that occurred at the family
farm outside Batavia, New York, in April 1945, when Gardner was twelve. Nutter's approach to this traumatic event is insightful, but because it emphasizes
repentance, forgiveness, and the return to community, it leads to a rather pre-
dictable conclusion. In stressing Gardner's redemptive vision, as well as his
writing's therapeutic value for the reader and for Gardner, Nutter tends to
sidestep both Gardner's treatment of the accident as an "original sin" and the

consequences of that treatment for his writing. Nutter also fails to consider fully the gruesome manner of Gilbert's death—crushed beneath a heavy piece of farm equipment as Gardner looked helplessly on—and its influence on the way bodies are figured in Gardner's fiction.

"It begins, of course, with the death of Beatrice," Gardner writes of Dante, one his favorite "true artists." He could just as well have been writing about himself; indeed, he probably was. The "wound" that Gardner dealt with directly for the first time in the 1977 story "Redemption" is one that he "had written around . . . from the beginning of his career." It is the "psychological wound" that figures so prominently in his neo-Romantic description of "the artist": the "fatal childhood accident for which one feels responsible and can never fully forgive oneself."[12] In much the same way that he transforms Gilbert's literal fatal injury into the artist's metaphorical psychological wound, Gardner transforms the broken Gilbert into Beatrice, the physical woman herself transformed into the ethereal and therefore deathless, as well as sexless, muse, still feminine but no longer fuckable. Gilbert appears throughout Gardner's guilt-ridden, guilt-driven work in a multiplicity of forms that generate the constellation of symptoms that make up "the Cain motif" in his stories and novels.[13] There are the dead children and young adults, often brothers and sisters, occasionally sons and daughters; the fatal accidents; the occasional murders and frequent suicides; the unpaid debts; the ghosts and ghostly presences; the betrayals of others and of one's ideals; the incestuous couplings (real or imagined); and an abundance of guilty but sympathetically portrayed Cains, Grendel in particular. Grendel's guilt is especially fascinating because so perversely assigned and accepted. He is punished, indeed masochistically seeks to be punished, for nothing more than becoming what others have claimed him to be: purely, monstrously, sadistically and cynically, as well as guiltily, "other." In "Redemption," Gardner magnifies the protagonist's responsibility for the death of his younger brother (also named Gilbert) and with it the guilt because, in Gardner's mind, for there to be redemption, there must be guilt, and for there to be guilt, there must be choice.[14]

Rather than explain this phenomenon wholly in terms of Lifton's analysis of survivor guilt, we would do well, given the pervasive influence of Gardner's Presbyterian upbringing, to connect that explanation with a distinction basic to Puritan thinking. As Bercovitch explains in *The Puritan Origins of the American Self*, the "basis of Puritan psychology lies in [the] contrast between personal responsibility and individualism. We can say, with William Haller, that [the Puritans] believed 'man's chief concern should be with the welfare of his own soul' only if we bear in mind their horror at the 'very name of Own,' their determination 'to *Hate* our *selves* and *ours*,' their opposing views of *soul* and *self*."[15] While a similar sense of failure, (ir)responsibility, and unworthiness mark Lifton's survivor, it is deepened in Gardner's case by a Calvinist sense of self-loathing, the "deep down inferiority" that he identified as his imagination's wellspring[16] and that left its trace on Gardner's writing—fiction and nonfiction alike—and on other aspects of his life. It is there in his attributing the failure of his first marriage to the success that came to him at the expense of his wife Joan's career as a musician. It is there too in the curious but strangely consistent mixture of self-deprecation and self-aggrandizement one finds in the interviews. And it is also evident in this "Lon Cheney of contemporary fiction" having written not only enough for two people (as if, his mother once suggested, he wrote both for himself and for Gilbert), but *as* two or more as well.[17]

Although his story "Redemption" is well known, *Stillness,* the novel from which it is drawn and which Gardner wrote as a form of bibliotherapy, is not, though it deserves to be. *Stillness* situates the limited events depicted in the story in the context of the protagonist's fuller life, his marriage and career in particular. Although the handling of sexual matters here is not much better, which is to say not much less squeamish, than in the other fiction, Gardner's depiction in *Stillness* of the main characters' brittle marriage, including several off-page infidelities, is unusually affecting. It is, however, a much earlier, though by no means unrelated betrayal that I wish to take note of here, along with its effect on the novel's protagonist, Martin ("Buddy") Orrick. In this passage, Martin recalls watching, with his cousin (later his wife) Joan, a home movie which in turn re-presents an even earlier period, before his brother's death:

> And then, with mild horror, Buddy realized that he himself was
> in this movie. His parents' car was parked beside the curb, and
> they were all getting out. He remembered before his picture
> appeared on the screen that as they walked toward the house
> Joan's father was running the movie camera, and he remembered
> that as he passed he, Buddy, had made a face. Only now did he
> realize the implications, and the skin of his face began to sting.
> His mother and father went past the camera—Joan's father had
> made them come one by one—and then Gilbert came by, smiling
> shyly—he had dark, slightly curly hair and eyes like his father's,

as though, perhaps, he had once been a child before and had not been happy, though he was happy now. He seemed wiser, gentler than the rest of his family—or was that, perhaps, a trick of Martin Orrick's memory, thinking back to that image on the screen long afterward? His brother Gilbert moved out of the picture and he saw himself coming, with none of his brother's confidence, though he was older, and he knew the stupid, obscene face must come, and waited, sick at heart, and it came— he stuck his tongue out, put his thumbs into his ears—and was gone almost instantly (Life is fleeting, Martin Orrick would write long afterward, even the worst of life is fleeting), and everyone laughed.[18]

The "stupid, obscene face," like the ambiguously directed laughter of the chorus of family members, is the measure of a guilt-induced self-loathing that manifests itself in Gardner's work not only thematically but in a love of grotesque characterizations. It is this grotesquerie that transforms his self-styled character-centered "moral fictions" into a literary freak show spread out over a quarter century and more than thirty books: novels, short stories, poetry, libretti, radio plays, children's fiction, and criticism. (Although one would not want to make too much of the fact that one of Gardner's last projects was a translation of a work, the epic *Gilgamesh*, that survives only in highly fragmented form, neither would one want to make too little of it, especially as Gardner's translation highlights the text's dismembered state.[19]) At times the grotesquerie clearly suggests an intertextual indebtedness to Nathanael West, Flannery O'Connor, and Sherwood Anderson. Often it is either comic or symbolic or both at once (for example, *Nickel Mountain*'s foul-smelling, absurdly trusting, perhaps conniving Goat Lady). For the most part, the mildly to wildly grotesque and deformed characters in Gardner's work are simply there. Indeed, they are everywhere: the deaf, the blind, the mute; the owl-faced and the one-eyed; the burned and scarred and the lame; the boy whom a genetic disorder has transmogrified into a giant ("nothing helps the ugly," his ludicrously doll-like father says). *Nickel Mountain*'s George Loomis keeps his boyish face but loses pieces of himself: his heart (to a Japanese whore), an ankle (in the Korean War), an arm (to a piece of farm equipment). Even the cats are grotesque, sprouting tumors and shedding their fur in unsightly patches. While it is certainly true that the grotesquerie serves Gardner's thematic purpose, it is also true that the grotesquerie is not only omnipresent; it is frequently gratuitous. In *Mickelsson's Ghosts*, Gardner describes a decidedly minor character's "pale hand twisted like a cripple's, signing the paper left-handed," and in the unfinished novel *Shadows*, begun in the 1970s, he mentions an even more minor character's "once pretty, grotesquely fat daughters."[20]

Admittedly, "the chalky-skinned, hydrocephalic little hunchback" whom Mickelsson voyeuristically spies atop a nude, goddesslike sociologist named Jessica Stark is a bit much even for Gardner, whose taste generally ran to the merely, if grotesquely, overweight. Yet it is not bulk alone that makes his many fat men so grotesque; it is the way their size feminizes them, shamefully so. There is the 290-pound Dr. Utt, "an old womanish man," in "The Old Men"; the suicidally fat Henry Soames in *Nickel Mountain*, son of an even fatter, more humiliatingly feminine father; and Koprophoros in *Jason and Medeia*, who was "vast—so fat he was frightening—and painted like a harlot." For them, weight is "a murderous solidity," and something more. *The Resurrection*'s protagonist, who is not fat, merely myopic and terminally ill, remembers how, years before, the sight of the "grotesque," bloated body of his pregnant wife reminded him of an art exhibit he had seen, "huge obscene images by Rico LeBrun, corruption lifted to the full heroic—great manlike turtles, struggling upward against the weight of their own monumental deformity—in another room sculpture by Mallarmy, old clothes cast in bronze, in human poses but no figure inside—helpless gestures of inextricable terror and joy!" Worse still, as Professor Utt says about himself at the outset of Gardner's career, he "began to put on the watery weight that comes to a body harboring a diseased mind." And as Professor Mickelsson speculates at the end of that same career about the relationship between illness and evil, "The unfortunate thing about the mentally ill . . . is that they're vile."[21] One would like to ascribe Mickelsson's remark to his unstable mental state. Unfortunately, Gardner's stories and novels, as well as his theory of moral fiction, tend to support rather than refute the position that Sander L. Gilman has spent much of his career detailing and critiquing: that the beautiful (sane and sanitary) body is the visible expression of human virtue, and the ugly (diseased or deformed) body the outward and visible sign of vice.[22]

In all but one respect, Gardner's grotesquerie has little in common with the grotesque realism about which Bakhtin has written so approvingly. For Bakhtin, the grotesque body is intensely, exuberantly physical and completely open. Partaking in and symbolic of carnival's joyful relativity, it is associated with the lower stratum and the people's unofficial truth. "The material bodily principle, earth, and real time become the relative center of the new picture of the world [emerging during the Renaissance]. Not the ascent of the individual soul into the higher sphere but the movement forward of all mankind, along the horizontal of historic time, becomes the basic criterion of all evaluations."[23] Of course, for Gardner it was not carnivalesque degradation, debasement, and decrowning that mattered most; it was redemption, "stillness," and transcendence—"some ultimate union, the dream of romantic reconciliation," as Coale calls it.[24] Yet in one important respect, Gardner's writing fully supports Bakhtin's position on the fate of grotesque realism once it is cut off from its roots in authentic popular culture. This is the "reduced," unregenerative laughter of the modern carnival and the purely private aspect of the grotesque body in its modern form. "In the private sphere of isolated individuals the image of the bodily lower stratum preserves the element of negation while losing almost entirely the positive regenerating force. Their link with life and with the cosmos is broken."[25] The distinction that Bakhtin makes between authentic popular culture and a modern times that is no less Freudian than it is Chaplinesque may be defined equally well in terms of the difference between the carnivalesque and the Calvinist. Where the former dealt with "the people's" primordial fears via mockery and laughter, the latter did so through guilt and shame. Thus, the relevance to Gardner's work of the argument Paul Semonin makes in an essay entitled "The Monster in the Marketplace: The Exhibition of Human Oddities in Early England": "In contrast to the frivolity of popular attitudes toward the monstrous, the Puritan attacks upon these 'anticke' figures often shrouded them in shame and fear. Yet, for all the foreboding portents in their prodigies, the Puritan critics clearly understood an important element of the psychology of the monstrous, even while they attempted to strip away the symbolic significance of the ludicrous[:] . . . that men were ashamed of the 'antickes' and 'chimeras' because they were part of the inner self, what the soul saw when it looked at its own image."[26]

As Semonin's remarks make clear, the figure of the disabled and deformed body that looms so large in Gardner's fiction has long been a prominent part of the Puritan mind (see, for example, Anne Bradstreet's 1678 poem, "The Author to Her Book"). Long before Freud's analysis of "prosthetic man," the Puritans thought of saving grace as the ultimate prosthesis. Benjamin Franklin's melioristic Enlightenment views on "the perfectibility of man" that were ridiculed by the staunchly anti-Puritan D. H. Lawrence have, of course, proven more palatable to Americans. This is what makes Gardner's forays into Puritan-style grotesquerie all the more striking and his distaste for, as well as fascination with, "extraordinary bodies" that "compel explanation, inspire representation, and incite regulation" all the more interesting.[27] We can gain a better understanding of what exactly is at stake in Gardner's use of grotesque figures by reviewing a number of the points Rosemarie Garland Thomson raises in her Foucauldian analysis of freak shows. There is the connection between the rise of freak shows along with penitentiaries and insane asylums in the mid-nineteenth century and the modern medical community's efforts to pathologize bodies that had formerly been seen as "prodigious" and "marvelous." And there is the way that the very presence (and exhibition) of the disabled and the deformed served to embody (as it were) fears about the American myth of autonomy and the Protestant work ethic upon which it is based. This seems particularly revealing when applied to a writer as energetic and prolific—some would say as literarily promiscuous and profligate—as Gardner, for whom work seemed a form of expiation (as well as a form of remembering). But most pertinent to Gardner's situation is the fact that "[f]reaks embodied the threat of individualism running rampant into chaos—the fear of antinomian logic that lurked under the optimistic surface of ardent American egalitarian democracy."[28]

The rampant antinomianism for which Anne Hutchinson and others were expelled from the Massachusetts Bay Colony, where the mere threat or spectacle of expulsion served as an effective means of social control, manifests itself in Gardner's work in two complementary ways. One is a perverse attraction to all that is marginal and monstrous, including Grendel (Gardner's best known example) and The Resurrection's John Horne (his most fascinating and underdiscussed grotesque).[29] The other is Gardner's compulsive need to regulate this figure. He accomplishes this in the fiction in two ways: either by reintegration into the community or by expulsion from it, often by death. And he regulates the monstrous figure outside his stories and novels via his "theory" of moral fiction. His disciplinary stance in On Moral Fiction is dismayingly simple to the point of being absurdly reductive: "Real art creates myths a society can live by instead of die by, and clearly our society is in need of such myths."[30] His position rests upon an appeal to common sense and the eternal verities, including those shopworn favorites, Truth, Beauty, and Goodness that Gilman has so exhaustively and effectively deconstructed. The underlying logic of these appeals underscores the more disturbing implications of the relationship Gardner posits between art and health and an obsessive, arguably prurient, decidedly puritanical interest in exposing impurity worthy of a Cotton Mather or a Kenneth Starr. Gardner's efforts here are understandable in light of Lifton's analysis of survivor guilt and "how guilt can lead to one's thinking he's contaminated and impure, not worthy of being part of the community."[31] Curiously, however, the uncompromising, table-banging polemic on true art that Ekelund contends Gardner wrote at least in part to atone for the many compromises he had been forced to make earlier in his career "fuses together all manners of style and rhetoric, logic and irrationality, reasoning and uncontrolled lashing out, self-exaltation and self-abnegation."[32] In sum, *On Moral Fiction* is a work that is itself extraordinarily confused, badly spliced, and grotesquely stitched together.

For a writer already disposed to thinking of the body as corrupt and corrupting, the fact that Gardner wrote or recast much of *On Moral Fiction* while recovering from surgery for colon cancer must surely have affected his polemical as well as puritanical thinking and manifested itself in ways less direct than the embarrassing difficulties occasioned by Gerald Craine's colostomy in the unfinished novel *Shadows*. It is there in *Mickelsson's Ghosts*, in a protagonist who describes himself as "pretty puritanical" to the young prostitute he frequents and in a pollution that is as much ethical as environmental. It is there in a treatment of sexuality that is characteristically evasive and in a depiction of bodies that is correspondingly excessive. It is there, too, at the beginning of Gardner's career, in the gothic brew of sex, guilt, and self-loathing of "The Old Men." Interestingly, the Puritan theme is perhaps most pronounced in *The Wreckage of Agathon*, in which the draconian means employed by the tyrant Lykourgos in an effort to purify Sparta seem suspiciously like Gardner's own efforts in *On Moral Fiction*. In *Stillness*, Gardner's namesake, Buddy Orrick, understands that his psychiatrist would have described his flight from San Francisco to Missouri "as a desperate attempt to shake the demons from his back, purify his sick heart by fire" by an act of self-assertion that Orrick realizes "was also an act of self-resignation: as people capable of believing in God can resign themselves completely to the will of God."[33]

The language here echoes that of Jonathan Edwards's *Personal Narrative*, in which Edwards expresses his desire to be metaphorically "swallowed up" by God. As even undergraduate readers are quick to point out, Gardner's own writing is rich in metaphor, indeed overrich. Although Gardner stressed the importance of metaphor in establishing character, which for him was the "heart" of all "good fiction," he failed to consider what such critics as Susan Sontag and Marita Sturken have demonstrated so convincingly, namely, metaphor's extraliterary implications.[34] Read culturally, the metaphorical binary oppositions Gardner deploys in *On Moral Fiction* and related works are at once illuminating and disturbing. For him, art is entirely either/or. It is either true or false, sane or insane, healthy or unhealthy, moral or immoral, normal or abnormal. Outside the "Big Tent" of "true art," Gardner posits a readily identifiable minor art of "literary sideshows" and "stunts," of "intellectual toys" and "linguistic sculpture," which prizes oddity and freakishness, such as "the humpback's peculiar (real or imagined) way of scratching his back."[35] Amazingly, of all those who responded negatively to the retrograde aesthetics of *On Moral Fiction* and its equally conservative social and political implications, only Harold Jaffe took the time to point out just how insidious Gardner's language actually is. And even Jaffe dealt only briefly with Gardner's pejorative use of "cripples" and "freaks" before moving on to what he felt was the more troubling question of Gardner's "literary McCarthyism."[36] Stranger still, Jaffe's whistle-blowing went unremarked until 1995, when Ekelund offered a footnote listing a number of worrisome passages. Gardner's harsh treatment of freakish, crippled art becomes even more interesting when considered in light of Gardner's espousal of "a disembodied faith," as Ekelund aptly calls it.[37]

As we have seen, the body in Gardner's fiction is almost always grotesque, but the grotesquerie is rarely liberating, rarely the antidote for, alternative to, or decrowning double of abstract, monologic authority. Rather, it is an expression of rejection and disgust. Much the same can be said for Gardner's treatment of textual bodies that prize metafiction over metaphysics, postmodern deconstructions over eternal verities, and *jouissance* over moral uplift. These are the texts that disrupt "the vivid and continuous dream in the reader's mind" by calling attention to their own physical and/or verbal selves. Interestingly enough, Gardner was part of the New Fiction movement that he later repudiated so vociferously and necessarily, for what is the New Fiction but a latter-day manifestation of the "new Hedonism that (as Lord Henry puts it in *The Picture of Dorian Gray*) was to re-create life and to save it from the harsh, uncomely puritanism that is having, in our own day, its curious revival."[38] "Every fair-minded person will readily admit that not all bad or mediocre artists should be dismissed from our republic," Gardner conceded, but since the true artist is neither fair-minded nor every person, he could, with all the self-righteousness of the elect, consider bad and mediocre art "a filth and a pestilence that must be driven out."[39] Here we have what Ekelund rightly calls the "unsettling flip side" of Gardner's theory of moral fiction: "that what is unhealthy is somehow responsible for being unhealthy."[40] And not just responsible. In an interview published in 1981, Gardner replaced his earlier biblical justifications (as in the passage quoted above) with a pseudo-scientific rationale for ridding the post-Platonic republic of all false artists and their pestilential art. Democracy and goodness, he said, are simply more fit to survive than tyranny and evil—excluding, one assumes, the tyranny of Gardner's own brand of literary McCarthyism.[41]

Gardner's use of disability, disfigurement, and freakishness in his work is certainly troubling. But what of the ease with which his critics have accepted them as purely symbolic? In the hands of his largely sympathetic critics, Gardner's grotesques have become nothing more than, for example, "a corpulent Asian," "a reclusive young giant," "an old, fat bank robber," a merely "pitiable" man like *The Resurrection's* John Horne or the police chief with "a physical flaw, a skin disease," "whose outward deformity signifies some inward distress," as Leonard Butts and Gregory Morris say of *The Sunlight Dialogues'* hairless, grublike Fred Clumly.[42] This marginalizing, or sanitizing, of the monstrous is understandable given the critics' desire to stay rather sheepishly in the moral fiction fold presided over by the pastorally inclined John Gardner, working well within the limits he himself established while further normalizing Gardner's policing of the freakish. Butts, then, only makes explicit what much of Gardner criticism implies when he emphasizes the "aesthetic wholeness" of the fiction. The term "aesthetic wholeness" is Gardner's own, and "wholeness" is an idea to which the "wounded" Gardner often returned. In one of the numerous interviews in which he proselytized for moral fiction while "challenging the literary naysayers" who "make us comfortable with our betrayals," Gardner makes his case for an art devoted to "keeping the kid alive"—by which he means not just the child's innocence but his "wholeness" too. As Gardner said in his "last interview," indirectly recalling his own prelapsarian days, great art "makes you whole."[43] Conversely, minor or immoral art disrupts and dismembers. Thus, Gardner's especially damning remarks about Kurt Vonnegut's *Slaughterhouse-Five*, and, even more to the point of this essay, Robert Coover's "A Pedestrian Accident."

It is worth recalling that when it was first published *On Moral Fiction* received a surprising number of approving, even enthusiastic reviews.[44] Although dismissed by many as a "mean-spirited" diatribe and "a shrill pitch to the literary right," it set off a well-publicized national debate that helped usher in, even if it did not directly cause, the period of literary and political conservatism in the United States that remains with us twenty years later.

Shockingly, yet not altogether surprisingly, the publication of *On Moral Fiction* earned Gardner the warm embrace of the Moral Majority, Inc. and an invitation to join the American Nazi Party. That Gardner rejected both in no uncertain terms is certainly to his credit, though the fact that both organizations believed they had found in him a like mind and a highly visible as well as culturally influential spokesperson is not. However, even as it looks ahead to Reaganomics and the rise of the political and religious right, *On Moral Fiction* connects with the past in two important ways. One is obvious. It promotes a dismayingly ahistorical aesthetic as well as a vaguely defined and valorized golden age. The other is less apparent but also more significant. This is the relationship between *On Moral Fiction* and an American Puritan tradition characterized by an obsessive interest in origins, preservation, and discrimination.45

Elsewhere, Gardner may have been more overt in acknowledging his "modern Protestant soul." There is, for example, his approval of Walt Disney's "Midwestern Protestantism" and his finding "more Christian feeling in late Mickey Mouse than in the 'Ave Maria.'" There is also the long, posthumously published essay in which Gardner claims that "the heart of good fiction is always religious"—"at least the American part of it," which Gardner then goes on to classify according to the "religious, or non-, or antireligious notions it expresses."46 The connections between Gardner's theory of moral fiction and the Puritan tradition are less specific but no less important. In his extolling "the true artist's faithfulness to his business" and in his complaining of a "loss of faith" on the part of many contemporary writers,47 one clearly discerns that "Judaic sense of wonder and millenarian promise" which, as Malcolm Bradbury and Richard Ruland have noted, characterize early Puritan thought and resulted not only in the Protestant work ethic but in a sense of "a dream gone wrong" as "the shortcomings of the sons were measured by the dreams of the fathers."48 Gardner's high-minded definition of "true art" echoes the typically Puritan (and by now characteristically American) belief in the "purposefulness and instructive intent" of writing. The Puritan "metaphysic of writing" so clearly expressed in the prefatory poem to Michael Wigglesworth's 1662 bestseller, *Day of Doom*—"No toys, nor fables (Poet's wonted crimes), / Here be, but things of worth, with wit prepar'd"—is just as evident in Gardner's statement of faith in fiction's essential morality: "not just that it entertains or distracts us from our troubles, not just that it broadens our knowledge of people and places, but also that it helps us know what we believe, reinforces those qualities that are noblest in us, leads us to feel uneasy about our faults and limitations."49

On Moral Fiction is Gardner's "Sinners in the Hands of an Angry God." In it he plays Jonathan Edwards's part, a latter-day prophet (or Senator McCarthy) bent upon a great awakening that requires exposing all false, trivial, and/or immoral art "for what it is"—the sign of a deep "sickness"—and outing all reprobate artists before banishing them from the American Eden.50 In doing so, *On Moral Fiction* not only betrays, as it were, its origin in American Puritan thought; it also underscores just how closely it conforms to that most enduring of all the Puritan literary forms, the American jeremiad as Bercovitch has defined it. *On Moral Fiction* takes "the American writers' tendency to see themselves as outcasts and isolates, prophets crying in the desert" about as far as anyone has gone or can go.51 *On Moral Fiction* combines castigation and celebration in order to stress reform rather than separation, afflictive correction rather than vindictive punishment, and it adapts an essentially religious form for national purposes. For all its reliance on Homer, Dante, Tolstoy, and Fowles, *On Moral Fiction* is in fact a book about contemporary *American* fiction. It appeared not long after Gardner's cleverly titled but otherwise cloyingly patriotic op-ed piece, "Amber (Get) Waves (Your) of (Plastic) Grain (Uncle Sam)" (*New York Times*, 29 October 1975) and the publication of his bicentennial novel, *October Light*, the following year. "Only in the United States," Bercovitch points out, "has nationalism carried with it the religious meaning of the sacred," and only here has the nation relied so heavily on defining itself in terms of what it is not. If the positive side of the American jeremiad has involved condemning the profane in order to commit the nation to a spiritual ideal and providing "an inexhaustible . . . source of exaltation through lament," then the negative side has involved "generat[ing] millennial frenzy out of self-doubt." It has "spawned an astonishing variety of official or self-appointed committees on un-American activities: 'progressivist societies' for eradicating the Indians, 'benevolent societies' for deporting blacks, 'Young Americans' for banning European culture, 'populists' obsessed with the spectre of foreign conspiracy, voluntary associations for safeguarding the Revolutionary traditions, male and female 'reform societies' for social regeneration through sexual purification."52

Gardner's call for morally uplifting fiction, with its "messianic voice,"53 exclusionary politics, and "totalitarian optimism,"54 derives as much from his own Calvinist sense of unworthiness, self-doubt, and self-loathing as it does from the anxious state of postwar American fiction and culture. Its high-minded ambitiousness is the inverse measure of a deep-seated ambivalence that, even as it led Gardner to castigate and cast out others, from Barth and Bellow to Updike and Vonnegut, brought down their righteous wrath on his (guilt-riven) head, as in a sense he may have expected, perhaps even hoped, believing he deserved no less. We may smile smugly at H. L. Mencken's witty definition of Puritanism—the haunting fear that someone somewhere may be happy—but Gardner's Hawthorne-imbued fiction suggests that what Puritanism is largely about is the fear of, or tragic awareness of, one's own unworthiness, especially unworthiness to be "saved." It is this fear that helps explain Gardner's desire to write, proselytize, and protest too much, and to do so not only for art—which he said must justify itself, must earn the right to exist (or rather to continue to exist)—but for the artist too. "The artist so debilitated by guilt and self-doubt that he cannot be certain real virtues exist" is doomed to be second-rate. He is guilty not of fratricide but of infidelity to the high calling of "true art" that was "not so much a profession as a yoga, or way," and guilty too of the "crippling defects" that are the outward and visible signs of far "graver faults of soul."[55] Gardner could concede that "our humanness is enriched by our increasingly sophisticated notion of guilt and of society's part in the guilt of individuals," but he could imagine nothing worse with which to charge the twentieth-century's unholy trinity of Freud, Wittgenstein, and Sartre than their having brought not sin or death but "free-floating guilt" into the world. What Gardner called "the inescapable bitterness of life" could only be explained by "the sin of Adam," an original sin that in Gardner's case grew into a self-doubt (and compensatory self-assertion) and self-loathing (and compensatory self-promotion) filtered through his Presbyterian upbringing and displaced onto the grotesque, obscenely physical "other."[56]

Putting this displacement in the context of the influence of American Puritanism on Gardner and his writing allows us both a fuller appreciation of the extent to which Puritanism continues to manifest itself in American culture and a keener understanding of Gardner's struggle with (as opposed to his and his critics' endorsement of) "aesthetic wholeness." As a passage from the novel *Stillness* demonstrates, Gardner himself was at least occasionally aware of both the nature and the implications of these displacements:

> Who it was he was angry at he could easily have said if he'd stop to
> think, but he couldn't, that moment, stop to think [immediately
> following an argument with his wife about an affair of hers
> which Martin, guilty about his own sexual betrayals, may only be

imagining]. He would remember later, thinking back to that
moment, that he'd done the same in London once. He and [his
son] Evan were crossing a wide, busy street—Evan smiling and
eager, looking up at the gables of the Parliament building—and
leading him through traffic, not holding his hand, Martin had
called back confusing signals, so that Evan had run when Martin
meant for him to wait, and a car had almost struck him. The
driver hit the brakes—a cripple in one of those state-provided
three-wheel cars—and Martin had turned and raged at the man,
though the driver had done nothing, nothing whatever except stop
with great skill in an emergency. But it was only after the poor
man had driven off that Martin had understood that he, he alone,
not the driver, not Evan, was in the wrong. So now.57

Here we see in condensed form the component parts of Gardner's deeply
Puritan art. There is the failure to protect a child and the displacement of
responsibility for and guilt over that failure not just onto someone else, but
onto a pathologized other. There is the linking of that failure (causally and
circumstantially) to sex both in the narrative and in the protagonist's decidedly Puritan mind. And there is the protagonist's eventual, self-excoriating
acceptance of his individual responsibility and guilt based upon his acceptance of that "deep-down inferiority" that was both the wellspring of
Gardner's imagination and a version of the Calvinist doctrine of innate
depravity. Here and throughout Gardner's varied and formidable body of
work one finds ample evidence of both the persistence and the perversity of
the American Puritan tradition, its pervasive influence and complex legacy.
At the very least, Gardner's example should lead us to question whether critics such as Joseph Adamson and Hilary Clark may not be overly optimistic in
their psychoanalytic reading of the relationship between shame and writing,
particularly the way in which "shame and guilt . . . work together in constructive ways." According to Adamson and Clark, "the ability to feel and
acknowledge genuine guilt and shame, rooted in human sympathy and feeling, defends against the destructive consequences of unconscious feelings of
shame—manifested, for example, in the narcissistic need to extend one's
power and control."58 It would be foolish to deny that much of the appeal of
Gardner and his fiction derives from the constructive uses to which he put
the guilt and shame he experienced so acutely. But it would be equally foolish, or worse, to deny that those uses entirely canceled out "the narcissistic
need to extend one's power and control" that is one of shame's "destructive

consequences." It is precisely this need that is so evident in Gardner's "shameful" handling of sexuality in the fiction, in his prurient interest in and policing of grotesque bodies, and in his obsession with purity and wholeness. Seeking to transmute his own shame and freakishness into asset and art, John Gardner became a latter-day John Winthrop proclaiming the city on a hill of moral fiction while warning of the deadly and deforming plagues that would be visited upon all who failed to keep the covenant with a wholly disembodied art of Truth, Beauty, and Goodness: a city where, as Robert Frost wistfully claimed, one could "drink and be whole again beyond confusion."59

Notes

1. See, e.g., Mikhail Bakhtin, *Rabelais and His World*, trans. Helene Iswolsky (Bloomington: Indiana University Press, 1984).

2. Liz Rosenberg, "What's It Like to Live with a Genius? Remembering John Gardner and How He Worked" (paper presented at the annual John Gardner conference, 4 April 1998, Batavia, N.Y.). Rosenberg's comment was cut from the version of her talk published in *Proceedings of the First Annual John Gardner Conference*, ed. Jim Fessenden (Batavia: The John Gardner Society, 1999), 85–89.

3. John Gardner, "The Old Men" (Ph.D. diss., University of Iowa, 1958), 626–27.

4. John Gardner, *Grendel* (New York: Knopf, 1971), 109.

5. *John Gardner: A Defense against Madness*, prod. and dir. Richard O. Moore, The Originals: The Writer in America series, Public Broadcasting System, 3 April 1978.

6. Raymond Carver, foreword to *On Becoming a Novelist*, by John Gardner (New York: Harper & Row, 1983), ix–xix.

7. Charles Johnson, "A Phenomenology of *On Moral Fiction*," in *Thor's Hammer: Essays on John Gardner*, ed. Jeff Henderson (Conway: University of Central Arkansas Press, 1985), 147–56.

8. Samuel Coale, "'Into the Farther Darkness': The Manichaean Pastoralism of John Gardner," in *John Gardner: Critical Perspectives*, ed. Robert A. Morace and Kathryn VanSpanckeren (Carbondale: Southern Illinois University Press, 1982), 17–18.

9. Bo Ekelund, *In the Pathless Forest: John Gardner's Literary Project* (Uppsala, Sweden: Acta Universitatis Upsaliensis, 1995), 110.

10. Ronald Grant Nutter, *A Dream of Peace: Art and Death in the Fiction of John Gardner* (New York: Lang, 1997).

11. Gregory L. Morris, *A World of Order and Light: The Fiction of John Gardner* (Athens: University of Georgia Press, 1984).

12. John Gardner, *On Moral Fiction* (New York: Basic Books, 1978), 31; John M.

Howell, "The Wound and the Albatross: John Gardner's Apprenticeship," in *Thor's Hammer*, 6; Gardner, *On Becoming a Novelist*, 62.

13. Ekelund, *In the Pathless Forest*, 354.

14. There is also a countermovement in Gardner's fiction, a tendency to share guilt by viewing responsibility in less narrowly private terms. After wondering what part Dale's wife may have played in his brother's suicide, Jay Corbie concludes, "But someone was responsible. Someone had to be" ("The Old Men," 172). At the other extreme is the view, "No use blaming anyone," expressed by a character in, and seemingly endorsed by the author of, *October Light*, a novel about the crippling effects of guilt. As James Page, one of that novel's two protagonists, eventually realizes: "Guilt. All this time he'd carried it, a burden that had bent his whole life double and when he caught it and held it in his two hands and opened them, there was nothing there" (John Gardner, *October Light* [New York: Knopf, 1976], 430).

15. Sacvan Bercovitch, *The Puritan Origins of the American Self* (New Haven: Yale University Press, 1975), 17.

16. Twyla Dell, "Dickey, Gardner; Impromptu Trialogue," *Broadside* (Fairfax, Va.: George Mason University) 21 (27 March 1978): 15–16.

17. Louise Sweeney, "John Gardner," *Christian Science Monitor*, 24 June 1980: B2–B3, B11; William Kennedy, rev. of *The King's Indian*, by John Gardner, *New Republic* 171, 7 December 1974, 19–20.

18. John Gardner, *"Stillness" and "Shadows"* (New York: Knopf, 1986), 56.

19. John Gardner and John Maier, trans., *Gilgamesh* (New York: Knopf, 1984).

20. John Gardner, *Mickelsson's Ghosts* (New York: Knopf, 1982), 41; Gardner, *Stillness*, 242.

21. John Gardner, *Jason and Medeia* (1973; reprint, New York: Ballantine, 1975), 12; Gardner, *Nickel Mountain* (New York: Knopf, 1974), 81; Gardner, *The Resurrection* (1966; reprint, New York: Ballantine, 1974), 154; Gardner, "The Old Men," 182; Gardner, *Mickelsson's Ghosts*, 432.

22. Sander L. Gilman, *Creating Beauty to Cure the Soul* (Durham, N.C.: Duke University Press, 1998).

23. Bakhtin, *Rabelais and His World*, 403–4.

24. Samuel Coale, "The Design of the Dream in Gardner's Fiction," in *Thor's Hammer*, 54.

25. Bakhtin, *Rabelais and His World*, 23.

26. Paul Semonin, "Monsters in the Marketplace: The Exhibition of Human Oddity in Early Modern England," in *Freakery: Cultural Spectacles of the Extraordinary Body*, ed. Rosemarie Garland Thomson (New York: New York University Press, 1996), 79.

27. Rosemarie Garland Thomson, introduction to *Freakery*, 1.

28. Rosemarie Garland Thomson, *Extraordinary Bodies: Figuring Physical Disability in American Culture and Literature* (New York: Columbia University Press, 1997), 66. Interesting to note, given Gardner's love of, and academic interest in, medieval litera-

ture, is Thomson's claim that "the medieval model that governs today's interpretation of disability assumes that any somatic trait that falls short of the idealized norm must be corrected or eliminated" (79).

29. "Congenitally shy" but arrogant too, with his "goatlike laugh" and ""sad-clown act," Horne hopes "to be reborn" even as he looks "for something in himself to love," all the while prattling about "remission of sin" and "art as atonement."

30. Gardner, *On Moral Fiction*, 126.

31. Nutter, *A Dream of Peace*, 174.

32. Ekelund, *In the Pathless Forest*, 337. In a telling instance of the Puritan pot calling the postmodern kettle black, Gardner accused William Gass and others of being "like the God of the Calvinists, [who] loves only his ideas" (*On Moral Fiction*, 72).

33. Gardner, *"Stillness,"* 4, 136. "Buddy" was the family's name for Gardner.

34. Susan Sontag, *"Illness as Metaphor" and "AIDS and Its Metaphors"* (1978, 1989; reprint, New York: Anchor Books, 1990); Marita Sturken, *Tangled Memories: The Vietnam War, The AIDS Epidemic, and the Politics of Remembering* (Berkeley: University of California Press, 1997).

35. Gardner, *On Moral Fiction*, 21.

36. Harold Jaffe, "Writer's Forum," *Fiction International* 12 (1980): 11–15.

37. Ekelund, *In the Pathless Forest*, 139(n87), 132.

38. *The Writings of Oscar Wilde*, ed. Isobel Murray (New York: Oxford University Press, 1989), 145.

39. Gardner, *On Moral Fiction*, 174.

40. Ekelund, *In the Pathless Forest*, 343.

41. John Gardner, "An Interview with John Gardner," interview by Per Winther, *English Studies* 62 (December 1981): 509–24.

42. Dean McWilliams, *John Gardner* (Boston: Twayne, 1990), 56, 88; Leonard Butts, *The Novels of John Gardner: Making Life Art as a Moral Process* (Baton Rouge: Louisiana State University Press, 1988), 21, 8, 73; Morris, *A World of Order and Light*, 76.

43. John Gardner, "Challenging the Literary Naysayers," interview by Daniel Laskin, *Horizon* 21 (July 1978): 32–36; John Gardner, "John Gardner's Last Interview," interview by Bruce Beans, *Today: The Inquirer Magazine* (Philadelphia), 17 October 1982, 1, 18–21.

44. For the critical response to *On Moral Fiction*, see Robert A. Morace, *John Gardner: An Annotated Secondary Bibliography* (New York: Garland, 1984), 148–62, and Morace, "John Gardner and His Reviewers," in *Thor's Hammer*, 17–32.

45. Jean Baudrillard, *America*, trans. Chris Turner (London: Verso, 1988), 7–8.

46. John Gardner, "Saint Walt" and "A Writer's View of Contemporary American Fiction," in *On Writers and Writing*, ed. Stewart O'Nan (Reading, Mass.: Addison-Wesley, 1994), 78–85, 163–98.

47. Gardner, *On Moral Fiction*, 55.

48. Malcolm Bradbury and Richard Ruland, *From Puritanism to Postmodernism: A History of American Literature* (New York: Penguin, 1992), 9, 12, 13.

49. Bradbury and Ruland, *From Puritanism to Postmodernism*, 19, 21; John Gardner, *The Art of Fiction: Notes on Craft for Young Writers* (New York: Knopf, 1984), 31.

50. Gardner, *On Moral Fiction*, 100–101, 105–6, 198.

51. Sacvan Bercovitch, *The American Jeremiad* (Madison: University of Wisconsin Press, 1978), 180.

52. Bercovitch, *American Jeremiad*, 176, 121, 159–60.

53. Carol MacCurdy, "*On Moral Fiction*: The Embattled John Gardner," in *Thor's Hammer*, 145.

54. Jeffrey Gillenkirk, "Surely Goodness and Mercy," *In These Times*, 31 May 1978, 23.

55. Gardner, *On Moral Fiction*, 145; John Gardner, "A Conversation with John Gardner," interview by Paul Ferguson and John Maier, in Morace, *John Gardner: An Annotated Secondary Bibliography*, 66; Gardner, *Art of Fiction*, 115.

56. Gardner, *On Moral Fiction*, 44, 46.

57. Gardner, "*Stillness*," 78.

58. Joseph Adamson and Hilary Clark, introduction to *Scenes of Shame: Psychoanalysis, Shame, and Writing*, ed. Adamson and Clark (Albany: State University of New York Press, 1999), 27.

59. Robert Frost, "Directive," *Selected Poems of Robert Frost* (New York: Holt, Rinehart and Winston, 1963), 253.

"Down Here in Paradise"

Toni Morrison's Americas

∽

Judith Wilt

In the American colonial period a series of cities appeared "on the hill[s]" from Massachusetts Bay to Providence to Philadelphia to Baltimore to Williamsburg, cities founded to express the purity of an aspiring and endangered religious sensibility. The cities faced away from an ensoiling mercantilist Europe, and from one another's corrupting and competing doctrines. The cities faced the wilderness, a symbolic space "out there" which was at once their opposite and their refuge, where the godless embraced the devil and the outlaw his will and the heretic her conscience, where the anti-city sustained the perfected community, and where at need, at inevitable need, the perfected community could flee—to western Pennsylvania, to Indiana, to Utah—to rebuild.

The strenuous seventeenth-century rhetoric of doctrinal purity lasted longer in America than in England, some historians have suggested, because the endless spaces of America allowed for these imaginable extremes, while the crowded purlieus of England were enforcing a spirit and then a theology of tolerance in the Protestant motherland. Where Young Goodman Brown danced with the devil and Hester Prynne made a new covenant with ardor, Cooper and Hawthorne, Dickinson and Whitman, made new polities in which to dream of still newer communes.

The work of Toni Morrison is an effort to reclaim, and impart to the official American idea, the African and African-American story. Her novels situate themselves steadfastly in "black history"; they are in and of the communities at the margin of the official American story. But in every important sense they recognize the one American world whose many communities go deeply to each other's making, and to the American definition. In her most recent novel, *Paradise*, the early American "Puritan" trajectories of purity and adultery, foundings and flights, are seen interpellated in, enforced on, enigmatically repeated in, the African-American story, with its own triumphant and yet cautionary tale of a city upon a hill.[1]

One of our original "captivity narratives," American-African slavery is both at odds with and yet deeply pliable to the "salvation history" of Protestant Christianity, which in its New England form went toward what Sacvan Bercovitch argues was the "Puritan origin" of the American self. For Morrison the work of nineteenth- and early-twentieth-century American literature was in part the half-conscious attempt to marshal awareness of the African-American other, playing *on* the darkness as a way to examine and foreground its own whiteness. And the work of twentieth- and twenty-first century African-American literature is in part to excavate and interrogate, on behalf of a continuing American idea, the rhetorics of purity and chosenness—racial and sexual, political and religious—that endure in and complicate the idea.

Nancy Armstrong and Leonard Tennenhouse have put newly into discourse the originary figure, "the generic intellectual ancestor,"[2] they call "the imaginary Puritan," in whose enabling shadow we define a modernity, a subjectivity. This ancestor seals the gap between old (God, Hebrew, English, speaking) and new (humankind, Christianity, American, reading/writing). Morrison's novel disrupts the binaries of *Paradise Lost/Regained* centered in the Miltonian key text of the time by making Paradise a work in time, cocreated by human and Divine "Down here in Paradise."[3]

As the culminating moment in "the succession of exoduses, at once repetitive and developmental"[4] going back to the Babylonian captivity and forward to the New Jerusalem, the American Foundation was to its clerical theorizers the meeting point of psycho- and socio-machia, the location where the formation of community dramatized, and actually accomplished, the release of "soul" from the thrall of "self." Yet the "repetition" of exoduses assumed, required, the persistence and recognition of captivities. As the "legend" of the founding divines of the seventeenth century and the Founding Fathers of the eighteenth century accommodated contention and critique, new captivities of sexuality (especially female) and raciality (especially African) emerged toward high consciousness, requiring new exercises of, new confirmations of, the redeemer nation.

Slavery, its histories and its consequences, is at once the sign of belonging to American salvation history and the sign of alienation from it. Double captives of cotton and Gospel, Africans in America could aspire to be owners of these things instead, or to the grace to be something beyond this dynamic. And so can all other Americans. Morrison has called us to recognize not just "her" but "our" "genderized, sexualized, wholly racialized world."[5] The accurate "placing" of slavery in every particular moment of the American historical consciousness is both a remedial and redemptive work, something never to look away from, always to see—and to see with.

Paradise is Morrison's newly sex-consecrating *Scarlet Letter*, her *Crucible*, her enigmatic slant of light on "The Soul Selects Her Own Society"; it is her "Strange Fruit" and *Grapes of Wrath*, her *Easy Rider*, her heartbreakingly cautioning *Linden Hills*, her intransigent and prophetic *Angels in America*, her northern and southern hemispheric magical realist Amerindian *House of Spirits*. It is an unsparing critique of the dangers of the Puritan myth of the Exodus and the existentialist myth of the "drift," but it also traces each of these kinds of movements to a threshold ("You see a door, I see a window" [305]) of grace.

"God's Bread"

Working from Milton's Paradise to the American scene, the (imaginary) Puritan reader encounters an allegorical topography of three spaces. "In here"—the garden or the city—a self-ordering activity reflects the Author. "Out there," Puritan divines warned, a wilderness "full of wild beasts and wild men" reflects the activity of the Author within the created world, the temptations and trials, the refining fire, "the flaile, the fan, the Milstone and the Oven" into whose jurisdiction "we must go . . . before we can be God's Bread."[6] And somewhere, a dimension and a condition in the mind of the Author as well, there is chaos, the nothing, the gap, the moving-moving. In *Paradise Lost* (or "Areopagitica" for that matter) the spaces in Law, (not)Law, and (lack)Law uphold and are porous to one another: In the territory of the Puritan imaginary, as Lacan might say, the Imaginary Puritan traverses these spaces carrying the orderings of Heaven/Paradise and Hell/world along, "nor am I out of it," even when, especially when, s/he is edging round the rifts where the lacklaw, no-thing, disrupts these binaries.

The urgencies of the African-American story, and its address to the American idea, direct Morrison's topography in the novel *Paradise*. Three dwelling places emerge. One is a community of Design, of design black, which has for ten generations been locked in purposeful oppositional gaze with a wilderness. It is emphatically "out there": "Out There: space, once beckoning and free, became unmonitored and seething; became a void where random and organized evil erupted when and where it chose—behind any standing tree, behind the door of any house, humble or grand. Out there where your children were sport, your women quarry, and where your very person could be annulled. . . . Out there where every cluster of whitemen looked like a posse, being alone was being dead" (16).

The second dwelling place is a community undesigned, of design impossible to color-fix, but fixed in gender. It is a wilderness of women abused, confused, drifted together out of the tender and brutal captivities of the nuclear family and gathered in random, bitchy grace in a polymorphous "bullet shaped" structure built in the 1920s by an embezzler on the lam, rebuilt shortly after by a Lady Patroness clumsily imposing charity, Christianity, and education on the dwindling Indian remnant of Oklahoma, and now named by its black Puritan neighbors, in awe and dread, the Convent.

Bordering both these communities lies a beckoning space unmistakably holy and terrible in the narrative, unruly except to its own elaborate order, inscribed in two erotic images of the American frontier landscape. One image is "real," located between the two human communities, and autoerotic in the sense explored by Luce Irigaray, a self-touching that brings the self to itself across the gap between subjectivity and its object. Near the town of Ruby, Oklahoma, it is rumored, is "a place where there was a lake in the middle of a wheat field. And . . . near this lake two trees grew in each other's arms. And if you squeezed in between them in just the right way, well, you would feel an ecstasy no human could invent or duplicate" (66). The other image, place, and sexuality can be imagined but not found, for it is in "Wish, Arizona," and its zone is the chaos that is its own imperturbable cosmos, the unauthored moving-moving: "A man and a woman fucking forever. When the light changes every four hours they do something new. At the desert's edge they fuck to the sky tide of Arizona. Nothing can stop them. Nothing wants to. . . . The black couple of Wish, Arizona. Moving, moving, all the time moving" (63).

Rock formation, tree formation, habitus of a god, the moving-moving is antitype, prototype, omegatype both to the patriarchal domesticity of the community of Design and to the haunted labyrinthine-shambles of the Convent. But like the family and the Convent, Morrison argues, this polysexual habitus is most human when most liminal, imagined. For this anti-Puritan paradise is subject to the dangerous process of reification that dogs all the activity of the human symbolic: Too soon one sees "a blessed utility become a shrine (cautioned against not only in scary Deuteronomy but in lovely Corinthians II as well)" (102).[7]

Paradise takes pains to situate its black community of Design with origins in the colonial period, building a lengthy history whose legends include "stories of great Migrations" (110) and foundations guided by God and prophets, undertaken in the context of mythic challenges to the soul and coherence of the community, challenges called "the Scattering" and "the Disallowing."[8] The families who live in Ruby, Oklahoma, in the novel's mainframe time, bicentennial summer 1976, are descendants of families who have lived with or near each other since 1755, "since before Bunker Hill" the narrative says pointedly (192). In colonial times, under whatever conditions of "owning" applied, Africans on the American continent lived as extended families as well as herded "hands," and worked as artisans and craftspeople, gunsmiths, seamstresses, cobblers, lace makers, shopkeepers, iron mongers, as well as crop pickers. The people of Ruby hold stubbornly to the pride of presence in this more fluid, prenational America, as well as to the memory of participation as educated men in the state governments of 1868–1875. They do it to claim an American (African) history richer than that assigned by even the most benign white-official history, in which African Americans figure as "ex-slaves," "ex-soldiers," never quite citizens.

Disenfranchised repeatedly between 1755 and 1890, men and women from the fifteen families whose ancestors knew each other when Mississippi was still the Louisiana Territory gathered with full ironic knowledge to hack their own trail of tears from the deep South to the imaginably free West. There were in the last part of the nineteenth century already a number of part- or all-black communities in this West, seeking "Negro homesteaders": The consortium of families led by onetime Mississippi judge and legislator Zecharia Morgan, once "Coffee" or "Kofi," did not initially intend to found a separate community in the thankfully treeless wilderness but to join one of these. But they kept themselves together out of pride in their history and out of fear of "the Scattering" that was God's curse on the tribes of the biblical Zechariah and that is the curse of any enforced migration. A more marked burden on the group was the refusal of the chance-met communities along their way—white, Indian, Negro—to welcome them in. "The Disallowing" that formed the African-American negative of the positive sense of American self-making and Christian mission in the Migration resulted in the founding of Haven in 1889 and 1890, after the guiding ancestral spirit-walker—godly in black suit, suspenders and satchel, incarnating the invisible, echoing footsteps of the leading Almighty—sat down finally on a plot of ground and began unpacking his satchel.

Zechariah Morgan's "This is Our Place" (98) had for his new city all the resonance of John Winthrop's injunction to be a "city upon a hill"—and all the enigma of shunning that goes with the shining of that light. For the objection of already-formed communities was not just to the size of the group, or its poverty, or its sense of righteousness, or even the sheer bad-luck fact that its still-migrating status unnerved the just-settled peoples whose new homes, schools, and churches were their guarantee of "difference" (14) from the moving-moving. The objection was to the blackness of their blackness: the Disallowing was to the strictness with which they had retained their African genetic heritage. After the foundation of Haven, the Morgans and the DuPreses, Fleetwoods, Pooles and Blackhorses, the Flood, Cato, Beauchamp and Best families retained enough savvy understanding of the Scattering principle not to be caught in the paralysis and decay when the other colored communities started dying in the 1930s and 1940s. They neither surrendered to the new Scattering that was the great migration north nor sat down among the going-out-of-business signs and mourned, but loaded up their household gods and moved a judicious distance farther west for a renewal and second foundation in Ruby, Oklahoma, in 1949 and 1950, consciously protecting their American dream. But an unconscious "rule . . . lived a quietly throbbing life" (195) underground, obscuring and obsessively establishing (black) racial "purity" as a founding dimension of the community.

As the secure and garden-mad 1950s became the disorientingly belligerent and Vietnam-haunted 1970s, the Ruby matron and teacher Patricia Best Flood started a founding families' genealogy as an educational tool for her students and then found the parents suddenly objecting to this rationalization of legend. She starts connecting the dots of her own and Ruby's past and uncovers its secret law. The mysterious alienation between her father and the other founders, once mythically read as a response to his work as a mortician, she now rereads as a response to his choosing a light-skinned wife. The weakening disease that has struck all four Fleetwood children may be a malignant outcome of Jeff's service among the Agent Orange and napalm in Vietnam—or a bite-back in the blood of a tribe that conceived its pride and its safety in marrying only each other. As the family tree turns from lines and names to narrative and memoir, Patricia Best imagines her way into the minds of ancestors who could not bear to be conscious of the sight that faced them in the 1890s: light-skinned African-American men allowed less degrading work than dark-skinned ones, and in turn disallowing the coal-black families, "8-rock" black African-Americans. "The sign of racial purity they had taken for granted had become a stain" (194), and the twice-threatened soul selected its own society, then shut the door.

A peek outside, during a trip by the Old Fathers in 1926 to explore the workings of other small towns in the West, confirmed this closing, as they were turned away from the hostile town of "Pura Sangre" with its cross at one end and its "No Niggers" sign at the other. Another trip outside in 1932 confirmed that the enemy was also inside the garden. Exploring another surviving black township, the adolescent sons of the Old Fathers, now the "Deacon" and "Steward" of contemporary Ruby, were literally knocked off their feet by an experience of desire buried even deeper than the half-conscious commitment to the African racial purity and "American" self-reliance—a snapshot burned on the eye of the "creamy sunlit skin" of women in pastel dresses moving gracefully in the spring air of another "colored" township, representing the obverse doctrine of "purity" to their own (110).

Fathers had good reasons to shun outsiders and take their own to wive; in threatened communities the half-biblically sanctioned informal ritual of the "takeover" parallels the sacred rites of marriage, when the widower or the widow or the orphaned is matched with the strongest male or female in the next house, the near blood (196). Sisters Soane and Dovey Blackhorse have married twin brothers Deacon and Steward Morgan in a newly naturalized rhythm. The raw edge of coercion that unites the last male Morgan with the one remaining healthy Fleetwood is naturalized too, by the unspoken urgencies of the future and the quiet pressure of the church blessing that, three years after the fact, licenses the sexual encounter of the couple, clumsily suturing the violence that accompanied it, and the disappeared pregnancy that was its outcome. But there is also that Morgan sterility, that Fleetwood sickness. There is the hint that the Ruby who gave her name to the town and who mothered the last male Morgan might herself have been a "takeover" within her own family and not the wife of her brothers' never-seen army buddy. And there is the spooky fact that Patricia Best's own daughter Billie Delia has fallen permanently in love with no less than two of the Poole brothers, desire falling helplessly into one of the many structures of incest.

The sublime and tragic enigma of the self-selected soul, the closed valves of attention in the city upon the hill, is manifest in the artifact chosen by the Old Fathers of Haven and reconstructed by the New Fathers of Ruby as the town center, temple, agora, an instrument that "both nourished them and monumentalized what they had done" (7). Cueing to an endless hermeneutics, that artifact is "an Oven. Round as a head, deep as desire" (6). The Old Fathers knew they were God's bread, not God. They made a further statement of their belief in the meeting place of the two concepts by establishing a central sphere, a hood, a head, for the communal fire in 1890. At the mouth of the head, a poet iron monger inscribed words, of which five remain in 1976: "the furrow of his brow." Some preceding letters have fallen off in the migration of the oven: Did the mouth of the head "originally" speak a caution, "Beware the furrow of his brow"? Or was it an authorizing command, "Be the furrow of his brow"? For nine generations the oven nourished its community without speaking, growing silently into its ambiguous monumentality.

Now in the 1970s, a new "black" generation of young people brings the oven into controversialist discourse. They are no longer Puritans, meant to "beware" a punishing God. As African-Americans, they affirm, they have been harrowed in the furrow of the white man's god's frown for too long. At stake is the power of origin, the idolatry that would *be* the frown of God, the fist of black power to the white world, of patriarchal authority in their own world. It is a frown directed at back-talking children or at the light skin that marks the Scattering and the Disallowing. It is a frown directed most forcibly at women. For if pure doctrine, pure African blood were, in the gaze of the monumentalizing Puritan Fathers, the deep desire of the Oven, "if that were their recipe" for its bread, then "everything that worries them," thinks Patricia Best, appalled, destroying the pages and notebooks that were the path to her terrifying insight, "must come from women" (217).

"They shot the white girl first," the novel begins, precipitating in the reader a search for a hermeneutics of color in gender that has licensed nine puritanical elders to bring shotguns to the Convent to exorcise their worries. And the reader is punished in the same way they are: a consciousness of doing helpless violence in the search. And at the end, the first law of detection is awry; there is no evidence of the crime. Habeas corpus, but we have no body. Entering the Convent, or coven of witches, the searchers find bread slowly rising on the abandoned kitchen shelves, and other signs of women and children—a sanitary napkin, a crib, a doll, a home-canned jar of peaches.

The Father who shot in the door, and the woman at the door, sees "the white girl" (3); the nephew who raises his gun moments later to shoot at three escaping women sees "bodacious black Eves" running at gun sound like track stars (18). But these interpretations are not entirely trustworthy. Having spent a lifetime tragically monumentalizing the blood color line, the men are now pulled by another vector of defense and desire to control feminine sexuality, of whatever color and blood, as the key to color and blood.

There are five women and one baby in the Convent when it is attacked in the novel's first section. By the ninth and last section we know that the oldest woman has the "brown" skin and the mixed blood and spirit of the "black," Portuguese, and Indio dwellers of Brazil. The narrative drops clues all along as to the blood, spirit, and color of the others—but it always complicates or undermines certainty. These are women who have fled or hid or drifted to the enigmatic sanctuary of the white-Catholic-founded Convent. They might be any or many colors: In this respect *Paradise* continues the "adversarial aesthetics" begun by Morrison in her first published fiction, "Recitatif," one meant to confound the way the category of race secures itself in its "visibility" as essential to being, denying its historical contingency as a made, made-up, thing.9

Mavis might be black: Her mind self-cauterized from withstanding years of abuse from a punishing husband and his fearfully behavior-repeating older children, she was "too dumb" to remember the baby twins smothering in the back seat of the gaudy Cadillac she left in the parking lot while buying hot dogs. Pallas might have a black father—he's getting rich in California managing black talent, but whatever color he is, he "married outside his own people" (254)—and a white mother (Is she? She's doing hippie art in New Mexico). Seneca has "chocolate eyes" (316); she might be black, growing up in public housing and weeping when she sees a weeping black woman, except that her mother is "not the same color" as the weeping black woman. And what color of skin is it that makes so eloquent a "map" of "roads" when she draws on it the red lines that emerge from her razor? Gigi, civil rights fighter, sexual dynamo seeking the moving-moving black couple of Wish, Arizona, is surely black. The colors "imperial black sporting a wild swipe of red, then thick feverish yellow" on the girl shot at the Convent door would fit the clothes she wore when K. D. Morgan first took her riding (4, 74). But wait, wasn't that body at the door "the white girl"?

Seeing by socioracial stereotype, by psychokinetic need, the Fathers of Ruby established the boundaries of black and white, female and male. They are devotees of a true womanhood based on a combination of Brer Rabbit and Frederick Douglass, not Thurgood Marshall or Malcolm X (82). The wives and daughters and crones of Ruby live within these boundaries too, but many of them will travel back and forth across them as they have done since Ruby came to the Convent in the 1950s. In those days the Convent was safely penned into its definition as a Roman Catholic mission-school, selling pecans and peppers and chickens for its financial support. But the order of nuns pulled out slowly in the 1950s as the supply of docile Indian girls dwindled, and the women who remained or arrived—one "superior," one "servant" and four drifters—while they see and say "black" and "white" about the world behind them, miraculously speak no racial discourse of each other *at all*.

As a male "embezzler's folly" taken over by a house of women, the Convent architecturally speaks two narratives of both gender and sexuality. For those exposed to violence or madness, mostly women and a few men, it speaks the ancient mercy of Sanctuary. To the patriarchs of Ruby it spells an invisible filching of assets—(male) sexual potency, heterosexual femininity. When the nuns moved into the embezzler's house they found male sexual potency and heterosexual femininity built obsessively and pornographically into its fabric—mightily endowed decorative cupids, vagina-shaped ashtrays, and a picture of St. Catherine of Siena offering red-tipped breasts and phalluses on a plate to God. The rage animating the nuns who took a hammer to these idolatries in the 1920s was feminist as well as Puritan, but by the 1970s the sanctuary is there as much for the stricken Ruby man with the DTs as for Pat Best's angry daughter, and the Fleetwood babies' maddened mother and the two women who came in different decades in the night with the tragic and deadly command "I can't have this baby."

To the citizens of Ruby, implicated in the folds of the Puritan origins of the American idea, the Convent also speaks an ancient spell of witch-sponsored heterodox sexuality—secret, underground, alternative, a polymorphous carnality licensed by the pagan superstitions of Catholic incarnation. These women let anyone in. Anything could be going on there: the ritual deaths of babies, the malignant sexuality of women sufficient to each other, the underground copulation of devil and witch, monk and nun.[10]

The sexual sufficiency of women to one another plays out in the intimate physical battles, the quiet slow dances, and one probable lesbian relationship. And the voices of dead and disappeared babies haunting the Convent speak a complex indictment of the forces that kill or condemn and an equally complex story of saving and "salvation" which is the most counter-Puritan thing about *Paradise*.

Save-Marie

At the novel's physical and moral center, two Baptist ministers face one another over the meaning of love as the nature of God. Pastor Senior Pulliam has the pulpit and speaks a very contemporary form of the pure doctrine of the Puritan God. This God is an in-itself, for-itself, to-itself Being uncontingent and "uninterested" in humans except as they seek to know—never fully to know, never to "graduate" from this curriculum—its Nature, which is love: love "divine only and difficult always. If you think it is easy you are a fool. If you think it is natural you are blind. It is a learned application without reason or motive except that it is God" (142).

Morrison plays fair. The stern appeal on the page of this high call to tight focus and clean radiance, nose cleared of the cheap perfume of self, is powerful. In response, Pastor Richard Misner can only lift the cross off the church wall and stand silently with it, hoping that the sight of this sign, which he believes is the first shape the conscious human mind draws, evocative of the placement of features on a face and the origin of consciousness in a body upright with arms outstretched toward another, will restore the human god. "The cross was abstract, the absent body was real," and its semiotic, prior even to the Christological story, is a crossing of the standing up and the holding out, a theology Teilhardian, Levinasian: Love is motion, love is "unmotivated respect" (146) from one's own body to the face of the Other.

One the one hand, the Puritan's caution:—Strait is the gate, unimaginable the diploma, who can say he is saved? On the other hand the Pauline elation:—Creation creates, and will ingather all of itself. Its most passionate expression comes in Richard Misner's sermon opening the last section of the novel, at the funeral of the Fleetwood infant who incomprehensibly was born fatally sick, and could not testify to the "quality" of her life nor "give" any return for the care lavished futilely on her except for the secret messages to the listening heart: "Oh, Save-Marie, your name always sounded like 'Save me.' 'Save me.' Any other messages hiding in your name? I know one that shines out for all to see: there never was a time when you were not saved, Marie" (307).

The body and its drives are the self-loving vertical of the sign of the cross: children represent its Other-open horizontal. Normative sexuality in the black Fathers of Ruby is poisoned by a tragic disconnect in their hard-tried souls. Proud and successful, yet burdened with the memory of outrage, toughened by wars and bowed by fear, they shut the valves of their attention, unable to take any more surprises, marry only their own, and apply discipline, "as though, rather than children," Reverend Misner muses, "they wanted duplicates" (161). "Slack" as the young Ruby males around the Oven seem in the 1970s, Misner can see the truth in their smart-aleck riposte to the Fathers' accusations of back talk—"What is talk if it's not 'back'? You all just want us not to talk at all" (85).

Ruby's women sympathize with the back-talking children too, but they are caught in their own deadly patterns of duplication and reversal. Soane Morgan, feeling the weight of two husbands in the marriage of sisters to twin brothers, bore two sons in two years and then went to the Convent for help to end a third pregnancy that would have been a daughter. Understood, soothed, refused, Soane turned back to wait her time, but the wish was the deed: The fetus was lost in violent miscarriage, and the two sons, in deadly harmony, came home from Vietnam as a mixed assemblage of parts in body bags two decades later. The teenaged Arnette Fleetwood, desiring and loathing the near-incestuous union with K. D. Morgan expected by the community, opened her body to him and then, "revolted by the work of her womb" (249), became the second Ruby girl to enter the Convent screaming "No! As if that made it so" (250). Harbored by the women, refused the abortion, Arnette continued her revolt, secretly assaulting her own womb with a mop handle so that a second violent miscarriage resulted.

Morrison's narrative, as it probes the reader's own stereotypes, allows the certainties of the Ruby males about the Convent women's assistance to abortion to drift unsupported and unchallenged for most of the novel, until the third cry of "no" to the work of the womb, this time from the drifter Pallas, triggers the confirmation that the Convent's nature is and has always been midwifery, not witchery. If the cries and whispers of ghostly children haunt the rooms there, it is because the mothers had not the will or the strength to hold them in bodily life. As with Mavis, whose twins, smothered in the Cadillac of her abusing husband, now slowly return, *Beloved*-wise, as accusing and then forgiving presences. As with Arnette's aunt, Sweetie Fleetwood, whose spirit revolted after six years of caring for four babies damaged in the womb: She walked by some blind instinct all seventeen miles from Ruby to the Convent, only to hear the rooms ring with the healthy cry she had never heard from one of her own. Jolted back into the grooves of

Ruby wifehood, she contributes her bit to the myth of the Convent's captivity of babies for sacrifice: "Babies cry here among these demons but not in her house?" (130). As with Seneca, who is perpetually missing the child-self who was abandoned by her mother, and whose drift toward the Convent started when her boyfriend was imprisoned for carelessly driving a car over a child "he thought was a . . . a . . . I forgot what he told me he thought it was" (133).

Morrison's explorations of the mystery of God as love, the sacred and terrible horizons opened by maternity, began, as I have written elsewhere, with her first novel, *The Bluest Eye* (1970), and reach a powerful culmination in *Beloved* (1987).[11] In *Paradise*, Morrison drives her narrative through the crucible of violence and waste toward illumination, redemption, and if necessary, flat-out miracle, pursuing the post-Puritan doctrine that there never was a time when we are not saved, Marie. A still more potent and complex maternal concept works itself out in the topos not of the dead or lost but the "stolen" child. It strangely links what is best both in the migrations of the black families of Haven/Ruby and the drift of the Convent's residents to womanspace. An impulse of grace, of exogamy, an openness to surprise, prompts each community to add to its numbers, but at the same time all the ambiguity of the world's own worldliness is in the narrative's audacious, ironic insistence on qualifying that act with the adjectives "stolen" or, later, "kidnapped."

Haven's founding group was seventy-nine persons, or eighty-one "if you counted the two stolen children . . . snatched up because the circumstances in which the children were found wouldn't let them do otherwise" (188, 189). The impulse there was not "imperial" but neither was it only saintly; they received the abandoned as an act of defiance to the communities that had earlier rejected the haven seekers. The founding mother superior of the Convent came from a mission in Brazil where she had "kidnapped three children, the easiest thing in the world in 1925," because "she flatly refused to leave them in the street garbage they sat in" (223). She left two of them in a South American orphanage but fell in love with the green-eyed nine-year-old Consolata and brought her as a ward to join the Arapaho children of the Convent's school, who welcomed her because "she was stolen as they had been" from a culture that seemed to white Christian charity to need tidying and taming (238).

The intractability of this stolen/saved paradox should put human moral thinking out of the God business, and it does, for the lifetime of the founders and foundress. Afterward, two of the stolen, one from each community, become the real carriers of the best of the founders' traditions, both of them mystic women, midwives denigrated as witches, descendants of that child of God in *Beloved*, with her "baby-catching hands," Baby Suggs. One is Lone DuPres, who in 1976 at the age of eighty-six is still seeking in the countryside near the Convent the herbs that mark her as the midwife of Ruby, though the community has now turned away from her easements to the starker comforts of science. The other is Consolata, who at nearly sixty has put in fifty years of serving, nourishing, healing, and in a sense "bearing" the nuns, the girls, and now the dislocated drifters from Ruby and from Route 70, including the one young nay-saying pregnant girl who has finally said yes to the Convent's offer to deliver her baby.

Lone DuPres was not yet two when a flash of insight took her stumbling away from the dead body of her nameless mother into the path of the Haven migration. She has a "gift" that expresses itself as part of her long career as a midwife. Seeing in, or even "stepping in," to the embodied consciousnesses of mothers and of babies in the womb, she has stored and "loaned" energy, pulling weak or reluctant new lives and exhausted maternal lives, forth (or back) into the world with God's own suction and sanction, until whatever poisoned Jeff and Sweetie Fleetwood's living force resisted even *her* imperative preternatural "step in," and the community lost faith in her.

Lone has seen and fostered her successor and equal in the woman who is now a reluctant new kind of reverend mother at the Convent. In the mid-1960s, as contact between Ruby's women and the Convent solidified behind the innocent exchanges of money and pies, chickens, medicines, and hot-pepper sauce, Lone DuPres offered her knowledge and her medicines to a Convent-miseducated Consolata unaware of her own menopause. She sensed in her the same "stepping in" gift. Body and spirit, created being and creating power, the natural magic Lone practices from an ancient tradition and the supernatural doctrines of Christian faith—these are integral to one another, Lone argues: "You stuck on dividing Him from His works. Don't unbalance His world" (244). When a Morgan son driving drunk crashed a car near the Convent, Lone rushed with Consolata to the scene, tried her aging strength on the just-dead body with its receding pinpoint of light, and then ordered the younger woman to put forth her own strength, which she did—seeing in, stepping in, drawing back the dead boy's light to see by, to see himself by, so that he finally opened his eyes and went back to his father—Deacon Morgan (245).

Morrison has linked this rebirth and gift-triggering scene with its origin, ten years before, in the forbidden ecstatic lovemaking of a man and a woman near the fig trees that grew in each other's arms, a form of the fable of the "black couple of Wish, Arizona." The man was Deacon Morgan, momentarily shocked loose from the monastic-dynastic imperatives of Ruby, and the woman was Consolata, momentarily shocked loose from the Jansenist pietism of the convent she served, now experiencing in the body the devouring/God-devouring energies implicit in the Catholic practices of Eucharist.

Like Hester and Dimmesdale, Deacon and Connie were certain of their consecration. For the moment at least, in loving sexual expression, Deacon knew himself as himself, not as a twin, a Morgan ("There are two of you?" "No, there's just one of me" [232]). For Connie, "the wing of a feathered thing, undead" through the waste of her childhood and the routines of the Arapaho school and the service of the nuns, shook and expanded in that contact that "good sex" promises and sometimes delivers: the moving-moving, the chaos, an intimacy for two neither "in here" nor "out there" but rapturously "out here" (226, 229).

This is not "the original world," and the "fall" happens soon after. Starved, mute, at the edge of idolatry, Connie bit Deacon's lips once too often and triggered his recoil: As his wife later put it, "He couldn't afford to fail. None of us could." Abandoned (again), Connie recoiled to mother church and to the mother superior, Mary Magna, whose arms were loving but who had no speech for the sexual awakening that had happened. "A sunshot seared her right eye" (241) as she left that phase of her life, the beginning of a transformation of her vision from day to night sight, of the winged sexuality connected to the world of origins to the insight/instepping gift, ultimately maternal, with which she pulls and holds life.

Acutely aware of the temptation to idolatry, the narrative creates no child from the ecstatic coupling of the Deacon and the nearly nun ecstatic, but replaces it in the zone of "Wish." Nor does the gift that is its trace in the world become a shrine, but remains a "blessed utility": Scout Morgan recovered from the car accident but not from the Vietnam War, and Consolata's later frantic "steppings in" to prolong the dying Mother Mary Magna's life were, as she notes herself, a curious kind of devouring of the woman who mothered her spiritual self, like her earlier hunger for the man with whom she discovered the wings of her embodied self.

The mother-daughter dyad of Mary Magna and Consolata is also Morrison's blessed utility, not a shrine, though it points to a complex and mobile spiritual fact. Mary Magna did her part of the world's work emphatically as mother, bearing and nourishing the world's imperfect children. But she was also Mary the Virgin, and that figure is only part of the story, and not the first part. In Mary Magna's last illness Connie played Eve to Mother's Mary, held her body in her arms and between her legs as if the younger woman were birthing the older one, Eve rescuing Mary to the body as Mary had rescued Eve from the body (223). But neither of these blessed utilities is sufficient apart from the other: The spirit's hunger for spirit shuts in the feathered and winged thing, while the body's hunger for body strips the body to bone alone: "My bones on hers the only good thing. Not spirit. Bones. No different for the man. My bones on his the only true thing. I wondering where is the spirit in this? It is true, like bones. It is good, like bones. . . . Hear me, listen. Never break them in two. Never put one over the other. Eve is Mary's mother. Mary is the daughter of Eve" (263). The two fig trees grow in each other's arms.

As Connie reaches this insight, her English breaking up under the thrusting forth of her first Brazilian speech, the four women in the Convent begin to hear her, to listen in a new, illuminating but also dangerous way. Connie herself has crossed toward a selfhood combining body and spirit, true and good, bones and breath, through a hallucinated (or realized) indwelling with a god figure who combines the physical lines and colors of her lost lover Deacon Morgan and herself (252). She calls Mavis, Gigi, Seneca and the pregnant Pallas to a similar exercise. They lay their bodies, bone and breath, on the ground, chalk round each other the outline of that position, and then each "fills in" her own outline with color and shape and symbol of history, need, desire, and dream. Slowly over months of quiet dream, speech, and ritual, each comes genuinely to inhabit that best self drawn on the cellar floor and revisited nightly, to make peace with the past and envision a future, while the garden continues to yield its food, the bread to be made and eaten each morning, and a baby, God's bread, is born to Pallas.

This is unmistakably sacred work, but a trick of the eye can turn it into the work of the devil. Preoccupied with their spiritual transformations and devotions, the Convent dwellers have missed the growing unease of Ruby with its women and its world, missed above all the significance of the "terrible discovery" in spring 1976 of a car full of bones, including a baby's, at the edge of Convent land. This was a (white) family who drove out, against advice from the humane in Ruby, into a blizzard three years before, and died, frozen in each others' embrace. Now they are the final evidence of malignance at the

Convent, the irrational trigger for the attack that begins and ends the novel. Women, properly the custodians of life, of man (men), become witches to the Puritan imagination when they turn their eyes and bodies to themselves, or each other, or to gods. The disappeared babies and rejected men and dissolving authorities of Ruby now appear as the objective correlative of death and the devil, the car of bones; the elders come for frontier justice, for Puritan exorcism. They are led, as is inevitable, by Deacon Morgan, avatar of an avenging God, whose spiritual crisis followed his own and Connie's ecstatic sexual awakening twenty years before, whose last child was miscarried twenty years before, on the land he crosses now with his gun.

Ruby, however, has a rescuing mission as well as a judging one, and so does even the Puritan God. The immediate rescuers, who arrive just minutes after the nine men with guns cease firing in the Convent, are led by Lone DuPres, who tries to stanch the blood of "the white woman" lying in the front hallway, who watches the Morgan wives cover the dead body of her friend Consolata. Remembering the power of "stepping in," she had whispered "Are you sure?" even to the body with the bullet hole in the center of its forehead. On second thought, though, she knows better than to want to witness the miracle, opting to leave the bodies alone with the powers of the Convent.

When the undertaker arrives and finds no body there, living or dead, and "the meaning of the ending" (297) goes up for multiple readings, Lone chooses her ending pitched halfway between Ezekiel and Paul. God, she believes, has miraculously intervened, swept the dead/alive directly to Himself, as a Sign to the outrageously prideful, the incorrigibly stupid, and the dimly hopeful, that redemption was not only needed, but available. And this belief bears fruit in one soul at least, as the community's leader, Deacon Morgan, wearing his banker's suit but no shoes or socks, and leaving behind for once in his life the automobile that projects his power, puts flesh to earth in a walk through his clientele to tell all the secret parts of his, and Ruby's, story to Pastor Richard Misner.

During the events at the Convent, Misner, passionately critical and hopeful newcomer to the glories and damages of Haven/Ruby, and Anna Flood, perspicacious and compassionate descendant of Haven's first families, were out of town on pastoral business, and in prickly amity deciding to love and marry. It is Ruby they want to rescue when they arrive at the Convent two days later and try to reconstruct "the meaning of the ending." Perhaps the women had returned, with or without Lone DuPres's assistance, to take care of themselves and their own, including the occupant of the still sheet-rumpled crib with the name "Divine" printed on it.

The reader is offered confirmation of this "meaning" in a series of brief final vignettes: four women, one carrying a baby, are seen briefly revisiting, edgily reconciling, the places from which they had come to the Convent. A fifth woman, with the features of the younger Consolata, lies daughterly in the lap of a singing black Mater Magna in the "unambivalent bliss" of the Oceanic (318). This last vignette has the narrative status of a dream vision, "solace" for the "disconsolate."[12] Reconsoled, the narrative sings, this creator/created dyad and all born from and into it "shoulder the work they were created to do down here in Paradise," a work emblematized in "speech shared and divided bread smoking from the fire" (318). It's the sort of scene and space, memory and prophecy, "neither life nor death—but there, just yonder" (307), that you might see if, like Anna Flood and Richard Misner, you went back to the Convent to reconstruct "the meaning of the ending," and sensed (one of you) a door, (the other of you) a window, and went all the way up to and through it.

Morrison's narrative offers this sense of threshold, with its laughing pessimism (Anna saw a closed door) and wary optimism (Richard saw a half-raised window) as the keystone of religious experience "down here in Paradise": "What would happen if you entered? What would be on the other side? What on earth would it be? What on earth?" (305). But the religious sensibility does not enter. Not just because of cowardice, Morrison suggests, but in obedience to the caution—scary Deuteronomy, lovely Corinthians, Puritan origin itself—that specifying the divine, or the origin and goal of the human, only separates what is of its nature integrated. Even at its best, religious sensibility can only paint a memorable fresco on the wall that the door becomes, that the window becomes: At its always available worst, religious sensibility makes a graven idol, a stone hood, of what should remain a liminal invitation to shoulder the world, make God's bread. The very Oven, we are told at the end of the novel, its foundations undermined by the rain that fell the morning of the attack, has shifted and tilted, retaining its blessed utility but revealing its blessed mortality.

Notes

1. Published soon after Morrison's novel, Russ Rymer's *American Beach: A Saga of Race, Wealth, and Memory* (New York: Harper Collins, 1998), a study of a more than

two-hundred-year-old black-founded Florida island community, makes a similar point: "The New World was colonized during the Reformation and the European wars of religion, a protracted and bitter dustup between the domain of religious virtue and the secular domains of business and law. . . . Black protest concurs in the centrality of [these contending values] whether it honors them in the breach by throwing racism in their face or buttresses them with stories of black achievement" (18).

2. Nancy Armstrong and Leonard Tennenhouse, *The Imaginary Puritan: Literature, Intellectual Labor, and the Origins of Personal Life* (Berkeley and Los Angeles: University of California Press, 1992), 8.

3. Toni Morrison, *Paradise* (New York: Knopf, 1998), 318. Henceforth cited by page number in the text. Critics have often treated Morrison's investment in revisioning multiple theologies, Christian and other. See Barbara Hill Rigney, *Lillith's Daughters: Women and Religion in Contemporary Fiction* (Madison: University of Wisconsin Press, 1982); Lauren Lepow, "Paradise Lost and Found: Dualism and Edenic Myth in Toni Morrison's *Tar Baby*," *Contemporary Literature* 23 (1987): 363–77; Ann-Janine Morey, "Margaret Atwood and Toni Morrison: Reflections on Postmodernism and the Study of Religion and Literature," *Journal of the American Academy of Religion* 60 (1992): 493–513.

4. Sacvan Bercovitch, *The Puritan Origins of the American Self* (New Haven: Yale University Press, 1975), 63.

5. Toni Morrison, *Playing in the Dark: Whiteness and the Literary Imagination* (Cambridge, Mass.: Harvard University Press, 1992), 4.

6. Bercovitch quotes William Bradford on the "wild beasts" (45) and William Perkins on "God's Bread" (15).

7. Deuteronomy is the Mosaic text authorizing migrations toward a land to be captured through alternating rhythms of ferocious war and equally ferocious fertility. It authorizes scary punishments for backsliders, like "stone them with stones till they die"; but it also enjoins the tribes to "love the stranger, for ye were strangers in Egypt" (10:19), and to shun the path by which the making of images becomes the worship of idols. Lovely Corinthians II commends the spirit not the letter, the house not made of hands, and particularly, the carrying of spiritual treasure in "earthen vessels" which, though they are easily and inevitably broken, can be replaced (3:6, 5:1, 4:7).

8. In *"Who Set You Flowin'?" The African American Migration Narrative* (New York: Oxford University Press, 1995), Farah Jasmine Griffin suggests that Toni Morrison's version of this story is now "the dominant one" among her novels, partly because her stories combine elements of the South/North flight-migration story central to the civil rights and black power movements with the re-membering movements central to much black women's narrative (8–12).

9. In "Recitatif," two schoolgirls grow into women speaking and feeling a black-white class-race discourse in which it is impossible to tell which person is black and which white. The argument about "adversarial aesthetics" is from a powerful reading of the story by my colleague Kalpana Seshadri-Crooks in her forthcoming *Desiring Whiteness: A Lacanian Analysis of Racial Visibility*.

10. See Nancy Lusignan Schultz, ed., *Veil of Fear: Nineteenth-Century Convent Tales* (West Lafayette, Ind.: Purdue University Press, 1999), for a reading of *Paradise* in the context of the American "convent-captivity" tradition.

11. In the last chapter of my book *Abortion, Choice and Contemporary Fiction: The Armageddon of the Maternal Instinct* (Chicago: University of Chicago Press, 1990) I studied a series of black women writers' texts in which "conversations with the aborted future end either in silence or in miracle" (154), locating particularly in *Beloved* a feminist concern with the Pietà-figure as a figure of sublimity. This essay is a continuation of that study, as *Paradise* is a continuation of Morrison's work with, among other things, the female Sublime, represented in this novel, as I argue, by a Mary/Eve dyad both erotic and maternal.

12. Writing about *Beloved* in "Postmodernism and Post-Utopian Desire in Toni Morrison and E. L. Doctorow," in Nancy J. Peterson, ed., *Toni Morrison: Critical and Theoretical Approaches* (Baltimore: Johns Hopkins University Press, 1997), Marianne DeKoven posits a textual form in which "an excess of apocalyptic material that cannot be integrated into the resolutions conventional narrative forms enforce pushes into the ending of each novel," and analyzes that novel as a study of "the maternal as the locus of defeated utopia," 114, 124. *Paradise*, with its wary investment in the liminal, is an extended reflection in post-Utopian mode.

Notes on Contributors

Renée L. Bergland teaches English at Simmons College in Boston. She is author of *The National Uncanny: Indian Ghosts and American Subjects* (University Press of New England, 2000). She is now at work on a manuscript about vision, gender, and subjectivity in prefilm America.

Carrie Tirado Bramen is an associate professor of English at the State University of New York, Buffalo, where she teaches courses in nineteenth-century U.S. literature and culture and contemporary Latino and multicultural fiction. She is the author of numerous articles as well as *The Uses of Variety: Modern Americanism and the Quest for National Distinctiveness* (Harvard University Press, 2000).

Margaret Soenser Breen is an assistant professor of English at the University of Connecticut, where she teaches courses in eighteenth- and nineteenth-century British literature, gay and lesbian literature, and queer theory. She has published a range of articles in these areas. She is also associate editor of the *International Journal of Sexuality and Gender Studies*.

Russ Castronovo is the director of the American Studies Program at the University of Miami. He is author of *Fathering the Nation: American Genealogies of Slavery and Freedom* (Berkeley: University of California Press, 1995). He has also written *Necro Citizenship: Death and the Public Sphere in the United States* and, with Dana D. Nelson, coedited *Materializing Democracy*, both forthcoming from Duke University Press.

Darryl Dickson-Carr is an assistant professor of English at Florida State University, where he teaches courses in African-American literature, twentieth-century American literature, postmodernism, and literary theory. He has published several essays on African-American satire, his primary research interest. His book *Sacredly Profane: The African American Satirical Novel in the Twentieth Century* is forthcoming from the University of Missouri Press.

Emory Elliott is director of the Center for Ideas and Society at the University of California, Riverside.

Tracy Fessenden is an associate professor of religious studies and women's studies at Arizona State University. She has published essays on religion and American literature and religious constructions of gender and race in nineteenth- and twentieth-century American culture. Her book *Culture and Redemption: Secularizing Desires in American Literature* is forthcoming from Princeton University Press.

Ed Ingebretsen, a Catholic priest, is an associate professor of English at Georgetown University. He is the author of numerous essays on popular American culture and several books, including *Maps of Heaven, Maps of Hell: Religious Terror as Memory from the Puritans to Stephen King* (1996) and *Dreadful Angels: Monsters and the Discourse of Fear*, forthcoming from the University of Chicago Press.

Robert A. Morace is chair of the English department at Daemen College. He has published numerous essays on contemporary fiction, and is the author of *The Dialogic Novels of Malcolm Bradbury and David Lodge* (Southern Illinois University Press, 1989) and *John Gardner: An Annotated Secondary Bibliography* (Garland, 1984). He is also coeditor (with Kathryn VanSpanckeren) of *John Gardner: Critical Perspectives* (Southern Illinois University Press, 1982).

Nicholas F. Radel is a professor of English at Furman University. He has published articles and reviews on early modern drama, sexuality, and gender theory. His most recent work focuses on queer theory and gay film and literature, particularly the works of Edmund White.

Jodi Schorb is completing her Ph.D. in English at the University of California at Davis, where she teaches in the English and the women and gender studies departments. Her dissertation on the early-American execution narrative examines the genre's relation to eighteenth-century sexual discourses, infanticide legislation, and emerging sentimental traditions of the new republic.

Gustavus Stadler is an assistant professor of English at Haverford College. He is at work on a book tentatively titled *The Sexual Politics of American Genius.*

Boris Vejdovsky teaches the literatures of the Americas and American culture at Lausanne University, Switzerland. He has published articles on literary and cultural theory and on a variety of American works from the early colonial period to the present. He is currently working toward the publication of a book tentatively entitled *Ideas of Order: Ethics and Topos in American Literature.*

Judith Wilt is a professor of English and the founding director of the Women's Studies Program at Boston College; she is also on the advisory board of the journal *Religion and the Arts.* Her most recent book is *Abortion, Choice, and Contemporary Fiction: The Armageddon of the Maternal Instinct.* She is now at work on a study of the novels of Mrs. Humphry Ward.

Magdalena J. Zaborowska is an associate professor in the Department of English and Center for Cultural Research at Aarhus University in Aarhus, Denmark. She has written *How We Found America: Reading Gender through East-European Immigrant Narratives* (University of North Carolina Press, 1995) and is the editor of *Other Americans, Other Americas: The Politics and Poetics of Multiculturalism* (Aarhus University Press, 1998). She is at work on a book about gender and erotics in transcultural narratives, and on an essay collection on posttotalitarian cultures, East and West.

Index

Goodell, William, 154
Gove, Mary, 159–160
Grace, 25, 26, 75, 255
Graham, Sylvester, 153–154, 160, 162, 163–165
Granger, Thomas, 145
Grant, Ulysses S., 177
Grapes of Wrath, 275
Gray, Thomas, 207
Greenblatt, Stephen, 173
Griffin, Susan, 172
Guilt, 253, 256, 267, 268
  "free-floating," 267
  "normalization of," 9
  shame and, 268–269
  survivor, 262
"Gynecological Consideration for the Sexual Act," 183

Haines, John, 48, 49
Hale, Sarah Josepha, 177
Halfway Covenant, 28
Hall, David, 24
Hall, Radclyffe, 244
Haller, William, 256
Halperin, David, 23
Hamlet, 12, 56, 58–61
Hancock, Geoffrey, 239
Hardwick, Elizabeth, 226
Harris, Henry, 129, 138
Harris, John, 138
Harry Potter books, 254
Hart, Gary, 34
Hawthorne, Nathaniel, 3, 13, 34, 37, 93–95, 99, 100–106, 145, 146, 229, 267, 273
Hawthorne, Sophia, 93, 99, 100–103
Health reform, 153, 159, 163
Heaven, 275
Hedged In, 178
"Hedonism, New," 263
Hell, 27, 275
"Helm effect," 68
Helms, Jesse, 32
Hentz, Caroline Lee, 175
Herbert, George, 47
Heresy, 26
Hertzberg, Arthur, 110
Heterosexism, 9, 235
Heterosexuality, 6, 7, 10
Higginson, Thomas Wentworth, 181
Hill, Anita, 7–9
Hinduism, 14, 192–193, 198, 202
  celibacy in, 201–204, 206
  Christian women and, 194–208
  masculinity and, 202–204

nationalism of, 203
  reconversion to, 202–203
Hispanics, 229
History of Redemption, A, 25
History of Sexuality, The, 4
Homer, 266
"Homo Will Not Inherit," 249
Homoeroticism
  of Levinsky, David, 220
  in religion, 10
  Wigglesworth, Michael, and, 42–52
Homophobia, 9, 52, 235
  Levinsky, David, and, 221
  of religious right, 237
Homosexuality, 33. *See also* Gay men; Lesbianism
  African Americans and, 140
  "Don't ask/don't tell" and, 32, 35–36
  heterosexual sodomy vs., 10
  of scholars of Puritans, 5, 6
  Wigglesworth, Michael, and, 41–52
Homosocial relations, 10, 47, 49–50
  acculturation and, 216
  among Protestant women, 176
  Douglass, Frederick, and, 127, 128, 129, 130
  Levinsky, David, and, 216, 218
  routed through women, 130
Hoover, Herbert, 2
House I Live In, The: or the Human Body, 161
House of Bondage, 179
House of Spirits, 275
How, Elizabeth, 64
How, James, Jr., 64
Howell, William Dean, 216
Hughes, Walter, 10, 42–43, 47, 49
Humanism, 95, 97
Humanists, 3
Hustler, 32
Hutchinson, Anne, 7, 22–23, 26, 27, 31, 34–37, 229, 261
Hypocrisy, 199

"I Lead Two Lives: Confessions of a Closet Baptist," 236
Identity
  "as difference," 218
  exclusionary notions of, 14
  non-, 219, 220
  prohibitions and, 4–5, 218
  Puritan sex and American, 10–12, 14, 56, 67, 68
  religion and national, 224
  sexual, 6, 52